Multinational Firms and the Theory of International Trade

Multinational Firms and the Theory of International Trade

James R. Markusen

The MIT Press
Cambridge, Massachusetts
London, England

This book was set in Palatino on 3B2 by Asco Typesetters, Hong Kong, and was printed and bound in the United States of America.

Library of Congress Cataloging-in-Publication Data

Markusen, James R., 1948–
  Multinational firms and the theory of international trade / James R. Markusen.
    p. cm.
  Includes bibliographical references and index.
  ISBN 0-262-13416-0 (hc. : alk. paper)
    1. International trade. 2. International business enterprises—Management. I. Title.
  HF1379 .M367   2002
  338.8′8—dc21   2002067072

For Ann, Daniel, and Peter

Contents

Acknowledgments

Much of this volume is built on previously published journal articles. My greatest debt is to my coauthors who worked with me over the years on those papers. Four chapters are derived from joint work with Ignatius Horstmann, three from work with Anthony Venables, and three from work with Keith Maskus. Wilfred Ethier, Kevin Honglin Zhang, and David Carr were coauthors on one paper each. Thomas Rutherford worked with me on a number of applied papers on multinationals that are not included, and he also developed the software that has been vital for producing both the original papers and the chapters in this volume.

Not only are all these folks fine scholars, but they are good friends and a lot of fun. I have never known quite where work stops and play begins, and I am not very good at research when I can't laugh and have a good time at the end of the day. Not only did my coauthors contribute a great deal intellectually, but we had fun in the course of our work. Chapter 5, for example, was originally conceived with Tony Venables on a set of cocktail napkins in a bar in Vigo, Spain. Sometimes I marvel at the fact that I am paid to do this work.

My wife, Ann Carlos, is also an economist, and we have suffered through many of each other's research pressures and anxieties over the years. Ann repeatedly encouraged me to write this book, and I gave in during the fall of 2000. But then she had to go through the traumas again with this manuscript, including periodic panic attacks when I thought I couldn't reproduce some earlier result and long weekends of silence. I am immensely grateful for her encouragement, support, and editorial comments.

My editor Kathy Caruso and designer Chrys Fox at The MIT Press were first-rate professionals. They identified and worked through difficult technical problems with me and, as with my coauthors, we had some laughs in the course of our work together. Asco Typesetters in Hong Kong were similarly great in helping solve some awkward issues, and they have left me thinking more about trade in knowledge-intensive services and the international fragmentation of production. The clarity and presentation of the book are much improved by all these folks.

I want to thank all of my friends and colleagues in Canada and in Europe, Sweden in particular. I have received a lot of support and interest from Canadians and Europeans who felt that these issues were far more important than the interest they generated initially in the United States. I gave my first seminar on multinationals and trade theory at the Institute for International Economic Studies in Stockholm in August 1980, and the encouragement I received has kept me going for more than twenty years.

Preface

1 Discontent with Traditional Theory

My training was in traditional international trade theory, which had been dominated for decades by the competitive, constant-returns general-equilibrium model. My first job out of graduate school was at the University of Western Ontario in Canada, where I found it hard to reconcile important aspects of the Canadian economy with what I had been taught and indeed with what I was teaching to students. The Canadian manufacturing sector included many large firms and was over 50 percent foreign owned. I discovered that, quite disjoint from international trade theory, there was another field that considered industrial organization aspects of trade and trade policy in partial-equilibrium and descriptive analysis. Here there were discussions of how policy influenced foreign ownership and attempts to measure the scale and market power inefficiencies caused by restrictive trade policies. Rather than consider trade liberalization, successive Canadian governments made clumsy attempts to restrict the foreign ownership generated by those trade barriers.

Our traditional theory of international trade left me ill-equipped to participate in the debate, so I began in the late 1970s to work on incorporating industrial organization aspects of industries into trade models. I wanted to maintain the general-equilibrium focus that is the great strength of trade theory. On the other hand, I wanted to give individual firms an important place in the theory and endogenize the location and ownership decisions that were obviously a crucial part of the story.

I searched the more formal international economics literature available at the time for guidance in this task. I was disappointed to find that direct investment and multinationals, if they were treated at all, were viewed as just part of the theory of portfolio capital flows. The view was that capital, if unrestricted, flows from where it is abundant to where it is scarce, and that was more or less all there was to say. There was no notion that the determinants and consequences of direct investments differ in any important way from those of portfolio capital investments.

This bias was also profoundly visible in data sources. Much data existed on direct investment stocks and flows, but very little existed on what the multinational firms actually produced and traded. Multinationals were viewed as investment and capital-flow phenomena, and not as real production units in the economy. You could get detailed data on trade flows from one source, data on investment stocks and flows from another source, but no data on multinational affiliate production activities.

It took very little staring at the available statistics to realize that viewing multinationals and direct investment as part of capital theory was largely a mistake. The latter theory suggested that direct investment should flow primarily from capital-rich to capital-poor countries, but this is clearly not the case as we will discuss in chapter 1. The overwhelming bulk of direct investment flows both from and to the high-income, developed countries, and there is a high degree of cross-penetration by firms from these countries into each other's markets.

Furthermore, the sourcing of finances for direct investment are often geographically disjoint from the actual parent country. The decision about whether and where to build a foreign plant is quite separate from how and where to raise the financing for that plant. I began to believe that the former decision should be the focus of a new microeconomic approach to direct investment while the latter could remain part of the more traditional theory of capital flows.

This is how I began working in 1977 on what is now known as the industrial organization approach to trade. It later turned out that others were beginning to do so at the same time, but with a different and generally more U.S. focus. As a consequence of my Canadian experience, I was primarily interested in oligopoly models in which the degree of competition and production efficiency were endogenous. Folks working in the United States were more fascinated than those elsewhere by the monopolistic competition model, which is devoid of these scale and procompetitive effects and concentrates instead on product diversity. I was also interested from the beginning in multinationals, again from the Canadian experience, while there was virtually no interest in multinationals among my colleagues in U.S. universities. In fact, many of them turned to normative analysis in the mid-1980s, a branch of theory now known as "strategic trade policy." The literature produced inevitably assumed single-plant nationally owned firms, despite the fact that the industries used to motivate the analysis were often dominated by multinationals.

After twenty years, I have to say that it has been a great journey, but it is time to wrap it up. This book is an attempt to do just that. Much in the book has been published previously, but I have spent a great deal of time rewriting and rearranging. With the benefit of hindsight, I believe that I have learned better ways to motivate and exposit key points, and better methods for integrating the disparate parts into a more unified and coherent theory. I hope this proves true.

2 Objectives

The purpose of this book is to present a microeconomic, general-equilibrium theory of multinational firms. This theory and its analytical constructions must pass several simple tests. First, it should be easily incorporated into the theory of international trade and existing general-equilibrium models of trade. I think of this book as an important extension and modernization of trade theory, not something that invalidates or displaces our traditional wisdom. In pursuing that objective, I try to build models that nest within the traditional industrial organization and factor proportions models. Second, the theoretical models must be consistent with important sylized facts about actual multinational activity. Thus the models must be able to generate outcomes in which, for example, there is a high degree of cross-investment and affiliate production among similar, high-income countries. Third, the theory should generate testable predictions and must survive more formal econometric testing.

3 What's In

The first part of the book is a series of models in which firms can choose a headquarters location that performs functions such as management, research and development, marketing, and finance. The firm also chooses the number and location of its production facilities. In chapters 2–4, I rely on partial-equilibrium models that capture crucial aspects of both technology characteristics and country characteristics.

These combine to determine the equilibrium "regime," the location of headquarters and the number and location of plants. The models nest familiar national firm models, such as those of the strategic trade policy literature, as special cases.

Chapters 5–9 provide general-equilibrium analyses, allowing for factor endowments to play important roles in determining equilibrium. Among the many questions analyzed are the relationship between trade and affiliate production, the effects of trade versus investment liberalization on factor prices, and the location of production. These general-equilibrium models provide testable hypotheses about how the pattern of affiliate production in the world economy should relate to country characteristics, such as total market size, differences in market size, relative factor endowments, and trade and investment barriers. Chapters 10–12 provide formal econometric tests and estimates of these predictions.

The final section of the book, chapters 13–15, considers "internalization." This involves an analysis of the mode by which firms serve foreign markets. While all of the earlier chapters restrict this choice to exports versus foreign production, chapters 13–15 add an additional arm's-length option such as licensing. Thus there are two modes of foreign production, one an owned subsidiary in which firm-specific assets are transferred internally within the firm, and the other a licensing agreement with an unaffiliated firm.

Six appendices to the book present and explain features of the software and actual code used in simulations.

4 What's Out

Truth in advertising requires that I also point out what is not in the book and provide brief explanations why.

Macroeconomics, capital flows. As noted above, a lot of evidence suggests that the decision to build or acquire a foreign factory is largely separate from the decision of where to raise the financial capital. The capital funds can come from the firm's internal retained earnings, from parent-country equity or debt financing, from host-country financing, or from third markets. In this book, I will abstract from the financing question entirely. Real factors of production, generally skilled labor and "other" factors, are required for the fixed costs for firms and plants. These physical factors do not flow between countries, but the services of assets produced with skilled labor do flow from parent to affiliate. Thus multinationals are exporters of services of real assets—such as management, engineering, and marketing services—to foreign locations. I believe that the financing decisions and accompanying capital flows are important and interesting, but I also believe that they can be largely separated from the real decisions about the location of production and the direction of trade. I concentrate entirely on the latter, and I hope that others can contribute the important but missing macroeconomics.

Firms organization and boundaries of the firm. My focus in this book is to incorporate the multinational firm into the general-equilibrium theory of international trade. This requires me to assume rather simple technologies and models of the firm itself. Thus the reader will not find much analysis of the boundaries, organization, and ownership determinants of the firm. I will not mention the "transactions-cost approach" to the multinational that has been popular in the international business literature. Part III of the book on internalization models will explicitly treat the firm's decision to transfer assets within the firm's ownership structure versus through some arm's-length alternative. But we will not probe deeper into the theory of the firm than this. As is the case of capital flows, I believe that models of the firm are important, but that they are not crucial to developing the basic general-equilibrium approach. Again, I very much hope that this work will be amended by others with richer models of the firm itself.

Dynamics. I have some (but not much) regret that there is only a minimal amount of dynamic analysis in the book. Once again, the principal focus is on incorporating endogenous production and location decisions into the mainstream general-equilibrium model of trade. This has proved quite enough for one book, and at many points I have resisted the temptation to expand the scope beyond its current boundaries. Interesting questions exist about multinationals such as the importance of early entry and initial knowledge advantages both on the growth and expansion of firms and on the choice of entry mode. I touch on some of these issues in two-period and infinite-horizon games in chapters 4 and 13–15, but a great deal is left to future researchers.

Normative policy analysis, strategic policies. This book focuses almost entirely on positive analysis. I provide analyses of a few policy experiments in order to show how endogenous choices by firms, largely ruled out by assumption in the strategic trade policy literature, yield a richer set of outcomes. But I am careful to avoid any discussion of optimal policy choice. The models in the book are easily adapted to this task, however, by anyone interested in such analyses.

5   Numerical versus Analytical Models

Chapters 2–4 and 13–15 of this book rely on analytical methods to derive results. Chapters 5–9 rely heavily on numerical simulations. The former chapters are partial-equilibrium while the latter are general-equilibrium models.

I and others in the trade industrial organization literature try to find analytical solutions to problems whenever possible. But although I try to use the simplest model suitable, even the basic general-equilibrium model that has the features I want suffers from two difficulties with respect to analytical methods. First, the dimensionality of even the minimal model in chapter 5 is high, having over forty unknowns. Second, many of the key relationships are inequalities, with associated nonnegative variables. The models are, in other words, nonlinear complementarity problems. Which inequalities hold with equality, and which as strict inequalities, is determined in the solution of the model. A comparative statics experiment in which some parameter is altered typically changes the set of inequalities that hold as equations, and therefore which endogenous variables are zero and which are strictly positive. An example would be which types of firms (national firms, horizontal multinationals, vertical multinationals) are active in equilibrium. This is not difficult with two-firm or three-firm types in a partial-equilibrium model, but with four or six in general equilibrium as in chapters 5–8 this becomes intractable.

Two responses to these difficulties are common in the trade-industrial organization literature. The first is to stick with partial-equilibrium models, as in the strategic trade policy literature. The second is to use general-equilibrium models but assume costless trade and factor price equalization between countries. The former sacrifices important issues on the factor-market side, while the latter does so on the product-market side.

In many cases, neither simplification is acceptable for my purposes. Therefore, following three chapters that use partial equilibrium models to obtain analytical solutions, I turn to numerical methods for simulation, relying on Rutherford's nonlinear complementarity solvers that are now subsystems of GAMS. In the general-equilibrium models, I lay out all of the inequalities and associated complementary variables that are solved in the simulations. I also try to provide intuition through the use of partial-equilibrium thought experiments and models-of-the-model. The analytical solutions to partial-equilibrium models in chapters 2–4 should also help lay out the basic intuition. Finally, I provide the actual GAMS code and documentation for some of the important models in six appendices. You might have a look at these early on in order to see how the simulation models work. Thanks for reading this preface. I hope that your investment in the book is worthwhile and that many of you continue to work in this important and interesting subfield.

Notation

I have tried to make notation as uniform as possible throughout the book. In a few cases, this is either impossible or inefficient, so there are a few instances where a variable may have a different definition in two chapters. Chapters 2–12 are quite homogeneous with respect to the underlying theory, and so the notation is closely consistent in those chapters. I try to highlight and emphasize the exceptions when they occur. You might want to refer back to these pages in the course of reading chapters 2–12 if your memory fails as mine often does in trying to remember notation. Chapters 13–15 use quite a different set of tools drawn from game theory, information theory, and contract theory such that the parameters and variables needed to specify the models referred to quite different entities from the earlier chapters. I eventually abandoned most efforts to make these last chapters notationally consistent with the rest of the book. What follows is then a general reference guide to chapters 2–12.

Goods

Y homogeneous good produced with constant returns to scale by competitive firms

X good produced by imperfect competitive firms with increasing returns to scale (X is homogeneous in chapters 2–12 except in chapter 6 where there are differentiated varieties of X)

U utility or welfare (in simulation models, U is a good produced from X and Y)

Factors

L unskilled labor

S skilled labor

Countries

i   often used to denote the parent (headquarters) country

j   often used to denote the host country

X firm types

d   domestic or national firm (single plant and headquarters in the same country)

h   horizontal multinational (plants in both countries, headquarters in one country)

v   vertical multinational (single plant and headquarters in different countries)

Costs

c   marginal cost of production (unit cost)

t   unit cost of shipping X between countries

F   firm-specific fixed cost (alternatively, skilled-labor requirements in fixed costs)

G   plant-specific fixed cost (alternatively, unskilled-labor requirements in fixed costs)

Prices

q   price of Y (typically chosen to equal one)

p   price of X

w   price of unskilled labor

z   price of skilled labor

Miscellaneous

m   markup on X production

N   number of firms

Superscripts are used to denote firm type. Double subscripts on variables are used to refer to countries. Let me present the general notation, and then try to carefully clarify the meaning of country subscripts.

Subscripts and Superscripts, etc.

d, h, v; k   as superscripts, denote firm type (also used to refer to firm types, as in type-d, type-h, type-v. d, h, v do not appear as variables). *k* is used as the general reference to firm type.

i, j   as subscripts, are the general references to countries

N_i^k	number of type-k firms headquartered in country i: $k = d, h, v$
X_{ij}	chapter 2 only: output of X *produced* in country i, *sold* in country j (there is only one firm in the model and its headquarters country is fixed)
X_{ij}^k	chapters 3, 5–8: output of X by a type-k firm, *headquartered* in country i, *sold* in j; where this output is *produced* depends on the firm type. The superscript is not needed in chapter 3.
X_{ij}	chapter 4 only: output of the firm *headquartered* in country i in *time period* j (all output is sold in the host country, so there is no need to distinguish country of sale)
X_j^k	chapter 9 only: output of type-k firm *sold* in country j (all firms are headquartered in one country, so there is no need to distinguish country of headquarters)
Y_{ij}	Y produced in country i and sold in country j
U_i	welfare of country i
q_i	price of good Y in country i (typically $= 1$ in both countries with no trade costs)
p_i	price of good X in country i
c_i	marginal cost of X production in country i (the same for all firm types)
m_{ij}^k	markup of type-k firm headquartered in i and selling in j
w_i	wage of unskilled labor in country i
z_i	wage of skilled labor in country i

Please note carefully the definitions of $X_{ij}^k, c_{ij}^k, m_{ij}^k$, where j is the country in which the output is *sold*. Consider the case where i is not equal to j. In chapter 2, there is only one firm in the model (headquartered in country i), so it is easiest to let the first subscript (i in this case) denote the country of production. In chapters 3–9 however, we need to distinguish between where a type-k firm is headquartered and where the output is produced. The convention I adopt in chapters 3 and 5–8 is therefore that the first subscript (i in this case) is where the firm is *headquartered*, which is not necessarily where that X quantity is produced. Chapters 5 and 9 require a somewhat different definition that I will introduce and explain when needed.

Where X_{ij}^k is *produced* depends on the firm type in chapters 3 and 5–8 (superscript k not used in chapter 3).

For a domestic firm $(k = d)$, X_{ij}^d is output produced in country i and shipped to country j.

For a horizontal firm $(k = h)$, X_{ij}^h is output produced in country j and sold in country j.

For a vertical firm $(k = v)$, X_{ij}^v is output produced in country j and sold in country j.

For a vertical firm $(k = v)$, X_{ii}^v is output produced in country j and shipped to country i.

Similar comments apply to m_{ij}^k. This is the markup of a type-k firm *headquartered* in country i and selling in country j. Where the relevant X carrying this markup is *produced* again depends on the firm type. For a type-d firm, it is produced in country i, but for a type-h or type-v firm it is produced in country j.

Consider finally cost variables such as c_i. Throughout the book, I will assume that all firm types producing in country i have the same marginal cost function, so there is no need to superscript this variable by firm type (or by where the output is sold) since trade costs are specified separately. In chapters 2–6, the X sector uses only one factor, so these variables are defined in real units of that factor. In chapters 7 and 8, the X sector uses both factors, so the c's are functions of factor prices in the country of production, and c is measured in units of the numeraire Y.

Infrequently used notation (typically used in describing simulation models)

c_{iu}	marginal cost of producing a unit of welfare (utility) in country i
c_{iy}	marginal cost of producing good Y in country i
p_{ui}	price of a unit of welfare (utility) in country i
p_{fci}^k	price of fixed costs for type-k firm headquartered in i
fc_i^k	total fixed costs for type-k firm headquartered in i
$cons_i$	income of the representative consumer in country i
$entre_i^k$	income of the "owner" of type-k firm headquartered in i
$mkrev_i^k$	markup revenue of type-k firm headquartered in country i

I

Technology, Costs, and
Market Structure

1   Statistics, Stylized Facts, and Basic Concepts

1.1   Introduction

The early 1980s saw majors developments in international economics as industrial organization aspects of international trade were integrated into more formal trade theory. Prior to the 1980s, two rather distinct literatures existed. There was general-equilibrium trade theory, which relied almost exclusively on the twin assumptions of constant returns to scale and perfect competition in production. Second, there was a partial-equilibrium literature that considered industrial organization effects of trade, such as the effect of trade barriers on concentration, competition, and production efficiency.

The so-called new trade theory and more recently the literature on "geography and trade" enriched our portfolio of theory by integrating these literature streams. Elements of increasing returns to scale, imperfect competition, and product differentiation were added to the more traditional comparative advantage bases for trade in general-equilibrium models. This new theory complements traditional comparative advantage models, in which trade and gains from trade arise as a consequence of differences between countries. In the new trade theory, trade and gains from trade can arise independently of any pattern of comparative advantage as firms exploit economies of scale and pursue strategies of product differentiation. The literature on geography and trade is a natural extension of this line of research, focusing on how industry agglomeration and regional differentiation can arise endogenously as a consequence of transport costs, market sizes, and the trade policy regime.

The new industrial organization (IO) models were an important step, but they nevertheless remained disjoint from any theory of the multinational enterprise. In the trade-IO models, a firm is generally synonymous with a plant or production facility; that is, a firm is a nationally owned organization that produces one good in one location. Multiplant production is generally excluded from the analysis. This is potentially troubling. After all, industries characterized by scale economies and imperfect competition are often dominated by multinationals. As a result, the policy and normative analysis that comes out of the new trade theory may be significantly off base. For example, conclusions of the "strategic trade policy" literature are fundamentally bound up with the notion of clearly defined national firms competing via trade with the national champions of other countries. Substantial foreign ownership of domestic production facilities radically alters the policy implications.

The purpose of this book, as I noted earlier, is to incorporate multinational firms into the general-equilibrium theory of trade. The purpose of this chapter is to survey some of the empirical evidence that we have accumulated to date. I have three separate objectives for this statistical abstract. The first is to convince you that the topic is too quantitatively important to disregard in trade theory, as has largely happened to date. The second is to convince you that the old view of direct investment as not fundamentally different from the theory of portfolio capital movements is completely wrong. The third objective is to provide motivation and support for assumptions employed in the theoretical models throughout the book. Section 1.4 introduces a general conceptual framework that is motivated by and draws on the empirical evidence.

For those interested in related theoretical treatments, complementary surveys of the individual elements I am combining here can be found in Beckman and Thisse (1986: location theory), Markusen (1995, 1998a: integrating multinationals into the IO theory of trade), and Fujita, Krugman, and Venables (1999: location theory, trade-IO models and "economic geography"). Caves (1996) and Ekholm (1995) are other sources for extensive references and literature reviews of multinational firms.

In the next two sections, I examine statistical and other data to create a general impression as to what key aspects of multinationals we need to capture in formal models. Section 1.4 presents the outline of a general conceptual framework that I refer to as the knowledge-capital model of the multinational, building on the earlier conceptual framework of Dunning (1977, 1981).

1.2 An Empirical Background

A preliminary note about terminology may be useful. Multinational enterprises (MNE) are firms that engage in foreign direct investment (FDI), defined as investments in which the firm acquires a substantial controlling interest in a foreign firm or sets up a subsidiary in a foreign country. I use the abbreviations MNE and FDI fairly interchangeably.

Horizontal direct investments refers to the foreign production of products and services roughly similar to those the firm produces for its home market. Vertical investments refer to those that geographically fragment the production process by stages of production. This terminology is not clearcut. All horizontal investments generally have some vertical element, in that services such as management, engineering, marketing, and finance are often supplied in one direction, from parents to subsidiaries. But the terms are convenient and in widespread use. So when I refer to horizontal investments or horizontal multinationals, I am referring to firms producing roughly the same final products in multiple countries as just noted, even though foreign plants are supplied with headquarters services. Vertical firms generally produce outputs not produced by the parent-country operation. A parent firm may ship designs and/or intermediate inputs to a foreign assembly plant, for example, and export the final output back to the parent-country market. While the horizontal-vertical distinction is not always clear empirically, it is well defined in the theoretical models that follow throughout the book.

Before plunging into the theory, I offer a much-needed background of stylized facts to provide a context within which to evaluate the theory and, indeed, to understand its origins. It is my view that much of the recent theory is fairly closely tied to the evidence, or at least consistent with it. Consider first some factors identified in aggregate data, which generally have to do with country characteristics, and then consider results found in analyses of industry- and firm-level data. The former have to do with characteristics of parent and host countries, while the latter generally refer to characteristics of multinational versus nonmultinational firms.

Country Characteristics

1. Direct foreign investment has grown rapidly throughout the world, with particularly strong surges in the late 1980s and late 1990s.[1]

2. The developed countries not only account for the overwhelming proportion of outward FDI but are also the major recipients of FDI.

3. Two-way FDI flows are common between pairs of developed countries, even at the industry level.[2]

4. Most FDI appears to be horizontal, at least insofar as most of the output of foreign affiliates is sold in the foreign country.[3]

5. A significant percentage of world trade is now intrafirm trade (about 30%). There is some evidence of complementarity between trade and investment.[4]

6. Little evidence exists that FDI is positively related to differences in capital endowments across countries, or alternatively to differences in the general return to capital. Skilled-labor endowments are strongly and positively related to outward direct investment.

7. Political risk and instability seems to be an important deterrent to inward FDI. Taxes appear to be of second-order importance (e.g., if a given U.S. company is going to invest in Europe, taxes help determine which location is chosen). I am not sufficiently knowledgeable to evaluate conflicting results in the international taxation literature.[5]

In summary, direct investment has been growing rapidly, and the bulk of it is horizontal direct investment among the high-income developed countries.

Firm and Industry Characteristics

1. Large differences exist across industries in the degree to which production and sales are accounted for by multinational firms.[6]

2. Multinationals tend to be important in industries and firms that (a) have high levels of R&D relative to sales, (b) employ large numbers of professional and technical workers as a percentage of their total workforces, (c) produce new and/or technically complex products, and (d) have high levels of product differentiation and advertising.[7]

3. Multinationals tend to be firms in which the value of the firms' intangible assets (roughly, market value less the value of tangible assets such as plant and equipment) is large relative to its market value.[8]

4. Limited evidence suggests that plant-level scale economies are negatively associated with multinationality.[9]

5. There seems to be a threshold size for multinationals, but above that level corporate size is not important. Corporate age is highly correlated with multinationality.[10]

6. There is evidence that FDI is positively related to the existence of trade barriers. Evidence by Brainard (1997) demonstrates that the *share* of foreign affiliate sales in the sum of exports and affiliate sales is positively related to trade barriers and transport costs.[11]

Thus trade barriers and transport costs do cause a substitution effect toward direct investment, although they may reduce the levels of both investment and trade. Carr, Markusen, and Maskus (2001) and Markusen and Maskus (2001, 2002) show that it depends on which country, parent, or host has the trade barriers. Host-country barriers clearly encourage FDI while parent-country barriers (weakly) discourage it. Distance between countries clearly discourages FDI.

In summary, multinationals are important in industries in which intangible, firm-specific assets are important. These assets can generally be characterized as "knowledge capital," ranging from proprietary product or process know-how to reputations and trademarks. Direct investment increases relative to trade (but not necessarily absolutely) as host-country trade barriers increase, but decreases with distance.

1.3 Key Statistics

Tables 1.1–1.8 present some statistics to back up and reinforce many of the points of the previous section. I refer to many of these at various points throughout the book to support certain theoretical assumptions.

Table 1.1 presents statistics on the growth of multinational activity over a fourteen-year period and compares them to figures on the growth of GDP, fixed capital, and trade in goods and nonfactor services. The top five rows show different measures of growth in multinational activity. Royalties and fees probably include payments between unaffiliated firms, which is not clear from the World Investment Report, but in any case they are payments for producer services much like that which is transferred within multinationals.

Trade has grown faster than GDP, which is a well-known statistic quoted by authors in the industrial organization approach to trade literature. Less well known, affiliate activity has grown much faster than GDP, capital stocks, and trade. Affiliate sales have generally grown significantly more slowly than FDI stocks and flows, and that is a

Table 1.1
Growth in FDI

	Annual growth rate (%), all countries		
	1986–1990	1991–1995	1996–1999
FDI inflows	24.7	20.0	31.9
FDI stocks	18.2	9.4	16.2
Sales of foreign affiliates	15.8	10.4	11.5
Gross product of foreign affiliates	16.4	7.1	15.3
Royalties and fees receipts	22.0	14.2	3.9
GDP at factor cost	11.7	6.3	0.6
Gross fixed capital formation	13.5	5.9	−1.4
Exports of goods and nonfactor services	15.0	9.5	1.5

Source: UNCTAD World Investment Report (2000, and earlier years).

puzzle in itself. The models in this book are addressed more closely to affiliate output and sales than to investment stocks. The mid-1990s was a slower period for FDI and sales relative to GDP and trade, but the former rebounded strongly in the late 1990s. The numbers in table 1.1 are key motivating statistics for this book and provide support for the notion that it is important to spend more time and effort trying to understand multinationals than remaining fixated on trade in international microeconomics.

Table 1.2 gives statistics on the sources and recipients of new direct investment flows, dividing the world into Developed, Developing, and Central and Eastern Europe (CEE) (this is the breakdown in the UNCTAD World Investment Report, not my choice). Not surprisingly, the developed countries are the major source of outward ("out") investment, but perhaps less well known, they are the major recipients ("in") as well. There is a period in the mid-1990s where this was less true, but a look at more refined statistics indicates that the boom in investment in the developing countries during the mid-1990s was almost entirely accounted for by the opening of China. The apparent boom in outward investment from developing countries in the same period was almost entirely accounted for by Taiwanese, American, and other firms funneling their investments into China through Hong Kong subsidiaries, so the funds appeared to be coming from a developing country. This investment boom in China significantly weakened in 1998–1999, and the world may return to a more historical pattern

Table 1.2
FDI inflows and outflows, share in total

	Developed		Developing		CEE	
Year	in	out	in	out	in	out
1983–1987	76	95	24	5	0	0
1988–1992	78	93	21	7	1	0
1993	62	85	35	15	3	0
1994	59	83	39	17	3	0
1995	65	85	32	15	4	0
1996	58	85	38	15	3	0
1997	58	86	38	14	4	1
1998	71	95	26	5	3	0
1999	74	91	24	8	1	0

Source: UNCTAD World Investment Report (2000, and earlier years).

in which the bulk of funds flows not only from but to developed countries.

The statistics in table 1.2 are a major challenge to theory that I alluded to in the preface and earlier in this chapter. Theory must be able to explain why so much FDI flows among the high-income developed countries. Clearly, a theoretical model in which FDI only flows from capital rich to capital poor countries should be dismissed out of hand.

Table 1.3 continues on somewhat the same theme. Table 1.3 presents data on stocks rather than flows, however. I do not know why there is a discrepancy between world inward and outward stocks, whether this is just a statistical discrepancy or not. But these stocks have clearly grown steadily and significantly faster than GDP, as the flow data in table 1.1 suggest. Again, note that the inward numbers for the developed countries are almost equal to the averages for the world as a whole.

Table 1.3 notes that developing countries are net recipients of direct investment, which is not surprising and consistent with the intuition one would get from a model of portfolio capital flows. However, table 1.3 also breaks out the "least-developed countries." This is a United Nations definition that includes forty-eight countries. Note that the least-developed countries have inward stocks that are much smaller than the world average. These are the world's most capital-scarce economies and, for whatever reasons, they do not attract much FDI.

Table 1.3
Ratio of inward and outward FDI stock to gross domestic product

	1980	1985	1990	1995	1998
World					
inward	4.9	6.7	8.6	9.6	13.7
outward	5.4	6.4	8.6	10.2	14.1
Developed countries					
inward	4.7	6.1	8.3	8.8	12.1
outward	6.4	7.5	9.8	11.7	16.4
Developing countries					
inward	5.4	9.1	10.5	13.4	20.0
outward	0.9	1.6	2.6	4.9	6.7
Least developed countries					
inward	1.8	3.4	4.4	6.9	7.4
outward	0.7	2.7	1.0	1.1	1.9
United States					
inward	3.1	4.6	7.1	7.6	9.5
outward	8.1	6.2	7.8	9.9	11.5
The Netherlands					
inward	11.1	19.5	25.9	31.5	48.0
outward	24.5	37.3	38.4	45.4	68.9
Sweden					
inward	2.9	5.0	13.4	19.1	21.5
outward	3.0	10.7	21.5	31.6	41.3
Switzerland					
inward	8.4	10.8	15.0	18.6	26.5
outward	21.1	27.0	28.9	46.3	69.1
United Kingdom					
inward	11.7	14.0	20.8	18.0	23.2
outward	15.0	21.9	23.4	27.4	35.9

Source: UNCTAD World Investment Report (2000). "Least Developed Countries" is a UN definition consisting of 48 countries.

In the bottom half of table 1.3, I present data on some smaller to moderate-sized high-income countries and include the United States for comparison. The Netherlands, Sweden, Switzerland, and the United Kingdom are all major sources of outward direct investment. But these countries are also major recipients of inward direct investment. The United States, by comparison, is moving toward a position in which inward and outward stocks are converging. These statistics figure importantly in the theory chapters that follow.

Table 1.4
Share of inward world FDI stock/share of world GDP

	Developed countries	Developing countries	Least developed countries
1980	0.96	1.10	0.37
1985	0.91	1.36	0.51
1990	0.97	1.22	0.51
1995	0.92	1.40	0.72
1998	0.88	1.46	0.54

Source: UNCTAD World Investment Report (2000); Zhang and Markusen (1999).

Table 1.4 presents data from the top of table 1.3 on inward investment stocks in a somewhat different form. The statistics in table 1.4 give a group's share of world inward FDI stock divided by its share of world GDP. Once again, the developed countries are major recipients or hosts of FDI. Developing countries have a larger share of inward investment than their share of world GDP. But the least-developed countries have a much smaller share of FDI than their share of income, and a much smaller share of FDI relative to income than the developed countries.

There are, of course, some obvious reasons why the least-developed countries might attract so little FDI. These include the absence of all forms of infrastructure, including physical, institutional, and legal, extending to the absence of rule of law. But there are other reasons as well, and these will be discussed in subsequent chapters. They include demand-side reasons, such as the nature of the products produced by multinationals, and cost-side reasons, such as the need for skilled labor in the production process. Both together suggest that it is in the nature of what multinationals do that their products and processes are not well suited to very poor countries.

Table 1.5 presents some data on labor-force composition, relative wages, and inward and outward FDI. Relative wage data is hard to get, but the GTAP data set has figures for a limited set of countries as shown. For the seven developed and fourteen developing countries noted, the former have a much larger proportion of the labor force classified as skilled, and a much lower relative wage for skilled labor. These are crucial stylized facts that are exploited in the theoretical assumptions later in this book. Table 1.5 also shows the FDI stock data as a percentage of GDP for comparison. The skilled-labor-abundant countries are strong outward investors but also very significant

Table 1.5
Selected statistics, unweighted averages, 1995

	Skilled worker as % of labor force	Ratio of skilled to unskilled wage	Inward FDI as % of GDP	Outward FDI as % of GDP
Seven developed countries (GTAP)	26.0	1.81	13.4	16.5
All developed			8.8	11.7
Fourteen developing countries (GTAP)	10.8	3.54	20.5	5.1
All developing			13.4	4.9

Sources: FDI data from UNCTAD World Investment Reports (1996, 1997, and 2000).
Labor force and wage data from GTAP data set, 1995.
Note: Seven developed countries are United States, Canada, Japan, Denmark, Germany, Great Britain, and Sweden. Fourteen developing countries are Mexico, Korea, Singapore, Philippines, Malaysia, Thailand, Indonesia, China, Brazil, Chile, Turkey, Venezuela, Columbia, and Sri Lanka.

recipients of FDI. The skilled-labor-scarce countries are significant recipients of investment but small outward investors.

Table 1.6 continues along similar lines but adds a twist in considering market size along with per capita income. Developing countries are first divided into groups on the basis of per capita income, and then each income class is divided into small and large countries. The right-hand column of table 1.6 then gives FDI per capita. First, clear evidence is visible that richer countries have more inward investment per person. This may be because there is a high income elasticity of demand for the products multinationals produce and/or the need for skilled labor and related factors in production. But there may well be some reverse causality as well, in that more inward FDI may help generate higher per capita incomes. Second, larger countries in a given per capita income class receive significantly more inward investment per capita (except for the very poorest class). This suggests to me that local sales are quite important in overall multinational activity.

Table 1.7 explicitly considers the role of the local market versus production for export and the role of imports from the parent firm. The data is all bilateral with the United States, giving U.S. parents' trade with their foreign affiliates (outward data) and foreign firms' trade with their U.S. affiliates (inward data). The country abbreviations should be obvious, except for OAP which is Other Asia-Pacific, and LAT which is Latin America.

Table 1.6
Inward FDI flows and their links with GDP per capita and national income of developing countries in 1993

Country groups by GDP per capita (US$)	Average FDI per capita (US$)	Country groups by country size in GDP (US$, millions)	Average FDI per capita (US$)
>5000	226.89	>55000	242.20
		<49000	53.83
2500–5000	45.30	>31000	45.73
		<17000	32.30
1200–2500	33.02	>10000	33.43
		<9600	30.60
600–1200	10.06	>10000	10.86
		<9300	2.59
300–600	6.56	>4800	6.91
		<3700	3.68
<300	0.63	>2000	0.34
		<1500	2.47

Sources: FDI data are from International Monetary Fund (1995), *Balance of Payments Statistics Yearbook 1995*. GDP data are from International Monetary Fund (1995), *International Financial Statistics Yearbook 1995*. See also Zhang and Markusen (1999) for more detailed definitions and discussions of these data.

The top panel gives 1997 data, and one sees that, for all countries, numbers in the left-hand column for all U.S. partner countries are quite modest, not exceeding 15 percent of total affiliate sales. Affiliates are, on the whole, clearly not just assembly operations for export back to the home country, nor do they source a major part of their inputs from home-country imports. U.S. imports from the foreign affiliates of U.S. corporations are quite small as a percentage of total affiliate sales, and similarly for U.S. exports by affiliates of foreign corporations to their foreign parents. The numbers for OAP and LAT are somewhat higher. But still, only a relatively small proportion of output is shipped back to the United States. U.S. affiliates in these countries are not primarily assembly or other "vertical" operations producing for export. The largest numbers for 1997 are for U.S. imports from affiliates in OAP (27% of sales) and LAT (26% of sales). This reinforces the point of table 1.6, that the local host-country market is, on the whole, quite important for multinational firms.

In the bottom row of the 1997 and 1987 panels, I present Grubel-Lloyd indices of cross- or intra-industry affiliates activity. The intra-industry affiliate sales index (IIAS) is defined as follows. Let AS_{ij} denote affiliate sales by affiliates in country i of country j parent firms.

Table 1.7
Parent-affiliate trade as a proportion of total affiliate sales, 1997 and 1987 (foreign affiliates of U.S. firms and U.S. affiliates of foreign firms)

	Countries										
	ALL	CAN	FRA	GER	NET	SWI	UK	AUS	JAP	OAP	LAT
1997 total manufacturing											
Outward data											
U.S. exports to affiliates	0.14	0.41	0.05	0.05	0.07	0.04	0.06	0.09	0.12	0.15	0.23
U.S. imports from affiliates	0.15	0.42	0.04	0.03	0.04	0.06	0.05	0.04	0.04	0.27	0.26
Inward data											
U.S. exports shipped by affiliates of foreign firms	0.10	0.10	0.13	0.13	0.07	0.11	0.10	0.09	0.11	0.12	0.07
U.S. imports shipped by foreign parents to their U.S. affiliates	0.15	0.14	0.16	0.15	0.13	0.08	0.09	0.10	0.23	0.11	0.22
Grubel-Lloyd indices	82.92	52.04	88.00	80.66	82.23	30.68	98.93	71.78	45.95	23.57	16.62
1987 total manufacturing											
Outward data											
U.S. exports to affiliates	0.14	0.38	0.04	0.03	0.08	0.04	0.05	0.08	0.07	0.24	0.18
U.S. imports from affiliates	0.12	0.33	0.03	0.03	0.02	0.04	0.05	na	0.07	na	0.17
Inward data											
U.S. exports shipped by affiliates of foreign firms	0.07	0.09	0.06	0.09	0.05	0.04	0.05	0.03	0.07	0.05	0.09
U.S. imports shipped by foreign parents to their U.S. affiliates	0.11	0.10	0.10	0.14	0.10	0.09	0.07	0.08	0.27	0.09	na
Grubel-Lloyd indices	73.38	72.09	72.48	67.01	94.88	22.73	91.02	47.92	93.51	47.42	28.73

Source: Calculated from Bureau of Economic Analysis data.

The Grubel-Lloyd index applied to cross-country affiliate sales is

$$IIAS_{ij} = \left[1 - \frac{|AS_{ij} - AS_{ji}|}{AS_{ij} + AS_{ji}}\right] * 100.$$

The IIAS index ranges from a low of zero, when affiliate activity is one way only, to a value of one hundred when affiliate sales are perfectly balanced. The Grubel-Lloyd indices in table 1.7 are high for developed-country partners of the U.S. except for Japan (1997: 46%) and Switzerland (1997: 31%), although even these are moderately high. Cross- or intra-industry penetration of each developed country's firms in the other market is high. The numbers of OAP and LAT are significantly smaller as one might expect. Once again, we see that much direct investment is among the developed countries, rather than a one-way trip from developed to developing countries.

Table 1.8 looks at firm characteristics. Data is very scarce on these issues, but I have assembled some data from the different sources noted. The top numbers give a proxy for skill level, which is compensation per employee. If we accept this as a rough proxy, then parents are skilled-labor-intensive relative to affiliates, but there is not a huge difference for developed-country affiliates. I have included the GTAP figure for the fourteen developing countries from table 1.5 for comparison with the number for affiliates in developing countries. The numbers indicate that developing-country affiliates pay an average wage that is close to the average earnings of skilled workers in developing countries. This in turn suggests that affiliates are skilled-labor-intensive relative to the developing host countries as a whole. I use these stylized facts in assumptions about factor intensities later in the book.

The second set of numbers gives the share of nonproduction workers in total employment of parents and affiliate. While nonproduction workers are at best a crude proxy for skilled or "knowledge workers," they again suggest that skilled or knowledge workers are somewhat, but not completely, concentrated in the parent operations. These numbers will be used to justify some assumptions on factor intensities used later in the book.

Assets per employee, the third set of numbers, serves as a proxy for physical capital and perhaps intangible capital (I am not sure) in parents and affiliates. Parents and affiliates in developed countries are

Table 1.8
Characteristics of U.S. multinational corporations in manufacturing (1989 data unless otherwise indicated)

Skill level (compensation per employee $000, World Investment Report 1993)	
Parents	38.9
Affiliates	25.2
Developed countries	33.3
Developing countries	9.5
Fourteen developing countries from table 1.5	
Average earnings of skilled workers	9.8
(GTAP data set)	
Share of nonproduction employees in total employment 1982 (Slaughter 2000)	
Parents	0.54
Affiliates	0.42
Assets per employee ($000 per employee, World Investment Report 1993)	
Parents	186
Affiliates	114
Developed countries	147
Developing countries	52
R&D expenditures as a percentage of sales (World Investment Report 1993)	
Parents	3.33
Affiliates	1.12
Developed countries	1.27
Developing countries	0.30
All U.S. R&D performing manufacturing firms	3.20
R&D employment as a percentage of total employment (World Investment Report 1993)	
Parents	5.46
Affiliates	2.42
All U.S. R&D performing manufacturing firms	4.90

Sources: UNCTAD World Investment Report (1993), Slaughter (2000), and 1995 GTAP data set converted to 1989 US$. All manufacturing from NSF data, Survey of Industrial Research and Development (1991).

not wildly different, but affiliates in developing countries are much less "asset intensive."

The final two sets of numbers are measures of R&D intensity for parents and affiliates, and I also include figures for all U.S. R&D performing manufacturing firms. Parents are significantly more R&D-intensive than their affiliates, including affiliates in developed countries. Parents are slightly more R&D-intensive than all R&D performing firms in the United States, but I do not know what share of manufacturing does not do R&D, and therefore do not know the R&D intensity of multinational parents relative to all of U.S. manufacturing. Obviously, the inclusion of all manufacturing firms would make the multinationals look considerably more R&D-intensive than just considering R&D-producing firms. In any case, these numbers complement statistics cited in the previous section that multinational firms have a high value of intangible assets, suggesting that multinationals are relatively intensive in knowledge-based assets.

1.4 A Knowledge-Capital Approach

A typical point of departure for theory has been the logical premise that firms incur significant costs of doing business abroad relative to domestic firms in those countries. Therefore, for a firm to become a multinational, it must have offsetting advantages. A limited but very useful organizing framework for inquiring into the nature of these advantages was proposed by John Dunning (1977, 1981). Dunning proposed that three conditions are needed for firms to have a strong incentive to undertake direct foreign investments.

1. Ownership advantage: The firm must have a product or a production process such that the firm enjoys some market power advantage in foreign markets.

2. Location advantage: The firm must have a reason to want to locate production abroad rather than concentrate it in the home country, especially if there are scale economies at the plant level.

3. Internalization advantage: The firm must have a reason to want to exploit its ownership advantage internally, rather than license or sell its product/process to a foreign firm.

An important task of theory is to connect these ideas with the firm (technology) and country characteristics in a consistent way. This is something that was undertaken in a number of papers including

Markusen (1984, 1997), Ethier (1986), Helpman (1984, 1985), Horstmann and Markusen (1987a,b; 1992), Brainard (1993a), Ethier and
Markusen (1996), and Markusen and Venables (1998, 2000). I will refer
to a synthesis of several approaches as the "knowledge-capital"
model, although I note that this is not a widely used term.

Consider first ownership advantages. Evidence indicates that multinationals are related to R&D, marketing, scientific and technical
workers, product newness and complexity, and product differentiation. This suggests that multinationals are firms that are intensive in
the use of knowledge capital. This is a broad term that includes the
human capital of the employees, patents, blueprints, procedures, and
other proprietary knowledge, and finally marketing assets such as
trademarks, reputations, and brand names.

The crucial question then is why should knowledge capital be associated with multinationals while physical capital is not? I have suggested that the answer lies in three features of knowledge capital,
although these should be referred to as assumptions pending econometric support. First, the services of knowledge capital can be easily
transported to foreign production facilities, at least relative to the services of physical capital. Engineers and managers can visit multiple
production facilities with some ease (although stationing them abroad
is costly) and communicate with them in a low-cost fashion via tele-
phone, fax, and electronic mail. This property of knowledge capital is
important to firms making either horizontal or vertical investments.

Second, knowledge-based assets are skilled-labor-intensive relative
to production. This creates a motive for the geographical fragmentation of production and vertical multinationals. Skilled-labor-intensive
"headquarters" activities such as R&D and management should be
located where skilled labor is abundant and relatively cheap while
production may be located in less-skilled-labor-abundant countries
and/or in large markets.

The third property of knowledge capital that leads to the association
of multinationals with knowledge capital is the fact that knowledge
capital often has a joint-input or "public-good" property within the
firm. Blueprints, chemical formulae, or even reputation capital may be
very costly to produce, but once they are created, they can be supplied
at relatively low cost to foreign production facilities without reducing
the value or productivity of those assets in existing facilities. The blueprint, for example, can yield a flow of services in multiple locations
simultaneously. This property of knowledge capital, which does not

characterize physical capital, is particularly important to horizontal multinationals. But it may be quite important to vertical multinationals as well, insofar as the "blueprint" indicates exactly how the geographically fragmented activities, components, and products must fit and work together. In the knowledge-capital framework, multinationals are then exporters of knowledge-based services: managerial and engineering services, financial services, reputations and trademarks.

The sources of location advantages are varied, primarily because they can differ between horizontal and vertical firms. Consider horizontal firms that produce the same goods and services in each of several locations. Given the existence of plant-level scale economies, there are two principal sources of location advantages in a particular market. The first is the existence of trade costs between that market and the MNE's home country, in the form of transport costs, tariffs, and quotas, and more intangible proximity advantages. Indeed, if trade costs were truly zero, production would be concentrated in a single location (again, assuming plant-level scale economies) with other locations served by exports. That is, some sort of trade cost seems to be a necessary condition for horizontal multinationals to exist. The second source of location advantage, again following from the existence of plant-level scale economies, is a large market in the potential host country. If that market is very small, it does not pay for a firm to establish a local production facility, and the firm will instead service that market by exports.

The sources of location advantage for vertical multinationals are somewhat different. Suppose, for example, that a particular MNE exports the services of its knowledge capital and perhaps other intermediate inputs to a foreign production facility for final assembly and shipment back to the MNE's home country. This type of investment is likely to be encouraged by low trade costs rather than by high trade costs. The most logical situation in which this type of fragmentation arises is when the stages of production have different factor intensities and the countries have different relative factor endowments. Then, for example, skilled-labor-intensive R&D and intermediate goods should be produced in the skilled-labor-abundant country, and less-skilled-labor final assembly should be done in a country with low-wage unskilled labor. Fragmentation arises to exploit factor-price differences across countries.

Internalization advantages are the most abstract of the three. The topic quickly gets into fundamental issues such as what is a firm, and

why and how agency problems might be better solved within a firm
rather than through an arm's-length arrangement with a licensee or
contractor. Basically, it is my view that internalization advantages
often arise from the same joint-input, public-goods property of knowledge that creates ownership advantages. The property of knowledge
that makes it easily transferred to foreign locations also makes it easily
dissipated. Firms transfer knowledge internally in order to maintain
the value of assets and prevent asset dissipation. Licensees can easily
absorb the knowledge capital and then defect from the firm or ruin
the firm's reputation for short-run profit. Internalization models will
be the focus of the last three chapters of the book (again, see Markusen 1995 for a survey).

This section can be summarized as follows.

Ownership advantages: Arise from knowledge capital, which (a) can
be easily transported or transferred to foreign production facilities and
(b) has a joint-input property across the different production facilities.

Location advantages: For horizontal firms, location advantages arise
when the host-country market is large and when trade costs (broadly
defined) are moderate to high. For vertical firms, location advantages arise when trade costs are low, stages of production differ in
factor intensities, and countries differ significantly in relative factor
endowments.

Internalization advantages: Although there are many facets to this
issue, internalization advantages can arise from the same joint-input
characteristic of knowledge capital that creates ownership advantages.
Transferring knowledge-based assets through arm's-length market
mechanisms runs the risk of asset dissipation.

1.5 Summary

The stylized facts and statistics presented in this chapter lay down a
network of facts that need explanation. The chapter also outlines a
rough idea, referred to as the knowledge-capital approach, that provides an organizing theoretical framework. Development of the formal theory is the task for chapters 2–9. Chapter 7 provides a more
rigorous statement as to exactly what I mean by the knowledge-
capital model, since we will not need the full model until that point.
I then subject the theory to formal econometric testing in chapters
10–12.

2

A Partial-Equilibrium, Single-Firm Model of Plant Location

2.1 Introduction

I have always believed that an effective approach to a topic is to start simple and build up to more complicated and realistic models. Following this philosophy, this chapter presents a model that contains the minimal technical structure that allows for interesting choices for the firm and at the same time permits a basic welfare analysis. Elements presented here reappear in more complicated structures throughout this book.

The purpose of this chapter is to establish basic results about how technology characteristics and country characteristics affect the firm's location choices. Technology characteristics include firm-level and plant-level scale economies. Country characteristics include total two-country market size, difference in market sizes, differences in marginal costs, and trade costs. Technology and country characteristics interact to determine the equilibrium number and location of plants. Later in the chapter, I consider a few simple policy experiments and show how regime shifts induced by parameter changes lead to policy results that differ substantially from the traditional wisdom derived from competitive models or "new trade-theory" models with fixed firm locations.

The model used in this chapter will be familiar to many readers since it uses the basic elements found in many models in the "strategic trade policy" literature. I have made that choice deliberately in order to make the presentation accessible and to permit the results to be related to the earlier literature.

2.2 A Single-Firm Model

Here are the principal elements of the model.

a. There are two countries, i and j.

b. There are two goods, X and Y.

c. There is one factor of production, L.

d. Y is produced with constant returns by a competitive industry in both countries.

e. X is produced by a single firm, headquartered in country i. Country j does not have a domestically owned firm.

f. The X firm can have either a single plant in country i: a type-d (domestic or national) firm, or plants in both countries: a type-h (horizontal multinational) firm, or a single plant in country j: a type-v (vertical multinational) firm.

g. Markets are segmented so that the X firm can price independently in the two markets without threat of arbitrage.

Double subscripts are used for X and Y, with the first indicating the country of *production* and the second the country of *consumption*. X_{ii} is the amount of X produced and sold in country i, positive if the firm is type-d or type-h. X_{ij} is the amount produced in country i and sold in j, positive only if the firm is type-d. X_{jj} is the amount produced and sold in country j, positive only if the firm is type-h or type-v. X_{ji} is the amount produced in country j and sold in i, positive only if the firm is type-v.

Y_{ii} is the total amount of Y produced and sold in country i and similarly for Y_{jj}. Y_{ij} denotes Y produced in i and sold (exported) to j and Y_{ji} denotes Y produced in j and sold (imported into) i. Some of these quantities will of course typically be zero in equilibrium. L_i is the population of country i, so X_{ii}/L_i and Y_{ii}/L_i are per capita quantities.

An individual consumer in country i has a quasi-linear utility function as commonly found in the trade industrial organization literature, with individual utility in country i denoted U_{mi}. Assume first that country i consumers are served from a local plant (the firm is type-d or type-h). Thus X_{ii} is positive and X_{ji} is zero.[1]

$$U_{mi} = \alpha(X_{ii}/L_i) - (\beta/2)(X_{ii}/L_i)^2 + (Y_{ii} + Y_{ji})/L_i \qquad (1)$$

Aggregating across individuals, total utility in country i is given by

$$U_i = L_i U_{mi} = \alpha X_{ii} - (\beta/2)X_{ii}^2/L_i + (Y_{ii} + Y_{ji}). \tag{2}$$

Production of Y in country i is given by a simple linear function, where γ is an efficiency parameter and L_{yi} is the labor allocated to Y.[2]

$$Y_{ii} + Y_{ij} = \gamma L_{yi} \tag{3}$$

Let Y be numeraire and let p_i denote the price of X in terms of Y in country i. γ is then implicitly the wage rate in terms of Y. The national budget constraint requires that the value of the labor endowment plus profits of the national firm (Π_i) equals consumption expenditure on X and Y.

$$\gamma L_i + \Pi_i = p_i X_{ii} + (Y_{ii} + Y_{ji}) \tag{4}$$

The left-hand side of (4) is also the value of production (payments to labor and profits exhaust output), so the alternative interpretation of (4) is that the value of production equals the value of consumption. Replace the Y terms in (2) with (4). The representative consumer in country i then solves the following maximization problem, viewing profits and the price of X as exogenous.

$$\text{Max}(X)U_i = \alpha X_{ii} - (\beta/2)X_{ii}^2/L_i + \gamma L_i + \Pi_i - p_i X_{ii} \tag{5}$$

Optimization yields a linear inverse-demand curve for X with demand independent of income.

$$p_i = \alpha - (\beta/L_i)X_{ii} \tag{6}$$

Let Π_{ii} denote profits for a domestic firm on domestic sales minus fixed costs. The domestic firm incurs three types of costs, all in units of Y. c_i is the marginal cost of production, G is a plant-specific fixed cost, and F is a firm-specific fixed cost. Using (6), the firm's profit equation is given by

$$\Pi_{ii} = p_i X_{ii} - c_i X_{ii} - G - F = [\alpha - (\beta/L_i)X_{ii}]X_{ii} - c_i X_{ii} - G - F. \tag{7}$$

The first-order condition with respect to X_{ii} is

$$\frac{d\Pi_{ii}}{dX_{ii}} = \alpha - 2(\beta/L_i)X_{ii} - c_i = 0. \tag{8}$$

This gives equilibrium supply of X to the local market.

$$X_{ii} = \frac{\alpha - c_i}{2\beta}L_i \tag{9}$$

Substituting (9) back into the profit equation allows us to derive an expression for profits on local sales.

$$\Pi_{ii} = (p_i - c_i)X_{ii} - G - F = [\alpha - (\beta/L_i)X_{ii} - c_i]\frac{\alpha - c_i}{2\beta}L_i - G - F \tag{10}$$

$$\Pi_{ii} = \left[\alpha - c_i - \frac{(\alpha - c_i)}{2}\right]\frac{\alpha - c_i}{2\beta}L_i - G - F = \frac{\alpha - c_i}{2}\frac{\alpha - c_i}{2\beta}L_i - G - F \tag{11}$$

$$\Pi_{ii} = \beta\left[\frac{\alpha - c_i}{2\beta}\right]^2 L_i - G - F = \beta\left[\frac{\alpha - c_i}{2\beta}L_i\right]^2\frac{1}{L_i} - G - F$$

$$= \frac{\beta X_{ii}^2}{L_i} - G - F \tag{12}$$

If the firm maintained a plant in the foreign country j (type-h or type-v), the profit expression for foreign sales (Π_{jj}) is the same with L_i and c_i altered to L_j and c_j. An addition G would be incurred by the firm, but not an addition F. Let t be the transport cost, in units of Y, incurred by export sales. If the firm exports to country j, its profit equation for export sales Π_{ij} (arbitrarily imputing fixed costs to the domestic profit equation (7)) is as follows:[3]

$$\Pi_{ij} = p_jX_{ij} - (c_i + t)X_{ij} = [\alpha - (\beta/L_j)X_{ij}]X_{ij} - (c_i + t)X_{ij} \tag{13}$$

Maximization of (13) yields the equilibrium export supply:

$$X_{ij} = \frac{\alpha - c_i - t}{2\beta}L_j. \tag{14}$$

Following the same procedure used in equations (10)–(12), export profits are given by

$$\Pi_{ij} = \beta\left[\frac{\alpha - c_i - t}{2\beta}\right]^2 L_j = \frac{\beta X_{ij}^2}{L_j}. \tag{15}$$

In the case of a vertical (type-v) firm, switching the subscripts in (15) (i to j, j to i) gives profits before fixed costs on exports from the plant in j to the parent country i.

We can now summarize the total profits the firm would obtain from each of its three alternative modes of serving market j. Superscripts refer to types d, h, and v.

$$\Pi_i^d = \Pi_{ii} + \Pi_{ij} = \beta\left[\frac{\alpha - c_i}{2\beta}\right]^2 L_i + \beta\left[\frac{\alpha - c_i - t}{2\beta}\right]^2 L_j - G - F \tag{16}$$

$$\Pi_i^h = \Pi_{ii} + \Pi_{jj} = \beta \left[\frac{\alpha - c_i}{2\beta}\right]^2 L_i + \beta \left[\frac{\alpha - c_j}{2\beta}\right]^2 L_j - 2G - F \tag{17}$$

$$\Pi_i^v = \Pi_{ji} + \Pi_{jj} = \beta \left[\frac{\alpha - c_j - t}{2\beta}\right]^2 L_i + \beta \left[\frac{\alpha - c_j}{2\beta}\right]^2 L_j - G - F \tag{18}$$

2.3 Technology and Country Characteristics as Determinants of Plant Location

These three equations yield a great deal of insight about the key factors that determine the firm's optimal choice. Consider first the relative sizes of the two markets holding total size, $L_i + L_j$ constant. Assume equal marginal costs in both countries. The profits of a type-h firm are not affected by the distribution of total demand between the countries. However, the profits of a type-d firm are increasing in the share of L in the home (country i) market and vice versa for the type-v firm. Furthermore, either the type-d or type-v structure must dominate as the size of one country goes to zero. If L_j goes to zero for example, the type-d and type-h firms earn the same "variable profits" (revenues net of marginal costs), but the type-h firm has higher fixed costs.

A type-h structure is more likely to be chosen if the countries are similar in size, and it will be chosen if t is sufficiently high and/or G is sufficiently low.

Figure 2.1 shows some simulation results for this model, with the horizontal axis showing the distribution of a fixed total L between the two countries.[4] Country i is small on the left and large on the right. As noted earlier, the profits of the type-h firm are independent of the distribution of L between L_i and L_j. When country i is small, the optimal choice is for the firm (headquartered in i) to be a type-v firm, producing in the foreign country and exporting back to the headquarters (home) country. For intermediate size differences, a two-plant type-h structure is chosen and when country i is large, a single plant at home (type-d) is optimal.

Figure 2.2 gives simulation results for the same model but with the total world L double that in figure 2.1. The figures are qualitatively the same, but the region in which the two-plant type-h option is chosen is significantly larger in figure 2.2. The two-plant horizontal structure is chosen even when the countries are quite different in size. Referring back to equations (16)–(18), an increase in $L = L_i + L_j$ shifts all three

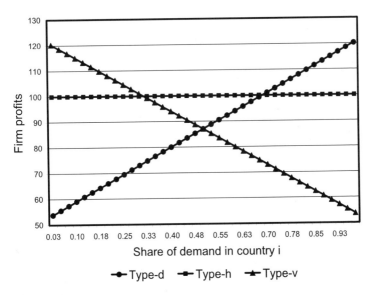

Figure 2.1
Relative size differences and the choice of regime, the base case

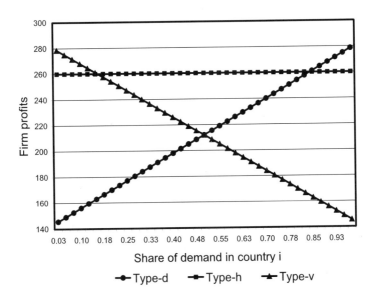

Figure 2.2
Total demand double the base case

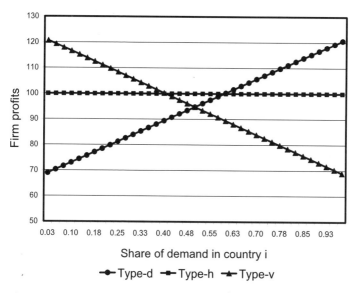

Figure 2.3
Trade costs 25 percent lower than in the base case

curves up, but shifts the type-h curve up more. Figures 2.1 and 2.2 give results that will appear repeatedly in the book, both in the theoretical chapters and in the empirical results: Multinationals will be "more likely" between two countries when they are large and relatively similar in size. When markets are very different in size, it does not pay to install costly capacity in the small market.

Figure 2.3 again uses the same model but lowers trade costs by 25 percent below the level used in figure 2.1 ($L_i + L_j$ is the same in figures 2.1 and 2.3). A lowering of trade costs shifts up the type-d and type-v curves while not affecting the type-h curve. This reduces the region where the type-h structure is chosen. As noted in chapter 1, multinational affiliate activity has grown faster than trade over the last two decades, consistent with market sizes growing somewhat faster than trade costs have fallen.

Figure 2.4 presents the trade-off between variables that leave the firm indifferent between a type-h structure and a type-d structure. The horizontal axis is the size of the world economy ($L = L_i + L_j$) as a proportion of the base case shown in figure 2.1. The left-hand Y-axis gives the share of demand located in country i that leaves the firm indifferent between one domestic plant and plants in both countries.

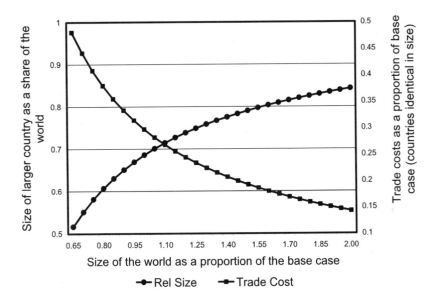

Figure 2.4
Relative size differences and trade costs that imply indifference between one and two plants, as a function of different levels of total world demand

This is the positively sloped relationship, indicating that the type-h form is consistent with larger size differences the larger total demand.

The right-hand Y-axis gives trade costs as a proportion of the base case that leave the firm indifferent when the counties are of identical size. This is the negatively sloped relationship, indicating that the critical level of trade costs falls as total market size increases. Firms may engage in horizontal investments at very low trade costs if markets are large. Exporting is a high variable-cost option, while a foreign branch plant is a high fixed-cost option, and thus the latter is chosen when markets are large.

Figure 2.5 again uses the base case model of figure 2.1 but alters the composition of fixed costs away from plant-specific costs G and toward firm-specific costs F holding $F + G$ constant. The result is rather obvious from inspecting (16)–(18). The profit curves for the type-d and type-v curves are unaffected, but the curve for the type-h firm shifts up. The type-h form will now be chosen for a wider range of differences in country size. This result is useful for thinking about technology changes over time. If technology changes in such a way that R&D and other initial costs become more important relative to

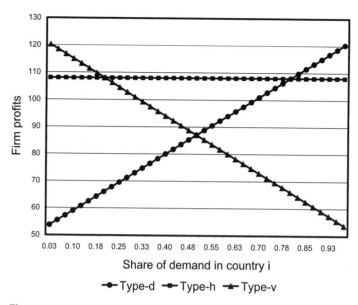

Figure 2.5
Composition of fixed costs altered toward F relative to the base case, holding $F + G$ constant

plant-level scale economies, we would expect that industry to become more multinationalized over time. Alternatively, it is useful for thinking about industries in cross-section, since some industries are far more dominated by multinationals than others. Industries are more likely to be multinationalized if firm-level scale economies are more important relative to plant-level scale economies. If firm-level scale economies are closely related to R&D, then we have an explanation for the common empirical finding that multinationals are more important in R&D-intensive industries.

Figures 2.6 and 2.7 illustrate the effects of differences in marginal production costs. In figure 2.6, marginal production costs are lower in host-country j than in parent country i. This has the rather obvious consequence that the type-v structure is chosen even when country j is relatively small. Low costs outweigh the small size of the local market. This will be important in later chapters when, in general-equilibrium models with skilled and unskilled labor, differences in relative factor endowments between countries combined with differences in factor intensities between firm-level and plant-level costs will be an explanation for vertical multinationals.

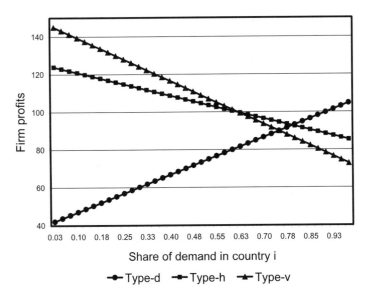

Figure 2.6
Marginal production costs lower in country *j*

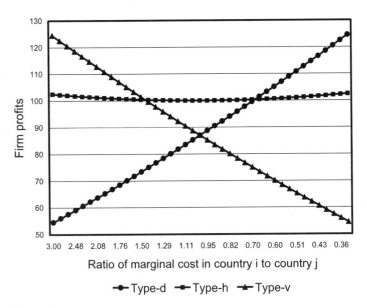

Figure 2.7
Relative production costs and choice of regime (country sizes identical)

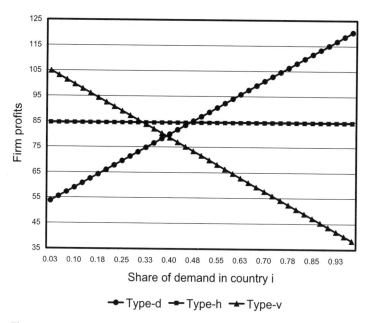

Figure 2.8
Technology transfer costs: Plant-specific fixed cost (G) 70 percent higher in foreign (country *j*) plant

Figure 2.7 plots the ratio of marginal costs in the two countries with country *i* being the high-cost country on the left. The countries are identical in size. The cost differences have some effect on the profits of a type-h firm because of the quadratic terms in (16)–(18), but this effect is quite small. Cost differences have large effects on the profits of a type-d firm relative to a type-v firm and both relative to a type-h firm. A type-h form is chosen when the countries have quite similar costs in this example, but a single plant located in the low-cost country is chosen when costs differ significantly. This result reappears in later chapters when readers will observe that horizontal multinationals are more important between two countries when they are similar in relative factor endowments (and thus relative costs) as well as in size.

Figure 2.8 considers what we could call technology transfer costs. It is not necessarily the case that firm-specific assets such as technology can be transferred without cost to foreign countries. Figure 2.8 uses the same parameters as the base case, except that it sets the fixed costs of a second plant 70 percent higher than the fixed costs for the home plant. This shifts the type-h and type-v profit curves down by equal amounts but does not affect the type-d profit curve. Figure 2.8 shows that this creates a bias toward home production, and a single home plant will be chosen when the countries are identical in size.

We can summarize this section by noting the conditions under which we are likely to see the firm choose the two-plant type-h structure:

1. Total "world" demand is high.

2. Countries are of similar size.

3. Trade costs are high.

4. Firm-specific fixed costs are large relative to plant-specific fixed costs.

5. Marginal costs are similar in the two countries.

6. Technology transfer costs are low.

2.4 Policy Experiments

It is beyond the scope of this book to offer a detailed policy analysis in each chapter. Futhermore, I have a distaste for exercises such as calculating "optimal" taxes or subsidies. Part of the difficulty is that in models with distortions such as those developed in this book, it is possible to get almost any result one wants through some set of assumptions. On the other hand, it is worthwhile to give some examples of how policies may work differently in models with endogenous location choices vis-à-vis models where the production regime is exogenously fixed.

First, it is necessary to derive welfare expressions for the model developed in section 2.2. Assume again that X_{ii} is postive and X_{ji} is zero (the firm is type-d or type-h). Substitute the expression for p_i in (6) into (5):

$$U_i = \alpha X_{ii} - \frac{\beta}{2L_i} X_{ii}^2 + \gamma L_i + \Pi_i - \alpha X_{ii} + \frac{\beta}{L_i} X_{ii}^2 \tag{19}$$

Denote consumer surplus, the utility derived from consuming X minus the cost of purchasing X, as CS (note Y costs the same as the utility derived). Equation (19) can be rewritten as

$$U_i = \frac{\beta X_{ii}^2}{2L_i} + \gamma L_i + \Pi_i = CS_i + \Pi_i + \gamma L_i \qquad CS_i = \frac{\beta X_{ii}^2}{2L_i} = \frac{\beta}{2}\left[\frac{\alpha - c_i}{2\beta}\right]^2 L_i.$$
$$\tag{20}$$

Now substitute in for profits from (16) to get country i's (the parent country's) welfare when the type-d firm is chosen:

$$U_i^d = CS_i + \Pi_i^d + \gamma L_i$$

$$= \frac{3\beta}{2} \left[\frac{\alpha - c_i}{2\beta} \right]^2 L_i + \beta \left[\frac{\alpha - c_i - t}{2\beta} \right]^2 L_j - G - F + \gamma L_i \quad (21)$$

Using (14), (17), and (18), country i's welfare under the type-h and type-v regimes are

$$U_i^h = CS_i + \Pi_i^h + \gamma L_i$$

$$= \frac{3\beta}{2} \left[\frac{\alpha - c_i}{2\beta} \right]^2 L_i + \beta \left[\frac{\alpha - c_j}{2\beta} \right]^2 L_j - 2G - F + \gamma L_i \quad (22)$$

$$U_i^v = CS_i + \Pi_i^v + \gamma L_i$$

$$= \frac{3\beta}{2} \left[\frac{\alpha - c_j - t}{2\beta} \right]^2 L_i + \beta \left[\frac{\alpha - c_j}{2\beta} \right]^2 L_j - G - F + \gamma L_i \quad (23)$$

Country j's welfare will be the same under the type-h or type-v firm at the same parameter values (of course which type is chosen does depend on parameter values) but will be lower under the type-d firm due to the higher price paid for the import good assuming $c_i = c_j$:

$$U_j^{h,v} = CS_j^{h,v} + \gamma L_j = \frac{\beta}{2} \left[\frac{\alpha - c_j}{2\beta} \right]^2 L_j + \gamma L_j \quad (24)$$

$$U_j^d = CS_j^d + \gamma L_j = \frac{\beta}{2} \left[\frac{\alpha - c_i - t}{2\beta} \right]^2 L_j + \gamma L_j \quad (25)$$

Note first that a small parameter change that leads the firm to switch from a type-d to a type-h structure has just a small effect on country i (i.e., if profits are just equal in the two modes so is welfare). However, country j is discretely better off with the type-h or type-v structure as long as its marginal cost does not exceed that in country i by more than the trade cost:

$$U_j^{v,h} - U_j^d = \frac{\beta}{2} \left[\frac{\alpha - c_j}{2\beta} \right]^2 L_j - \frac{\beta}{2} \left[\frac{\alpha - c_i - t}{2\beta} \right]^2 L_j \geq 0 \quad \text{for } c_j \leq c_i + t \quad (26)$$

This is positive if $(c_i + t) > c_j$ as noted. Assuming that it is the fixed cost or small market size that deters the firm from investing in country j and not a higher marginal cost in j, then j is better off with a local plant than without.

A small parameter change that shifts the firm from a type-d or type-h structure to a type-v structure causes a discrete fall in country i's welfare. When the firm is indifferent between modes d and v or between h and v, consumers are not, having discretely lower consumer surplus under mode v:

$$\Pi_i^v = \Pi_i^d \quad \text{or}$$

$$\Pi_i^v = \Pi_i^h \Rightarrow U_i^{d,h} - U_i^v = \frac{\beta}{2}\left[\frac{\alpha - c_i}{2\beta}\right]^2 L_i - \frac{\beta}{2}\left[\frac{\alpha - c_j - t}{2\beta}\right]^2 L_i \quad (27)$$

This expression is positive assuming $c_i < c_j + t$.

The point of this discussion is that the choice of mode by the firm does not necessarily maximize social welfare in either country. The term *maximize welfare* is used here in a second-best sense, referring to the best choice of mode *given* that the firm produces as a monopoly. The firm may be indifferent between two modes, but consumers (and national welfare maximization) may not be. Note that when the firm is indifferent between two modes and $c_i = c_j$, at least one country's consumers will not be indifferent. Each country will want a plant in its country, so country i will not want type-v and country j will not want type-d.

Figures 2.9 and 2.10 present simulation results for two policy experiments. Country i is four times the size of country j so that the firm initially prefers mode d. Marginal costs are the same in the two countries. I ignore γL_i and γL_j in calculating welfare numbers and report only the sum of consumer surplus and profits.

In figure 2.9, I vary country j's trade cost (cost of exporting from i to j), holding country i's cost at 2.0, the value used for both countries in the base case of figure 2.1. I also look at the case where the cost is a revenue-generating tariff for country j rather than a resource-using trade cost. In the case of the tariff, tariff revenue must be added to the budget constraint for country j (equation (4) for country j), and thus tariff revenue will appear as a term in the welfare expression as well. The result shown in figure 2.9 is that increases in the trade cost/tariff reduce country i's welfare and have a stronger negative effect on country j, due to size differences. The tariff, of course, reduces country j's welfare less. There is, however, a discrete jump in country j's welfare when the cost becomes large enough to induce a mode shift where the firm builds a plant in country j, shifting to a type-h structure. This shift is sufficiently strong that country j is better off relative

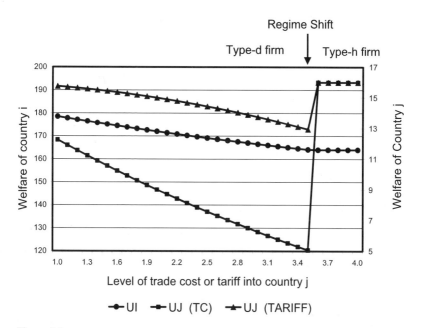

Figure 2.9
Welfare effects of changing country j's trade costs (TC) or tariff (country i four times the size of j)

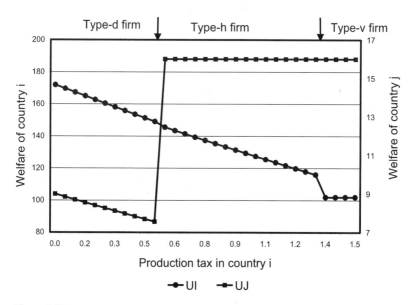

Figure 2.10
Welfare effect of a production tax in country i (country i four times the size of country j)

to the initial situation with the trade cost equal to 1.0, and indeed this must be the case as is shown in (26) with the assumption that $c_i = c_j$. Note that there is no discrete change in country i's welfare at the regime shift, which also follows from the previous discussion. Figure 2.10 shows the effects of the imposition of a production tax in country i. Production tax revenues must be added to the budget constraint for country i in (4) and will then appear as a term in the welfare expression when there is domestic production in country i. Parameter values are the same as in the base case except for the difference in country size. The tax has a negative effect on country i and on country j under the type-d regime. At a tax equal to 0.5 (marginal cost c_i is 2.0), the firm shifts to a type-h structure, incurring the fixed cost G to build a plant in country j to serve j's market. This results in a large, discrete improvement in country j's welfare. There is a small discrete fall in country j's welfare as tax revenue is lost, but this jump is quantitatively very small in figure 2.10. Welfare continues to fall in country i as the tax increases but country j is not affected. A second regime shift occurs when the tax becomes so punitive that the firm abandons production in country i altogether, becomes a type-v firm, and serves its home market by exports. Country j is indifferent to this shift, but there is a discrete drop in country i's welfare due to two effects: the discrete loss of tax revenue, and the higher price paid for X due to the trade cost of importing.

These experiments are hardly exhaustive. Nor are the results completely robust for the experiments that we have considered. As noted above, if the firm is prevented from entering country j due to its higher marginal cost rather than because of the fixed cost of entry, then a tariff by country j that induces entry may result in a discrete fall in welfare for country j. Cheap imports plus tariff revenue are displaced by costly domestic production. This is a case modeled in Levinsohn (1989). However, I wish to caution again that my purpose here is to provide illustrations of the effects of allowing for regime shifts, not to provide policy recommendations.

2.5 Summary and Conclusions

The purpose of this chapter is thus to provide a minimal model of a firm's location decisions and to show how firm or technology/cost factors combine with country characteristics to determine the equilibrium regime. I noted the conditions under which one is likely to see the firm choose the two-plant type-h structure:

1. Total "world" demand is high.
2. Countries are of similar size.
3. Trade costs are high.
4. Firm-specific fixed costs are large relative to plant-specific fixed costs.
5. Marginal costs are similar in the two countries.
6. Technology transfer costs are low.

If a firm is going to have only a single plant, the relationship between domestic and foreign market size, the relationship between domestic and foreign production costs, and the existence of technology transfer costs determine the optimal choice.

In section 2.4 I turned to policy and considered the effects of policies that induce regime shifts on welfare. I showed that the firm's choice does not necessarily maximize (second-best) welfare of either country. If the firm is indifferent between two modes, then one of the countries must be worse off under one of those two modes in terms of both consumer surplus and total welfare.[5]

With respect to the specific policies considered, I showed that a trade barrier to induce local production in the host country may benefit that country, but this result can be reversed with an alternative specification of costs. A production tax in the parent country will at some point induce "capital flight," the shift of production abroad to the detriment of the parent country and to the benefit of the host country.

3

International Duopoly
with Endogenous Market
Structures

3.1 Introduction

A large literature on trade and trade policy under conditions of imperfect competition and increasing returns to scale now exists. Much of the literature is normative, a subfield that has been dubbed strategic trade policy and that seeks to understand "optimal" policies under various sets of assumptions. Almost all of this literature assumes an exogenously specified market structure. Indeed, the number of firms is generally fixed at one in each country. Thus no entry or exit is considered, and no firm has any option other than a single integrated operation in its home country. I have always found these twin assumptions odd, given that most of the industries referred to as motivational examples have seen both significant entry and exit and are often dominated by multinationals.

In this chapter, I follow the strategic trade policy literature and assume at most two firms, with at most one headquartered in each of two countries. However, each firm may choose among three options. It may have a single plant in its home country and serve the other country by exports. This is, of course, the "classic" case (and generally the only case considered) in the strategic trade policy literature. In my model, each firm may choose instead to maintain plants in both countries or to not enter the market. Other principal assumptions of the model, including functional forms for demand and costs, follow the strategic trade policy literature quite closely. This is a deliberate choice so that readers can relate the results here to earlier literature, such as Dixit (1984), Brander and Spencer (1985), and Eaton and Grossman (1986).

Before continuing, I find it useful to note what I will *not* consider in the chapter. First of all, the number of firms will be limited to one or zero in each country. I will not consider free entry, although I believe strongly that it is important to do so in policy analysis. Policy conclusions can differ substantially in models with free entry and exist, and readers are referred to Venables (1985), Dixit and Kyle (1985), Horstmann and Markusen (1986), and Markusen and Venables (1988) for models with national firms only, but with free entry and exit. The latter assumptions are used in chapters 5–7. Second, I do not consider asymmetries in countries such as size and cost differences, as I did in chapter 2, and surely do in subsequent chapters. I stick to a model of identical countries and show that a rich set of possibilities emerges even in such a restricted model. Asymmetries may emerge in equilibrium, and the otherwise identical countries can enjoy quite different welfare levels in equilibrium.

Third, I stick to positive analysis. I do not attempt to solve for "optimal" policies but note instead how a given policy may have quite different effects from traditional analysis when it induces a regime shift. Although some authors are reluctant to acknowledge the fact, most of the normative strategic policy literature is just Pigouvian marginal analysis in the presence of distortions. This chapter departs from this tradition. In the original article on which this chapter is based (Horstmann and Markusen 1992), Horstmann and I subtitled the paper "natural facit saltum" (nature proceeds by leaps), a play on the subtitle to Marshall's famous *Principles of Economics*, "natural non facit saltum." Examples presented at the end of the chapter will make it clear that by inducing a regime shift, a policy may have far larger benefits or costs, or may have opposite effects from those predicted by marginal analysis.

Section 3.2 introduces the duopoly model, and I hope that notation and choice of functions allow the reader to exploit previous investments made in the strategic trade policy literature, even if my focus is on positive not normative economics.

3.2   A Duopoly Model of International Competition

I use the same notation and functional forms as in the previous chapter. However, I restrict the analysis to identical economies. This allows me to exploit symmetry and to eliminate unnecessary notation. First, normalize market size in each country to one, so that $L_i = L_j = 1$. Second, assume that there is a small cost penalty for type-v firms relative to type-d firms for splitting the headquarters and plant. Since the countries have identical sizes and costs, type-v firms are never active in this model and will not be referred to again. Third, drop the subscript i on marginal cost c, assumed identical across countries. G and F again denote plant and firm fixed costs, respectively.

X_{ij} will denote output of the firm *headquartered* in i and *sold* in j. Please note that this is a different definition from the previous chapter, since it's now necessary to keep track of an additional factor—namely, which firm is being talked about. I use this notation for chapters 5–8 as well. Where X_{ij} is *produced* depends on the firm type.

X_{ij} for a type-d firm (headquartered in i) is produced in i and exported to country j.

X_{ij} for a type-h firm (headquartered in i) is produced in the branch plant in country j.

The duopoly equilibrium is determined as a solution to a two-stage game. In the first stage, the firms decide (simultaneously) on the number of plants $(0, 1, 2)$, and in the second stage they compete in a Cournot output game. Markets are segmented as in chapter 2.

The utility function and budget constraint for country i are given by

$$U_i = \alpha(X_{ii} + X_{ji}) - (\beta/2)(X_{ii} + X_{ji})^2 + (Y_{ii} + Y_{ji})$$

$$\gamma L_i + \Pi_i = \gamma + \Pi_i = p_i(X_{ii} + X_{ji}) + (Y_{ii} + Y_{ji}). \tag{1}$$

Substituting from the budget constraint for good Y, we have the consumer's choice problem, where profits (Π_i) are viewed as exogenous.

$$\text{Max}(X)U_i = \alpha(X_{ii} + X_{ji}) - (\beta/2)(X_{ii} + X_{ji})^2 + \gamma + \Pi_i - p_i(X_{ii} + X_{ji}) \tag{2}$$

The inverse demand function is given by the first-order condition, and is linear in X.

$$p_i = \alpha - \beta(X_{ii} + X_{ji}) \tag{3}$$

Hold the market structure or regime fixed for the moment. That is, consider the second-stage output decisions first. Let Π_{ij} denote the profits of firm i on it sales in market j before (net of) all fixed costs. Profits for firm i on its domestic sales are given by

$$\Pi_{ii} = p_i X_{ii} - c X_{ii} = [\alpha - \beta(X_{ii} + X_{ji})]X_{ii} - c X_{ii}. \tag{4}$$

Assume Cournot competition, so that each firm makes a best response to the other firm's output, maximizing profits while holding the other firm's output fixed.

$$\frac{d\Pi_{ii}}{dX_{ii}} = \alpha - 2\beta X_{ii} - \beta X_{ji} - c = 0 \tag{5}$$

Assume first that firm i faces a rival producing in the domestic market; that is, firm j is a type-h firm. Then, exploiting cost symmetry, solve (5) for the Cournot output of the firm i (equal to the country j firm's output from its plant in country i) by setting $X_{ii} = X_{ji}$.

$$X_{ii} = \frac{\alpha - c}{3\beta} = X_{ji} \qquad \text{(if firm } j \text{ is type-h)} \tag{6}$$

Substitute (6) back into the profit equation (4).

$$\Pi_{ii} = (p_i - c)X_{ii} = [\alpha - \beta(X_{ii} + X_{ji}) - c]\frac{\alpha - c}{3\beta} \tag{7}$$

$$\Pi_{ii} = \left[\alpha - c - \frac{2(\alpha - c)}{3}\right]\frac{\alpha - c}{3\beta} = \frac{\alpha - c}{3}\frac{\alpha - c}{3\beta} \tag{8}$$

$$\Pi_{ii} = \beta\left[\frac{\alpha - c}{3\beta}\right]^2 \tag{9}$$

Now suppose that firm j is type-d, exporting to market i from its plant in country j. The first-order condition for firm i is the same as in (5) for market i, but the trade cost t must be added to the cost c for firm j. The first-order conditions are

$$\frac{d\Pi_{ii}}{dX_{ii}} = \alpha - 2\beta X_{ii} - \beta X_{ji} - c = 0$$

$$\frac{d\Pi_{ji}}{dX_{ji}} = \alpha - 2\beta X_{ji} - \beta X_{ii} - c - t = 0. \tag{10}$$

Substitute the first equation of (10) into the second.

$$\alpha - 2\beta X_{ji} - \frac{\alpha}{2} + \frac{\beta}{2}X_{ji} + \frac{c}{2} - c - t = 0 \tag{11}$$

$$\frac{\alpha}{2} - \frac{3}{2}\beta X_{ji} - \frac{c}{2} - t = \alpha - 3\beta X_{ji} - c - 2t = 0 \tag{12}$$

$$X_{ji} = \left[\frac{\alpha - c - 2t}{3\beta}\right] \tag{13}$$

Now solve for X_{ii} using the first equation of (10).

$$\alpha - 2\beta X_{ii} - \frac{\alpha - c - 2t}{3} - c = 0 \tag{14}$$

$$\frac{2}{3}\alpha - 2\beta X_{ii} - \frac{2}{3}c + \frac{2}{3}t = \frac{\alpha}{3} - \beta X_{ii} - \frac{c}{3} + \frac{t}{3} = 0 \tag{15}$$

$$X_{ii} = \left[\frac{\alpha - c + t}{3\beta}\right] \tag{16}$$

Now substitute (16) into the profit equation for firm i to get profits on domestic sales before (net of) fixed costs.

$$\Pi_{ii} = \left[\alpha - \beta\left[\frac{2(\alpha - c - t/2)}{3\beta}\right] - c\right]\left[\frac{\alpha - c + t}{3\beta}\right] \tag{17}$$

$$\Pi_{ii} = \left[\alpha - \frac{2}{3}\alpha + \frac{2}{3}c + \frac{t}{3} - c\right]\left[\frac{\alpha - c + t}{3\beta}\right] = \left[\frac{\alpha - c + t}{3}\right]\left[\frac{\alpha - c + t}{3\beta}\right] \tag{18}$$

$$\Pi_{ii} = \beta\left[\frac{\alpha - c + t}{3\beta}\right]^2 \tag{19}$$

Follow the same procedure for firm j, substituting (13) into its profit equation.

$$\Pi_{ji} = \left[\alpha - \beta\left[\frac{2(\alpha - c - t/2)}{3\beta}\right] - c - t\right]\left[\frac{\alpha - c - 2t}{3\beta}\right] \tag{20}$$

$$\Pi_{ji} = \left[\alpha - \frac{2}{3}\alpha + \frac{2}{3}c + \frac{t}{3} - c - t\right]\left[\frac{\alpha - c - 2t}{3\beta}\right]$$

$$= \left[\frac{\alpha - c - 2t}{3}\right]\left[\frac{\alpha - c - 2t}{3\beta}\right] \tag{21}$$

$$\Pi_{ji} = \beta\left[\frac{\alpha - c - 2t}{3\beta}\right]^2 \tag{22}$$

In examining these results, notice that β is just a scaling parameter, so it can be normalized at one, without any loss of generality. Second, note that shifting c is equivalent to shifting α in the opposite direction. Thus c is also a redundant parameter, and marginal cost can be set equal to zero, however offensive to reality that might be. Thus let $\beta = 1$, $c = 0$. Equations (9), (19), and (22) are all that is needed to find profits in each market structure when subtracting the relevant fixed costs. Let $\Pi_i(n_i, n_j)$ be the profits (inclusive of fixed costs) of firm i when firm i chooses n_i plants and firm j chooses n_j plants, and similarly for $\Pi_j(n_i, n_j)$. n_i and n_j take on the values $(0, 1, 2)$. Profits in monopolistic market structures such as $(1, 0)$ and $(2, 0)$ can be found by referring back to chapter 2. Profits in the various possible market structures are as follows:

$$\Pi_i(2, 2) = 2\left[\frac{\alpha}{3}\right]^2 - 2G - F = \Pi_j(2, 2) \tag{23}$$

$$\Pi_i(1, 1) = \left[\frac{\alpha + t}{3}\right]^2 + \left[\frac{\alpha - 2t}{3}\right]^2 - G - F = \Pi_j(1, 1) \tag{24}$$

$$\Pi_i(2, 1) = \left[\frac{\alpha}{3}\right]^2 + \left[\frac{\alpha + t}{3}\right]^2 - 2G - F = \Pi_j(1, 2) \tag{25}$$

$$\Pi_i(1, 2) = \left[\frac{\alpha}{3}\right]^2 + \left[\frac{\alpha - 2t}{3}\right]^2 - G - F = \Pi_j(2, 1) \tag{26}$$

$$\Pi_i(2, 0) = 2\left[\frac{\alpha}{2}\right]^2 - 2G - F = \Pi_j(0, 2) \tag{27}$$

$$\Pi_i(1, 0) = \left[\frac{\alpha}{2}\right]^2 + \left[\frac{\alpha - t}{2}\right]^2 - G - F = \Pi_j(0, 1) \tag{28}$$

Profits are zero when a firm chooses zero plants.

These profit levels in the second-stage output game can be inserted into a three-by-three payoff matrix, where the rows will denote the strategies of firm i and the columns the strategies of firm j. The payoff matrix is as follows where the first number in a cell is the profits of firm i and the second number is the profits of firm j.

		Firm j number of plants		
		0	1	2
Firm i	0	$0, 0$	$0, \Pi_j(0, 1)$	$0, \Pi_j(0, 2)$
number of	1	$\Pi_i(1, 0), 0$	$\Pi_i(1, 1), \Pi_j(1, 1)$	$\Pi_i(1, 2), \Pi_j(1, 2)$
plants	2	$\Pi_i(2, 0), 0$	$\Pi_i(2, 1), \Pi_j(2, 1)$	$\Pi_i(2, 2), \Pi_j(2, 2)$

$$(29)$$

This is a symmetric matrix, a result which follows from the fact that costs and market sizes are the same (see equations (23)–(28)).

Before solving the game for various parameter values, look first at the intuition as to when a $(2, 2)$ market structure might generate more profits than a $(1, 1)$. Of course, high profits in the former is neither necessary nor sufficient to ensure that it is an equilibrium, but that discussion is postponed for a moment.

Refer back to equations (23) and (24). It is clear that higher total fixed costs reduce the profits of the firms in both $(2,2)$ and $(1,1)$, so neither of these regimes might be an equilibrium at high fixed costs. Changes in the composition of fixed costs toward F and away from G, such as $dF = -dG > 0$, will favor $(2,2)$ over $(1,1)$ and vice versa.

The relationship between profits in $(1,1)$ and trade costs t is, however, nonmonotonic. This was noted by Brander and Krugman (1983). Beginning at free trade $(t = 0)$, increases in t reduce profits up to the point where $t = \alpha/5$, where the derivative of (24) with respect to t is zero. For values of t higher than that, profits increase and eventually at autarky $(t = \alpha/2$ from (13)), profits are higher for the firms than in free trade (autarky profits before fixed costs are $(\alpha/2)^2 > 2(\alpha/3)^2$ where the right-hand side is free-trade profits from (24)). The fact that autarky profits are higher than free trade is a manifestation of the pro-competitive effect of trade in this model (Markusen 1981). For the calibrations used in the numerical examples, this will not be much of a problem. Furthermore, it certainly does not follow that trade costs above $t > \alpha/5$ make $(1,1)$ more likely, because higher trade costs also make each firm more likely to deviate to a two-plant strategy, given that the other firm has only one plant.

Figures 3.1–3.4 present general results relating the Nash equilibrium regime to key parameters. While these figures are drawn for particular numerical values of certain other parameters, they must have the general shapes shown. Figure 3.1 shows the regime as a function of F and G holding α and t at fixed values. Figure 3.3 allows F and t to vary, and figure 3.4 allows G and t to vary. Each line represents a locus of points at which one or both firms are indifferent between two choices, given the choice of the other firm.

Let's go through figure 3.1 in detail. Figure 3.2 expands on a key region of this diagram. Note from symmetry that if $(2,0)$ is an equilibrium, $(0,2)$ must be as well and similarly for $(1,0)$ and $(0,1)$. Several loci are defined by the following conditions:

a. Boundary between $(2,2)$ and $(2,0)$, $(0,2)$. At points on this locus, profits for the two firms in $(2,2)$ are zero, so each firm is indifferent to exiting, given that the rival has two plants.

b. Boundary between $(2,0)$, $(0,2)$ and $(0,0)$. Fixed costs are so high that the single multinational firm operating just breaks even and is indifferent to exiting. Boundaries (a) and (b) have slopes of -2 because, with two plants, an increase of $G = 1$ must be matched by a decrease of $F = 2$.

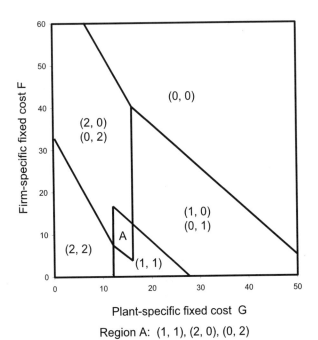

Figure 3.1
Regimes as a function of F and G ($t = 3$)

c. Boundary between $(1,1)$ and $(1,0)$, $(0,1)$. Profits for the two firms in $(1,1)$ are zero, so each firm is indifferent to exiting given that the other firm has one plant.

d. Boundary between $(1,0)$, $(0,1)$ and $(0,0)$. The single one-plant firm just breaks even and is indifferent to exiting. Boundaries (c) and (d) have slopes of -1 because, with one plant, an increase of $G = 1$ must be matched by a decrease of $F = 1$.

There is a central region of the diagram in which there are multiple equilibria. This will be explained with reference to the labeling in figure 3.2. Consider first the vertical line in figure 3.1 separating $(2,2)$ and $(1,1)$. This has two separate components, that below point A^0 in figure 3.2 and that between A^0 and A^1. Below A^0, firm $i(j)$ is indifferent between one and two plants, and the value of G at which this occurs is the same regardless of whether firm $j(i)$ has one or two plants. That is, this boundary is defined by

$$\Pi_i(2,1) = \Pi_i(1,1) \geq 0, \qquad \Pi_i(2,2) = \Pi_i(1,2) \geq 0$$

$$\text{(vertical line below } A^0\text{)}. \qquad (30)$$

Within A: $\Pi_i(1,1)$, $\Pi_i(2,0) > 0$, $\Pi_i(1,2)$, $\Pi_i(2,2) < 0$

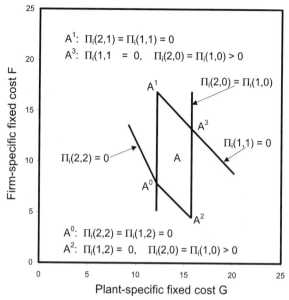

Between A^0 and A^2: $\Pi_i(2,0) > 0 = \Pi_i(1,2) > \Pi_i(2,2)$
Between A^0 and A^1: $\Pi_i(2,1) = \Pi_i(1,1) > 0 > \Pi_i(2,2) = \Pi_i(1,2)$
Line below A^0 : $\Pi_i(2,1) = \Pi_i(1,1) > 0$ $\Pi_i(2,2) = \Pi_i(1,2) > 0$

Figure 3.2
The region of multiple equilibria in figure 3.1

These two equations are both satisfied at the same G, given from (23)–(26) by

$$G = \left[\frac{\alpha}{3}\right]^2 - \left[\frac{\alpha - 2t}{3}\right]^2. \tag{31}$$

To the left of this boundary, neither firm wants to deviate from two to one or zero plants, and to the right, neither wants to deviate from one to two or zero plants.

The vertical segment between A^0 and A^1 in figure 3.2 is defined by the first inequality in (30) holding, but the second one failing. Note in comparing (23) and (25) that revenues for firm i in $(2,1)$ exceed those in $(2,2)$. A^0 is the critical value of F at which the second inequality in (30) holds as an equality at zero, so that firm i just breaks even with either one or two plants if firm j has two plants. Above A^0, we have

$\Pi_i(2,1) = \Pi_i(1,1) \geq 0, \qquad \Pi_i(2,2) = \Pi_i(1,2) < 0$

$$\text{(vertical line from A}^0 \text{ to A}^1). \qquad (32)$$

On both sides of this boundary, firm i will not enter if firm j has two plants. But to the right of it, firm i will enter with one plant if firm j has one plant.

Now consider the vertical line separating $(2,0)$, $(0,2)$ and $(1,0)$, $(0,1)$ in figure 3.1. This vertical line also has two segments, one above A^3 in figure 3.2 and one between A^3 and A^2 in figure 3.2. Above A^3, this line is the condition that the monopoly firm is indifferent between one and two plants, and firm j cannot profitably enter regardless if firm i has one or two plants.

$\Pi_i(2,0) = \Pi_i(1,0) \geq 0, \qquad \Pi_j(1,1), \Pi_j(1,2), \Pi_j(2,1), \Pi_j(2,2) < 0$

$$\text{(vertical line above A}^3). \qquad (33)$$

Between A^3 and A^2 in figure 3.2, these same inequalities hold except that firm j could profitably enter if firm i has one plant (but not two).

$\Pi_i(2,0) = \Pi_i(1,0) > 0, \qquad \Pi_j(1,1) > 0,$

$\Pi_j(1,2), \Pi_j(2,1), \Pi_j(2,2) < 0 \qquad \text{(between } A^3 \text{ and } A^2) \qquad (34)$

The vertical boundaries in (33) and (34) are, from (27) and (28), given by

$$G = \left[\frac{\alpha}{2}\right]^2 - \left[\frac{\alpha - t}{2}\right]^2. \qquad (35)$$

Comparing (31) and (35), it is clear that (35) occurs at a higher level of G as shown in figures 3.1 and 3.2. The first term in (35) exceeds that in (31) and similarly for the second term. The $(2,0)$, $(1,0)$ boundary must lie to the right of the $(2,2)$, $(1,1)$ boundary as shown. Intuitively, the active firm effectively has a bigger market when there is no competitor and thus will still choose the high fixed-cost two-plant option at values of G where as a duopolist would chose one plant.

Only two pieces of the puzzle remain. Between A^0 and A^2, profits for firm i in $(1,2)$ are zero but profits in $(1,1)$ are positive, so i would enter against a one-plant firm j above this line but not against a two-plant firm j. The slope of this locus is -1 so as to preserve $\Pi_i(1,2) = 0$. The relevant locus ends at point A^2 because to the right of A^2 firm j would never choose two plants, so $(0,2)$ cannot be an equilibrium.

Between A^1 and A^3 in figure 3.2, $\Pi_i(1,1) = 0$ so this locus also has a slope of -1. This segment is in the region where $\Pi_i(2,2) < 0$, so above the segment firm i would not enter against either a one- or two-plant competitor, while below it firm i would enter against a one-plant competitor but not a two-plant competitor. This segment ends at A^1 because at any point further to the northwest, $(1,1)$ is no longer an equilibrium. One firm should deviate to a second plant, and the best response of the other firm is then to exit. Here is a partial summary of what I have shown about region A.

• Below A^0A^2, $(2,0)$ cannot be an equilibrium because firm j should deviate to $(2,1)$.

• Above A^1A^3, $(1,1)$ cannot be an equilibrium because each firm makes losses.

• Right of A^3A^2, $(2,0)$ cannot be an equilibrium because firm i should deviate to $(1,0)$.

• Left of A^1A^0, $(1,1)$ cannot be an equilibrium because firm i should deviate to $(2,1)$.

Apologies for the complexity. (It took Horstmann and me many attempts before we correctly drew this picture.) What all of the analysis tells us is that moving into region A in figure 3.1 or 3.2 from any direction implies that $(1,1)$ generates positive profits, so that a firm will always enter against a one-plant rival. But it will not choose two plants against a one-plant rival, and it cannot profitably enter with either one or two plants against a two-plant rival. A two-plant monopoly does not want to deviate to one plant. Thus there are three equilibria in region A, the $(1,1)$ exporting duopoly and the symmetric multinational monopolies $(2,0)$ and $(0,2)$.

Much of what figure 3.1 shows is intuitive. Beginning at $F = 0$, increases in F holding G constant generally change the number of firms active in equilibrium, but not the number of plants per firm. Obviously, F has no direct effect on the decision to be a national or a multinational firm and had no effect on that mode choice in chapter 2. The exception occurs when beginning below region A in figure 3.1 and increasing F to move up vertically in the graph. At some point, $(1,1)$ changes to $(2,0)$ or $(0,2)$. The intuition is that as F rises, one firm is eventually forced out. But when that occurs it is as if the remaining firm experiences an expansion in market size. Thus while it chose one plant when competing with the other firm, it will now choose two plants as a monopolist.

Beginning at $G = 0$ and increasing G while holding F constant leads, at some point, to a shift from two-plant to one-plant production. This makes sense since G has a direct impact on that choice. But increases in G also have the effect of raising total costs so that, as in the case of increases in F, increases in G also tend to force one firm out of the market. That region A exists is perhaps also intuitive once one gets past the messy notation and need to check every deviation. It is a region in which $(1, 1)$ generates positive profits, but neither firm wants to deviate to two plants, and a firm cannot profitably enter against a two-plant rival.

Region A is quite important for policy and fits nicely with some of the recent literature in "economic geography," which loves instances of multiple equilibria. It is important for policy because the different equilibria have very different implications for the welfare of the two countries. If one country can somehow gain a first-mover advantage and enter first, a blockaded equilibrium results in which the first entrant blocks the second firm without in any way acting strategically to prevent entry. This problem is the focus of chapter 4.

Figure 3.3 graphs regimes as a function of F and t. I will spare you the pain of going through region A again; all of the principles about checking profitable and unprofitable deviations apply in exactly the same way as they did in figure 3.1. As in the case of figure 3.1, increases in F holding t constant generally have an impact on the number of firms rather than on the number of plants per firm. But beginning below region A and passing through it has the same intuition about an effective increase in the market size for the remaining firm as described above. Like increases in G in figure 3.1, increases in t in figure 3.3 holding F constant generally change the number of plants. But once only two-plant firms are active (either $(2, 2)$ or $(2, 0)(0, 2)$), further increases in t have no effect. Boundaries between $(1, 0)$–$(2, 0)$ and $(1, 1)$–$(2, 2)$ are vertical because, while F impacts the ability of the market to support two firms, it does not directly impact on the choice of one versus two plants.

Figure 3.4 graphs the regime as a function of G and t. I have not shown the region $(0, 0)$ because of a scaling issue (it occurs at quite a large value of G), but it exists outside the area depicted in the figure. If your geometric sense is pretty good, you can see that figure 3.4 is not that wildly different from figure 3.3. As just noted, the boundaries be-

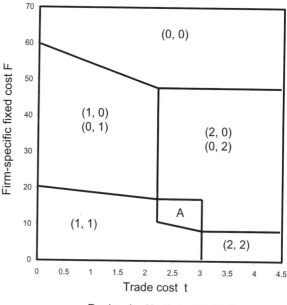

Region A: (1, 1), (2, 0), (0, 2)

Figure 3.3
Regime as a function of F and t ($G = 12$)

tween $(1, 0)$–$(2, 0)$ and $(1, 1)$–$(2, 2)$ are vertical in figure 3.3. But they cannot be vertical in figure 3.4. Increases in G have a direct impact on the profitability of one versus two plants, and any increases in G must be met by an increase in t so as to maintain indifference. Indeed, the $(1, 1)$–$(2, 2)$ boundary in figure 3.4 must go through the origin: A firm is indifferent between one and two plants (however many plants the other firm has) if both G and t are zero. Take the $(1, 0)$–$(2, 0)$ and $(1, 1)$–$(2, 2)$ boundaries in figure 3.3 and make them positively sloped, and you will have almost produced figure 3.4.

As an exercise in testing your intuition, consider raising total demand in each country. What happens to figures 3.1–3.4? I suspect that region A should move toward the northeast in figure 3.1, and toward the northwest in figures 3.3–3.4.

3.3 Welfare Analysis

Your pain and suffering in chapter 2 now pay off. The welfare expressions are the same, except that we must be sure to include all sources

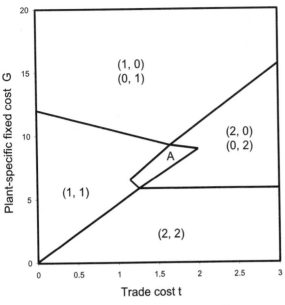

Region A: (1, 1), (2, 0), (0, 2)

Figure 3.4
Regime as a function of G and t $(F = 20)$

of supply in calculating a country's consumer surplus. Profits are already derived in equations (23)–(28) above. Refer back to equations (19) and (20) in chapter 2, and note that here $L_i = 1$ and $\beta = 1$. In regime (n_i, n_j), country i's welfare is given by

$$U_i = CS_i + \Pi_i(n_1, n_2) + \gamma = \frac{1}{2}(X_{ii} + X_{ji})^2 + \Pi_i(n_1, n_2) + \gamma. \qquad (36)$$

An X can take on one of five distinct values in addition to zero. Consider the five possibilities for supplies to country i's consumers. (6) gives $X_{ii}(1,2)$ or $X_{ii}(2,2)$. (13) gives $X_{ji}(2,1)$ or $X_{ji}(1,1)$. (16) gives $X_{ii}(1,1)$ or $X_{ii}(2,1)$.

$$X_{ii}(1,2) = X_{ii}(2,2) = \left[\frac{\alpha}{3}\right] \qquad (37)$$

$$X_{ji}(1,1) = X_{ji}(2,1) = \left[\frac{\alpha - 2t}{3}\right] \qquad (38)$$

$$X_{ii}(1,1) = X_{ii}(2,1) = \left[\frac{\alpha + t}{3}\right] \tag{39}$$

Monopoly quantities are

$$X_{ii}(1,0) = X_{ii}(2,0) = X_{ji}(0,2) = \left[\frac{\alpha}{2}\right] \quad X_{ji}(0,1) = \left[\frac{\alpha - t}{2}\right]. \tag{40}$$

Painful though it is, I will write out country i's six possible welfare levels, excluding $(0,0)$.

$$U_i(2,2) = \frac{1}{2}\left[\frac{2\alpha}{3}\right]^2 + 2\left[\frac{\alpha}{3}\right]^2 - 2G - F \tag{41}$$

$$U_i(2,0) = \frac{1}{2}\left[\frac{\alpha}{2}\right]^2 + 2\left[\frac{\alpha}{2}\right]^2 - 2G - F \quad U_i(0,2) = \frac{1}{2}\left[\frac{\alpha}{2}\right]^2 \tag{42}$$

$$U_i(1,1) = \frac{1}{2}\left[\frac{2\alpha - t}{3}\right]^2 + \left[\frac{\alpha + t}{3}\right]^2 + \left[\frac{\alpha - 2t}{3}\right]^2 - G - F \tag{43}$$

$$U_i(1,0) = \frac{1}{2}\left[\frac{\alpha}{2}\right]^2 + \left[\frac{\alpha}{2}\right]^2 + \left[\frac{\alpha - t}{2}\right]^2 - G - F \quad U_i(0,1) = \frac{1}{2}\left[\frac{\alpha - t}{2}\right]^2 \tag{44}$$

In order to illustrate the importance of the regime and regime shifts for welfare, take figure 3.1 and move horizontally at $F = 12$ (and $t = 3$ as in that figure). Note that in a traditional strategic trade policy model with market structure fixed at one national firm in each country, this would be a completely boring exercise. Nothing would happen except that the profits of each firm would be reduced by exactly the amount of the increase in G. Our model here is much more fun. This increase in F will take us through a sequence of equilibria starting at $F = 0$: $(2,2)$, $(2,0)$–$(0,2)$, $(1,1)$, $(1,0)$–$(0,1)$.

I used a GAMS model to solve for the set of all (pure strategy) Nash equilibria at five different values of G. This is also a quick numerical check that there are no mistakes in the construction of figure 3.1. The equilibria that emerged were as predicted by figure 3.1. The values of G and the resulting equilibria are shown in table 3.1. It is particularly interesting and important for policy to note the large difference between the two countries' welfare levels in the asymmetric equilibria. $G = 14$ is in region A of figure 3.1. Country i enjoys a much higher welfare level at $(2,0)$ than at $(1,1)$, which is in turn much higher than in $(0,2)$. Blockading entry has a very beneficial effect and being

Table 3.1
Sequence of equilibria, profits, and welfare, for different levels of G in figure 3.1 ($F = 12$, $t = 3$)

$G = 8$								
NE: $(2,2)$								
Π_i	4.0							
Π_j	4.0							
U_i	36.0							
U_j	36.0							
$G = 11$			$G = 11$					
NE: $(2,0)$			NE: $(0,2)$					
Π_i	38.0		Π_i	0.0				
Π_j	0.0		Π_j	38.0				
U_i	56.0		U_i	18.0				
U_j	18.0		U_j	56.0				
$G = 14$			$G = 14$			$G = 14$		
NE: $(2,0)$			NE: $(1,1)$			NE: $(0,2)$		
Π_i	32.0		Π_i	3.0		Π_i	0.0	
Π_j	0.0		Π_j	3.0		Π_j	32.0	
U_i	50.0		U_i	27.5		U_i	18.0	
U_j	18.0		U_j	27.5		U_j	50.0	
$G = 16$								
NE: $(1,1)$								
Π_i	1.0							
Π_j	1.0							
U_i	25.5							
U_j	25.5							
$G = 18$			$G = 18$					
NE: $(1,0)$			NE: $(0,1)$					
Π_i	26.3		Π_i	0.0				
Π_j	0.0		Π_j	26.3				
U_i	44.3		U_i	10.1				
U_j	10.1		U_j	44.3				

blockaded a very detrimental effect. A higher value of $G = 18$ creates an even worse outcome for country i in $(0, 1)$, since it now pays the transport cost on X in addition to the high monopoly price. I will make additional comments about the implications of this for strategic trade policy in section 3.4.

One final result in region A of figure 3.1 ($G = 14$ in table 3.1) is interesting. In the symmetric equilibrium $(1, 1)$ not only are total industry profits lower, but total two-country welfare is as well. The explanation for this must lie in wasteful cross-hauling as mentioned in the chapter 2: The gain in consumer surplus from competition is outweighed by the loss of real resources used in transport (Brander and Krugman 1983). When trade costs use real resources, more competition via trade is not necessarily better. Equilibrium market structures neither maximize welfare nor industry profits.

3.4 Policy Experiments

As noted in chapter 2, detailed analyses of policies are beyond the scope of this book. But as in the case of chapter 2, a couple of examples are helpful in illustrating how policies can work in ways very different from those of traditional analysis. Figure 3.5 takes an example where countries are initially identical and trade costs are low relative to plant-specific costs so that the equilibrium regime is $(1, 1)$ (values are $F = 10$, $G = 12$, $t = 1$). Country j increases a non-revenue-generating barrier to trade, such as time-consuming inspections. One then needs to differentiate between trade costs in the two directions, so that the trade cost from i to j is denoted tc_j. tc_i is the cost of shipping from j to i (shipping into i).

An asymmetry has now been introduced into the model, and $(2, 1)$ can be an equilibrium when $tc_j > tc_i$. Figures 3.5 and 3.6 show the effects of raising tc_j from an initial position of $tc_j = tc_i = 1$ on profits (figure 3.5) and total welfare (figure 3.6). In figure 3.5, we initially get the result that is now well known from strategic trade policy: The cost increase reduces the profits of firm i and increases the profits of firm j. There is nothing new here. But for values of $tc_j > 2.75$, firm i finds it more profitable to build a branch plant in country j, but firm j sticks with one plant. Referring to (24) and (26), firm j must be made worse off by this regime shift since it now faces a lower cost competitor in its own market. This regime shift makes firm j worse off than in the

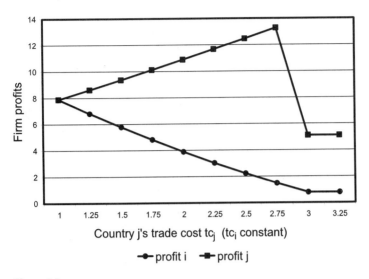

Figure 3.5
Regime shift induced by an increase in country j's trade cost tc_j $(tc_i = 1)$, $(1,1)$ to $(2,1)$

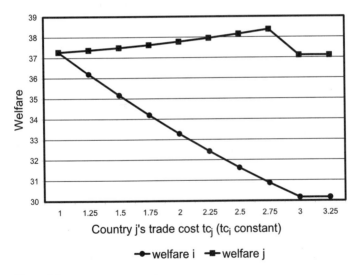

Figure 3.6
Regime shift induced by an increase in country j's trade cost tc_j $(tc_i = 1)$, $(1,1)$ to $(2,1)$

original position with $tc_j = 1$. Using trade costs to help the domestic firm can backfire if it induces the foreign firm to jump the trade barrier.

Figure 3.6 shows the effects on domestic welfare of the two countries. It is obvious that the welfare of country i is going to decrease, since this change is just the change in firm i's profits. It is not so clear how either the tax increase at $(1, 1)$ or the regime shift will affect country j. The reason for the theoretical ambiguity is the conflict between consumer surplus and profits, which move in opposite directions in this example. (Much of the strategic trade policy literature avoids this problem with the ridiculous assumption that both firms sell to a third market.) In the initial phase of the tax increase where $(1, 1)$ continues to be the market structure, consumer surplus in country j declines but the profits of firm j rise. The regime shift causes consumer surplus to rise due to a pro-competitive effect in the local market but causes the profits of firm j to fall. Figure 3.6 shows that the profit effect dominates, and welfare at first rises and then falls at the regime shift. Welfare as well as profits fall in country j below the initial level at $tc_j = 1$ after the regime shift. Inducing entry reduces both profits and welfare.

Note that this last result on welfare does not hold if initial trade costs are zero. Then inducing entry would just return country j and firm j to their initial free trade levels. Firm i and country i would, however, be worse off by exactly G, the cost of the plant in country j. Furthermore, I am sure that these results could be reversed by different functional forms, so figure 3.6 should not be taken as a robust policy conclusion.

It is also the case that the increase in tc_j could lead to a different regime shift. Figures 3.7 and 3.8 use exactly the same parameter values, except that F is increased from ten to twelve. In this case, the higher cost of shipping to country j drives the profits of firm i to zero. At $tc_j > 2.5$, firm j exits and the regime shifts to $(0, 1)$ and firm j becomes an exporting monopoly. This has a large positive effect on the profits of firm j as shown in figure 3.7. Figure 3.8 shows that country i loses at the regime shift. There is both a loss of profits and a loss of consumer surplus since country i's consumers must now pay the monopoly price rather than the duopoly price for X. As in the case of figure 3.6 (but opposite in sign), the positive effect of the regime shift on firm j's profits outweighs the loss of consumer surplus in country j.

This is reminiscent of Krugman (1984) and also Tyson's (1992) discussion of the U.S.-Japan semiconductor dispute. Clearly, using

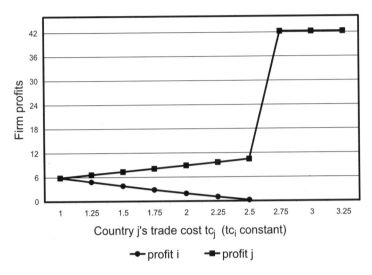

Figure 3.7
Regime shift induced by an increase in country j's trade cost tc_j $(tc_i = 1)$, $(1,1)$ to $(0,1)$

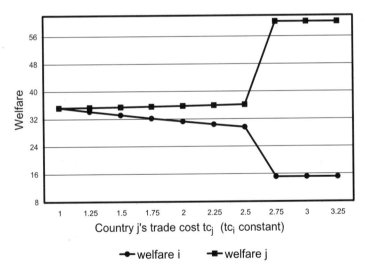

Figure 3.8
Regime shift induced by an increase in country j's trade cost tc_j $(tc_i = 1)$, $(1,1)$ to $(0,1)$

protection to force out foreign rivals can be a very powerful tool—if it works. U.S. protectionism and the threat of protectionism against imported Japanese cars in the 1980s, on the other hand, are credited/blamed on forcing the entry of Japanese firms into the United States. Figures 3.5–3.8 illustrate why I am very hesitant to make policy recommendations from this analysis. One can generally find models and parameter values to support any case one desires to support. This lack of robustness in strategic trade policy is well understood, and if anything, allowing for endogenous market structures makes the problem worse.

3.5 Summary and Conclusions

This chapter considers a simple duopoly model of international competition in an increasing returns sector. The model is deliberately constructed to be similar to a number of models in the strategic trade policy literature. Assumptions used here include linear demand and constant marginal cost. The twist here is that competition is modeled as a two-stage game. In stage one, each firm makes a choice among three discrete strategies: not entering, building one plant in the home market that serves the foreign market by exports, and building two plants, thereby serving each market by local production. In the second stage, firms play a Cournot output game.

Firms have firm-specific as well as plant-specific fixed costs, as in chapter 2. But the firm-specific costs now play a bigger role in determining the equilibrium market structure. I have shown that changes in firm-specific fixed costs largely impact the number of firms that can survive in equilibrium, whereas plant-specific fixed costs impact both the number of plants chosen by firms and the number of firms surviving in equilibrium. Trade costs impact largely on the number of plants per firm. Nevertheless, changes in firm-specific fixed costs can indirectly lead to changes in the number of plants per firm. Beginning from a $(1, 1)$ exporting market structure, for example, increases in F can lead to the exit of one firm, after which the remaining firm switches to two plants due to an increase in its effective market size.

The existence of multiple equilibria is a generic part of this model in a certain subregion of parameter space. There are parameter values such that a firm can profitably enter against a one-plant rival but not against a two-plant rival, so that the exporting duopoly $(1, 1)$ and the multinational monopoly $(2, 0)$, $(0, 2)$ are all equilibria. This is more than a theoretical curiosity and has important welfare and policy implications. The distribution of welfare is much different among these three equilibria, with a country having a significantly higher welfare level if it gets the single firm versus a two-firm duopoly that is in turn much superior to the other country having the single multinational firm. In a dynamic model or game in which one firm gets to move first, that firm can blockade entry of its foreign rival by entering with its optimal nonstrategic choice of two plants. This is important for public policy such as direct or indirect (via tax credits) support for R&D and education, for example. In this model, it may pay heavily to be first, *provided* that country and technology variables happen to be in this region of parameter space.

The final section of the chapter considered two versions of the same policy experiment, in which the initial regime is $(1, 1)$. One country raises its (inward) trade costs. Initially, we get the usual result from the strategic trade policy literature that welfare for that country increases even if the barrier generates no revenue. In the first experiment, parameters are chosen such that at some point the regime shifts such that the foreign firm enters the cost-imposing country with a branch plant, shifting the regime to $(2, 1)$ if country j is the cost-imposing country. In a numerical example, this leads to a fall in both profits and welfare for country j, although I doubt that this is a general result. In the second parameterization, the foreign firm cannot make profits with two-plant production, so at some point country j's trade barrier leads the country i firm to exit and the market structures shifts to $(0, 1)$. This leads to a large increase in the profits of firm j and in the welfare of country j.

The purpose of this exercise is not to make policy recommendations. Indeed, it is rather the opposite. I am trying to show that in this type of model one can generate opposite welfare prescriptions merely by changing parameter values, a pessimistic result for strategic trade policy.

4

Incumbency, Preemption, and Persistence

4.1 Introduction

The model in chapter 3 assumed identical countries. The symmetry properties of such an assumption yield tremendous analytical advantages. In doing so, they make the model appropriate and productive for analyzing trade and investment among similar high-income countries. Yet it is clear that the world is composed of quite different countries at various stages of development, and that differ in a variety of other respects. The world's best known and most successful multinationals developed first in high-income countries, then spread their activities to the next tier of economies, and so forth.

In a sense, this chapter combines important elements of the previous two chapters. I follow chapter 2 in assuming an asymmetry in which one country has an existing, incumbent firm at the beginning of the model time line while the other country has none. I then incorporate entry and duopoly aspects of chapter 3, allowing for the possibility that a local firm could enter the second, or "host," country. The incumbent multinational can serve the host economy by either exporting or by building a local plant. Following a tradition already established, we assume a firm-specific fixed cost or asset that is a joint input across multiple production facilities. The multinational has already sunk this cost or created this asset at the beginning of the model time line. Thus the multinational can build a plant in the host country for only an added plant-specific fixed cost, while a local entrant must incur both firm- and plant-specific fixed costs. Local production gives the multinational a lower marginal cost relative to exporting, and hence more of an advantage in the duopoly output game over a local entrant.

I am particularly interested in issues of preemptive entry by the multinational, whether this is a nonstrategic decision (blockaded entry) or a strategic decision. In the latter case, I mean that the multinational might prefer to export if there were no threat of local entry but builds a local plant to obtain the lower marginal cost, and hence larger strategic advantage, to prevent entry of the local firm. Preemption in this model equals persistence of market domination by the multinational and if the model is realistic, it predicts a strong serial correlation among top market-share firms in a growing world.

This chapter is a simplified and reworked version of Horstmann and Markusen (1987a). That paper was a dynamic model in continuous time, with the multinational able to pick the exact timing of entry. Here I have simplified that model to a two-period case. The advantage of this is that it flows quite naturally from the previous two chapters and little new notation or analytics is needed. There are a few disadvantages of the two-period model (besides generality) such as having to make arbitrary "tie-break" type rules; for example, assuming that the incumbent must decide its mode at period one, it cannot wait until period 2 when the local entrant can enter. Interested readers are referred to this earlier paper for a more complete analysis.

Finally, I should also note that Horstmann and Markusen (1987a) owes some debt to earlier papers, most notably Eaton and Lipsey (1979). A very important and empirically relevant (to international economics) addition made to Eaton and Lipsey's findings is the choice the incumbent firm has between exporting and branch-plant production, something that didn't occur in the spatial context of Eaton and Lipsey.

4.2   The Duopoly Model with First-Mover Advantage for the Multinational

The functional forms used in this chapter will be the same as those in chapter 3, with somewhat different notation to account for different market sizes, growth in market size, and two time periods. Basically, I deal with only the host-country market. The incumbent firm is referred to as "the multinational" regardless of whether or not that firm exports to or invests in the host country. The multinational has sunk investments in the home country, the home-country market is segmented from the host-country market, and any host-country entrant cannot export to or invest in the home country. Thus in what follows, all references are to the host-country market only. Important notation that differs from the previous chapter is as follows:

m	incumbent or multinational firm
n	potential entrant in the host country
$1, 2$	time periods 1 and 2
L_1	host-country market size at $t = 1$
L_2	host-country market size at $t = 2$
δ	discount factor for period 2 ($\delta < 1$)
E	export mode for the multinational (not quantity of exports)
D	domestic production mode by the multinational and/or domestic entrant
0	no-entry mode for the (potential) domestic entrant
F	firm-specific fixed cost incurred by the entrant
G	plant-specific fixed cost incurred by the entrant or by multinational if the latter chooses mode D.
$\Pi_{ki}(M_m, M_n)$	profits *before fixed costs* of firm k in time period i, when the multinational chooses mode M_m and the entrant chooses mode M_n.

$$k = \{m, n\} \qquad i = \{1, 2\}$$
$$M_m = \{E, D\} \qquad M_n = \{D, 0\}$$

As in the case of the previous two chapters, host-country demand is linear and differs between periods only in market size. X_{mi} and X_{ni} are the supplies of firms m and n, respectively, in period i. Price in period i is given by

$$p_i = \alpha - (\beta/L_i)(X_{mi} + X_{ni}) \qquad i = 1, 2. \tag{1}$$

Set marginal cost of production equal to zero for both the multinational and the potential entrant as in chapter 3 ($c = 0$). t denotes the specific transport cost if the multinational chooses mode E. Using (1), the firm profit equations *before fixed costs* are given by

$$\Pi_{mi}(E, M_{ni}) = p_i X_{mi} - t X_{mi} = [\alpha - (\beta/L_i)(X_{mi} + X_{ni})]X_{mi} - t X_{mi} \tag{2}$$

$$\Pi_{mi}(D, M_{ni}) = p_i X_{mi} = [\alpha - (\beta/L_i)(X_{mi} + X_{ni})]X_{mi} \tag{3}$$

$$\Pi_{ni}(M_{mi}, D) = p_i X_{ni} = [\alpha - (\beta/L_i)(X_{mi} + X_{ni})]X_{ni} \tag{4}$$

Four possible profit levels exist for the multinational, and two for the domestic entrant (plus zero profit from not entering). Since we have already calculated these in the chapter 3, I won't write out and solve the first-order conditions again. Let $\beta = 1$ as in chapter 3. Before fixed-cost profits in Cournot equlibrium as a function of the regime are

$$\Pi_{mi}(E,0) = \left[\frac{\alpha - t}{2}\right]^2 L_i \qquad \Pi_{mi}(D,0) = \left[\frac{\alpha}{2}\right]^2 L_i \tag{5}$$

$$\Pi_{mi}(E,D) = \left[\frac{\alpha - 2t}{3}\right]^2 L_i \qquad \Pi_{mi}(D,D) = \left[\frac{\alpha}{3}\right]^2 L_i \tag{6}$$

$$\Pi_{ni}(E,D) = \left[\frac{\alpha + t}{3}\right]^2 L_i \qquad \Pi_{ni}(D,D) = \left[\frac{\alpha}{3}\right]^2 L_i \tag{7}$$

Most of the properties of this model are robust to different parameter values. But I will use a numerical example throughout, partly to construct diagrams with reference to a real example. These numerical values are given as follows, followed by the values of pre-fixed costs profits given in (5)–(7).

Numerical example: $\alpha = 12$, $t = 3$, $L_1 = 1$, $\delta = 1/2.5$, $L_2 = 7.5$, $\delta L_2 = 3$.

$\Pi_{m1}(E,0) = 20.25$ $\Pi_{m1}(D,0) = 36$ $\Pi_{m1}(E,D) = 4$ $\Pi_{m1}(D,D) = 16$

$\delta\Pi_{m2}(E,0) = 60.75$ $\delta\Pi_{m2}(D,0) = 108$ $\delta\Pi_{m2}(E,D) = 12$ $\delta\Pi_{m2}(D,D) = 48$

$\Pi_{n1}(E,D) = 25$ $\Pi_{n1}(D,D) = 16$ $\delta\Pi_{n2}(E,D) = 75$ $\delta\Pi_{n2}(D,D) = 48$

Note that I am assuming that the second-period market size is much larger than the first and also that the discount factor is quite high. One could think of this as an example where the first period is actually a number of years (e.g., 5) and the second period is the present value of forever after.

There are a number of ways to model the timing and entry restrictions of the game. I have picked one that seems at least as reasonable as other alternatives, although in discrete time no alternative is totally persuasive to me. There is some arbitrariness in all alternatives. To begin with, I exclude the possibility that the entrant can enter at $t = 1$, perhaps reflecting prohibitively high costs at $t = 1$ due to lagging technological development (e.g., firm n has a higher F and G at $t = 1$ than at $t = 2$). Possibly, firm n has to study or reverse-engineer the product for one period before it is capable of entering, or the multinationals sales cost (through exporting or domestic production) in-

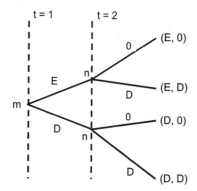

Extension: multinational moves first, but firm n can
also choose to enter at t =1 or wait until t = 2

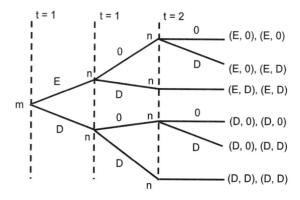

Figure 4.1
Multinational's entry decision (firm n cannot enter at $t = 1$)

clude developing the market for this product. I relax this assumption
later.

I also assume that the multinational must decide at $t = 1$ whether or
not to build a branch plant at $t = 1$ and cannot switch from exporting
to a branch plant at $t = 2$. Perhaps the multinational fears that the
local government will favor a local firm once it is capable of entering
at $t = 2$. Plant fixed costs are sunk, so the multinational will not switch
from branch-plant production to exporting at $t = 2$.

The game tree is shown in the top panel of figure 4.1. Firm m
chooses E or D at $t = 1$, and then firm n chooses D or 0 at $t = 2$. Figure
4.2 divides parameter space (F, G) into equilibrium regimes using

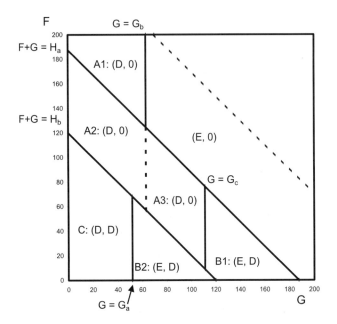

REGION: A1: natural monopoly
          A2: blockaded entry
          A3: strategic preemption
          B1: accommodation

Below H_a: firm n can enter against exports, but not against
              a local plant
Below H_b: firm n can enter against a local plant

Figure 4.2
Regime as a function of F and G at $t = 2$ (firm n cannot enter at $t = 1$)

the numerical values shown above in equations (5)–(7). The relative positions of the loci in figure 4.2 are robust with respect to parameter values, but do of course rely on the functional forms chosen.

The two diagonal loci refer to zero-profit conditions for firm n, and have slopes -1, since only the sum of F and G matters (ignore the dotted diagonal line in the northeast of the diagram for the moment). I use the notation $H = F + G$. Locus H_a gives the maximum fixed costs that allow firm n to enter at $t = 2$ competing against *exports* of the multinational.

Locus $(F + G) = H_a$:   (numerical example: $H_a = F + G = 187.5$)

$$\delta(\Pi_{n2}(E, D) - H_a) = 0 \qquad H \equiv F + G \qquad (8)$$

Above locus H_a in figure 4.2, firm n cannot enter in period 2, below H_a, firm n can enter in competition with an exporting multinational, but not against a locally producing multinational. Locus H_b gives the zero-profit condition for firm n to be able to enter against a *local plant* of the multinational at $t = 2$.

Locus $(F + G) = H_b$:   (numerical example: $H_b = F + G = 120$)

$$\delta(\Pi_{n2}(D, D) - H_b) = 0 \qquad H \equiv F + G \tag{9}$$

Below locus H_b in figure 4.2, firm n can enter in period 2 in competition with a locally producing multinational. Note that $H_a > H_b$, since firm n earns more competing against imports from the multinational than against a local branch plant.

There are similarly several loci relating to conditions of indifference for firm m. These are vertical, since firm m does not incur F. G_a is a condition of indifference between a local plant and exporting *given* that firm n will enter at $t = 2$.

Locus $G = G_a$:   (numerical example: $G_a = 51.75$)

$$\Pi_{m1}(D, 0) - G_a + \delta\Pi_{m2}(D, D) = \Pi_{m1}(E, 0) + \delta\Pi_{m2}(E, D) \tag{10}$$

This is the locus of indifference for the multinational between exporting and a local plant, *given* that the local firm n will have a plant at $t = 2$ under either choice. G_b is a condition of indifference between a local plant and exporting *given* that firm n will *not* enter at $t = 2$.

Locus $G = G_b$:   (numerical example: $G_b = 63$)

$$\Pi_{m1}(D, 0) - G_b + \delta\Pi_{m2}(D, 0) = \Pi_{m1}(E, 0) + \delta\Pi_{m2}(E, 0) \tag{11}$$

To the right of this locus, the multinational may still enter local production as I note shortly, but I refer to this entry as strategic preemption rather than blockaded entry. Combining these last two equations, we see that $G_b > G_a$, since the added profits of a local plant over exporting are greater when there is no local competition.

$$G_b - G_a = \delta(\Pi_{m2}(D, 0) - \Pi_{m2}(E, 0))$$

$$- \delta(\Pi_{m2}(D, D) - \Pi_{m2}(E, D)) > 0 \tag{12}$$

Finally, there is the locus of indifference for the multinational between preempting entry by building a local plant and accommodating entry by choosing exporting.

Locus $G = G_c$:   (numerical example: $G_c = 111.25$)

$$\Pi_{m1}(D,0) - G_c + \delta\Pi_{m2}(D,0) = \Pi_{m1}(E,0) + \delta\Pi_{m2}(E,D) \qquad (13)$$

Comparing this locus with that for G_b, one gets $G_c > G_b$. This is because G_c adds the firm's preemption incentive to its cost decision, the latter being all that is involved in G_b.

$$G_c - G_b = \delta(\Pi_{m2}(E,0) - \Pi_{m2}(E,D)) > 0 \qquad (14)$$

The positions of three G loci in figure 4.2 are robust to the numerical values chosen.

Figure 4.2 puts the H and G loci together to complete the picture. Only relevant sections of each G locus are shown. The G_a locus is only relevant when firm n is going to enter against either imports or a local plant, and thus is only relevant below H_b. G_b involves firm m's choice between exports and a local plant given that firm n does not enter. Locus G_c is relevant where the multinational's entry via a local plant blocks entry by firm n at $t = 2$, but entry by exporting will not block entry. Thus G_c is relevant between H_a and H_b.

One final point to note, the dotted line in the northeast region of figure 4.2 is a locus of zero profits for firm n if firm m did not enter at all. This is not a possible outcome of the model, but I am simply noting the position of this locus for reference, and emphasize that it has nothing to do with equilibrium.

The regions marked A1, A2, A3, and B1 in figure 4.2 are interesting from the point of view of the theory of the multinational and can be contrasted to the symmetric model of chapter 3. All the A regions have the regime $(D,0)$, but for different reasons. One could call region A1 a "natural monopoly" in that firm n could not have entered even if firm m had just chosen to export. Region A2 is referred to as "blockaded entry," in that firm n could enter if firm m chose to export, but firm m's optimal choice is a local plant given that firm n does not enter. In other words, the choice of a local plant is a nonstrategic choice of the multinational.

Region A3 of figure 4.2 is called "strategic preemption." If there were no threat of entry, firm m would choose exports (points are to the right of G_b). But below H_a, firm n will enter the market if firm m chooses exports. Thus the multinational's choice is being a monopolist with a local plant or an exporter in a duopoly competition with the local firm. To the right of G_b but to the left of G_c, the firm's optimal choice is a branch plant that then excludes firm n. Thus the decision to invest in region A3 is a strategic decision.

B1 is interesting in that in this area, the multinational could exclude the local firm, but with $G > G_c$ it is simply too costly to do so. I label this region of figure 4.2 "accommodation." It is optimal for the multinational to bear the unit costs of exports rather than the high fixed cost of a local plant.

Below H_b in figure 4.2, firm n is going to enter regardless of whether or not firm m chooses a local plant or exports. Thus the multinational's mode choice is simply a matter of a nonstrategic calculation of the profits of exporting versus local production, given that the local firm will enter in either case. Locus G_a gives the value of G at which the multinational is indifferent between the two modes, given firm n entry at $t = 2$. Regions B2 and B1 both have the equilibrium regime (E, D), but for different reasons. In B1, the multinational could prevent entry by choosing a local plant but chooses not to, while in B2 it cannot prevent entry by its choice of mode.

4.3 An Extension

There are many possible ways to formulate the timing and sequence of moves in a game such as this one. These modeling choices matter for certain results, but no alternative open to me seemed to dominate, and no alternative seemed without some arbitrariness. In this section, I consider a small extension of the game in section 4.2. In the end, I think that the results largely reinforce the findings of section 4.2, so I have tried to write this section so that it can be skipped without loss of continuity. Again, see Horstmann and Markusen (1987a) for a continuous-time analog of this model.

One limitation of the game is that it is rather stark, a once-and-for-all decision to preempt local competition. A more complex model might, among many other things, allow for the multinational to delay but not permanently prevent entry of a local rival. That is what I examine in this section. Consider the lower panel of figure 4.1. Suppose that the multinational can credibly commit before $t = 1$ to entering at $t = 1$. I believe that this is a reasonable assumption about large multinationals. This assumption allows the multinational to move first, but it still incurs its fixed costs and receives its first revenues at $t = 1$. This may or may not be the most elegant assumption, but it allows one to use all the same algebraic expressions derived in the previous section. Again, one might assume that the multinational's entry by either exports or local production makes the market for the product, so that the local firm cannot enter until the multinational credibly commits to doing so.

Firm n can enter at $t = 1$ or delay until $t = 2$. Entry costs for both firms are sunk so they will not change their decision at $t = 2$ (price will exceed marginal cost) and the multinational must choose at $t = 1$ as in the previous section. The advantage to delaying is that the market is larger later, and there is a delay in the incurring of fixed costs for the entrant. To solve the model, consider first the locus of points along which firm n can just break even entering at $t = 1$ against exports. This is denoted H_c in figure 4.3.

Locus $(F + G) = H_c$:   (numerical example: $H_c = F + G = 100$)

$$\Pi_{n1}(E, D) - H_c + \delta\Pi_{n2}(E, D) = 0 \qquad H \equiv F + G \tag{15}$$

Above locus H_c in figure 4.3, firm n cannot enter in period 1, while below H_c, firm n can enter in competition with an exporting multinational, but not against a locally producing multinational.

In general, locus H_c can be above or below locus H_b, which is reproduced from figure 4.2 in figure 4.3. H_b refers to whether or not firm n can enter in the *second* period against a *local plant* of the multinational, whereas H_c refers to whether or not firm n can enter in the *first period* against a multinational *exporter*. For the numerical example I am using, H_c is below H_b as shown in figure 4.3. Referring to our earlier definitions and results, note that these values of H can be written as

$$H_b = \Pi_{n2}(D, D) = \left[\frac{\alpha}{3}\right]^2 L_2 \tag{15}$$

$$H_c = \Pi_{n1}(E, D) + \delta\Pi_{n2}(E, D) = \left[\frac{\alpha + t}{3}\right]^2 L_1 + \delta\left[\frac{\alpha + t}{3}\right]^2 L_2 \tag{16}$$

These two can be solved to yield

$$H_c < H_b \qquad \textit{iff} \ (L_1 + \delta L_2) < \left[\frac{\alpha}{\alpha + t}\right]^2 L_2. \tag{17}$$

Thus H_c will lie below H_b as in our example of figure 4.3 if second-period demand is large compared to the first period and the discount

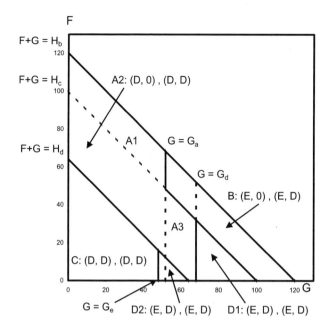

REGION: A1: natural monopoly at t = 1
          A2: blockaded entry at t = 1
          A3: strategic preemption at t = 1
          D1: accommodation at t = 1

Below H_b: firm n can enter against a local plant at t = 2
Below H_c: firm n can enter against exports, but not
             a local plant at t = 1
Below H_d: firm n can enter against a local plant at t = 1

Figure 4.3
Regime as a function of F and G (lower portion of figure 4.2, firm n can enter at $t = 1$)

factor is small (discounting is high). Much larger future demand and high discounting both mean that there is a larger benefit to waiting until the second period to incur fixed costs for firm n. When this benefit is sufficiently larger such that (17) holds, firm n can enter against a local plant in the second period at higher fixed costs than it can enter against an exporter in the first period.

Inequality (17) holds in our numerical example. Although this is not robust to different parameter values, it is a convenient outcome. With $H_c < H_b$, the portion of figure 4.3 above H_b is preserved exactly as is in the original game with firm n allowed to enter at $t = 1$. If $F + G > H_b$, then firm n will never choose to enter at $t = 1$ and thus the solution to the game is the same as in figure 4.2. One need only look at values of H less than H_b in the extension, which is what I do in figure 4.3. At even lower levels of fixed costs than H_c, firm n could enter in the first period against a local plant of the multinational. This critical value of H is given by

Locus $(F + G) = H_d$:   (numerical example: $H_d = F + G = 64$)

$$\Pi_{n1}(D, D) - H_d + \delta \Pi_{n2}(D, D) = 0 \qquad H \equiv F + G \qquad (18)$$

Above locus H_d in figure 4.3, firm n can enter in period 1 in competition with an exporting multinational, but not against a locally producing multinational, whereas below H_d, firm n can enter in period 1 in competition with a locally producing multinational.

Two more loci are needed to complete the picture in figure 4.3 (locus $G = G_a$ is the same as in figure 4.2). Locus G_d gives the condition for firm m to be indifferent between choosing a branch plant to deter the local firm's entry for one period and choosing exporting, thereby accommodating first-period entry.

Locus $G = G_d$:   (numerical example: $G_d = 68$)

$$\Pi_{m1}(D, 0) - G_d + \delta \Pi_{m2}(D, D) = \Pi_{m1}(E, D) + \delta \Pi_{m2}(E, D) \qquad (19)$$

At both points to the right and left of G_d, firm m could deter entry of firm n until the second period by building a local plant, but to the right of G_d it does not pay firm m to do so.

Finally, when fixed costs are so small that firm n is going to enter in the first period regardless of what firm m does, there is a condition of indifference for firm m between exports and local production.

Locus $G = G_e$:   (numerical example: $G_e = 48$)

$$\Pi_{m1}(D, D) - G_e + \delta \Pi_{m2}(D, D) = \Pi_{m1}(E, D) + \delta \Pi_{m2}(E, D) \qquad (20)$$

Firm m cannot prevent entry on either side of this boundary, so this boundary is just giving a simple nonstrategic choice of exporting versus local production.

The pattern of equilibrium regimes in figure 4.3 is similar to that in figure 4.2. Regions A1–A3 in figure 4.3 are analogous to similarly labeled regions in figure 4.2 Area A1 is something like natural monopoly: Firm n could not enter even against exports at $t = 1$. A2 is a blockaded entry: firm n could enter against exports, but firm m's optimal (nonstrategic) choice is local production. In A3, firm m would choose exporting if it was not threatened by first-period entry but chooses local production to block entry for one time period. A3 in figure 4.3 is part of area B2 in figure 4.2, so A3 is a region where the choice of the multinational is reversed as a consequence of the threat of first-period entry. Preserving its monopoly position for one period is worth the fixed costs for firm m in region A3 of figure 4.3.

Region D1 of figure 4.3 is one in which the multinational could deter first-period entry by local production, but it is too costly to do so. Thus this is also labeled as a region of accommodation. Region D2 has the same regime but for different reasons. In the case of D2, the multinational cannot deter first-period entry regardless of its mode choice, and exporting is the optimal (nonstrategic) choice in this area.

Region B of figure 4.3 gives the same outcome as regions B1 and B2 of figure 4.2. In B of figure 4.3, exports are sufficient to prevent first-period enty and (to the right of G_a) exporting is then the multinational's optimal choice.

Overall, figure 4.3 has much the same shape as figure 4.2, provided again that parameters are chosen such that (17) holds. Indeed, when (17) holds, the section of figure 4.2 below H_b can just be replaced by figure 4.3 below H_b, and one has the complete picture.

4.4 Interpretations of and Comments on Welfare

As I noted earlier, there are surely many alternative ways of modeling the sequencing of moves and the timing of the games. Alternatives may exist that are more empirically appealing than the choices I have made. But I am going to limit myself to the above, which I believe captures some important aspects about incumbency and preemption. To the extent that we do find my modeling choices appealing or plausible, what general ideas emerge? I suppose that the important point brought out by figures 4.2 and 4.3 is the persistence of early advantages in an expanding world economy. In each figure, regions exist in which local firms are deterred or at least temporarily deterred from entering their local market due to investment decisions of an incumbent multinational firm. Over some of the parameter space, this entry decision by the incumbent is nonstrategic, as in regions A2 of the two figures, but it has the side effect of blockading local entry. In another region, A3, the multinational chooses entry into local production precisely to prevent local entry.

A second general idea that this chapter offers is another way of looking at firm-specific assets. The fact that the local firm has to incur a firm-specific cost to enter production that the multinational has already sunk is crucial to the results. Note in figure 4.2 that if $F = 0$, the multinational never preempts and little of interest emerges. In figure 4.3, there is a very small section of the horizontal axis with the regime $(D, 0)$, (D, D), but this is due solely to the assumption that the multinational gets to move first and that the market is not big enough in the first period to support two local plants. If the firms could move simultaneously, a symmetric equilibrium would occur with the local firm getting the local plant as in chapter 3. Thus the existence of sunk, firm-specific assets is the principal determinant of the ability to preempt and explains the persistence of monopoly.

I should make a few comments about welfare. I believe that most of the intuition about welfare from the previous two chapters applies here, and that there is not enough that is sufficiently novel to add to justify a lot of algebra. The basic tensions that I have discussed in chapters 2 and 3 apply here. Having a foreign firm is beneficial if it adds to competition, but not if it merely transfers rents that would have been earned by a local entrepreneur in the absence of the multinational. Refer to table 3.1, and consider $G = 14$ where there are multiple equilibria. The ability of the multinational to preempt entry of a local firm in this chapter is like allowing the foreign firm to enter first as in chapter 3, thereby dooming the host country to the worst outcome of the three equilibria.

This raises the possibility of a whole host of new strategic-trade policy papers in which inward investment policy is a choice variable, but I will surely leave those to others. In actual policy situations, I can only point out that it would be extraordinarily difficult to know in advance what would happen if the country did ban inward investment. Such a policy can only be beneficial if there is indeed an efficient local firm waiting to enter who is or would be blocked by the multinational. In addition, there are complicated timing issues. A multinational entering today might blockade a local firm that would have entered ten years from now. The host country then has a ten-year welfare improvement, followed by lower welfare than in the counterfactual (the multinational not allowed to enter).

4.5 Summary and Conclusions

This chapter is an extension of the duopoly model of the previous chapter, in which I now allow for an incumbent firm with a first-mover advantage. This is particularly relevant to a dynamic world, in which some countries and their national firms have enjoyed early success. The question is whether or not this early success is self-perpetuating, and whether or not the developing countries will be able to develop firms to compete successfully with the first entrants.

A primary feature of the model, as in the previous chapter and indeed in the whole book, is the existence of firm-specific assets that are joint inputs across plants and the service of which can be transferred to foreign locations. If these are sunk costs, then incumbent firms have an advantage over entrants in new markets.

The incumbent firm in this chapter can serve the new market by exports or by building a local plant. Any local entrant can compete more successfully against exports because of the higher (delivered) marginal cost of exports relative to local production. Because the incumbent multinational has already sunk its firm-specific costs, it can often preempt local competition by building a plant in the country. This preemption may be strategic or nonstrategic (blockaded entry) depending on parameter values. However, I also noted that the multinational will not always preempt when it is able to do so, since it has the option of exporting instead of local production. The local entrant must build a plant as the only way of entering.

This last possibility notwithstanding, there does seem to be some presumption in the model that, given the existence of knowledge-based assets, the market power and dominance of early entrants can persist from market to market in an expanding world economy.

5   A General-Equilibrium Oligopoly Model of Horizontal Multinationals

5.1 Introduction

Chapters 2 and 3 introduce many of the basic ideas that form the cornerstones of the theory of the multinational enterprise. Chapter 4 provides dynamic extensions to the theory by allowing an incumbent the option of moving first. There are important limitations to these models, and I wish to stress two in particular. First, these are partial-equilibrium models, and the great strength of our theory of international trade is its general-equilibrium approach. If one is to integrate the multinational into the theory of international trade, one needs to turn to a general-equilibrium framework.

There are several reasons why a general-equilibrium framework is important. First, one wants to know and subsequently test how the pattern of multinational activity is related to country characteristics including factor endowments. The discussion in chapter 1 demonstrates that most multinational activity occurs among the high-income developed countries, and one wants the theory to be able to explain that fact. Conversely, one wants to understand why so little investment goes to the poorest countries in the world in spite of low wages in these countries. One also wants to understand the reverse causality—namely, how the liberalization of restrictions on direct investment affect country characteristics, such as skilled versus unskilled wages and the location of employment.

Second and closely related, I have limited the analysis to at most a small number of firms. While this may be appropriate for a small minority of industries, it cannot capture important characteristics of many industries in which entry and exit are important features of the industry's history. The effects of policies can differ dramatically depending on whether or not there is free entry and exit of firms. The difficulty is that our analytical tool kits are not well equipped to deal with problems where the number of firms is endogenous and greater than two but less than infinity. In chapter 3, we saw that just having two firms with three options each gets complicated quickly, and having a larger number of firms turns the problem into one in which we must solve a set of inequalities with discrete variables.

A system of inequalities, each with an associated nonnegative continuous variable, is referred to as a complementarity problem in mathematical programming. Techniques for solving these problems are now well developed, and I exploit them heavily in the next few chapters. But not much can be done with integer variables, such as the number of firms. In this chapter and in the next few to follow, I therefore adopt the time-honored if not completely satisfactory technique of allowing the number of firms to be a continuous variable. This is the standard assumption in monopolistic-competition models in particular. A free-entry inequality, restricting profits to nonnegative values, will then be complementary to a (continuous) variable giving the number of firms that are active in equilibrium. Models that make use of this assumption include Venables (1985), Horstmann and Markusen (1986), and of course the entire monopolistic-competition approach. This chapter is based on Markusen and Venables (1998).

The model has two countries, two goods, and two factors. One sector, X, produces a homogeneous good with increasing returns to scale. Firms may choose to supply a foreign market with exports or to build a branch plant in the foreign country. I will not consider vertical firms; that is, single-plant firms with a headquarters in one country and a plant in the other country. A much richer model that includes the possibility of vertical fragmentation is offered in chapter 7.

The model is useful in allowing us to show how the equilibrium regime is related to country characteristics, including market size and asymmetries in market size, and differences in relative factor endowments. These interact with the technology characteristics that we examined in chapter 3, including firm versus plant-level scale economies and trade costs. It also allows us to determine the pattern of trade and affiliate production as a function of country charateristics.

Results from the model are that multinationals are most important when countries are relatively similar in size and in relative factor endowments. This fits well with casual empirical evidence and, as this book later demonstrates, with formal testing as well.

5.2 Specification of the Model

I have tried to make notation as uniform as possible throughout the book. As I noted earlier, the model has two countries, 1 and 2, with i, j used as nonspecific references to 1 and 2. Where relevant, I use i as the parent country and j as the host country, or in the case of a national firm i as the exporting country/firm and j as the importing country/firm as in "from i to j." The countries produce two homogeneous goods, Y and X. Y is produced with constant returns by a competitive industry, and the price of Y is used as numeraire throughout the chapter and the book. The X sector is where the action is.

There are two factors of production, S (skilled labor) and L (unskilled labor). In this chapter, I concentrate on horizontal motives for multinational production, so I will assume that all costs of X use factors in the same proportion. Having made that assumption, it is costless to make the further assumption that the X industry uses only skilled labor and thus that unskilled labor is used only in the Y industry. In order to avoid a strict interpretation of L as unskilled labor, I also refer to L as a "composite factor." Empirical evidence suggests that skilled labor is generally a crucial factor in understanding multinationals, so I tend to lump other factors such as physical capital and land into the second factor L. L is a specific factor in the Y sector. S is used for transporting X between countries. There are no shipping costs for good Y.[1]

Subscripts (i, j) are used to denote the countries. The output of Y in country i is a Cobb-Douglas function, where L_i is country i's endowment of L. The production function for Y is

$$Y_i = S_{iy}^\alpha L_i^{1-\alpha} \qquad i = 1, 2. \tag{1}$$

The skilled wage rate z and unskilled wage rate w are given by the value marginal products of these factors in Y production.

$$z_i = \alpha(S_{iy}/L_i)^{\alpha-1}, \quad w_i = (1-\alpha)(S_{iy}/L_i)^\alpha \qquad i = 1, 2 \tag{2}$$

Expansion of the X sector draws skilled labor from the Y sector, lowering the S/L ratio in the Y sector, thereby raising the cost of skilled labor measured in terms of Y. The supply of skilled labor to the X sector is thus upward sloping in the wage rate, adding some "convexity" to the model.

Superscripts d and h will be used to designate a variable as referring to national firms and multinational firms respectively. N_i^k ($k = d, h,$

$i = 1, 2$) will denote the number of firms of type-k active in equilibrium in country i.

Consider X firms in country i, with equivalent definitions for country j. X_{ij}^d denotes the sales in country j of a national firm based in country i. A national firm undertakes all its production in its base country, so the skilled labor used by one national firm in country i is given by

$$cX_{ii}^d + (c + t)X_{ij}^d + G + F, \qquad i \neq j, \tag{3}$$

where c is the constant marginal production cost, and G is the plant-specific and F the firm-specific fixed costs—all measured in units of country i's skilled labor. t is the amount of skilled labor needed to transport one unit of X from country i to country j. All of these cost parameters are the same for both countries.

A multinational based in country i has sales in country j, X_{ij}^h. It operates one plant in each country but incurs its firm-specific fixed cost, F, in its base country. Sales are met entirely from local production and not trade, so a country i multinational has demand for country i skilled labor given by[2]

$$cX_{ii}^h + G + F. \tag{4}$$

Operating a plant in the host country means that a country i multinational has demand for country j labor,

$$cX_{ij}^h + G \qquad i \neq j. \tag{5}$$

Let S_i denote the total skilled-labor endowment of country i. Adding labor demand from N_i^d national firms, N_i^h multinationals based in country i, and N_j^h multinationals based in country j gives country i factor market clearing

$$S_i = S_{iy} + (cX_{ii}^d + (c + t)X_{ij}^d + G + F)N_i^d$$
$$+ (cX_{ii}^h + G + F)N_i^h + (cX_{ji}^h + G)N_j^h. \tag{6}$$

In equilibrium, the X sector makes no profits so country i national income, denoted M_i, is

$$M_i = w_i L_i + z_i S_i. \tag{7}$$

Variable p_i denotes the price of X in country i, and X_{ic} and Y_{ic} denote the consumption of X and Y. Utility of the representative consumer in each country is Cobb-Douglas:

$$U_i = X_{ic}^\beta Y_{ic}^{1-\beta}, \qquad X_{ic} = N_i^d X_{ii}^d + N_j^d X_{ji}^d + N_i^h X_{ii}^h + N_j^h X_{ji}^h, \tag{8}$$

giving demands

$$X_{ic} = \beta M_i / p_i, \qquad Y_{ic} = (1 - \beta) M_i \tag{9}$$

Equilibrium in the X sector is determined by pricing equations (marginal revenue equals marginal cost) and free-entry conditions (profits are nonpositive). I denote proportional markups of price over marginal cost by m_{ij}^k, $(k = d, h)$, so, for example, m_{ij}^h is the markup of a country i multinational in market j. Pricing equations of national and multinational firms in market i are (written in complementary-slackness form with associated variables in brackets):[3]

$$p_i(1 - m_{ii}^d) \leq z_i c \qquad (X_{ii}^d) \tag{10}$$

$$p_j(1 - m_{ij}^d) \leq z_i(c + t) \qquad (X_{ij}^d) \tag{11}$$

$$p_i(1 - m_{ii}^h) \leq z_i c \qquad (X_{ii}^h) \tag{12}$$

$$p_j(1 - m_{ij}^h) \leq z_j c \qquad (X_{ij}^h) \tag{13}$$

Corresponding equations apply to country j.

Revenue for a Cournot firm type-k serving j from i is given by $R_{ij}^k = p_j(X_{jc})X_{ij}^k$. The Marshallian price elasticity of demand is denoted η. η is just -1 in our formulation with Cobb-Douglas demand in (9). Cournot conjectures imply that $\partial X_{jc}/\partial X_{ij}^k = 1$; that is, a one-unit increase in one's own supply is a one-unit increase in market supply. Marginal revenue is then

$$\frac{\partial R_{ij}^k}{\partial X_{ij}^k} = p_j + X_{ij}^k \frac{\partial p_j}{\partial X_{jc}} \frac{\partial X_{jc}}{\partial X_{ij}^k} = p_j + p_j \frac{X_{ij}^k}{X_{jc}} \left[\frac{X_{jc}}{p_j} \frac{\partial p_j}{\partial X_{jc}} \right] \frac{\partial X_{jc}}{\partial X_{ij}^k}$$

$$= p_j \left[1 - \frac{X_{ij}^k}{X_{jc}} \frac{1}{\eta_j} \right] = p_j(1 - m_{ij}^k)$$

$$\eta_j \equiv - \left[\frac{p_j}{X_{jc}} \frac{\partial X_{jc}}{\partial p_j} \right] = 1 \text{ (Cobb-Douglas)}$$

$$\frac{\partial X_{jc}}{\partial X_{ij}^k} = 1 \text{ (Cournot conjecture)}$$

$$m_{ij}^k = \frac{X_{ij}^k}{X_{jc}} = \frac{p_j X_{ij}^k}{\beta M_j} \qquad \text{since } X_{jc} = \beta \frac{M_j}{p_j} \text{ (Cobb-Douglas).} \tag{14}$$

The Cournot markup with Cobb-Douglas demand (and identical products) is just the firm's market share. Using this last expression in (10)–(13) gives expressions for output:

$$X_{ii}^d \geq \beta M_i \frac{p_i - z_i c}{p_i^2} \tag{15}$$

$$X_{ij}^d \geq \beta M_j \frac{p_j - z_i(c + t)}{p_j^2} \tag{16}$$

$$X_{ii}^h \geq \beta M_i \frac{p_i - z_i c}{p_i^2} \tag{17}$$

$$X_{ij}^h \geq \beta M_j \frac{p_j - z_j c}{p_j^2} \tag{18}$$

Each of these holds with equality if the right-hand side is positive, otherwise output is zero.

The production regime refers to the combination of firm types that operate in equilibrium. This is determined by free entry of firms of each type, which can be represented by four zero-profit conditions. Given inequalities (10)–(13), zero profits can be written as the requirement that markup revenues are less than or equal to fixed costs. Complementary variables are the number of firms of each type.

$$p_i m_{ii}^d X_{ii}^d + p_j m_{ij}^d X_{ij}^d \leq z_i(G + F) \qquad (N_i^d) \tag{19}$$

$$p_j m_{jj}^d X_{jj}^d + p_i m_{ji}^d X_{ji}^d \leq z_j(G + F) \qquad (N_j^d) \tag{20}$$

$$p_i m_{ii}^h X_{ii}^h + p_j m_{ij}^h X_{ij}^h \leq z_i(G + F) + z_j G \qquad (N_i^h) \tag{21}$$

$$p_j m_{jj}^h X_{jj}^h + p_i m_{ji}^h X_{ji}^h \leq z_j(G + F) + z_i G \qquad (N_j^h) \tag{22}$$

If outputs are positive, then using (14)–(18), these free entry conditions can be expressed as follows:

$$\beta \left[M_i \left(\frac{p_i - z_i c}{p_i} \right)^2 + M_j \left(\frac{p_j - z_i(c + t)}{p_j} \right)^2 \right] \leq z_i(G + F) \qquad (N_i^d) \tag{23}$$

$$\beta \left[M_i \left(\frac{p_i - z_j(c + t)}{p_i} \right)^2 + M_j \left(\frac{p_j - z_j c}{p_j} \right)^2 \right] \leq z_j(G + F) \qquad (N_j^d) \tag{24}$$

$$\beta \left[M_i \left(\frac{p_i - z_i c}{p_i} \right)^2 + M_j \left(\frac{p_j - z_j c}{p_j} \right)^2 \right] \leq z_i(G + F) + z_j G \qquad (N_i^h) \tag{25}$$

$$\beta \left[M_i \left(\frac{p_i - z_i c}{p_i} \right)^2 + M_j \left(\frac{p_j - z_j c}{p_j} \right)^2 \right] \leq z_j(G + F) + z_i G \qquad (N_j^h) \tag{26}$$

To summarize the X sector in the model, the eight inequalities (15)–(18) are associated with the eight output levels (two each for four firm types), and the four inequalities in (23)–(26) are associated with the number of firms of each type. Additionally goods prices are given by (9), income levels from (7), and factor prices from factor-market clearing equation (6) together with labor demand from the Y sector, (2).

5.3 Intuition from Impact Effects

In this section, I use inequalities (23)–(26) to conduct some "thought experiments" to help provide intuition to the general-equilibrium results to follow. These are "impact effects" in which I change one variable holding other endogenous variables constant. The inequalities (23)–(26) have markup revenues on the left-hand side and fixed costs on the right-hand side. Moving all terms to the left gives firm profits (recall that markup revenues are total revenues minus variable costs). Let Π_j^k denote the (potential or actual) profit of a type-k firm headquartered in country j. Inequalities (23)–(26) can be written as follows:

$$\Pi_i^d = a_i M_i + b_j M_j - d_i \leq 0 \tag{27}$$

$$\Pi_j^d = b_i M_i + a_j M_j - d_j \leq 0 \tag{28}$$

$$\Pi_i^h = a_i M_i + a_j M_j - d_i - e_j \leq 0 \tag{29}$$

$$\Pi_j^h = a_i M_i + a_j M_j - d_j - e_i \leq 0 \tag{30}$$

where (a, b, d, e) are all positive. Suppose that one assumes initially that the countries are identical, so that commodity prices, factor prices, and incomes are the same in both countries. Then $a_i = a_j > b_i = b_j$, $d_i = d_j$, $e_i = e_j$, and $M_i = M_j$.

Consider first the effects of raising total world income holding all prices constant. Because $a_i > b_i$, the following result occurs:

Change in Total Income: $dM_i = dM_j > 0$

$$d\Pi_i^h = d\Pi_j^h > d\Pi_i^d = d\Pi_j^d \geq 0$$

Because of the transport costs, an increase in total world income raises multinationals' markup revenues more than national firms' (potential or actual) revenues, suggesting that multinationals will be associated with higher world income. Intuitively, a branch plant is a high fixed cost option, while exporting is a high variable cost option. The increase in equilibrium firm scale associated with higher world income will induce some shift toward multinationals.[4]

Next, hold total world income fixed but change the distribution of income:

Change in the Distribution of Income: $dM_i = -dM_j > 0$

$$d\Pi_i^d > d\Pi_i^h = d\Pi_j^h = 0 > d\Pi_j^d$$

This change is most favorable to (potential or actual) type-d_i firms since their sales, due to transport costs, are concentrated in the large country. Multinationals are "indifferent" to the change under the maintained assumption that commodity and factor prices are the same in the two countries. Type-d_j firms "lose" since their sales are concentrated in country j, now the smaller country.

Next consider a rise in one wage rate and an equal fall in the other. Given the assumption that $p_i = p_j$ and $z_i = z_j$ initially, one has

Change in z: $dz_j = -dz_i > 0$

$$d\Pi_i^d > d\Pi_i^h > 0 > d\Pi_j^h > d\Pi_j^d.$$

Type-d_i firms benefit the most, since they have their markup revenues raised and their fixed costs fall. Next comes multinationals head-quartered in country i: Their markup revenues are unaffected given the equality of prices initially, and their fixed costs fall (but by less than those of type-d_i firms). Type-h_j firms have their revenues unaffected, but their fixed costs rise. Type-d_j firms are affected the worst, losing markup revenues and bearing a larger increase in fixed costs than are borne by type-h_j firms. One can summarize this and the previous point by saying that differences between countries in size and in relative endowments is disadvantageous to multinationals, not so much because they are directly affected, but because national firms located in the "favored" country (in terms of size, endowments) have an advantage.

Now suppose that firm-level scale economies become more important relative to plant-level scale economies. Or suppose that the transactions costs of being a multinational fall, so that $(F + 2G)/(F + G)$, the ratio of type-h to type-d fixed costs, falls. These changes could occur in several different ways, all of which seem to lead to the same result. I offer the following definition:

Change in Firm versus Plant Cost Ratio: $dF = -dG > 0$

$$d\Pi_i^h = d\Pi_j^h > 0 = d\Pi_i^d = d\Pi_j^d$$

Fixed costs of national firms are unaffected under this change, while multinational firms have their fixed costs lowered.

Finally, consider a change in transport costs, which yields an obvious result.

Change in Transport Costs: $dt > 0$

$$d\Pi_i^h = d\Pi_j^h = 0 > d\Pi_i^d = d\Pi_j^d$$

An increase in transport costs improves the relative profitability of multinational firms.

Now let me summarize these results.

Multinational firms will have an advantage relative to type-d_i and/ or type-d_j firms when

1. The overall market is large.

2. The markets are of similar size.

3. Labor costs are similar.

4. Firm-level scale economies are large relative to plant-level scale economies. (The added fixed costs of becoming a multinational firm are low.)

5. Transport costs are high.

These are impact effects derived by treating wages and prices as exogenous. I now endogenize these, computing the full general-equilibrium model.

5.4   The Numerical General-Equilibrium Model

Two difficulties hinder actually solving the model outlined above. First, there are many dimensions to the model. Second, it consists of many inequalities in addition to a few equalities. For both reasons, traditional comparative statics techniques are of limited value. Changing a parameter value will generally change which inequalities hold as strict inequalities and which hold as equalities.

Recent advances in numerical methods allow this model to be formulated as a nonlinear complementarity problem—that is, as a set of inequalities each with an associated non-negative variable. The variable is strictly positive when the inequality holds as an equality in equilibrium, and zero if it holds as a strict inequality in equilibrium.

I will use the nonlinear complementarity algorithm developed by Rutherford to formulate and solve this model and code it using Rutherford's higher-level language MPS/GE (mathematical programming system for general equilibrium), which is now a subsystem of GAMS (general algebraic modeling system) (Rutherford 1995, 1999). This is really the only suitable software for solving this type of problem. Many alternative packages will solve systems of equations, but in a model of this type that would require an awkward procedure in which a regime is assumed, the model solved, and then any (assumed) inactive firm types checked to see if they can enter profitably. Iterating in this way over the many possible regimes would be very tedious. For that reason, I include the code for this model in appendix 5.

The numerical model is thus a system of inequalities with associated non-negative variables. I write these out below. Recall that $i, j = \{1, 2\}$ and $k = \{d, h\}$. A few additional items of notation are used that were not needed previously, and they are generally consistent with the notation table that follows the preface. c_{yi} and c_{ui} are the cost of producing a unit of Y and a unit of utility in country i, respectively, both measured in units of Y (this is slightly awkward because the unit cost of X as defined above is in physical units of skilled labor). c_{yi} is thus a function of factor prices and c_{ui} is a function of commodity prices. p_{ui} is the price of a unit of utility and the price of Y is one. fc_i^k denotes the cost of producing fixed costs for a type-k firm headquartered in country i (for type-h firms, this depends on the price of skilled labor in both countries). p_{fci}^k is the price of a unit of fixed costs for a type-k firm headquartered in country i. N_i^k will denote the activity that produces fixed costs for a type-k firm headquartered in country i and also the number of those firms active in equilibrium (i.e., units are chosen such that the equilibrium activity level is the number of firms). $mkrev_i^k$ is the markup revenue (total from both markets) of a type-k firm headquartered in country i.

Three sets of inequalities exist. Pricing inequalities have activity levels as complementary variables. Market-clearing inequalities have prices as complementary variables. Income balance inequalities have incomes as complementary variables. Note that firm owners are "consumers" who receive income from markup revenues and demand fixed costs. The activity level for fixed-costs is the number of firms active in equilibrium.

Inequalities	Complementary variable	Number of inequalities
Pricing inequalities	Activity level	Number
$q_i \leq c_{yi}$	Y_i	2
$p_{ui} \leq c_{ui}$	U_i	2
$p_i(1 - m_{ii}^d) \leq z_i c$	X_{ii}^d	2
$p_j(1 - m_{ij}^d) \leq z_i(c + t)$	X_{ij}^d	2
$p_i(1 - m_{ii}^h) \leq z_i c$	X_{ii}^h	2
$p_j(1 - m_{ij}^h) \leq z_j c$	X_{ij}^h	2
$p_{fci}^k \leq fc_i^k$	N_i^k	4
Market-clearing inequalities	Price	Number
$\sum_i$ demand $Y_{ic} \leq \sum_i$ supply Y_i	q	1
demand $U_i \leq$ supply U_i	p_{ui}	2
demand $X_{jc} \leq \sum_{k,i}$ supply X_{ij}^k	p_j	2
demand $N_i^k \leq$ supply N_i^k	p_{fci}^k	4
demand $L_i \leq$ supply L_i	w_i	2
demand $S_i \leq$ supply S_i	z_i	2
Income balance	Incomes	Number
expend $cons_i =$ income $cons_i$	income $cons_i$	2
demand $N_i^k =$ mkrev$_i^k$	income $entre_i^k$	4
Auxiliary constraints	Markups	Number
$m_{ij}^k = (Cournot\ formula)_{ij}^k$	m_{ij}^k	8

The numerical model is thus solving forty-three inequalities/ equalities in forty-three unknowns. But the price of Y is used as numeraire ($q = 1$) and so the market-clearing inequality for Y is dropped.

5.5 The Equilibrium Regime

Table 5.1 shows the values used in the calibration of the general-equilibrium model, with countries identical and type-h firms active. Columns of this matrix are production and consumption activities while rows are markets. A zero column sum implies product exhaustion (zero profits) for an activity while a zero row sum implies market clearing for that market. Even though these are just arbitrary numbers, calibrating the model allows for an important "replication check": If the initial solution to the model does not replicate the input data, then there is a modeling error. For those who are interested, this is

Table 5.1
Calibration of the model at the center of the Edgeworth box

	YI	YJ	XMIII	XMIIJ	XMJII	XMJIJ	NMI	NMJ	UI	UJ	CONSI	CONSJ	ENTI	ENTJ	ROWSUM
CYI	100								−100						0
CYJ		100								−100					0
CXI			50		50				−100						0
CXJ				50		50				−100					0
FCI							20						−20		0
FCJ								20						−20	0
LI	−50		−40	−40			−15	−5			150				0
SI	−50										50				0
LJ		−50			−40	−40	−5	−15				150			0
SJ		−50										50			0
UTILI									200		−200				0
UTILJ										200		−200			0
MKII			−10										10		0
MKIJ				−10									10		0
MKJJ						−10								10	0
MKJI					−10									10	0
COLSUM	0	0	0	0	0	0	0	0	0	0	0	0	0	0	0

Notes: Fixed costs of inactive type-*d* firms = 13.8 (total for 2.5 firms, same number as in the benchmark for type-*h*):

Row sums equal zero are market clearing conditions (e.g., supply equal demand).

Column sums equal zero are product exhaustion conditions (e.g., zero profits).

Positive entries are receipts (e.g., sales revenues for firms, factor sales to firms by consumers).

Negative entries are payments (e.g., factor payments to consumers, markup revenues to entrepreneurs).

discussed further and the notation for activities and markets is defined in appendix 5.

The elasticity of substitution in Y is 3.0, while all X-sector activities have fixed coefficients. At the bottom of table 5.1, I show the input requirements for the initially inactive type-d firms that is chosen so that type-h firm fixed costs are 1.45 times the level of type-d firm fixed costs at initial factor prices. All activity levels and prices are one initially, except for inactive sectors and the number of firms. There are 2.5 firms of type-h_i and type-h_j initially, 5 in all, so markups are one-fifth or 20 percent. See appendix 5 for more details.

Figures 5.1–5.3 present the world Edgeworth box familiar to most readers, where the vertical dimension is the total world endowment of S (skilled labor) and the horizontal dimension is the total world endowment of L (unskilled labor). Any point within the box is a division of the world endowment between the two countries, with country i measured from the southwest (SW) corner and country j from the northeast (NE) corner. Along the SW-NE diagonal of the box, the two countries have identical relative endowments but differ in size, while along the NW-SE (northwest-southeast) diagonal they differ in relative endowments. In figures 5.1–5.3, I repeatedly solve the model, altering the distribution of the world endowment in 5-percent steps so each cell is a solution to the model. A note to readers of the original article (Markusen and Venables 1998): The axes are reversed here from the original in order to make the diagrams consistent across several chapters. The calibration in table 5.1 just described above is for the center of these Edgeworth boxes.

Figure 5.1 presents a general characterization of the equilibrium regime over this parameter space. I refer to this simulation as the "base case": It has a transport cost of $t = .15$ (expressed as a proportion of marginal cost) and a ratio of MNE fixed costs to NE (national enterprise, type-d firms) fixed costs of 1.45 if wages are equalized between countries. In the center of the box, there is a region in which all firms are type-h in equilibrium. At the edges of the box are regions in which only national firms are active in equilibrium. In between are regions of mixed regimes of national and multinational firms. One sees that in a qualitative sense, multinationals are associated with similarities in country size and in relative endowments. But multinationals can also dominate when a moderately small country is also moderately skilled-labor-abundant.

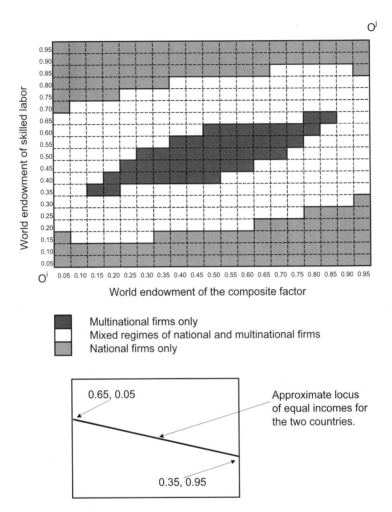

Figure 5.1
Equilibrium regimes $(t = 0.15)$

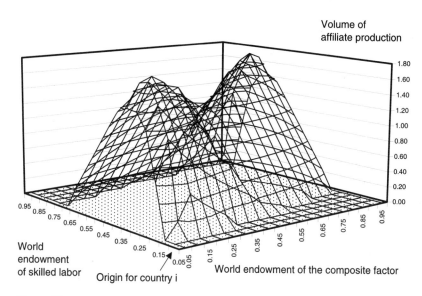

Figure 5.2
Volume of affiliate production

Table 5.2 gives the full set of firm types active in each cell, with the note at the bottom of the table explaining what the numbers mean. For example, the number 10.11 means that types h_i, d_i, and d_j are active. Up to three types of firms can be active in equilibrium, but we find no case where more than three types are active. I have been asked how three firm types can exist simultaneously, and even had one author claim this is impossible (but he used a partial-equilibrium model). The reason that multiple firm types can be supported in general equilibrium often has to do with general-equilibrium factor-market effects that do not arise in a partial-equilibrium model. Suppose, for example, that the two countries have identical relative endowments but that country i is three times the size of country j. The regime will not be type-h_i and type-h_j firms, with three-quarters of them headquartered in country i and one-quarter in country j. While factor demands for headquarters would be in proportion to country size, each country will have the same number of plants, meaning that factor demands for plants will be much higher in proportion to size in the small country, with correspondingly higher prices for skilled labor there. To put it another way, if there are zero profits earned in country j in this proposed equilibrium, there will be positive profits for national firms to enter in country i. Thus the regime may be h_i, h_j, d_i and indeed one

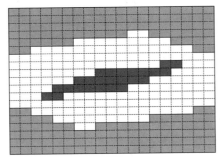

Countries smaller: 65%

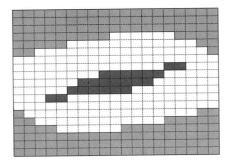

Trade costs smaller: 12%

Multinational firms only
Mixed regimes
National firms only

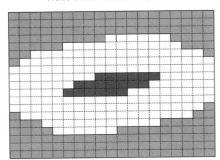

Firm scale economies smaller: 1.60

Figure 5.3
Comparative statics

Table 5.2
Types of firms active in equilibrium: Regime (the number in the cell) = $I_i^d + I_j^d + I_i^h + I_j^h$ (I is for "indicator")

World endowment of skilled labor (O^i) \ World endowment of the composite factor (O^j)	0.05	0.10	0.15	0.20	0.25	0.30	0.35	0.40	0.45	0.50	0.55	0.60	0.65	0.70	0.75	0.80	0.85	0.90	0.95
0.95	0.10	0.10	0.10	0.10	0.10	0.10	0.10	0.10	0.10	0.10	0.10	0.10	0.10	0.10	0.10	0.10	0.10	0.10	0.10
0.90	0.10	0.10	0.10	0.10	0.10	0.10	0.10	0.10	0.10	0.10	0.10	0.10	0.10	1.10	1.10	1.10	1.10	1.10	0.11
0.85	0.10	0.10	0.10	0.10	0.10	0.10	0.10	0.10	10.10	10.10	10.10	10.10	0.10	1.10	1.10	1.10	1.10	1.11	0.11
0.80	0.10	0.10	0.10	0.10	0.10	0.10	0.10	10.10	10.10	10.10	10.10	10.10	11.10	1.10	1.10	1.10	1.10	1.10	1.11
0.75	0.10	0.10	0.10	0.10	0.10	0.10	10.10	10.10	10.10	10.10	10.10	10.10	11.10	1.10	1.10	1.10	1.10	1.10	1.11
0.70	10.10	10.10	10.10	10.10	10.10	10.10	10.10	10.10	10.10	10.00	10.00	11.00	11.10	1.10	1.10	1.10	1.10	1.10	1.11
0.65	10.10	10.10	10.10	10.10	10.10	10.10	10.10	10.10	10.00	10.00	11.00	11.00	11.00	1.00	1.00	1.00	1.00	1.10	1.11
0.60	10.10	10.10	10.10	10.10	10.10	10.10	10.10	10.00	10.00	11.00	11.00	11.00	11.00	1.00	1.00	1.00	1.01	1.01	1.11
0.55	10.10	10.10	10.10	10.10	10.10	10.10	10.00	10.00	11.00	11.00	11.00	10.00	11.00	1.00	1.00	1.01	1.01	1.01	1.01
0.50	10.10	10.10	10.10	10.10	10.10	10.00	10.00	10.00	11.00	10.00	10.00	11.00	1.00	1.00	1.00	1.01	1.01	1.01	1.01
0.45	10.10	10.10	10.10	10.10	10.00	10.00	10.00	11.00	11.00	1.00	11.00	10.00	1.00	1.00	1.01	1.01	1.01	1.01	1.01
0.40	10.10	10.10	10.10	10.00	10.00	10.00	10.01	11.00	1.00	1.00	11.00	1.00	1.00	1.00	1.01	1.01	1.01	1.01	1.01
0.35	10.11	10.00	10.00	10.00	10.01	10.01	11.01	1.01	1.01	1.01	1.01	1.01	1.01	1.01	1.01	1.01	1.01	1.01	1.01
0.30	10.11	10.01	10.01	10.01	10.01	10.01	10.01	1.01	1.01	1.01	1.01	1.01	1.01	1.01	1.01	1.01	1.01	1.01	1.01
0.25	10.11	10.01	10.01	10.01	10.01	10.01	10.01	0.01	1.01	1.01	1.01	1.01	1.01	1.01	1.01	1.01	1.01	1.01	0.01
0.20	10.11	10.01	10.01	10.01	10.01	10.01	0.01	0.01	0.01	1.01	1.01	1.01	1.01	1.01	1.01	1.01	1.01	1.01	0.01
0.15	0.11	10.01	10.01	0.01	0.01	0.01	0.01	0.01	0.01	0.01	1.01	1.01	1.01	1.01	1.01	1.01	1.01	1.01	0.01
0.10	0.11	0.01	0.01	0.01	0.01	0.01	0.01	0.01	0.01	0.01	0.01	0.01	0.01	0.01	0.01	0.01	0.01	0.01	0.01
0.05	0.01	0.01	0.01	0.01	0.01	0.01	0.01	0.01	0.01	0.01	0.01	0.01	0.01	0.01	0.01	0.01	0.01	0.01	0.01

World endowment of the composite factor

$I_i^d = 0.1$ if type-d_i firms active, 0 otherwise
$I_j^d = 0.01$ if type-d_j firms active, 0 otherwise

$I_i^h = 10$ if type-h_i firms active, 0 otherwise
$I_j^h = 1$ if type-h_j firms active, 0 otherwise

sees this outcome in table 5.2 when country i has 65 percent of both factors. This point should also help support the focus on general-equilibrium analysis in this book.

Figure 5.1 illustrates, in a qualitative sense, a principal idea of this chapter and indeed of this book. Convergence of countries in either size or in relative endowments (a movement toward the center of the Edgeworth box) shifts the regime from national to multinational firms. The poorest, smallest countries do not receive direct investment, suggestive of the statistics presented earlier.

Now consider movements inside the box, first moving from the NW corner of figure 5.1 to the center. The sequence of regimes in this convergence in relative endowments is given in table 5.2:

$$d_i, (d_i\ h_i), h_i, (h_i\ h_j)$$

When the countries are very different in relative endowments but similar in size, type-d_i firms have a great advantage due to the lower skilled wage in country i. As convergence proceeds, this advantage is eroded and some type-h_i firms can enter. With further convergence, all firms are type-h_i. Finally, when the countries approach symmetry the regime shifts to intra-industry direct investment, $(h_i\ h_j)$.

Now consider moving from the SW corner of figure 5.1 to the center, so that countries are converging in size. The result is now a bit more complicated. Once multinationals enter, the *share* of multinationals in all firms increases monotonically until all firms are multinationals. However the *location* of headquarters (type-h_j versus type-h_i) is complicated. The sequence of firm types is

$$d_j, (d_j\ h_i), (d_j\ h_i\ h_j), (h_i\ h_j).$$

When country i is very small at the SW corner, all firms are type-d ones headquartered and producing in country j. It does not pay to install capacity in the small market. As the countries converge somewhat in size, some multinationals can enter and they will be headquartered in country i, the small country, because skilled labor will be cheaper in the small country where little X is produced.

One next reaches points in which type-h firms from both countries are active plus national firms from the large country. Three firm types can coexist due to market size and factor market effects in general equilibrium. Let me provide an alternative explanation to the one offered earlier. Suppose that the countries differ "enough" in size and that only $(h_i\ h_j)$ firms are active. The total number of plants in each country is the same in spite of the difference in their sizes. Therefore, markups will be the same for firms in each market. But then markup revenues for a given firm will be higher in the large market. Each type-h firm will choose the location of its headquarters solely on the basis of the price of skilled labor, and therefore if the regime is $(h_i \, h_j)$ then the price of skilled labor must be the same in both countries. What this adds up to is the possibility of positive profits for type-d firms to enter in the large country, possibly serving only the domestic market. And this is indeed what happens when the countries have identical relative endowments and differ "enough" but not "too much" in size: Multinationals from both countries coexist with national firms headquartered and producing in the large country.

As noted above, multinationals tend to dominate when countries are similar in size and in relative endowments. But they also may dominate when one country is moderately small and skilled-labor-abundant. This is another general-equilibrium effect. A relatively small market size, which discourages type-h firms, can be offset by a relatively low price for skilled labor. Another way of thinking about this is to consider a firm entering in such a country. The firm wants its headquarters in the small, skilled-labor-abundant country due to the price of skilled labor there. However, it may want to build a branch plant in the large market even if the cost of skilled labor is moderately higher there in order to save transport costs. While headquarters locations are chosen only on the basis of the cost of skilled labor, plant locations depend on market size as well as on factor prices.

Figure 5.2 shows a 3-D picture of the volume of affiliate production in the world economy corresponding to the same output data that generated figure 5.1. Affiliate production is defined as the value of the output of type-h_i firms in country j and type-h_j firms in country i: $p_j X_{ij}^h + p_i X_{ji}^h$. Affiliate production is large when the countries are relatively similar in size. But the "twin humps" of figure 5.2 require some explanation. When the countries are identical in the center of the box, all firms are type-h and each firm has half its production in the other (nonheadquarters) country. Thus exactly half of all world production of X is affiliate production. When the countries differ "somewhat" in size and the smaller country is "moderately" skilled-labor-abundant, type-h firms still dominate the X sector. But most of the firms will be headquartered in the skilled-labor-abundant country while more than half of the production will be in the other (large) country. Thus more than half of world production will be affiliate production. In cell

(.35, .15) of figure 5.1 and table 5.2, type-h$_i$ firms are the only type active in equilibrium while about three-quarters of all X output is in country j. About three-quarters of all output is affiliate output by definition and affiliate output is greater than at the center of the box.

This explains the twin humps in figure 5.2. For future reference in later empirical chapters in this book, I note that the height of the peaks above the central "saddle" in figure 5.2 depends on the necessary split of fixed costs between the two markets for a type-h firm. Figures in this chapter are constructed on the assumption of a 3/4–1/4 split between the headquarters and host country. This is motivated, for example, by supposing that F is half the type-h firm's fixed costs, and $2G$ is the other half. A type-h firm thus has three-quarters of its fixed costs $(F + G)$ in the headquarters country and one-quarter (G) in the host country. If I make this difference smaller, then the peaks move toward each other in figure 5.2 and the difference in the heights between the peaks and the saddle shrinks.

Comparative statics is somewhat imprecise in this type of model compared to a model with an interior solution to a set of equations where a derivative may have the same sign over a parameter space. With regime shifting, the effects of a parameter change can have very different effects depending on the value of both that parameter and other parameters. Figure 5.3 recomputes the simulation of figure 5.1 by changing underlying parameters. (The axes labels and values are the same in figure 5.3 as in figure 5.1; I left them off to save space to in turn permit a larger font size.)

In the top panel of figure 5.3, I lower country sizes to 65 percent of their original value. This favors national firms as noted in section 5.3 or, more precisely, harms national firms less than multinational firms. In terms of figure 5.1, the area of type-h firms only shrinks in the top panel and the region of type-d firms only expands. Thus regime shifting occurs near these boundaries whereas at other points such as the center of the box there is no regime shifting, although the number of type-h firms falls.

The center panel of figure 5.3 lowers trade costs from 15 percent to 12 percent of marginal cost. This improves the profitability of a national firm while leaving the profits of a multinational firm unchanged. Region shifting again occurs near the boundaries of the original regions in figure 5.1, while in the center of the box there is no change in any endogenous variable.

The bottom panel of figure 5.3 raises the fixed costs for a type-h firm from a 1.45 multiple of type-d fixed costs to 1.6. Thus firm-level scale economies are less significant than in the base case of figure 5.1. This also favors type-d firms over type-h firms, and the region of multinationals only shrinks and the region of national firms only expands. I could of course combine several changes, and that is what I look at in the empirical chapters using multiple regression analysis. For example, the world might be characterized by both falling trade costs and rising incomes, which tend to have offsetting influences in shifting between national and multinational production.

5.6 Assessing the Consequences of Multinationals by Counterfactual

Answers to the question, What are the effects of multinationals? require some sort of counterfactual or standard of comparison. In our case, a relatively obvious counterfactual is provided by running the model with multinationals suppressed. I refer to this as the "NE model" (national enterprise), and it is essentially a two-factor version of the (free entry) models of Brander and Krugman (1983) and Venables (1985). Figures 5.4 and 5.5 present comparisons of our model with endogenous multinationals (referred to as the MNE model) with the restricted NE model. Figure 5.4 considers the NW-SE diagonal of the Edgeworth box so that countries may differ in relative endowment but not much in size. In figure 5.4, the left-hand end of the horizontal axis corresponds to the NW corner of the Edgeworth box in figures 5.1 and 5.2, and the right-hand end corresponds to the SE corner. Figure 5.5 considers the SW-NE diagonal along which countries differ in size but not in relative endowments. For figure 5.5, the left-hand end of the horizontal axis corresponds to the SW corner of the Edgeworth box in figures 5.1 and 5.2, and the right-hand end corresponds to the NE corner.

The top panel of figure 5.4 shows the share of world X production located in country i minus its share of the world unskilled labor with multinationals permitted and with multinationals suppressed. At the left corner (the NW corner of the Edgeworth box), country i is very skilled-labor abundant and unskilled-labor scarce, and at the right corner the opposite is true. To the left of center on the horizontal axis (the center of the Edgeworth box), country i produces a larger share of X than its share of the world labor endowment in the absence of multinationals, exporting X to country j. Both the price of X and the skilled-labor wage are low in country i. When multinationals are allowed to enter, it is rather obvious that they should be type-h_i,

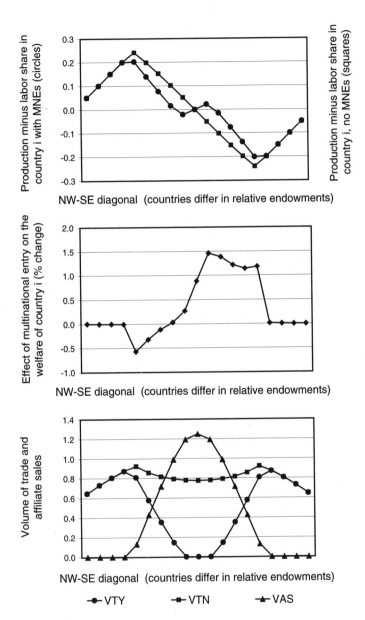

Figure 5.4
Effect of multinational entry on the location of production, welfare, and the volume of trade: NW-SE diagonal

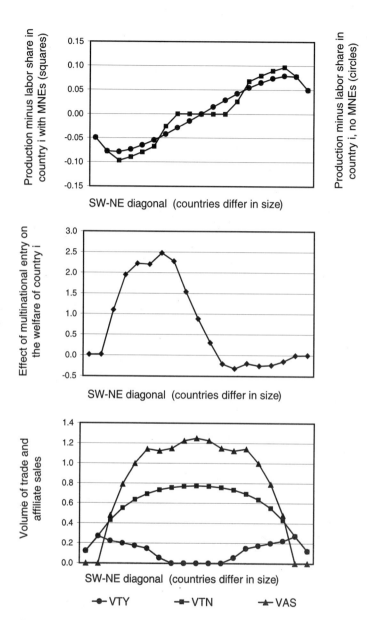

Figure 5.5
Effect of multinational entry on the location of production, welfare, and the volume of trade: SW-NE diagonal

locating their headquarters where skilled-labor is cheap. This involves a substitution of type-d_i firms by type-h_i, economizing on skilled-labor demand in country j and permitting a higher production level in equilibrium. When country i becomes skilled-labor scarce to the right of the midpoint of the box, one gets the symmetric but opposite effect (the curves are positively sloped in the right end of the box because the country h's share of world labor is decreasing, but there is no X production). The general conclusion from the top panel of figure 5.4 is that the entry of multinationals evens out production of X, shifting production from the skilled-labor-abundant country to the skilled-labor-scarce country when countries are roughly the same size.

The second panel of figure 5.4 considers the welfare of country i with multinationals minus welfare with multinationals excluded. Note that there is no reason for this to be symmetric around the midpoint. Country i can lose a little from investment liberalization when it is the skilled-labor-abundant country but always gains when it is the skilled-labor-scarce country, remembering again that the countries have roughly the same income along the NW-SE diagonal of the Edgeworth box. This phenomenon could be termed a procompetitive effect or a home-market effect, although the latter term has been used to refer to somewhat different concepts in the literature. When multinationals are excluded, most firms are headquartered and producing in the skilled-labor-abundant country. While there are no profits in this free-entry model, there is still a surplus of price minus marginal cost that is captured by the producing country (a type of Harberger triangle). Alternatively, plant scale is high in the skilled-labor-abundant country, meaning that real factor productivity is high. The skilled-labor-abundant country enjoys an income level that is higher than the skilled-labor-scarce country. When multinationals are permitted to enter, production is transferred to the skilled-labor-scarce country, resulting in gains for that country and possible losses for the skilled-labor-abundant country.

The bottom panel of figure 5.4 shows the volume of trade in X with and without multinationals, and the volume of affiliates sales with multinationals (i.e, the production and sales of type-h_i firms in country j and type-h_j firms in country i as shown in figure 5.2). VTY denotes volume of trade "yes" as in multinationals permitted, VTN denotes volume of trade "no" (multinationals excluded) and VAS denotes volume of affiliate sales. VTN is M-shaped as per a standard factor proportions model, except that here positive trade remains when the countries are identical, a Brander-Krugman "reciprocal dumping" effect. Multinational entry reduces the volume of trade over the region in which multinationals are active and substitutes affiliate sales. VTY is zero when countries are similar in relative endowments. Affiliate sales are very high at the center of the box because only type-h firms are active there, and each of them has an equal share of production at home and abroad. Thus in the center, exactly half of all world X production is affiliate sales as noted in connection with figure 5.2.

Figure 5.5 shows the corresponding results for the SW-NE diagonal where countries differ in size. Country i is small at the left and large at the right. The pattern for production shifts following investment liberalization in the top panel is similar to that in figure 5.4 near the center of the box where multinationals' entry evens out the distribution of X production, transferring a larger share to the small country. Now it is the small country that gains production share due to liberalization. The reason is another "home-market effect" created by transport costs in the absence of multinationals. Firms in the small country are disadvantaged by the combination of their small domestic market and having to bear transport costs to the large foreign market. Production of X in the smaller country is proportionately much less than its share of the world factor endowment in the absence of multinationals. Investment liberalization increases the small country's initially small production share when the countries are not too different in size.

When the difference between the country sizes is larger, the small country actually loses production as shown in the top panel of figure 5.5. This is because type-d_i firms (if i is the small country) are displaced by type-h_i firms following liberalization. If you are going to be a firm headquartered in a small country, it is better ceteris paribus to be a two-plant firm producing in both countries rather than exporting to the large country.

Welfare effects of permitting multinational entry are shown in the middle panel of figure 5.5. The small country is the big winner due to a fall in its price index as it gains more local production. The large country can in fact lose, due to an increase in its price index, but this loss is extremely small in the simulations. Investment liberalization causes the large country to lose its home-market advantage, which keeps the price index low in the big country in the absence of multinationals. However, it is interesting to note that the small country can also gain when it loses production (points 3–6 on the horizontal axis of the middle panel of figure 5.5). It is not completely clear to me what is happening here, but it appears to be a real income effect from the factor-market side rather than from the price index for X. Demand for skilled labor increases due to an expansion in the number of firms headquartered in the small country that outweighs the contraction in the demand for skilled labor due to the fall in production.

The lower panel of figure 5.5 completes the discussion by plotting trade volumes and affiliate sales. The trade-volume curves with and without multinationals are similar in shape to those in figure 5.4, but the volume is smaller. The volume-of-affiliate-sales curve exhibits some nonmonotonicity. The fall in affiliate sales between points 6 and 7 is due to the replacement of type-h_i firms by type-h_j firms as I discussed with respect to headquarters locations in figure 5.2. Only a type-h firm's overseas sales are defined as affiliate sales. When country i is small and a type-h_j firm replaces a type-h_i firm, identical except to headquarters location, affiliate sales will fall (e.g., most of the type-h_i firm's sales were in j and therefore "affiliate sales"). This is an artifact of the definition of affiliate sales and is consistent with total production by type-h firms growing between points 5 and 6.

I can summarize this section by saying that permitting multinational firms to enter generally shifts production to the smaller country and/or the country that is scarce in the factor used intensively in the multinational sector (S in this case). Welfare always improves in the small or skilled-labor-scarce country but could possibly decrease for a large or skilled-labor-abundant country that loses its home-market advantage when multinationals enter. Affiliate sales displace trade following investment liberalization. Affiliate sales and trade in X are necessarily substitutes in this model.

5.7 Summary and Conclusions

This chapter develops a model in which multinational (multiplant) firms may arise endogenously in competition with national (single-plant) firms. In many respects, the model is deliberately constructed to be similar to a standard oligopoly model of the "new trade theory" in which multinational firms are excluded by assumption. This permits a clear comparison between that literature and this chapter. I believe that the need to do this is clearly motivated by the large and growing proportion of international economic activity carried out by multinational firms.

Some of the key elements of the model have been discussed in previous papers, in particular the distinction between firm-level and plant-level scale economies. I obtain the general results, found also in papers by Horstmann and Markusen (1992) and Brainard (1993a) that multinationals tend to be found in equilibrium when firm-level scale economies and tariff/transport costs are large relative to plant-level scale economies. This chapter departs from these earlier works by explicitly considering the role of asymmetries between countries, an important exercise in that many of the stylized facts concerning trade and investment have to do with differences among countries. The general finding is that multinationals become more important relative to trade as countries become more similar in size, and in relative endowments and as world income grows. It is interesting to note that the "new trade theory" concentrates on competition between national firms of similar countries, which is precisely the place where one expects activity to be dominated by multinationals, not national firms.

I believe that the model points the way for formal empirical work insofar as the results embody testable hypotheses on the volume of investment (or affiliate sales) relative to GDP or exports as a function of cross-section and time-series variables. Cross-section variables are differences in country size, differences in relative endowments, levels of trade costs, and investment costs. Time-series evidence helps establish the hypothesized role of growth in world income: the displacement of trade by affiliate sales. Other hypotheses derive from figures 5.4 and 5.5, suggesting that investment liberalization in the world economy should shift production to economies that are smaller and poorly endowed with the factor used intensively in the multinationalized sector. Further discussion and references to empirical results occur later in the book.

6

A General-Equilibrium
Monopolistic-Competition
Model of Horizontal
Multinationals

6.1 Introduction

The previous chapters have used a simple Cournot oligopoly model with homogeneous goods. An alternative approach, using the Dixit-Stiglitz monopolistic-competition model, has been equally popular in international economics. Indeed, I suspect that the general-equilibrium literature has made more use of this approach than the oligopoly approach. The latter has been used relatively more extensively in the strategic trade policy literature.

In this chapter, I rework chapter 5 using the "large-group" monopolistic-competition model. X is differentiated at the firm level, but there are a sufficiently large number of firms in equilibrium such that individual firms are assumed to take the number and prices of other firms as given. This results in the familiar property that markups are constant.

The chapter is based on Markusen and Venables (2000), although I have modified it quite a bit in order to make it compatible with the previous chapter. Markusen and Venables (2000) assumed three firm types, so that there was only one type of multinational that drew fixed costs from both countries depending on factor prices. This makes it difficult not only to compare to the previous chapter but also to discuss the volume of multinational production, since there is no meaningful way to define which plant is in the home country and which is a branch plant (therefore an affiliate with affiliate production). Thus, I have substituted the four-firm-type model of the previous chapter. Second, Markusen and Venables (2000) had the X sector using both factors, and I have retained the assumption that only skilled labor is used in X to make it easily comparable to chapter 5. I am actually able to use exactly the same data in the simulation model of this chapter as used in chapter 5, calibrated at the center of the Edgeworth box.

One inconsistency between chapter 5 and Markusen and Venables (2000) is that the former modeled trade costs as adding to marginal costs while the latter used "iceberg" trade costs. After some debate, I decided that it would be difficult to reconcile this chapter to Markusen and Venables (2000) if I changed the formulation (e.g., understanding the CES price indices), so I have retained the iceberg formulation. Since the two are ultimately technically identical, this does not affect results. It seems logical in this particular case to maintain the comparability to the original formulation and a small expense in terms of comparability to chapter 5.

Many of the results, such as equilibrium regimes and the volume of affiliate activity, are strikingly similar over the endowment space of the Edgeworth box. I view this as a strength of the underlying approach to the problem, and for that reason choose to include this chapter in the book in spite of the similar results.

Actually, a couple of results do differ. Much higher trade costs are needed to generate multinational activity in the monopolistic-competition case. I interpret this as being due to the imperfect substitutability of the products, implying that trade costs hurt national firms less than in the case of homogeneous products. Second, there is no world market size effect in the monopolistic-competition model. This effect was shown in the top panel of figure 5.3. In the oligopoly model, a larger world market must lower markups and increase firm scale, thereby encouraging national firms to switch from high marginal-cost exporting to high fixed-cost branch plants. There is no markup effect and hence no firm-scale effect in the large-group monopolistic-competition model. Doubling the world factor endowment does not encourage a switch to multinational production. I am not very comfortable with this result, because it then requires more arcane explanations for the increase in affiliate production relative to trade I document in chapter 1.

I should note that I focus on horizontal activity for reasons discussed earlier, and thus I continue with the assumption of chapter 5 that a firm does not have the option of fragmenting a headquarters and single plant. This makes it impossible to compare the model to the work of Helpman (1984) and Helpman and Krugman (1985), who focus on this "vertical" case to the exclusion of horizontal activity (due in part to the odd assumption of zero trade costs). I do, however, present an integrated model of vertical and horizontal activity in the next chapter.

Finally, I have left out some valuable parts of Markusen and Venables (2000) since they are not directly relevant to this book. There are some important results about the pattern of national firm activity, factor prices, and agglomeration with positive trade costs that I do not discuss here.

6.2   Specification of the Model

I have tried to make notation as uniform as possible throughout the book. The model has two countries, 1 and 2, with i, j used as non-specific references to 1 and 2 ($\{i, j\} = \{1, 2\}$). Where relevant, I use i as the parent country and j as the host country or, in the case of a national firm, i as the exporting country/firm and j as the importing country/firm as in "from i to j." The countries produce two goods, Y and X. Y is a homogeneous good produced with constant returns by a competitive industry and will be used as numeraire throughout the chapter. X firms produce symmetric but imperfectly substitutable goods in the usual Dixit-Stiglitz fashion.

Two factors of production, S (skilled labor) and L (unskilled labor), exist. In this chapter, I concentrate on horizontal motives for multinational production, so I assume that all costs of X use factors in the same proportion. Having made that assumption, it is costless to make the further assumption that the X industry uses only skilled labor and thus that unskilled labor is used only in the Y industry. While this unfortunately departs from Markusen and Venables (2000), it does have the advantage of making the model and its results directly comparable to those in chapter 5 and therefore to Markusen and Venables (1998).

To avoid a strict interpretation of L as unskilled labor, I also refer to L as a "composite factor." Empirical evidence suggests that skilled labor is generally the crucial factor in understanding multinationals, so I tend to lump other factors such as physical capital and land into the second factor L. L is a specific factor in the Y sector. Transport costs for X are iceberg, defined below. There are no shipping costs for good Y.

Subscripts (i, j) are used to denote the countries. The output of Y in country i is a Cobb-Douglas function, where L_i is country i's endowment of L. The production function for Y is

$$Y_i = S_{iy}^{\gamma} L_i^{1-\gamma} \qquad i = 1, 2. \tag{1}$$

The skilled wage rate z and unskilled wage rate w are given by the value marginal products of these factors in Y production.

$$z_i = \gamma(S_{iy}/L_i)^{\gamma-1}, \quad w_i = (1-\gamma)(S_{iy}/L_i)^{\gamma} \quad i = 1, 2 \tag{2}$$

Expansion of the X sector draws skilled labor from the Y sector, lowering the S/L ratio in the Y sector, thereby raising the cost of skilled labor measured in terms of Y. The supply of skilled labor to the X sector is thus upward sloping in the wage rate, adding some "convexity" to the model. In equilibrium, the X sector makes no profits so country i national income, denoted M_i, is

$$M_i = w_i L_i + z_i S_i. \tag{3}$$

Superscripts d and h are used to designate a variable as referring to national firms and multinational firms, respectively. N_i^k ($k = d, h$, $i = 1, 2$) denotes the number of type-k firms headquartered in country i that are active in equilibrium.

Consider X firms in country i, with equivalent definitions for country j. X_{ij}^d denotes the sales in country j of a national firm based in country i. X_{ic} and Y_{ic} denote the consumption of X and Y in country i where X_{ic} is a CES aggregate of the individual varieties, a procedure that is probably familiar to most readers. Following the convention in the previous chapter, I allow p_{ij}^k to denote the price of an X variety produced by a type-k firm headquartered in country i and sold in j, although additional assumptions make possible the use of much simpler notation. Utility of the representative consumer in each country is Cobb-Douglas, and the symmetry of varieties within a group of goods allows one to write utility as follows ($0 < \alpha < 1$):

$$U_i = X_{ic}^{\beta} Y_{ic}^{1-\beta}, \quad X_{ic} \equiv [N_i^d(X_{ii}^d)^{\alpha} + N_j^d(X_{ji}^d)^{\alpha} + N_i^h(X_{ii}^h)^{\alpha} + N_j^h(X_{ji}^h)^{\alpha}]^{\frac{1}{\alpha}} \tag{4}$$

This function permits the use of two-stage budgeting, in which the consumer in country i first allocates total income (M_i) between Y_{ic} and X_{ic}. Let X_{ic} be as defined above, and let e_i denote the minimum cost of buying one unit of X_{ic} at price p_{ij}^k for the individual varieties (i.e., e_i is the unit expenditure function for X_{ic}). Y is numeraire. First-stage budgeting yields

$$Y_{ic} = (1-\beta)M_i \qquad X_{ic} = \beta M_i/e_i \qquad e_i(p_{ji}^k) = \min(X_{ji}^k)\sum_{i,j,k} p_{ji}^k X_{ji}^k$$

$$\text{subject to } X_{ic} = 1. \tag{5}$$

Let $M_{ix} = \beta M_i$ be the expenditure on X in aggregate in country i. It is necessary to solve for the demand for a given X variety, and for the price index e. In order to simplify the messy notation, I use a single subscript on the X_{ij}^k recognizing that subscript i now indexes varieities from *all* firm types in *all* countries. Similar comments apply to p, and I return to the general notation shortly. The consumer's subproblem maximizing the utility from X goods subject to an expenditure constraint (using λ as a Lagrangean multiplier) and first-order conditions are

$$\max X_c = \left[\sum X_i^\alpha\right]^{\frac{1}{\alpha}} + \lambda\left(M_x - \sum p_i X_i\right)$$

$$\Rightarrow \frac{1}{\alpha}\left[\sum X_i^\alpha\right]^{\frac{1}{\alpha}-1}\alpha X_i^{\alpha-1} - \lambda p_i = 0. \tag{6}$$

Let σ denote the elasticity of substitution among varieties. Dividing the first-order condition for variety i by the one for variety j results in the following:

$$\left[\frac{X_i}{X_j}\right]^{\alpha-1} = \frac{p_i}{p_j} \qquad \frac{X_i}{X_j} = \left[\frac{p_i}{p_j}\right]^{\frac{1}{\alpha-1}} = \left[\frac{p_i}{p_j}\right]^{-\sigma} \qquad \text{since } \sigma = \frac{1}{1-\alpha} \tag{7}$$

$$X_j = \left[\frac{p_i}{p_j}\right]^\sigma X_i \qquad p_j X_j = p_j p_j^{-\sigma} p_i^\sigma X_i$$

$$\sum p_j X_j = M_x = \left[\sum p_j^{1-\sigma}\right] p_i^\sigma X_i \tag{8}$$

Inverting this last equation reveals the demand for an individual variety i:

$$X_i = p_i^{-\sigma}\left[\sum p_j^{1-\sigma}\right]^{-1} M_x \qquad \sigma = \frac{1}{1-\alpha}, \quad \alpha = \frac{\sigma-1}{\sigma} \tag{9}$$

Now X_i can be used to construct X_c and then solve for e, noting the relationship between α and σ.

$$X_i^\alpha = X_i^{\frac{\sigma-1}{\sigma}} = p_i^{1-\sigma}\left[\sum p_j^{1-\sigma}\right]^{\frac{1-\sigma}{\sigma}} M_x^\alpha \tag{10}$$

$$\sum X_i^\alpha = \left[\sum p_i^{1-\sigma}\right]\left[\sum p_j^{1-\sigma}\right]^{\frac{1-\sigma}{\sigma}} M_x^\alpha = \left[\sum p_j^{1-\sigma}\right]^{\frac{1}{\sigma}} M_x^\alpha \tag{11}$$

$$X_c = \left[\sum X_i^\alpha\right]^{\frac{1}{\alpha}} = \left[\sum X_i^\alpha\right]^{\frac{\sigma}{\sigma-1}} = \left[\sum p_j^{1-\sigma}\right]^{\frac{1}{\sigma-1}} M_x \tag{12}$$

$$e = \left[\sum p_j^{1-\sigma} \right]^{\frac{1}{1-\sigma}} \qquad (13)$$

Having derived e, I then use equation (13) in (9) to get the demand for an individual variety.

$$X_i = p_i^{-\sigma} e^{\sigma-1} M_x \qquad \text{since } e^{\sigma-1} = \left[\sum p_j^{1-\sigma} \right]^{-1} \qquad (14)$$

It is necessary to clarify subscripts and superscripts. First, note how iceberg trade costs are reflected in prices and demand. For a domestic firm, X_{ij}^d is the amount produced in country i and shipped to country j. Similarly, p_{ij} is the export price per unit in country i. Let t $(t > 1)$ be the ratio of the amount of X exported to the amount that arrives "unmelted." Alternatively $1/t$ is the proportion of a good that "survives" transit (the proportion "unmelted"). If X_{ij} is shipped, the amount received in country j is X_{ij}/t.

Second, make the usual assumption that there is no price discrimination and so the home price of a good for local sales equals its export price. Third, assume that type-d and type-h firms producing in a country have the same marginal cost, and hence the prices of all goods *produced* in one country have the same price *in equilibrium*. Thus one can use the notation p_i and p_j for the price of all goods *produced* in country i and country j, respectively. The revenues received by the exporter are equal to the costs paid by the importer: $p_i X_{ij}^d$ is the revenue received by the exporter and X_{ij}^d/t are the number of units arriving in the importing country, so the price per unit in the importing country must be $p_i t$ $(p_i X_{ij}^d = (p_i t) X_{ij}^d/t)$. Rather than introduce additional notation, I therefore use X_{ij}/t and $p_i t$ as the quantity and price in country j of a country i variety exported to country j.

The price index for country i is then given by

$$e_i = [N_i^d p_i^{1-\sigma} + N_j^d (p_j t)^{1-\sigma} + N_i^h p_i^{1-\sigma} + N_j^h p_i^{1-\sigma}]^{\frac{1}{1-\sigma}}. \qquad (15)$$

Assuming that the relevant firm types are active in equilibrium, the demand functions for the various X varieties sold in country i are given by

$$X_{ii}^d = X_{ii}^h = X_{ji}^h = p_i^{-\sigma} e_i^{\sigma-1} M_{ix} \qquad X_{ji}^d/t = (p_j t)^{-\sigma} e_i^{\sigma-1} M_{ix}, \qquad (16)$$

where the second equation can also be written as

$$X_{ji}^d = p_j^{-\sigma} t^{1-\sigma} e_i^{\sigma-1} M_{ix}. \qquad (17)$$

A national firm undertakes all its production in its base country, so the skilled labor used by one national firm in country i is given by

$$cX_{ii}^d + cX_{ij}^d + G + F \qquad i \neq j, \tag{18}$$

where c is the constant marginal production cost and G and F are the plant-specific and firm-specific fixed costs all measured in units of skilled labor. All of these cost parameters are the same for both countries. Note the difference from chapter 5 in that transport costs do not appear in (18), but rather they are accounted for by the "melting" shown in (16) and (17).

A multinational based in country i has sales in country j, X_{ij}^h. It operates one plant in each country but incurs its firm-specific fixed cost, F, in its base country. Sales are met entirely from local production not trade, so a country i multinational has demand for country i skilled labor given by

$$cX_{ii}^h + G + F. \tag{19}$$

Operating a plant in the host country means that a country i multinational has demand for country j labor,

$$cX_{ij}^h + G \qquad i \neq j. \tag{20}$$

Let S_i denote the total skilled-labor endowment of country i. Adding labor demand from the Y sector, from N_i^d national firms, N_i^h multinationals based in country i, and N_j^h multinationals based in country j, gives country i factor market clearing:

$$S_i = S_{iy} + (cX_{ii}^d + cX_{ij}^d + G + F)N_i^d + (cX_{ii}^h + G + F)N_i^h + (cX_{ji}^h + G)N_j^h \tag{21}$$

Equilibrium in the X sector is determined by pricing equations (marginal revenue equals marginal cost) and free-entry conditions. We follow the now well-known large-group monopolistic-competition approach, which assumes a large number of firms such that each firm is assumed to take the price index e_i in (16) and country income as exogenous. A firm's price then depends (is perceived to depend) only on its own price. Inverting the demand function in (16), one can solve for an individual firm's marginal revenue (e.g., a firm producing and selling in country i). Let R_{ii} denote a country i firm's revenue on sales in market i:

$$R_{ii}^k = p_i(X_{ii}^k)X_{ii}^k \qquad MR_{ii}^k = p_i + X_{ii}^k \frac{\partial p_i}{\partial X_{ii}^k} = p_i\left[1 + \frac{X_{ii}^k}{p_i}\frac{\partial p_i}{\partial X_{ii}^k}\right] = p_i\left[1 - \frac{1}{\eta}\right]$$

$$(22)$$

where η is the Marshallian price elasticity of demand for X (defined as positive). Referring to the demand equation (16), this is simply given by the elasticity of substitution σ among varieties, given that the firm perceives e_i and income as constant. With firms viewing e_i as exogenous, one has the well-known result that the markup is just the constant $1/\sigma$.

Pricing equations of national and multinational firms in market i (written in complementary-slackness form with associated variables in brackets) are as follows. These exploit the *equilibrium* result that all goods produced in a country must sell for the same price in order to simplify notation.

$$p_i(1 - 1/\sigma) \le z_i c \qquad (X_{ii}^d) \tag{23}$$

$$p_i(1 - 1/\sigma) \le z_i c \qquad (X_{ij}^d) \tag{24}$$

$$p_i(1 - 1/\sigma) \le z_i c \qquad (X_{ii}^h) \tag{25}$$

$$p_j(1 - 1/\sigma) \le z_j c \qquad (X_{ij}^h) \tag{26}$$

Corresponding equations apply to country j. Each of these holds with equality if the right-hand side is positive, otherwise output is zero.

The production regime refers to the combination of firm types that operate in equilibrium. This is determined by free entry of firms of each type, which can be represented by four zero-profit conditions. Given inequalities (23)–(26), zero profits can be written as the requirement that markup revenues are less than or equal to fixed costs. Complementary variables are the number of firms of each type.

$$p_i X_{ii}^d + p_i X_{ij}^d \le z_i c X_{ii}^d + z_i c X_{ij}^d + z_i(G + F) \qquad (N_i^d) \tag{27}$$

$$p_j X_{jj}^d + p_j X_{ji}^d \le z_j c X_{jj}^d + z_j c X_{ji}^d + z_j(G + F) \qquad (N_j^d) \tag{28}$$

$$p_i X_{ii}^h + p_j X_{ij}^h \le z_i c X_{ii}^h + z_j c X_{ij}^h + z_i(G + F) + z_j G \qquad (N_i^h) \tag{29}$$

$$p_j X_{jj}^h + p_i X_{ji}^h \le z_j c X_{jj}^h + z_i c X_{ji}^h + z_j(G + F) + z_i G \qquad (N_j^h) \tag{30}$$

Assume positive production by some firm type in country i, so that (23)–(25) hold with equality. Then multiply (23) and (24) through by output levels, add these two equations together, and divide (27) by this sum. This leaves the following relatively simple expression for the zero-profit condition (27), with a corresponding expression (28) for the national firms in country j.

$$\frac{1}{(1-1/\sigma)} \leq 1 + \frac{G+F}{c(X_{ii}^d + X_{ij}^d)} \qquad \frac{1}{(\sigma-1)} \leq \frac{G+F}{c(X_{ii}^d + X_{ij}^d)} \tag{31}$$

$$X_{ii}^d + X_{ij}^d \leq (\sigma-1)(G+F)/c \tag{32}$$

$$X_{jj}^d + X_{ji}^d \leq (\sigma-1)(G+F)/c \tag{33}$$

Thus the output of any active national firm in either country is a constant and independent of prices and incomes (but of course the *number* of active firms depends on these variables). The scale of firm output is increasing in the ratio of fixed to marginal cost, and increasing in the elasticity of substitution between varieties.

The corresponding equations for type-h firms are not as simple, and total firm output depends on prices in the two countries. Multiply (25) and (26) (holding with equality) by outputs, add the two equations together, and subtract them from the zero-profit equations (29) and (30). Multiplying both sides by σ produces

$$(p_i X_{ii}^h + p_j X_{ij}^h) \leq \sigma z_i (F+G) + \sigma z_j G \tag{34}$$

$$(p_i X_{ji}^h + p_j X_{jj}^h) \leq \sigma z_j (F+G) + \sigma z_i G \tag{35}$$

These equations are clearly not as simple as those in (32) and (33), but they are in fact more helpful for analyzing the optimal regime. Therefore, I convert (32) and (33) into the same form as (34) and (35) by multiplying (32) through p_i/σ and (33) through by p_j/σ. (32) and (33) thus become

$$(p_i X_{ii}^d + p_j X_{ij}^d) \leq \sigma z_i (F+G) \tag{36}$$

$$(p_j X_{ji}^d + p_j X_{jj}^d) \leq \sigma z_j (F+G) \tag{37}$$

Now replace the X's in (34)–(37) with the demand functions from (16) and (17). This gives us four inequalities, where the complementary variables are the number of firms of each type active in equilibrium:

$$p_i^{1-\sigma} e_i^{\sigma-1} M_{ix} + p_i^{1-\sigma} t^{1-\sigma} e_j^{\sigma-1} M_{jx} \leq \sigma z_i (F+G) \qquad N_i^d \tag{38}$$

$$p_j^{1-\sigma} t^{1-\sigma} e_i^{\sigma-1} M_{ix} + p_j^{1-\sigma} e_j^{\sigma-1} M_{jx} \leq \sigma z_j (F+G) \qquad N_j^d \tag{39}$$

$$p_i^{1-\sigma} e_i^{\sigma-1} M_{ix} + p_i^{1-\sigma} e_j^{\sigma-1} M_{jx} \leq \sigma z_i (F+G) + \sigma z_j G \qquad N_i^h \tag{40}$$

$$p_i^{1-\sigma} e_i^{\sigma-1} M_{ix} + p_j^{1-\sigma} e_j^{\sigma-1} M_{jx} \leq \sigma z_j (F+G) + \sigma z_i G \qquad N_j^h \tag{41}$$

6.3   Intuition from Impact Effects

In this section, I conduct some "thought experiments" using inequalities (38)–(41) to help provide intuition to the general-equilibrium results just as I did in the previous chapter. These are "impact effects" where one variable is changed holding other endogenous variables constant.

Start with a symmetric situation, such as the center of the world Edgeworth box used in chapter 5. There one knows commodity prices are the same in the two countries. When this is true, and $p_i = p_j = p$, the price index in (15) for country i is given by

$$e_i = p[N_i^d + N_j^d t^{1-\sigma} + N_i^h + N_j^h]^{\frac{1}{1-\sigma}} \tag{42}$$

$$e_i^{\sigma-1} = p^{\sigma-1}[N_i^d + N_j^d t^{1-\sigma} + N_i^h + N_j^h]^{-1} \tag{43}$$

$$p^{1-\sigma}e_i^{\sigma-1} = [N_i^d + N_j^d t^{1-\sigma} + N_i^h + N_j^h]^{-1} \equiv \delta_i \tag{44}$$

and similarly

$$p^{1-\sigma}e_j^{\sigma-1} = [N_i^d t^{1-\sigma} + N_j^d + N_i^h + N_j^h]^{-1} \equiv \delta_j. \tag{45}$$

Assumptions that imply equal prices for X production in the two countries allow an enormous simplification of (38)–(41). Using δ as defined in (44) and (45), conditions (38)–(41) can now be written as

$$\delta_i M_{ix} + t^{1-\sigma}\delta_j M_{jx} \le \sigma z_i(F+G) \qquad N_i^d \tag{46}$$

$$t^{1-\sigma}\delta_i M_{ix} + \delta_j M_{jx} \le \sigma z_j(F+G) \qquad N_j^d \tag{47}$$

$$\delta_i M_{ix} + \delta_j M_{jx} \le \sigma z_i(F+G) + \sigma z_j G \qquad N_i^h \tag{48}$$

$$\delta_i M_{ix} + \delta_j M_{jx} \le \sigma z_j(F+G) + \sigma z_i G \qquad N_j^h \tag{49}$$

Assume that one is indeed at the center of the world Edgeworth box so that incomes as well as X prices are the same in the two countries. Then referring back to the definitions of δ_i and δ_j in (44) and (45), one has $\delta_i = \delta_j$ and by extension $z_i = z_j$. These assumptions then provide the critical relationship between trade costs and firm/plant scale economies such that type-d and type-h firms could just coexist at the center of the box ((46)–(49) all hold with equality).

$$\frac{(1+t^{1-\sigma})}{2} = \frac{F+G}{F+2G} \qquad 2 > (1+t^{1-\sigma}) = \frac{2F+2G}{F+2G} > 1 \tag{50}$$

Assume that one calibrates the model with high trade costs or low plant-specific fixed costs, so that only type-h firms are active initially (with the same number in both countries). Now it is easy to conduct thought experiments as in chapter 5, remembering that an increase in the left-hand side of an inequality (46)–(49) means an improvement in actual or *potential* profitability of that firm type holding the initial numbers and type of active firms constant. Let Π_i^k and Π_j^k denote the (potential or actual) profit of a type-k firm headquartered in countries i and j, respectively.

Consider first the effects of raising total world income (world factor endowment) holding all prices constant. At first glance, it appears that one has the same result as in the previous chapter, which is that this improves the profitability of type-h firms relative to type-d firms. Raising M_i and M_j in the same amount should increase the revenues of type-h firms more than type-d firms since the former do not bear transport costs ($t^{1-\sigma} < 1$ since $\sigma > 1$, $t > 1$). However, note from the definition of δ in (44) and (45) that δ^{-1} is homogeneous of degree 1 in the total number of firms of all types. Thus a neutral (proportional) expansion in the size of the world economy leaves $\delta_i M_i$ unchanged. Similarly, the potential profitability of inactive firm types is left unchanged. Thus the following result occurs:

Change in Total Income: $dM_i = dM_j > 0$

$$d\Pi_i^h = d\Pi_j^h = d\Pi_i^d = d\Pi_j^d = 0$$

This is an artifact of the fixed markup assumption of the monopolistic-competition model. There are no firm-scale effects in equilibrium, and expanding the size of the world economy leads only to the entry of additional firms and not to increases in firm scale. Thus a larger world economy does not lead to a switch from high-marginal-cost exports to high-fixed-cost foreign plants. Frankly, I am uncomfortable with respect to the empirical relevance of this result. It is contradicted by both casual empiricism and formal econometric work. It is one of several reasons why I am not a great supporter of the large-group monopolistic-competition model.

Next, hold total world income fixed but change the distribution of income (i.e., change the distribution of the total world factor endowment), assuming again that one is calibrated to the center of the Edgeworth box and that only type-h firms are active initially. Holding the deltas and therefore the number of active firms constant produces a clear result.

Change in the Distribution of Income: $dM_i = -dM_j > 0$

$$d\Pi_i^d > d\Pi_i^h = d\Pi_j^h = 0 > d\Pi_j^d$$

This change is most favorable to (potential or actual) type-d_i firms since their sales, due to transport costs, are concentrated in the large country. Multinationals are "indifferent" to the change under the maintained assumption that commodity and factor prices are the same in the two countries. Type-d_j firms "lose" since their sales are concentrated in country j, now the smaller country. With only type-h firms active initially, this result should continue to hold locally allowing the δ's to vary, since there should just be a shuffling of type-h_i firms replacing type-h_j firms, thus (locally) leaving the δ's unaffected.

One factor that does affect firm scale and hence the equilibrium regime is the elasticity of substitution among X varieties. It is not very obvious from (46)–(49), and it appears from those inequalities that an increase in σ raises the costs of type-h firms more than type-d firms. But referring to earlier equations such as (33) and (34), one notes that increased substitutability lowers markups and raises firm output in equilibrium. This raises revenues for type-h firms more than for type-d firms. In equilibrium, simulations show the expected result: that an increased elasticity of substitution increases the likelihood of multinational firms. Thus one has

Change in the Elasticity of Substitution among X Varieties: $d\sigma > 0$

$$d\Pi_i^h = d\Pi_j^h > d\Pi_i^d = d\Pi_j^d.$$

Next consider a rise in one wage rate and an equal fall in the other, again holding the number and types of active firms constant. Given the assumption that $p_i = p_j$ and $z_i = z_j$ initially, one has

Change in z: $dz_j = -dz_i > 0$

$$d\Pi_i^d > d\Pi_i^h > 0 > d\Pi_j^h > d\Pi_j^d.$$

Type-d_i firms benefit the most, since they have their fixed costs fall. Next comes multinationals headquartered in country i: Their fixed costs fall (but by less than those of type-d_i firms). Type-h_j firms have their revenues unaffected, but their fixed costs rise. Type d_j are affected the worst, bearing a larger increase in fixed costs than are borne by type-h_j firms. One can summarize this and the previous point by saying that differences between countries in size and in relative endowments is disadvantageous to multinationals, not so much because they are directly affected, but because national firms located in the "favored" (size, endowments) country have an advantage.

Note also that, when only type-h firms are active, the choice of whether to be a type-h_i or a type-h_j firm is determined solely by differences in the price of skilled labor in the two countries. In general-equilibrium, firm headquarters will be concentrated in the skilled-labor-abundant country. I noted this effect in connection with figure 5.2 and note it again shortly.

Now suppose that firm-level scale economies become more important relative to plant-level scale economies. Or suppose that the transactions costs of being a multinational fall, so that $(F + 2G)/(F + G)$, the ratio of type-h to type-d fixed costs falls. These changes could occur in several different ways, all of which seem to lead to the same result. I present the following definition:

Change in Firm versus Plant Cost Ratio: $dF = -dG > 0$

$$d\Pi_i^h = d\Pi_j^h > 0 = d\Pi_i^d = d\Pi_j^d$$

Fixed costs of national firms are unaffected under this change, while multinational firms have their fixed costs lowered. Note also with reference to (46)–(49) that if F is zero, then type-h firms will never be active (assuming transport costs are not prohibitive). Firm-level scale economies are a necessary condition for multinational firms. On the other hand, if $G = 0$ and $F > 0$ (maintaining the assumption of commodity and factor-price equalization), then only type-h firms will be active in the symmetric equilibrium.

Finally, consider a change in transport costs, which yields an obvious result.

Change in Transport Costs: $dt > 0$

$$d\Pi_i^h = d\Pi_j^h = 0 > d\Pi_i^d = d\Pi_j^d$$

An increase in transport costs improves the relative profitability of multinational firms.

Now let me summarize these results.

Multinational firms will have an advantage relative to type-d_i and/ or type-d_j firms when:

1. The markets are of similar size.

2. Labor costs are similar.

3. Firm-level scale economies are large relative to plant-level scale economies. (The added fixed costs of becoming a multinational firm are low.)

4. Transport costs are high.

5. Varieties are good substitutes for one another.

6. But unlike the oligopoly model of chapter 5, a larger world economy does not induce a shift from national to multinational firms since there are no firm scale effects. A larger market induces entry of proportionately more firms.

7. $F > 0$ is a necessary condition for multinationals. Given commodity and factor-price equalization and $F > 0$, $G > 0$ is a necessary condition for national firms.

These are impact effects derived by treating wages and prices as exogenous. I now endogenize these, computing the full general-equilibrium model.

6.4 The Numerical General-Equilibrium Model

I don't want to keep repeating my earlier discussions on the virtues of numerical modeling for this type of problem. Very briefly, two difficulties interfere with actually solving the model outlined above. First, there are many dimensions to the model. Second, it consists of many inequalities in addition to a few equalities. For both reasons, traditional comparative statics techniques are of limited value. Changing a parameter value will generally change which inequalities hold as strict inequalities and which hold as equalities.

For this model I used Rutherford's (1995, 1999) nonlinear complementary solver (called MILES), which is a subsystem of GAMS and is used in the higher-level language MPS/GE described earlier. The model is simple enough that it is not difficult to write out all the equations and inequalities. Second, there are problems with the Arrow-Debreu formulation inherent in MPS/GE. The variable number of goods creates some coding difficulties, not to mention an inherent problem of multiple equilibria with fixed markups. If marginal revenue and zero profits hold when a firm type is active, they may also hold with that firm type inactive (marginal revenue equals marginal cost, and markup revenues are less than fixed cost when output is zero). Thus I use the solver directly on a set of equations and inequalities. This problem also leads to difficulties with the classic complementarity formulation in which output levels are complementary to price-cost equations. Thus I associate prices with the marginal-revenue equal marginal-cost inequalities and outputs with supply-equals-demand inequalities rather than the other way around. I include the code for this model in appendix 6.

The numerical model is a system of equations and inequalities with associated non-negative variables. I hope the notation is familiar (c_{iyz} and c_{iyw} are derivatives of c_{iy} with respect to the prices of skilled and unskilled labor, and thus unit factor demands by Shepard's lemma).

Inequalities	Complementary variable
$q \leq c_{iy}(w_i, z_i), \qquad q \leq c_{jy}(w_j, z_j)$	Y_i, Y_j
$e_i = [N_i^d p_i^{1-\sigma} + N_j^d (p_j t)^{1-\sigma} + N_i^h p_i^{1-\sigma} + N_j^h p_i^{1-\sigma}]^{\frac{1}{1-\sigma}}$	e_i
$e_j = [N_j^d p_j^{1-\sigma} + N_i^d (p_i t)^{1-\sigma} + N_j^h p_j^{1-\sigma} + N_i^h p_j^{1-\sigma}]^{\frac{1}{1-\sigma}}$	e_j
$p_i(1 - 1/\sigma) \leq z_i c, \qquad p_j(1 - 1/\sigma) \leq z_j c$	p_i, p_j
$Y_i + Y_j = (1 - \beta)M_i/q + (1 - \beta)M_j/q$	(q set to one, equation dropped)
$X_{ii}^d = p_i^{-\sigma} e_i^{\sigma-1} \beta M_i$	X_{ii}^d
$X_{ij}^d = p_i^{-\sigma} t^{1-\sigma} e_j^{\sigma-1} \beta M_j$	X_{ij}^d
$X_{jj}^d = p_j^{-\sigma} e_j^{\sigma-1} \beta M_j$	X_{jj}^d
$X_{ji}^d = p_j^{-\sigma} t^{1-\sigma} e_i^{\sigma-1} \beta M_i$	X_{ij}^d
$X_{ii}^h = p_i^{-\sigma} e_i^{\sigma-1} \beta M_i$	X_{ii}^h
$X_{ij}^h = p_j^{-\sigma} e_j^{\sigma-1} \beta M_j$	X_{ij}^h
$X_{jj}^h = p_j^{-\sigma} e_j^{\sigma-1} \beta M_j$	X_{jj}^h
$X_{ji}^h = p_i^{-\sigma} e_i^{\sigma-1} \beta M_i$	X_{ji}^h
$X_{ii}^d + X_{ij}^d \leq (\sigma - 1)(G + F)/c$	N_i^d
$X_{jj}^d + X_{ji}^d \leq (\sigma - 1)(G + F)/c$	N_j^d
$(p_i X_{ii}^h + p_j X_{ij}^h) \leq \sigma z_i(F + G) + \sigma z_j G$	N_i^h
$(p_i X_{ji}^h + p_j X_{jj}^h) \leq \sigma z_j(F + G) + \sigma z_i G$	N_j^h
$M_i = w_i L_i + z_i S_i, \qquad M_j = w_j L_j + z_j S_j$	M_i, M_j
$c_{iyw} Y_i \leq L_i, \qquad c_{jyw} Y_j \leq L_j$	w_i, w_j
$c_{iyz} Y_i + (cX_{ii}^d + cX_{ij}^d + G + F)N_i^d +$ $(cX_{ii}^h + G + F)N_i^h + (cX_{ji}^h + G)N_j^h \leq S_i$	z_i
$c_{jyz} Y_j + (cX_{jj}^d + cX_{ji}^d + G + F)N_j^d +$ $(cX_{jj}^h + G + F)N_j^h + (cX_{ij}^h + G)N_i^h \leq S_j$	z_j

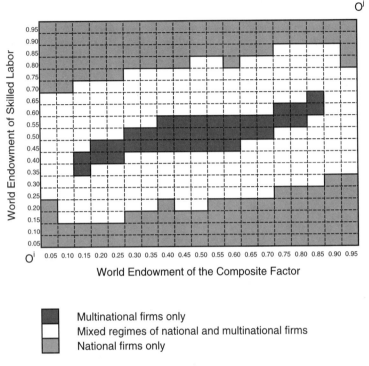

Figure 6.1
Markusen-Venables four-firm type model with large-group monopolistic competition
$(t = 0.35)$

The numerical model is thus solving twenty-four inequalities in twenty-four unknowns.

6.5   The Equilibrium Regime

Figures 6.1–6.3 present the world Edgeworth box familiar from chapter 5. The vertical dimension is the total world endowment of S (skilled labor), and the horizontal dimension is the total world endowment of L (unskilled labor). Any point within the box is a division of the world endowment between the two countries, with country i measured from the southwest (SW) corner and country j from the northeast (NE) corner. Along the SW-NE diagonal of the box, the two countries have identical relative endowments but differ in size, while along the NW-SE (northwest-southeast) diagonal they differ in relative

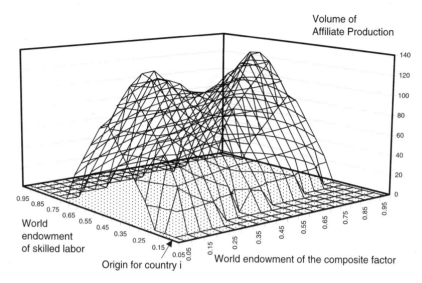

Figure 6.2
Volume of affiliate production

endowments. In figures 6.1–6.3 I repeatedly solve the model, altering the distribution of the world endowment in 5 percent steps so each cell is a solution to the model. Recall that the axes are reversed here from the original (Markusen and Venables 2000) in order to make the diagrams consistent across several chapters. The calibration of the numerical model, presented in an appendix, uses exactly the same data as that in the previous chapter. In the present case, the observed markups of 20 percent mean that the elasticity of substitution is calibrated at 5.

Figure 6.1 presents a general characterization of the equilibrium regime over this parameter space. The "base case" simulation produces a picture that is strikingly similar to figure 5.1. The principal difference is that figure 6.1 requires a much higher transport cost, 35 percent (expressed as a proportion of marginal cost), than the the 15 percent used to produce figure 5.1. I believe that this difference is due largely to the fact that varieties were perfect substitutes in the previous chapter but imperfect substitutes here. Notice from (17) that a given value of t reduces demand more when the X varieties are better substitutions (σ larger). In this case, trade costs hurt exporting firms less due to the lower value of σ relative to chapter 5 (σ infinite), and thus higher trade costs are needed to accomplish the switch to multinational

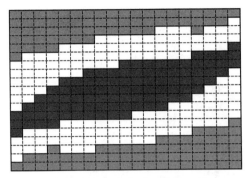

Elasticity of substitution higher: 8

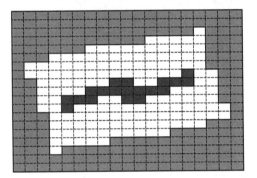

Trade costs smaller: 30%

Multinational firms only
Mixed regimes
National firms only

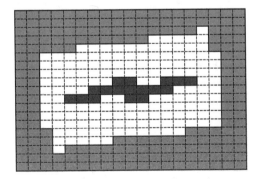

Firm scale economies smaller: 1.54

Figure 6.3
Comparative statics

production, other things being equal. Other values, including the ratio of MNE fixed costs to NE fixed costs, markups, and so forth, are the same.

In the center of the box in figure 6.1, there is a region in which all firms are type-h in equilibrium. At the edges of the box, there are regions in which only national firms are active in equilibrium. In between are regions of mixed regimes of national and multinational firms. We see that in a qualitative sense, multinationals are associated with similarities in country size and in relative endowments. But multinationals can also dominate when a moderately small country is also moderately skilled-labor-abundant.

Figures 6.1 illustrates, in a qualitative sense, a principal idea of this book. Convergence of countries in either size or in relative endowments (a movement toward the center of the Edgeworth box) shifts the regime from national to multinational firms. The poorest, smallest countries do not receive direct investment, suggestive of the statistics presented earlier in the book. It is indeed somewhat comforting that the oligopoly model with homogeneous goods and endogenous markups of chapter 5 and the monopolistic-competition model with fixed markups of this chapter produce essentially the same results.

Figure 6.2 shows a 3-D picture of the volume of affiliate production in the world economy corresponding to the same output data that generate figure 6.1, and it corresponds to figure 5.2. Affiliate production is defined as the value of the output of type-h_i firms in country j and type-h_j firms in country i: $p_j X_{ij}^h N_i^h + p_i X_{ji}^h N_j^h$. Affiliate production is large when the countries are relatively similar in size. The "twin humps" of figure 6.2 have the same explanation as those in chapter 5. When the countries are identical in the center of the box, all firms are type-h and each firm has half its production in the other (non-headquarters) country. Thus exactly half of all world production of X is affiliate production. When the countries differ "somewhat" in size and the smaller country is "moderately" skilled-labor-abundant, type-h firms still dominate the X sector. But most or all of the firms will be headquartered in the skilled-labor-abundant country while more than half of the production will be in the other (large) country. Thus more than half of world production will be affiliate production. In cell (.35, .15) of figure 6.1, type-h_i firms are the only type active in equilibrium while about three-quarters of all X output is in country j. Thus about three-quarters of all output is affiliate output by definition, and affiliate output is greater than at the center of the box.

This explains the twin humps in figure 6.2, just as in the case of the oligopoly model. I note again for future reference in later empirical chapters that the height of the peaks above the central "saddle" in figure 6.2 depends on the necessary split of fixed costs between the two markets for a type-h firm. Figures in this chapter are constructed on the assumption of a 3/4–1/4 split between the headquarters and host country. This is motivated, for example, by supposing that F is half the type-h firm's fixed costs, and $2G$ is the other half. A type-h firm thus has three-quarters of its fixed costs $(F + G)$ in the headquarters country and one-quarter (G) in the host country. If I make this difference smaller, then the peaks move together in figure 6.2 and the difference in the heights between the peaks and the saddle shrinks.

Figure 6.3 performs some comparative statics exercises similar to figure 5.3. I have dropped the axis labels in figure 6.3 to save space and permit larger font size as I did in figure 5.3, since the labeling is exactly the same as in figure 6.1. Changing the size of the total world endowment is not an interesting exercise in this case, and nothing happens. So instead of looking at the size of the world economy as in the top panel of figure 5.3, here I increase the elasticity of substitution among X varieties from 5 to 8. This increases firm scale and favors multinational firms noted in section 3 above. Referring back to figure 6.1, the area of type-h firms only expands in the top panel and the region of type-d firms only shrinks somewhat. Thus we get regime shifting near these boundaries whereas at other points such as the center of the box no regime shifting occurs, although the number of type-h firms falls as firm scale increases.

The center panel of figure 6.3 lowers trade costs from 35 percent to 30 percent of marginal cost. This improves the profitability of a national firm while leaving the profits of a multinational firm unchanged. Regime shifting again occurs near the boundaries of the original regions in figure 6.1, while in the center of the box there is no change in any endogenous variable.

The bottom panel of figure 6.3 raises the fixed costs for a type-h firm from 1.45 multiple of type-d fixed costs to 1.54. Thus firm-level scale economies are less significant than in the base case of figure 6.1. This also favors type-d firms over type-h firms, and the region of multinationals only shrinks and the region of national firms only expands.

I could of course combine several changes and that is what I look at in the empirical chapters. For example, the world might be characterized by both falling trade costs and rising firm-level scale economies, which tend to have offsetting influences in shifting between national and multinational production. Or if products are becoming better substitutes for some reason, there is an increased incentive to invade each other's markets through investment possibly in spite of falling trade costs.

In chapter 5, I turned to assessing the effects of multinationals by comparing equilibrium with multinationals to one in which they are banned by assumption. It is probably clear at this point that the present monopolistic-competition formulation produces very similar results to those of the oligopoly model. I believe that this is a strength of the general approach.

6.6 Summary and Conclusions

The Dixit-Stiglitz model of monopolistic competition has been popular among trade economists and was developed in particular by Krugman, Ethier, Helpman, and others. The purpose of this chapter was to rework the horizontal model of chapter 5 using this alternative framework. It is interesting and indeed reassuring to see that the results of the analysis are very similar to those from the oligopoly framework. Multinationals dominate when countries are relatively similar in size and in relative endowments, but they can also dominate if the smaller country is also skilled-labor-abundant. Multinationals are encouraged by higher trade costs and higher firm-level scale economies, but changing the world factor endowment toward skilled labor has little effect (actually even less than in chapter 5 since there is no firm scale effect).

One exception to the similarity of the results is that the oligopoly model predicts a switch to multinational production as the world becomes richer and demand increases. This does not occur in the large-group monopolistic-competition model where proportionately higher demand leads to entry at constant firm scale, so that there is no incentive for firms to switch from national to multinational production. This bothers me somewhat, since it makes it more difficult to explain the switch toward multinational affiliate production rather than exports that occurs in the world economy between richer pairs of countries or as world GNP increases. Of course, product differentiation can be combined with variable markups ("small-group" monopolistic competition). Such models are analytically difficult and messy, although computer simulation is just as simple.

7   The Knowledge-Capital Model

7.1 Introduction

Now it is time to expand the basic horizontal model of the last few chapters to include additional options for the firm. In particular, firms may consider a more vertically fragmented structure, in which different stages of production occur in different countries. The horizontal model does have, of course, a vertical component in that the headquarters is located in one country and hence there is a one-way flow of headquarters services from the parent to the host. Yet insofar as final production occurs in both the parent and host country, it is convenient to refer to this model as horizontal multinational activity. A vertical firm in our notation is then a single-plant firm with the headquarters and plant in different countries.

Two papers offering general-equilibrium models of multinationals appeared in 1984. Helpman (1984) has a model in which production involved two activities, one capital-intensive and the other one labor-intensive, which could be geographically separated. I took a rather different approach, assuming the existence of firm-level scale economies arising from the joint-input nature of knowledge capital across geographically separated production facilities (Markusen 1984). Helpman mentions firm-level scale economies in his model, but because he assumes zero trade costs, firms never choose multiple plants. Helpman's model thus focuses on the notion of vertically integrated firms that geographically fragment the two activities, but no investments actually take place between very similar countries due to the assumption of zero trade costs. My model captures the notion of horizontally integrated firms that undertake the same activity in multiple countries but excludes any motive for vertical specialization.

As just noted, I have been concentrating on horizontal motives for multinationality with the exception of chapter 2, which also allows for a vertical structure. I have done this partly to keep matters simple, but mostly because I believe that the weight of empirical evidence suggests the dominance of horizontal motives for foreign production. This chapter broadens the horizontal analysis of the previous chapters by allowing firms to choose a single plant, but to locate that single plant in the other country from its headquarters location.

The four-firm-type oligopoly model of chapter 5 is now expanded to six firm types, with the addition of two types of single-plant vertical firms, one with its headquarters in country i and plant in country j and the other with its headquarters in country j and plant in country i. The firm type will be identified by the headquarters country, so a type-v_i firm is a firm with headquarters in i and plant in j.

As is implicit in Helpman's paper, the existence of vertical firms in equilibrium is more likely and more interesting when there are differences in factor intensities among activities. For example, headquarters activities may be more skilled-labor-intensive than plants. This requires a second modification and complication from the model of chapters 5 and 6 in that we must model the X sector as using both factors. I should note, however, that differences in factor intensities among X-sector activities is not a necessary condition for vertical firms. The reason is that the headquarters location is chosen solely on the basis of factor prices, whereas the location of the single plant depends both on factor prices and on market size. Thus even if all X activities used a single factor, an equilibrium with a type-v_i firm could result if country i has a slightly lower price for this factor, but country j had a bigger market. The firm would want its headquarters in country i for factor-price reasons, but the market-size motive could dominate in its plant-location decision. Since I use a two-factor X sector in the model that follows, I will not mention this possibility again but merely note it for completeness.

Section 7.2 develops what I call the "knowledge-capital model" of the multinational. I am not going to claim that it is entirely novel, since its individual elements are well known. But I believe that clarifying and integrating its distinct components is a contribution to the theory of the multinational enterprise. In particular, I think that there has been some failure to distinguish between what I refer to as "jointness" and what I will call "fragmentation."[1] The two are related, and both stem from a common property of knowledge-based assets, but they are not at all the same thing. Jointness is the key concept in explaining motives for horizontal multinationals while fragmentation is key for understanding vertical firms.

The methodology and technical exposition in this chapter follows very closely that of chapter 5. I develop the equations and inequalities, then try to use partial-equilibrium reasoning to get intuition into general-equilibrium results. Then I turn to numerical simulations. The general-equilibrium model of this chapter has over sixty equations and inequalities, and general-equilibrium interactions between goods and factor markets are key to the interesting results. The most interesting questions simply cannot be asked in a small-dimension model capable of an analytical solution.

7.2 The Knowledge-Capital Model

The general-equilibrium model of this chapter is much the same as that in chapter 5, built around the key idea that there are knowledge-based assets or fixed costs that create firm-level scale economies. But this present chapter has a more complex structure in the X sector and more options for firms. I refer to this extended model, which allows for both vertical and horizontal activity, as the "knowledge-capital" model.

There are three defining assumptions for the knowledge-capital model.

1. *Fragmentation*: the location of knowledge-based assets may be fragmented from production. Any incremental cost of supplying services of the asset to a single foreign plant versus the cost to a single domestic plant is small.

2. *Skilled-labor intensity*: knowledge-based assets are skilled-labor-intensive relative to final production.

3. *Jointness*: the services of knowledge-based assets are (at least partially) joint ("public") inputs into multiple production facilities. The added cost of a second plant is small compared to the cost of establishing a firm with a local plant.

The first two properties, fragmentation and skilled-labor intensity motivate vertical (type-v) multinationals that locate their single plant and headquarters in different countries depending on factor prices and market sizes. The third property, jointness, gives rise to horizontal (type-h) multinationals that have plants producing the final good in multiple countries. Jointness was the key property of the models in chapters 5 and 6.

It is important to note that (1) and (3) are not the same thing. A knowledge-based asset, such as a skilled engineer, may be easily transported to a foreign plant, but may be fully rivaled or nonjoint in that his or her services cannot be supplied to two plants at the same time. Using alternative terminology, a firm may be able to geographically fragment production at low cost without having firm-level scale economies. Fragmentation is related to the concept of "technology transfer cost," the ease of supplying services to a foreign plant. Fragmentation relates to supplying services to a foreign plant, regardless of whether or not the firm has a domestic plant as well.

Jointness refers to the ability to use the engineer or other headquarters asset in multiple production locations without reducing the services provided in any single location. A blueprint is the classical example of a joint input. Jointness inherently referrs to the costs of running two plants rather than one.

Two numerical examples might help. Comparing the two, jointness is relatively high but fragmentation is relatively costly in the first example, while in the second it is the other way around. First, suppose it takes ten units of skilled labor to produce a blueprint but there are no additional costs to open a domestic plant. Suppose five units of skilled labor are required to implement that blueprint in a foreign plant. Then in this first example, the total fixed costs of the three types of firms are

Example 1: fixed costs for different firm types: high jointness, high fragmentation costs.

domestic (type-d) $10 = 10 + 0$
horizontal (type-h) $15 = 10 + 5$
vertical (type-v) $15 = 10 + 5$

In this case, one would say that there exists a high degree of jointness, since the second plant can be opened for only 50 percent of the costs of the first one (the blueprint). But the cost of fragmentation is high, since it costs 50 percent more to open a single foreign plant than a single domestic plant.

Now consider a second case. Suppose that only four units of skilled labor are needed to make the blueprint, and that six units are required to implement the blueprint in a domestic plant, and eight units to implement it in a foreign plant. These are the fixed costs of the three firm types.

Example 2: fixed costs for different firm types: low jointness, low fragmentation costs.

domestic (type-d) $10 = 4 + 6$

horizontal (type-h) $18 = 4 + 6 + 8$

vertical (type-v) $12 = 4 + 8$

Compared to the first case, a lower degree of jointness is apparent, since a second plant costs 80 percent of the first plant plus blueprint, instead of only 50 percent in the previous example. But there is a lower cost to fragmentation since it costs only 20 percent more to implement the blueprint in a foreign plant than in a domestic plant instead of 50 percent as in example 1.

More generally, jointness could be measured by the ratio of fixed costs for a horizontal multinational to the fixed costs for a domestic firm. I assume that this ratio is between one and two, with a value of 2 meaning no jointness and 1 meaning perfect jointness. Costs of fragmentation can be measured by the ratio of fixed costs for a vertical firm to the fixed costs for a domestic firm. It seems reasonable to restrict this ratio to between 2 and 1, with 2 meaning very high costs to fragmentation and 1 meaning costless fragmentation.

Defined in this way, Helpman's (1984) model had costless fragmentation in that, at equal factor prices, there were no added fixed costs for fragmenting the headquarters and plant. Markusen and Venables's (1998, 2000) models and chapters 5 and 6 implicitly had very high fragmentation costs in that type-*v* firms were not considered.

In this and in chapters 8 and 9, I assume both jointness and fragmentation exist and generally assume that a horizontal firm has higher fixed costs than a vertical firm as in example 2 above. Type-h fixed costs (at equal factor prices across countries) will be less than double the costs of a type-d firm (jointness), and the fixed costs of a type-v firm will be less than those of a type-h firm but generally more than those for a type-d firm.

In summary, the knowledge-capital model refers to a technology in which firm-fixed costs are characterized by relatively low costs of geographically fragmenting headquarters and a single plant, skilled-labor intensity of firm fixed costs relative to production, and jointness of firm-fixed costs across multiple plants.

7.3   Model Structure

The model has two countries (1 and 2, or generally i, j) producing two homogeneous goods, Y and X. There are two factors of production, L (unskilled labor), and S (skilled labor). L and S are mobile between industries but internationally immobile. Y is used as numeraire throughout the chapter.

Subscripts (i, j) will be used to denote the countries $(1, 2)$. The output of Y in country i is a CES function, identical in both countries. The production function for Y is

$$Y_i = (aL_{iy}^{\alpha} + (1-a)S_{iy}^{\alpha})^{1/\alpha} \qquad i = 1, 2, \tag{1}$$

where L_{iy} and S_{iy} are the unskilled and skilled labor used in the Y sector in country i. The elasticity of substitution $(1/(1-\alpha))$ is set at 3.0 in the simulation runs reported later in the chapter.

Good X is produced with increasing returns to scale by imperfectly competitive Cournot firms. There are both firm-level (arising from joint inputs such as R&D) and plant-level scale economies. There is free entry and exit of firms, and entering firms choose their "type." The term *regime* denotes the set of firm types active in equilibrium. There are six firm types, defined as follows:

Type-h_i Horizontal multinationals that maintain plants in both countries, with headquarters located in country i.

Type-h_j Horizontal multinationals that maintain plants in both countries, with headquarters located in country j.

Type-d_i National firms that maintain a single plant, with headquarters in country i. Type-d_i firms may or may not export to country j.

Type-d_j National firms that maintain a single plant, with headquarters in country j. Type-d_j firms may or may not export to country i.

Type-v_i Vertical multinationals that maintain a single plant in country j, with headquarters in country i. Type-v_i firms may or may not export to country i.

Type-v_j Vertical multinationals that maintain a single plant in country i, with headquarters in country j. Type-v_j firms may or may not export to country j.

Factor-intensity assumptions are crucial to the results derived below. These are guided by what I believe are some empirically relevant assumptions. First, headquarters activities are more skilled-labor-intensive than production plants (including both plant-specific fixed costs and marginal costs). This implies that an "integrated" type-d firm, with a headquarters and plant in the same location, is more skilled-labor-intensive than a plant alone. Second, assume that a plant alone (no headquarters) is more skilled-labor-intensive than the composite Y sector. This is much less obvious, but some evidence suggests that this is probably true for developing countries: Branch plants of foreign multinationals are more skilled-labor-intensive than the economy as a whole.[2] Assumptions about the skilled-labor intensity of activities are therefore

Activities

[headquarters only] > [integrated X] > [plant only] > [Y].

Third, assume that two-plant type-h firms are more skilled-labor-intensive than single-plant type-d or type-v firms. Two-plant firms are assumed to need additional skilled labor in the source country in order to manage the overseas facility and to require some skilled labor in the host-country branch plant as well. Single-plant type-d or type-v firms are assumed to use the same factor proportions as in marginal costs for shipping costs (as in iceberg costs) if they supply the market in which the plant is not located. Assumptions on the skilled-labor intensity of firm types are therefore

Firm Types

[type-h firms] > [type-v and type-d firms].

This last property is unimportant for this chapter, but will be of some importance in chapter 8 when I discuss factor-market effects of trade and investment liberalization.

Superscripts (d, v, h) will be used to designate a variable as referring to domestic or national firms, vertical multinationals, and horizontal multinational firms respectively. (N_i^h, N_i^v, N_i^d) will indicate the number of active h, v, and d firms based in country i. Important notation in the model is as follows:

p_i price of X (in terms of Y) in country i $(i = 1, 2)$

w_i wage of unskilled labor in country i

z_i wage of skilled labor in country i

c_i marginal cost of X production in country i, for all firm types (the functional form for c is identical across countries).

c_{iw}, c_{iz} factor-price derivatives of c give X-sector unit input requirement for factors L and S (by Shepard's lemma) in country i

t_i transport cost for X (uses factors in the same proportion as c)

M_i income of country i

X_{ij}^k sales of a type-k firm $(k = d, v, h)$ headquartered in country i with sales in market j

m_{ij}^k markup of a type-k firm $(k = d, v, h)$ headquartered in country i with sales in market j

fc_i^k fixed costs of a type-k firm headquartered in country i

Assume that both marginal costs, transport costs, and fixed costs in X are fixed-coefficient technologies. This allows us to know the factor intensities of production and fixed costs across countries even if factor prices are different in the two countries. In the case of marginal and transport costs, combined with the assumption that the functions are the same for all firm types and countries, this implies that the derivations of these functions with respect to factor prices are quantities that are independent of factor prices and the same for all firm types and countries. Thus the marginal costs functions can be written as

$$c_i(w_i, z_i) = w_i c_w + z_i c_z, \qquad t_i(w_i, z_i) = w_i \tau c_w + z_i \tau c_z = \tau c_i(w_i, z_i), \qquad (2)$$

where τ is a constant of proportionality between trade costs and marginal production costs. With fixed coefficients, unit input requirements are not subscripted by country.

I will, with apologies, depart somewhat from the notation of the previous chapters in defining fixed costs. In this chapter, F denotes costs incurred in units of skilled labor and G denotes fixed costs incurred in units of unskilled labor. Superscripts d, h, and v continue to denote firm type. It is assumed that G is associated with plants and that the same amount of unskilled labor is required for a plant regardless of whether or not it is in the home or host country. Subscripts

i and j will be attached to skilled-labor requirements. F_i will be the skilled-labor requirements in the home or parent country, and F_j, in the case of type-h and type-v firms, will be skilled-labor requirements in the foreign or host country. Fixed costs for firms headquartered in country i are

$$fc_i^d(w_i, z_i) = z_i F_i^d + w_i G \tag{3}$$

$$fc_i^h(w_i, z_i, w_j, z_j) = z_i F_i^h + w_i G + z_j F_j^h + w_j G \tag{4}$$

$$fc_i^v(z_i, w_j, z_j) = z_i F_i^v + w_j G + z_j F_j^v \tag{5}$$

Quantitative results, and perhaps some qualitative results, are going to be sensitive to assumptions about these costs. I already assume that G is the same for any plant regardless of firm type and country. I make three other assumptions in what follows. First, assume that skilled-labor requirements for a type-h firm are greater than (but less than double) the skilled-labor requirements of a type-d firm. This is the jointness assumption: Total fixed costs for a type-h firm are less than double the fixed costs of a type-d firm. Second, the additional skilled-labor requirements of a type-h firm over a type-d firm are incurred partly in the home (parent) country and partly in the host (foreign) country. The last assumption is that managerial and coordination activities require some additional parent country skilled labor for a type-h firm. For firms based in country i,

$$2F_i^d > F_i^h + F_j^h > F_i^d < F_i^h. \tag{6}$$

Finally, assume that type-v firms have higher skilled-labor requirements than type-d firms (but less than for type-h firms), so that fragmentation is not perfect (technology transfer incurs some costs).

$$F_i^h + F_j^h > F_i^v + F_j^v > F_i^d$$

In the specific examples given later, assume also that the parent country skilled-labor requirement for a type-v firm is less than for a type-d firm (the added skilled labor comes from the host country), although I don't believe this assumption is important in any of the results.

This probably has your head spinning, so let me give a specific example, which is the parameterization used in the numerical model that appears later in the chapter. The values are

$$G = 2, \quad F_i^d = 11, \quad [F_i^h = 12, F_j^h = 4], \quad [F_i^v = 9, F_j^v = 4]. \tag{7}$$

Total fixed-cost factor requirements for firms are then

	type-d_i	type-h_i	type-v_i	type-d_j	type-h_j	type-v_j
L_i	2	2	—	—	2	2
S_i	11	12	9	—	4	4
L_j	—	2	2	2	2	—
S_j	—	4	4	11	12	9

The numerical model used later in the chapter is calibrated so that at the center of the Edgeworth box, with high trade costs so that type-h firms are the equilibrium regime, the prices of both factors in each country equal one. Given this calibration, measures of the degree of jointness and fragmentation at this center point are found by just summing the factor requirements of the firm types. The fixed costs of a type-h firm (20) are 1.54 times greater than the fixed costs of a type-d firm $(20/13)$, and the fixed costs of a type-v firm are 1.15 times greater than the fixed costs of a type-d firm $(15/13)$. These ratios will of course vary in general equilibrium as I move over the Edgeworth box due to factor-price changes both within and between countries.

In equilibrium, the X sector makes no profits so country i income, denoted M_i, is

$$M_i = w_i L_i + z_i S_i \qquad i = 1, 2, \tag{8}$$

where L_i and S_i are total factor endowments of country i. p_i denotes the price of X in country i, and X_{ic} and Y_{ic} denote the consumption of X and Y. Utility of the representative consumer in each country is Cobb-Douglas:

$$U_i = X_{ic}^{\beta} Y_{ic}^{1-\beta}, \quad X_{ic} \equiv N_i^d X_{ii}^d + N_j^d X_{ji}^d + N_i^h X_{ii}^h + N_j^h X_{ji}^h + N_i^v X_{ii}^v + N_j^v X_{ji}^v \tag{9}$$

giving demands

$$X_{ic} = \beta M_i / p_i, \qquad Y_{ic} = (1 - \beta) M_i. \tag{10}$$

Equilibrium in the X sector is the solution to a complementarity problem. First, there are marginal revenue–marginal cost inequalities associated with outputs per firm. For firms headquartered in country i, these are given by (11)–(16). Another six inequalities correspond to firms headquartered in country j. Remember in reviewing these inequalities that the first subscript on X is the headquarters country, and the second is the country of *sale* (not necessarily production). X_{ji}^d

is produced in country j and exported to country i. X_{ji}^v is produced in country i and also sold in country i.

$$p_i(1 - m_{ii}^d) \leq c_i(w_i, z_i) \qquad (X_{ii}^d) \qquad (11)$$

$$p_j(1 - m_{ij}^d) \leq c_i(w_i, z_i) + t_i(w_i, z_i) = c_i(w_i, z_i)(1 + \tau) \qquad (X_{ij}^d) \qquad (12)$$

$$p_i(1 - m_{ii}^h) \leq c_i(w_i, z_i) \qquad (X_{ii}^h) \qquad (13)$$

$$p_j(1 - m_{ij}^h) \leq c_j(w_j, z_j) \qquad (X_{ij}^h) \qquad (14)$$

$$p_j(1 - m_{ij}^v) \leq c_j(w_j, z_j) \qquad (X_{ij}^v) \qquad (15)$$

$$p_i(1 - m_{ii}^v) \leq c_j(w_j, z_j) + t_j(w_j, z_j) = c_j(w_j, z_j)(1 + \tau) \qquad (X_{ii}^v) \qquad (16)$$

Note that marginal costs (and trade costs) depend only on factor prices in the country of production and that they are independent of firm type.

In a Cournot model with homogeneous products, the optimal markup formula is given by the firm's market share divided by the Marshallian price elasticity of demand in that market. In our model, the price elasticity is one (see equation (10)), reducing the firm's markup to its market share. This gives, also using demand equations (10),

$$m_{ij}^k = \frac{X_{ij}^k}{X_{jc}} = \frac{p_j X_{ij}^k}{\beta M_j} \qquad k = d, h, v \qquad i, j = 1, 2. \qquad (17)$$

Six zero-profit conditions correspond to the number of firms of each type. Given equations (11)–(16), zero profits can be written as the requirement that markup revenues equal fixed costs, with the number of firms as the associated complementary variable.

$$p_i m_{ii}^d X_{ii}^d + p_j m_{ij}^d X_{ij}^d \leq fc_i^d(w_i, z_i) \qquad (N_i^d) \qquad (18)$$

$$p_j m_{jj}^d X_{jj}^d + p_i m_{ji}^d X_{ji}^d \leq fc_j^d(w_j, z_j) \qquad (N_j^d) \qquad (19)$$

$$p_i m_{ii}^h X_{ii}^h + p_j m_{ij}^h X_{ij}^h \leq fc_i^h(w_i, z_i, w_j, z_j) \qquad (N_i^h) \qquad (20)$$

$$p_j m_{jj}^h X_{jj}^h + p_i m_{ji}^h X_{ji}^h \leq fc_j^h(w_i, z_i, w_j, z_j) \qquad (N_j^h) \qquad (21)$$

$$p_i m_{ii}^v X_{ii}^v + p_j m_{ij}^v X_{ij}^v \leq fc_i^v(z_i, w_j, z_j) \qquad (N_i^v) \qquad (22)$$

$$p_j m_{jj}^v X_{jj}^v + p_i m_{ji}^v X_{ji}^v \leq fc_j^v(w_i, z_i, z_j) \qquad (N_j^v) \qquad (23)$$

Substituting markups into MR = MC inequalities results in outputs for X produced in country i:

$$X \geq \beta M_i \frac{p_i - c_i(w_i, z_i)}{p_i^2}, \qquad \text{for } X_{ii}^d, X_{ii}^h, X_{ji}^h, X_{ji}^v \tag{24}$$

$$X \geq \beta M_j \frac{p_j - c_i(w_i, z_i)(1 + \tau)}{p_j^2}, \qquad \text{for } X_{ij}^d, X_{ij}^v \tag{25}$$

Similar inequalities hold for goods produced in country j.

Substitute these inequalities into the zero-profit conditions in order to derive some awful-looking quadratic equations.

$$\beta \left[M_i \left(\frac{p_i - c_i}{p_i} \right)^2 + M_j \left(\frac{p_j - c_i(1 + \tau)}{p_j} \right)^2 \right] \leq fc_i^d(w_i, z_i) \qquad (N_i^d) \tag{26}$$

$$\beta \left[M_i \left(\frac{p_i - c_j(1 + \tau)}{p_i} \right)^2 + M_j \left(\frac{p_j - c_j}{p_j} \right)^2 \right] \leq fc_j^d(w_j, z_j) \qquad (N_j^d) \tag{27}$$

$$\beta \left[M_i \left(\frac{p_i - c_i}{p_i} \right)^2 + M_j \left(\frac{p_j - c_j}{p_j} \right)^2 \right] \leq fc_i^h(w_i, z_i, w_j, z_j) \qquad (N_i^h) \tag{28}$$

$$\beta \left[M_i \left(\frac{p_i - c_i}{p_i} \right)^2 + M_j \left(\frac{p_j - c_j}{p_j} \right)^2 \right] \leq fc_j^h(w_i, z_i, w_j, z_j) \qquad (N_j^h) \tag{29}$$

$$\beta \left[M_i \left(\frac{p_i - c_j(1 + \tau)}{p_i} \right)^2 + M_j \left(\frac{p_j - c_j}{p_j} \right)^2 \right] \leq fc_i^v(z_i, w_j, z_j) \qquad (N_i^v) \tag{30}$$

$$\beta \left[M_i \left(\frac{p_i - c_i}{p_i} \right)^2 + M_j \left(\frac{p_j - c_i(1 + \tau)}{p_j} \right)^2 \right] \leq fc_j^v(w_i, z_i, z_j) \qquad (N_j^v) \tag{31}$$

There are several things to note about inequalities (26)–(31) when combined with earlier assumptions about factor intensities. Results relating to horizontal type-h firms relative to single-plant type-d or type-v firms largely follow from the impact-effect discussions in chapters 5 and 6, so I note those findings without analysis.

1. Type-h multinationals will have higher markup revenues than type-d or type-v single-plant firms, since the latter bear transport costs.

2. Type-h multinationals will have higher fixed costs than either a type-d or a type-v firm from at least one country.

3. Type-h multinationals will tend to dominate when total world income is high $(M_i + M_j)$, when trade costs are relatively high (τ), and when the two countries are relatively symmetric in both incomes $(M_i = M_j)$ and in factor prices.

4. When total income is low, trade barriers are low, or countries are asymmetric in size or factor prices, then type-v or type-d firms will dominate.

These results should be familiar from the previous chapter. Vertical firms, which are new in this chapter, deserve more comment. Compare inequality (26) and (31). At a given set of world income levels, commodity prices and factor prices, a type-d_i firm and a type-v_j firm have the same markup revenues. Similar comments apply to type-d_j and type-v_i. Thus which type is more profitable depends on fixed costs and therefore on international factor-price differences, and one more point can be added to the above list.

5. The particular advantage for type-v firms relative to type-d firms lies in situations with unequal factor prices: type-v firms can "arbitrage": locating headquarters activities where skilled labor is cheap, and the plant where unskilled labor is cheap and the market large.

Because I have assumed that technology transfer is costly (fragmentation is not costless), the type-d_i firm will always dominate the type-v_i firm if factor prices are equal or nearly equal across countries. Note also in this regard that there will never be a regime with both type-v_i and type-v_j firms active, because one could replace a type-v_i with a type-d_j and a type-v_j with a type-d_i and generate the same revenues but lower fixed costs. Any vertical activity in the model will be strictly one-way.

Type-v firms will arise in preference to or in addition to type-d firms when factor prices are different between countries. But this is not a sufficient condition. The most obvious case where a vertical firm type would dominate is when one country is small and skilled-labor-abundant. Referring again to (26)–(27) and (30)–(31), if country j is large then either a type-d_j or type-v_i firm will dominate a type-d_i or type-v_j firm from a revenue point of view. The type-d_j firm incurs all of its skilled-labor fixed costs in country j, while the type-v_i firm incurs them primarily in country i. Thus if the smaller country i is skilled-labor-abundant relative to country j, then the type-v_i firm will dominate the type-d_j. But if it is the large country that is skilled-labor-abundant, then the factor-price motive for locating a headquarters will coincide with the market-size motive for locating a plant, and the type-d_j firm will dominate. Thus one is most likely to find vertical firms when one country is small and skilled-labor-abundant.

But type-v firms can also be found in combination with some other firm type when the countries are of similar size. Suppose that countries i and j have the same income, but that country i is skilled-labor-abundant relative to country j. Then in the absence of multinationals, one might expect that all firms might be type-d_i or at least that there are many more type-d_i than type-d_j firms. But this implies a significant commodity-price difference between the two markets, with a higher price in country j. This in turn suggests that some type-v_i firms can profitably enter, capturing high revenues in country j but paying low fixed costs by locating its headquarters in country i. There might be a relatively balanced number of plants between the two countries, but all firms would be headquartered in country i (the regime is d_i, v_i).

7.4   The Numerical General-Equilibrium Model

In this section, I briefly present the actual equations and inequalities solved in the numerical model used to investigate the theory presented earlier. Table 7.1 shows the calibration of the model to the center of the Edgeworth box, where type-h_i and type-h_j firms are active at high trade costs (20%). Fixed costs correspond to the numbers given earlier in the text.

The numerical model is a system of inequalities with associated non-negative variables. Below, I write these out. Recall that $i, j = \{1, 2\}$ and $k = \{d, h, v\}$. A few additional items of notation are used below that were not needed above and are generally consistent with the notation table that follows the preface. c_{iy} and c_{iu} are the cost of producing a unit of Y and a unit of utility in country i, respectively, both measured in units of Y. c_{iy} is thus a function of factor prices and c_{iu} is a function of commodity prices. p_{ui} is the price of a unit of utility, and the price of Y is fixed at one. p_{fci}^k is the price of a unit of fixed costs for firm type-k headquartered in country i. N_i^k will denote the activity that produces fixed costs for firm type-k headquartered in country i, and also the number of those firms active in equilibrium (i.e., units are chosen such that the equilibrium activity level is the number of firms). $mkrev_i^k$ is the markup revenue (total from both markets) of a firm type-k headquartered in country i.

Three sets of inequalities exist. Pricing inequalities have activity levels as complementary variables. Market-clearing inequalities have prices as complementary variables. Income balance inequalities have incomes as complementary variables. Note that firm owners are "con-

Table 7.1
Calibration of the model at the center of the Edgeworth box

	YI	YJ	XMIII	XMJII	XMJJJ	XMIJ	NMI	NMJ	UI	UJ	CONSI	CONSJ	ENTI	ENTJ	ROWSUM
CYI	100								−100						0
CYJ		100								−100					0
CXI			50	50					−100						0
CXJ					50	50				−100					0
FCI							20						−20		0
FCJ								20						−20	0
LI	−90		−30			−30	−2	−2			154				0
SI	−10		−10			−10	−12	−4			46				0
LJ		−90		−30	−30		−2	−2				154			0
SJ		−10		−10	−10		−4	−12				46			0
UTILI									200		−200				0
UTILJ										200		−200			0
MKII			−10										10		0
MKIJ						−10							10		0
MKJJ					−10									10	0
MKJI				−10										10	0
COLSUM	0	0	0	0	0	0	0	0	0	0	0	0	0	0	0

Notes: Fixed costs of initially inactive firm types

	d_i	d_j	v_i	v_j
LI	2		9	
SI	11		2	
LJ		2		4
SJ		11		9

These are the total fixed costs for 2.5 firms, the number of type-h firms in the data above. See table 5.1 for the meaning of row sums, column sums, positive entries, and negative entries.

sumers" who receive income from markup revenues and demand fixed costs. The activity level for fixed costs is the number of firms active in equilibrium. Recall that $i = \{1, 2\}$ in what follows:

Inequalities	Complementary variable	Number of inequalites
Pricing inequalities	Activity level	Number
$q_i \leq c_{iy}$	Y_i	2
$p_{ui} \leq c_{iu}$	U_i	2
$p_i(1 - m_{ii}^d) \leq c_i(w_i, z_i)$	X_{ii}^d	2
$p_j(1 - m_{ij}^d) \leq c_i(w_i, z_i)(1 + \tau)$	X_{ij}^d	2
$p_i(1 - m_{ii}^h) \leq c_i(w_i, z_i)$	X_{ii}^h	2
$p_j(1 - m_{ij}^h) \leq c_j(w_j, z_j)$	X_{ij}^h	2
$p_i(1 - m_{ii}^v) \leq c_j(w_j, z_j)(1 + \tau)$	X_{ii}^v	2
$p_j(1 - m_{ij}^v) \leq c_j(w_j, z_j)$	X_{ij}^v	2
$p_{fci}^k \leq fc_i^k$	N_i^k	6
Market clearing inequalities	Price	Number
$\sum_i demand\ Y_{ic} \leq \sum_i supply\ Y_i$	q	1
$demand\ U_i \leq supply\ U_i$	p_{ui}	2
$demand\ X_{jc} \leq \sum_{k,i} supply\ X_{ij}^k$	p_j	2
$demand\ N_i^k \leq supply\ N_i^k$	p_{fci}^k	6
$demand\ L_i \leq supply\ L_i$	w_i	2
$demand\ S_i \leq supply\ S_i$	z_i	2
Income balance	Incomes	Number
$expend\ cons_i = income\ cons_i$	$income\ cons_i$	2
$demand\ N_i^k = mkrev_i^k$	$income\ entre_i^k$	6
Auxiliary constraints	Markups	Number
$m_{ij}^k \leq (Cournot\ formula)_{ij}^k$	m_{ij}^k	12

The general-equilibrium model is thus solving fifty-seven equations and inequalities for fifty-seven unknowns.

7.5 Equilibrium Regimes and Affiliate Production

Table 7.1 shows the values used in the calibration of the general-equilibrium model at the center of the Edgeworth box with only type-h firms active. Trade costs are 20 percent. The elasticity of substitution in Y is 3.0, while all X-sector activities have fixed coefficients. At the

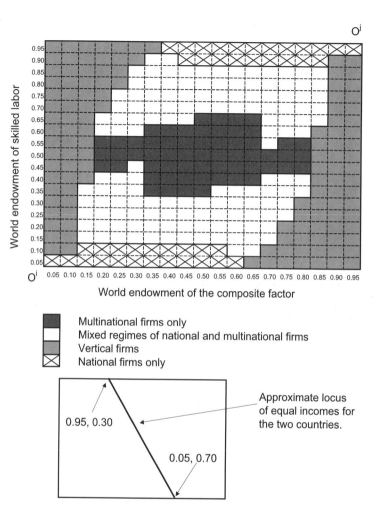

Figure 7.1
Equilibrium regimes ($t = 0.20$)

Table 7.2
Types of firms active in equilibrium: Regime (the number in the cell) $= I_i^d + I_j^d + I_i^v + I_j^v + I_i^h + I_j^h$ (I is for "indicator")

																			O^j
100.000	100.000	100.000	100.000	100.000	100.000	100.000	100.000	100.000	100.000	100.000	100.000	100.000	100.000	100.000	100.000	100.000	100.000	100.000	100.000
100.000	100.000	100.000	100.000	100.000	100.000	100.000	100.000	100.000	100.000	100.000	100.000	100.000	100.000	100.000	100.000	100.000	100.200	100.200	100.200
100.010	100.010	100.010	100.010	100.010	100.010	100.010	100.010	100.010	100.010	100.010	100.010	100.011	100.011	100.001	100.001	100.001	100.200	100.200	100.200
100.010	100.010	100.010	100.010	100.010	100.010	100.010	100.010	100.010	100.010	100.010	100.010	100.011	100.011	100.001	100.001	100.001	100.201	100.201	100.201
100.010	100.010	100.010	100.010	100.010	100.010	100.010	100.010	100.010	100.010	100.010	100.010	100.011	100.001	100.001	100.001	100.001	100.201	100.201	100.200
100.010	100.010	100.010	100.010	100.010	100.010	100.010	0.010	0.010	0.010	0.011	0.011	100.001	100.001	100.001	100.001	100.001	100.001	0.201	0.200
100.010	100.010	100.010	100.010	100.010	0.010	0.010	0.010	0.010	0.010	0.011	0.011	0.011	0.001	100.001	100.001	100.001	100.001	0.201	0.200
0.010	0.010	0.010	0.010	0.010	0.010	0.010	0.011	0.011	0.011	0.011	0.011	0.001	0.001	0.001	0.001	0.001	0.201	0.201	0.201
0.010	0.010	0.010	0.011	0.011	0.011	0.011	0.011	0.011	0.011	0.011	0.011	0.001	0.001	0.001	0.001	0.001	10.201	0.201	0.201
10.010	10.010	10.010	10.011	10.011	0.011	0.011	0.011	0.001	0.001	0.001	0.001	0.001	0.001	10.001	10.001	10.001	10.201	10.201	0.201
10.010	10.010	10.010	10.011	10.011	10.001	10.001	0.001	0.001	0.001	0.001	0.001	10.001	10.001	10.001	10.001	10.201	10.201	10.201	0.201
10.010	10.010	10.010	10.011	10.001	10.001	10.001	10.001	10.001	10.001	10.001	10.001	10.001	10.001	10.001	10.201	10.201	10.201	10.201	0.201
10.010	10.010	10.010	10.001	10.001	10.001	10.001	10.001	10.001	10.001	10.001	10.001	10.001	10.001	10.201	10.201	10.201	10.201	10.201	10.201
10.010	10.010	10.001	10.001	10.001	10.001	10.001	10.001	10.001	10.001	10.001	10.001	10.201	10.201	10.201	10.201	10.201	10.201	10.201	10.200
10.011	10.011	10.001	10.001	10.001	10.001	10.001	10.001	10.001	10.001	10.001	10.001	10.201	10.201	10.201	10.201	10.201	10.200	10.200	10.200
10.011	10.011	10.001	10.001	10.001	10.001	10.001	10.001	10.001	10.001	10.001	10.001	10.201	10.201	10.201	10.201	10.200	10.200	10.200	10.200
10.010	10.010	10.000	10.000	10.000	10.000	10.000	10.000	10.001	10.001	10.001	10.001	10.201	10.201	10.201	10.200	10.200	10.200	10.200	10.200
10.000	10.000	10.000	10.000	10.000	10.000	10.000	10.000	10.000	10.201	10.200	10.200	10.200	10.200	10.200	10.200	10.200	10.200	10.200	10.200
10.000	10.000	10.000	10.000	10.000	10.000	10.000	10.000	10.000	10.200	10.200	10.200	10.200	10.200	10.200	10.200	10.200	10.200	10.200	10.200
102.000	102.000	102.000	102.000	102.000	102.000	102.000	102.010	102.010	2.010	2.010	2.010	2.000	2.000	12.000	12.000	12.000	12.000	10.000	O^i

$I_i^d = 100$ if type-d_i firms active, 0 otherwise
$I_j^d = 10$ if type-d_j firms active, 0 otherwise

$I_i^v = 2.0$ if type-v_i firms active, 0 otherwise
$I_j^v = 0.2$ if type-v_j firms active, 0 otherwise

$I_i^h = 0.01$ if type-h_i firms active, 0 otherwise
$I_j^h = 0.001$ if type-h_j firms active, 0 otherwise

bottom of the table, I show the input requirements for inactive firm types. All activity levels and prices are one initially, except for inactive sectors and the number of firms. There are 2.5 firms of type-h_i and type-h_j initially, which implies five plants in each market (with no exports or imports), so markups are one-fifth or 20 percent.

Figure 7.1 shows the general pattern of regimes over the Edgeworth box, and table 7.2 gives the full detail. Figure 7.1 is simplified into regions of type-h firms only, type-d firms only, regions in which some type-v firms are active (alone or with other firm types), and all other regions (white region). The locus along which the incomes of the two countries are approximately equal is steeper than the NW-SE diagonal and runs from (approximately) cell row 0.95/column 0.30 southeasterly to the cell row 0.05/column 0.70.

The pattern of equilibrium regimes is consistent with impact-effect reasoning of section 7.3. With high trade costs, only type-h firms are active in the central region where countries are similar in size and in relative endowments. Type-v firms are active when one country is both small and skilled-labor-abundant. Only type-d firms are active when one country is large and skilled-labor-abundant. Results with respect to type-h firms are similar to those in chapters 5 and 6. The difference in this model is that more multinational activity occurs when one country is both small and skilled-labor-abundant, due to the introduction of type-v firms.

Table 7.2 gives the full set of firm types active in each cell, with the table note explaining what the numbers mean. For example, the number 102.010 means that types d_i, v_i, and h_i are active. Up to three types of firms can be active in equilibrium, but we find no case where more than three types are active.

Let me repeat one earlier comment from chapter 5, which also helps justify the general-equilibrium approach used in this book. I have been asked how three firm types can exist simultaneously and even had one author claim this is impossible, but in a partial-equilibrium model. The reason that multiple firm types can be supported in general equilibrium often has to do with general-equilibrium factor market effects that do not arise in a partial-equilibrium model. Suppose, for example, that the two countries have identical relative endowments but country i is three times the size of country j. The regime will not be type-h_i and type-h_j firms, with three-quarters of them headquartered in country i and one-quarter in country j. While factor demands for headquarters are in proportion to country size, each

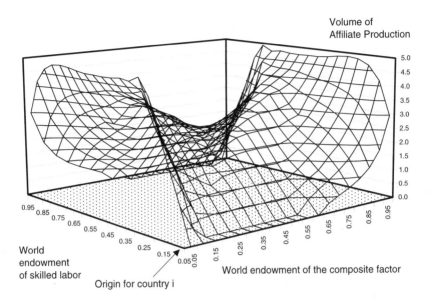

Figure 7.2
Volume of affiliate production (Y numeraire)

country will have the same number of plants, meaning that factor demands for plants are much higher in proportion to size in the small country, with correspondingly higher prices for skilled labor there. To put it another way, if there are zero profits earned in country j in this proposed equilibrium, there will be positive profits for national firms to enter in country i. Thus the regime may be h_i, h_j, d_i, an outcome that is demonstrated in table 7.2 when country i has 70 percent of both factors.

I do not observe good data that give firm types in a way that even remotely resembles the theoretical model of this chapter. But I do have data on affiliate production and sales in the world economy. Thus as I did in chapters 5 and 6, I can plot the volume of affiliate sales over the Edgeworth box. This will be used later to generate testable hypotheses for econometric estimation.

Figure 7.2 gives affiliate sales over the box. These are values that use good Y as numeraire, as I have done throughout this book. This diagram has a definite saddle pattern, with an inverted U-shaped curve along the SW-NE diagonal where countries differ in size but not in relative endowments. The highest affiliate production occurs when one country is small and skilled-labor-abundant. The intuition here is similar to that discussed earlier in the book. At the center of the

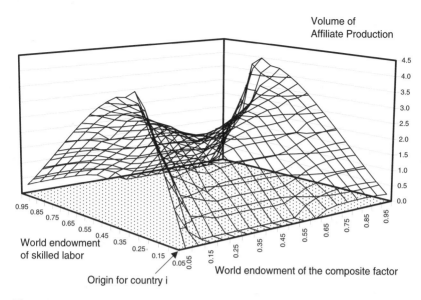

Figure 7.3
Volume of affiliate production (X numeraire)

Edgeworth box, all firms are type-h and are divided evenly between countries, with each firm's local and branch plant having the same output and sales. Since only branch-plant output is considered affiliate activity, affiliate production is exactly half of total world X output. When one country is small and skilled-labor-abundant, all or almost all of the firm headquarters will be located there, but all or almost all of the production will be in the other, large country. In this case, all or almost all of world X output is considered affiliate output. In table 7.2, for example, note that when country i has 0.35 of total world skilled labor but only 0.05 of total world unskilled labor, the regime is type-v_i firm only. So all world production of X is affiliate production.

Figure 7.3 raises an issue that was not important in earlier chapters. Figure 7.2, like those in earlier chapters, uses Y as numeraire. Figure 7.3 plots physical units of X, or uses X as numeraire. For much of the box, this doesn't make much difference. The exception is in the NW and SE corners, where there is substantial difference for the two alternative numeraires. The reason is that in this region, X becomes very expensive relative to good Y, so affiliate activity measured in terms of Y (figure 7.2) is much greater than when measured in terms of good X. This was not important in chapters 5 and 6 since there was not much affiliate activity in this region.

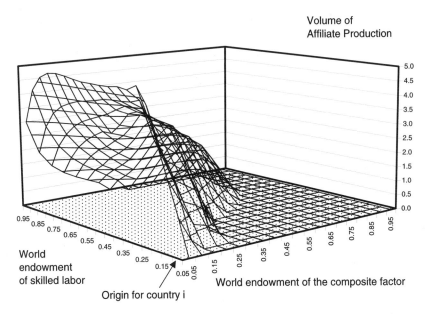

Volume of
Affiliate Production

Figure 7.4
Volume of affiliate production by country *i* firms in country *j*

Keeping this in mind, I continue to use the diagrams with Y as numeraire in the analysis, partly since I think that corresponds better to what is in the data and is thus more appropriate for formulating empirical tests later in the book. I also think that the crucial difference between the extended knowledge-capital model and the horizontal model of chapters 5 and 6 remains valid under either numeraire, although it is clearly a less spectacular difference using units of X. If you refer back to figures 5.2 and 6.2, you see that the increased importance of multinational activity when one country is both small and skilled-labor-abundant in the knowledge-capital model remains true whether we use figure 7.2 or figure 7.3. Parenthetically, I also used the real consumer price index (the unit expenditure function) to deflate X, and that results in something a bit in between figure 7.2 and figure 7.3, as one would expect. But it is much closer to figure 7.2, so again, that is the approach that I use.

Figure 7.4 considers just the production of affiliates of country *i* firms located in country *j*. Here one sees quite dramatically the fact that headquarters of either type-h or type-v firms are concentrated in the skilled-labor-abundant country. I use this result later in the book to formulate empirical tests.

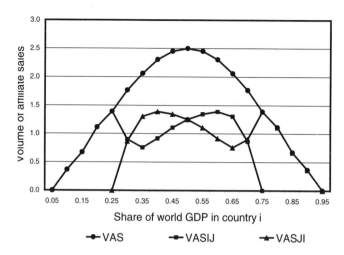

Figure 7.5
Volume of affiliate production along the SW-NE diagonal

Figures 7.5–7.7 clarify some results that are difficult to see from figures 7.2–7.3. Figure 7.5 plots affiliate production along the SW-NE diagonal of the Edgeworth box when the countries differ in size but not in relative endowments. *VAS* is the total volume of affiliate sales and *VASIJ* is the volume of sales by affiliates of country *i* headquartered firms in country *j*. *VASJI* is similarly defined. The curve for total affiliate sales has the inverted U-shape that I have discussed before. When the countries are of quite different size, type-d firms headquartered in the larger country have an advantage and compete with type-h firms headquartered in the small country.

The curves for the individual countries are not monotonic. Consider *VASIJ* beginning at the left corner of the box in figure 7.5 where country *i* is small. With reference to table 7.2, when country *i* is small type-d_j firms are active, and either type-v_i or type-h_i firms are active, so all affiliate activity is by country *i* firms, but there is simply not much of it. When the share of skilled (and unskilled) labor in country *j* reaches 30–35 percent, type-d_j firms switch to being type-h_j firms. These firms have higher sales in country *i* than in type-d_j firms since the former do not bear transport costs. Thus they force the exit of some type-h_i firms, which is why *VASIJ* falls. At 0.35 all firms are type-h, but since country *j* is larger, most affiliate sales are by country *j* firms in country *i*. These two country curves then reconverge at the center of the box. Thus the initial rise in *VASIJ* is a country size effect.

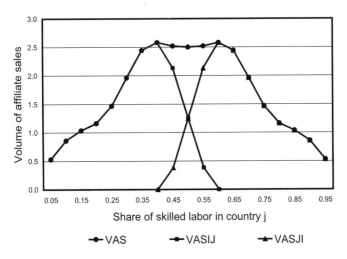

Figure 7.6
Volume of affiliate production along the (approximate) equal income locus NW-SE
(shown in figure 7.1)

The subsequent fall in *VASIJ* is due to a regime shift. Once the shift
from type-d_j to type-h_j firms is complete, the slope of *VASIJ* turns
positive again due to a country size effect. The same story in reverse
applies to points to the right of the center point in figure 7.5.

Figure 7.6 shows affiliate sales along the (approximate) equal-income
locus noted in figure 7.1. Movements to the right on the horizontal
axis correspond to a movement from NW to SE in figure 7.1. Note
with reference to figures 7.2 and 7.3 that these curves are not sensitive
to the numeraire issue. It only becomes important when income levels
are very different.

Total affiliate sales in figure 7.6 has an inverted *U* shape, with some
small nonmonotonicity near the center. Thus is due to a relative concentration of headquarters in the skilled-labor-abundant country but a
relative concentration of production in the unskilled-labor-abundant
country, so that slightly over half of world production of *X* is affiliate
production when there is a small difference in relative endowments.
For an individual country, its affiliate's activity is highest when it is
"moderately" skilled-labor-abundant. Total affiliate activity is the same
when one country has three-quarters of the world's supply of skilled
labor as at the center of the box, but in the former case it is all one-
way instead of perfectly balanced at the center of the box. As the
countries become very different in relative endowments, the dominant
firm type becomes domestic firms headquartered in the skilled-labor-

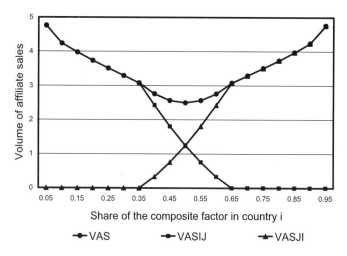

Figure 7.7
Volume of affiliate production, countries have equal (and constant) shares of world skilled labor

abundant country, together with a few type-v firms also headquartered in that country. Thus there are single-plant firms producing in both countries, but all firms are headquartered in the skilled-labor-abundant country.

Figure 7.7 shows affiliate sales along a horizontal line through the midpoint of the Edgeworth box, so that both countries have equal shares of skilled labor. Note again with reference to figures 7.2 and 7.3 that this curve is not really affected by the numeraire choice. Along this locus, affiliate sales have a U shape due once again to a familiar cause: Headquarters are concentrated in the small, skilled-labor-abundant country while production is concentrated in the large market. Thus most of world production is affiliate production near the ends of the horizontal axis in figure 7.7.

The latter point also explains the monotonic fall in $VASIJ$ moving from left to right. At the left edge, country i has all the headquarters but virtually no production (the regime is v_i, h_i, see table 7.2) while at the right-hand edge it has the opposite: no headquarters but branch plants of type-v_j and type-h_j firms.

7.6 Summary and Conclusions

This chapter extends the horizontal model to allow for the geographic fragmentation of activities within single-plant firms. The vertical model of Helpman (1984) then arises as a special case. The introduction of the type-v firms is most important when one country is small and skilled-labor-abundant. With relatively high trade costs as assumed in this chapter, type-v firms do not arise when countries are similar in size and in relative endowments.

It is the combination of small size and skilled-labor abundance that leads to type-v firms. Headquarters are chosen on the basis of factor prices, so the skilled-labor-abundant country is the headquarters country. The location of a single-plant depends critically on market size, however, and relatively less on factor prices. Thus, when one country is small and skilled-labor-abundant, the motives for headquarters and plant location reinforce each other in creating type-v firms.

These results weaken the strong results of the previous two chapters that multinationals are most likely to arise between countries that are similar in both size and in relative endowments. This statement is amended to include small skilled-labor-abundant countries. At a casual level, this might explain why countries such as Sweden, the Netherlands, and Switzerland are such important home countries to multinational firms. At the same time, it explains why large unskilled-labor-abundant countries such as China are large recipients of FDI, but don't supply much of it. More formal empirical work follows.

8

Extensions to the Knowledge-Capital Model: Trade versus Affiliate Production, Factor-Price Effects, and Welfare Effects of Trade and Investment Liberalization

8.1 Introduction

The purpose of this chapter is to provide extensions to the analysis of the knowledge-capital model. My focus is on the relationship between affiliate production and trade in X. A second focus is on the relationship between the degree of liberalization in trade and investment barriers and on factor prices. Welfare effects of liberalization when countries are asymmetric is another interesting exercise that I examine at the end of the chapter. The model is exactly the same as in chapter 7, so that you are saved any new notation and equations. I use, however, a slightly different calibration for the numerical examples, which I explain shortly.

Throughout the chapter, I refer repeatedly to four scenarios, which differ in the degree of restrictions on trade in X and restrictions on the existence of multinational firms. I have already used the term *regime* to denote the set of firm types active in equilibrium. But the term is also frequently used to refer to the degree of restrictions on trade and investment, as in "trade regime" or "investment regime." I am not sure this is the best decision, but because of this common usage, I use the word regime to mean three different things, trying to be careful to always use the appropriate adjective with the noun:

"Market regime" denotes the types of firms active in equilibrium.

"Trade regime" denotes the level of trade costs.

"Investment regime" denotes restrictions on the existence of multinational (type-h and type-v) firms.

In order to keep things manageable, I consider only two levels of trade restrictions and two levels of investment restrictions. Numerically, I look at 20 percent versus 1 percent trade costs for good X.

With respect to restrictions on multinational firms, costs of doing business abroad are built into the fixed-cost assumptions for the different firm types. So, for example, if jointness is not perfect or fragmentation is not costless, then some of those added costs of being a type-h or type-v firm, respectively, could be interpreted as policy-induced barriers. I consider just two alternatives. One is a stark but convenient reference point, which is that multinational firms are simply banned. Type-h and type-v firms cannot exist. The other is some modest level of investment restrictions built into the fixed costs used in the model calibration. I do not attempt to divide the added fixed costs of being a type-h or type-v firm above those of a type-d firm into a policy component and a technology component. The four combinations of trade and investment restrictions considered are denoted as follows:

NL   "no liberalization": 20 percent trade costs, multinational firms prohibited

TL   "trade liberalization": 1 percent trade costs, multinational firms prohibited

IL   "investment liberalization": 20 percent trade costs, multinationals permitted at base-calibration fixed costs

FL   "full liberalization": 1 percent trade costs, multinationals permitted

In the section 8.2, I review some of the basic equations of the model and look again at the intuition as to how trade and investment restrictions affect the market regime. In section 8.3, I examine the base calibration for the simulation model.

Sections 8.4 and 8.5 then turn to the relationship between affiliate production and trade in X. The findings here relate to many issues discussed in the literature, including whether or not trade and affiliate production are complements or substitutes. I feel that these terms have been used somewhat loosely in the literature and include references to simple correlations between the trade and affiliate production. For instance, one could say that trade and affiliate production are complements if both are observed to rise together. I find this unsatisfactory since, for example, both could be rising due to some third factor such as growth in world income or the simultaneous lowering of all costs of international business. I examine two types of experiments. In the first, I look at the effect of lowering trade costs with investment liberalized—that is, going from IL to FL. In this case, one could say that trade and investment are complements if the lowering of trade costs raises the volume of affiliate production. In the second set of experiments, I eliminate investment restrictions for a given level of trade costs. This really involves two separate experiments, liberalizing investment given high trade costs (NL to IL) and liberalizing investment given low trade costs (TL to FL). Here one could say that trade and affiliate production are complements if eliminating investment restrictions increases the volume of trade.

In section 8.5, I consider the effects of investment liberalization on the direction of trade in X. For some values of size and relative-endowment differences between countries, investment liberalization can reverse the direction of trade. Investment liberalization permits a fragmentation or unbundling between the headquarters services and actual X production. A country that exports the combined bundle of services and physical output when investment is banned may choose to specialize in the headquarters services component and import the physical good after liberalization.

Section 8.6 considers factor market issues and the effects of investment liberalization on the real and relative prices of skilled labor. An important result in this section is that there is something of a skilled-labor bias to affiliate production in the model. For a range of differences in relative country sizes and relative endowments, investment liberalization raises the real and relative (to unskilled labor) return to skilled labor for both countries. The reason behind this is reminiscent of the model of Feenstra and Hanson (1996a,b; 1997). What happens in my model is that investment liberalization leads the skilled-labor-abundant country to specialize less in X production and more in head-quarters services, and it leads the unskilled-labor-abundant country to specialize less in Y production and more in X. In both cases, the countries are moving from a less-skilled-labor-intensive activity to a more skilled-labor-intensive activity, thus raising the real and relative wage of skilled labor in equilibrium.

Section 8.7 considers the effects of investment liberalization on welfare of the two countries. Results indicate that the larger country may lose from liberalization. This, I believe, has to do with home-market effects that favor the large country when multinationals are prohibited. Thus contrary to many political arguments, it is the FDI-exporting countries that may lose from liberalization rather than the FDI-importing countries.

Section 8.8 considers a narrow but very interesting special case in which one country is relatively large and skilled-labor-abundant. This case is interesting insofar as the four trade and investment regimes all generate quite different allocations inside the small skilled-labor-scarce country. Furthermore, it is a case where the large country loses from investment liberalization under high trade costs (NL to IL) and a case in which investment liberalization under either high or low trade costs leads to an increase in the real and relative price of skilled labor in both countries. A detailed examination of this case helps clarify the causes of these outcomes.

8.2 Review of the Model

This chapter uses the six-firm-type model of chapter 7. All of the notation and analytics are the same. Nevertheless, I think it is valuable to review some of the key equations again in order to gain intuition into the numerical general-equilibrium results that follow. The following equations reproduce equations (26)–(31) in chapter 7. These were derived by substitution of the pricing equations and markup formulae into the zero-profit conditions. The complementary variables are the numbers of each firm type active in equilibrium.

$$\beta\left[M_i\left(\frac{p_i-c_i}{p_i}\right)^2 + M_j\left(\frac{p_j-c_i(1+\tau)}{p_j}\right)^2\right] \le fc_i^d(w_i,z_i) \qquad (N_i^d) \qquad (1)$$

$$\beta\left[M_i\left(\frac{p_i-c_j(1+\tau)}{p_i}\right)^2 + M_j\left(\frac{p_j-c_j}{p_j}\right)^2\right] \le fc_j^d(w_j,z_j) \qquad (N_j^d) \qquad (2)$$

$$\beta\left[M_i\left(\frac{p_i-c_i}{p_i}\right)^2 + M_j\left(\frac{p_j-c_j}{p_j}\right)^2\right] \le fc_i^h(w_i,z_i,w_j,z_j) \qquad (N_i^h) \qquad (3)$$

$$\beta\left[M_i\left(\frac{p_i-c_i}{p_i}\right)^2 + M_j\left(\frac{p_j-c_j}{p_j}\right)^2\right] \le fc_j^h(w_i,z_i,w_j,z_j) \qquad (N_j^h) \qquad (4)$$

$$\beta\left[M_i\left(\frac{p_i-c_j(1+\tau)}{p_i}\right)^2 + M_j\left(\frac{p_j-c_j}{p_j}\right)^2\right] \le fc_i^v(z_i,w_j,z_j) \qquad (N_i^v) \qquad (5)$$

$$\beta\left[M_i\left(\frac{p_i-c_i}{p_i}\right)^2 + M_j\left(\frac{p_j-c_i(1+\tau)}{p_j}\right)^2\right] \le fc_j^v(w_i,z_i,z_j) \qquad (N_j^v) \qquad (6)$$

Note that markup revenues (the left-hand sides of these inequalities) minus fixed costs (right-hand sides) equal profits. These inequalities can then be written in more compact form as follows:

$$\Pi_i^d = a_i M_i + b_j M_j - fc_i^d \leq 0 \tag{7}$$

$$\Pi_j^d = b_i M_i + a_j M_j - fc_j^d \leq 0 \tag{8}$$

$$\Pi_i^h = a_i M_i + a_j M_j - fc_i^h \leq 0 \tag{9}$$

$$\Pi_j^h = a_i M_i + a_j M_j - fc_j^h \leq 0 \tag{10}$$

$$\Pi_i^v = b_i M_i + a_j M_j - fc_i^v \leq 0 \tag{11}$$

$$\Pi_j^v = a_i M_i + b_j M_j - fc_j^v \leq 0 \tag{12}$$

Note that $a_i > b_i$ if trade costs are positive (as I always assume). This implies that, at equal factor prices, national (type-d) firms will headquarter in the larger market and vertical firms (type-v), if they exist, may headquarter in the smaller market. In fact, (7) and (8) suggest that if factor prices were the same in the two countries, then only type-d firms would exist in the larger country. This is not necessarily true due to the endogeneity of markups.

The determination of equilibrium markups is of some importance to the issues in this chapter, so we need to take a moment to examine how they might differ between countries in equilibrium. Refer back to inequalities (11)–(16) of the previous chapter. Suppose that there is local production in market i. Then a_i can be written as

$$a_i = \beta\left[1 - \frac{c_i}{p_i}\right]^2 = \beta[1 - (1 - m_{ii}^k)]^2 = \beta[m_{ii}^k]^2 \qquad k = (d, h). \tag{13}$$

Thus, assuming that local production exists in both markets, $a_i > a_j$ if and only if the markup on local production is higher in market i. Referring again to chapter 7, the markup is given by a firm's market share:

$$m_{ii}^k = \frac{X_{ii}^k}{X_{ic}} \qquad k = d, h, v, \tag{14}$$

where X_{ic} is total sales (consumption) in market i.

With apologies for partial-equilibrium reasoning, consider the following thought experiment. Suppose that there are only national firms in existence (the regime is (d_i, d_j)), and that most of these are headquartered in country i. Suppose also that all firms sell in both markets, and finally that factor prices are the same in the two markets. Given these assumptions, the amount each importing firm sells in a market is less than the amount that a local firm sells. Thus for a firm in country i, most of the firms in the denominator of (14) are high-sales local firms and few are low-sales foreign firms. The opposite is true for country j, where most of the firms in the denominator are low-sales foreign (country i) firms. Thus, given our assumptions, the equilibrium markup will be higher in country j than in country i.

Suppose that there are N_i firms in country i and N_j firms in country j, $N_i > N_j$. Markups are given by

$$m_{ii}^d = \frac{X_{ii}^d}{N_i X_{ii}^d + N_j X_{ji}^d} \qquad m_{jj}^d = \frac{X_{jj}^d}{N_i X_{ij}^d + N_j X_{jj}^d}. \tag{15}$$

Refer again to equations (11)–(16) in the previous chapter, and (1)–(5) in this chapter. Maintaining the thought-experiment assumption that factor prices are the same in the two countries, quotients of these conditions tell us that

$$\frac{1 - m_{ii}^d}{1 - m_{ji}^d} = \frac{1 - m_{jj}^d}{1 - m_{ij}^d} = \frac{1}{1 + \tau} < 1 \Rightarrow \frac{m_{ii}^d}{m_{ji}^d} \quad \text{and} \quad \frac{m_{jj}^d}{m_{ij}^d} > 1. \tag{16}$$

This in turn implies that

$$\frac{X_{ii}^d}{X_{ji}^d} \quad \text{and} \quad \frac{X_{jj}^d}{X_{ij}^d} > 1. \tag{17}$$

Using (15), (17), and (1)–(5), given $N_i > N_j$, it must be the case that

$$m_{ii}^d < m_{jj}^d \Rightarrow c_i(w_i, z_i)/p_i > c_j(w_j, z_j)/p_j. \tag{18}$$

The real price of at least one factor must be higher in the low-markup country (country i in this example). When the markup differences are related to country size with identical relative endowments, the ratio of the large to the small country's income can exceed the ratio of their endowments (size).

Two consequences of this result will be important later in the chapter. First, a relatively small and/or skilled-labor-scarce country may have some production by local firms, but the markup will be higher than in the large and/or skilled-labor-abundant country. In terms of (1)–(2) or (7)–(8), suppose that $M_i > M_j$ but factor prices were equalized. Then both inequalities could hold with equality if markups in the smaller country j were higher. The same reasoning applies if incomes were the same in the two countries, but costs were higher in country j.

In summary, with the regime (d_i, d_j), one expects that the smaller and/or skilled-labor-scarce country will have a higher markup on domestic production.

Second, the higher markup in the small and/or skilled-labor-scarce country will have important consequences for the effects of liberalization of trade and/or investment on welfare and factor prices. If relative factor prices were equalized between countries, the country with the higher markup would have lower real wages as noted following inequality (18). This is what I will refer to as the "home-market effect." Liberalization may then move welfare in opposite directions in the two countries.

I should also review the fixed-cost functions from chapter 7 that appear in (1)–(6) and (7)–(12). These are as follows for firms headquartered in country i ($i = 1, 2$):

$$fc_i^d(w_i, z_i) = z_i F_i^d + w_i G \tag{19}$$

$$fc_i^h(w_i, z_i, w_j, z_j) = z_i F_i^h + w_i G + z_j F_j^h + w_j G \tag{20}$$

$$fc_i^v(z_i, w_j, z_j) = z_i F_i^v + w_j G + z_j F_j^v \tag{21}$$

Type-h firms have higher fixed costs than at least one type of domestic or vertical firm. Assuming that Y is produced in both countries and, as I have always assumed, fixed costs are skilled-labor-intensive relative to Y, fixed costs are higher for a given firm type for firms headquartered in the country with the higher relative price for skilled labor. If factor prices are sufficiently different to outweigh any fragmentation costs, a type-v firm headquartered in the country where skilled labor is relatively cheap has lower fixed costs than a type-d firm headquartered in the other country.

I can now summarize some of the principal determinants of the equilibrium regime much as I did in chapter 7, referring to (7)–(12) and (19)–(21). Type-h firms are likely to arise when countries' total incomes are high, countries are similar in size, and trade costs are high. Type-d firms headquartered in the larger country exist when the countries are quite different in size and/or trade costs are low. Type-v firms arise when countries are asymmetric in relative factor endowments and in size. In particular, type-v firms are likely to dominate when one country is skilled-labor-abundant and small. In such a situation, factor-price and market-size motives reinforce one another for type-v firms headquartered in the skilled-labor-abundant country.

8.3   Calibration, Equilibrium Market Regimes

Once again, I calibrate the model to the center of the Edgeworth box with high trade costs, such that only type-h firms are active. The model is thus calibrated at the IL equilibrium. While the model is identical to that in chapter 7, I use a somewhat different calibration for the numerical model. This is shown in table 8.1. There are two differences from the calibration shown in table 7.1. First, a smaller difference in factor intensities exists between the Y and X sectors in this chapter. Second, a smaller fragmentation cost occurs in this chapter. At the center of the world Edgeworth box where all factor prices are the same, fixed costs for a type-v firm are fourteen in this chapter as opposed to fifteen in chapter 7, with the fixed costs for a type-d firm being thirteen in both cases. The fixed-cost functions for type-h firms are twenty in both chapters. These changes turn out to make little difference to general results, but generate somewhat larger effects in trade and investment-liberalization experiments.

Tables 8.2 and 8.3 give the market regime for the four different combinations of trade and investment regimes. Table 8.2 gives the two investment regimes for high trade costs (NL and IL), and table 8.3 gives the investments regimes for low trade costs (TL and FL). I realize that these are not very helpful per se, and I will not have much to say about them at the moment. But one needs them to understand the effects of moving from one investment or trade regime to another. So from time to time throughout the chapter, I refer to these numbers in order to explain which market regime shifts are associated with other changes (e.g., trade volumes, factor prices).

8.4   Effects of Trade Costs on the Volume of Affiliate Production

Figures 8.1 and 8.2 show the volume of affiliate production (investment liberalized) over the world Edgeworth box for high and low trade costs, respectively. Figure 8.1 is thus trade/investment regime IL and figure 8.2 is trade/investment regime FL. Figure 8.1 is quite similar to the corresponding diagram in chapter 7, figure 7.2, which has a somewhat different calibration.

The saddle shape of figure 8.1, discussed in the previous chapter, bears repeating here, referring to the bottom panel in table 8.2. At the center of the box with countries identical, the regime is (h_i, h_j) with equal numbers of firms headquartered in each country. With equal

Table 8.1
Calibration of the model at the center of the Edgeworth box

	YI	YJ	XMII	XMIJ	XMJJ	XMJI	NMI	NMJ	UI	UJ	CONSI	CONSJ	ENTI	ENTJ	ROWSUM
CYI	100								-100						0
CYJ		100								-100					0
CXI			50	50	50	50			-100						0
CXJ										-100					0
FCI							20						-20		0
FCJ								20						-20	0
LI	-80		-35	-35			-2	-2			154				0
SI	-20		-5	-5			-12	-4			46				0
LJ		-80			-35	-35	-2	-2				154			0
SJ		-20			-5	-5	-4	-12				46			0
UTILI									200		-200				0
UTILJ										200		-200			0
MKII			-10										10		0
MKIJ				-10									10		0
MKJJ					-10									10	0
MKJI						-10								10	0
COLSUM	0	0	0	0	0	0	0	0	0	0	0	0	0	0	0

Notes: Fixed costs of initially inactive firm types

	d_i	d_j	v_i	v_j
LI	2		9	2
SI	11		2	3
LJ		2	3	
SJ		11		9

See table 5.1 for the meaning of row sums, column sums, positive entries, and negative entries.

Table 8.2
Types of firms active in equilibrium, high trade costs: Regime (the number in the cell) $= I_i^d + I_j^d + I_i^v + I_j^v + I_i^h + I_j^h$ (I is for "indicator")

Investment prohibited (case NL)

O^j (columns) / O^i (rows)

110.000	110.000	110.000	110.000	110.000	110.000	100.000	100.000	100.000	100.000	100.000	100.000	100.000	100.000	100.000	100.000	100.000	100.000
110.000	110.000	110.000	110.000	110.000	110.000	110.000	100.000	100.000	100.000	100.000	100.000	100.000	100.000	100.000	100.000	100.000	100.000
110.000	110.000	110.000	110.000	110.000	110.000	110.000	110.000	100.000	100.000	100.000	100.000	100.000	100.000	100.000	100.000	100.000	100.000
110.000	110.000	110.000	110.000	110.000	110.000	110.000	110.000	110.000	100.000	100.000	100.000	100.000	100.000	100.000	100.000	100.000	100.000
110.000	110.000	110.000	110.000	110.000	110.000	110.000	110.000	110.000	110.000	100.000	100.000	100.000	100.000	100.000	100.000	100.000	100.000
110.000	110.000	110.000	110.000	110.000	110.000	110.000	110.000	110.000	110.000	110.000	100.000	100.000	100.000	100.000	100.000	100.000	100.000
110.000	110.000	110.000	110.000	110.000	110.000	110.000	110.000	110.000	110.000	110.000	110.000	100.000	100.000	100.000	100.000	100.000	100.000
10.000	110.000	110.000	110.000	110.000	110.000	110.000	110.000	110.000	110.000	110.000	110.000	110.000	100.000	100.000	100.000	100.000	100.000
10.000	10.000	110.000	110.000	110.000	110.000	110.000	110.000	110.000	110.000	110.000	110.000	110.000	110.000	100.000	100.000	100.000	100.000
10.000	10.000	10.000	110.000	110.000	110.000	110.000	110.000	110.000	110.000	110.000	110.000	110.000	110.000	110.000	100.000	100.000	100.000
10.000	10.000	10.000	10.000	110.000	110.000	110.000	110.000	110.000	110.000	110.000	110.000	110.000	110.000	110.000	110.000	100.000	100.000
10.000	10.000	10.000	10.000	10.000	110.000	110.000	110.000	110.000	110.000	110.000	110.000	110.000	110.000	110.000	110.000	110.000	100.000
10.000	10.000	10.000	10.000	10.000	10.000	110.000	110.000	110.000	110.000	110.000	110.000	110.000	110.000	110.000	110.000	110.000	110.000
10.000	10.000	10.000	10.000	10.000	10.000	10.000	110.000	110.000	110.000	110.000	110.000	110.000	110.000	110.000	110.000	110.000	110.000
10.000	10.000	10.000	10.000	10.000	10.000	10.000	10.000	110.000	110.000	110.000	110.000	110.000	110.000	110.000	110.000	110.000	110.000
10.000	10.000	10.000	10.000	10.000	10.000	10.000	10.000	10.000	110.000	110.000	110.000	110.000	110.000	110.000	110.000	110.000	110.000
10.000	10.000	10.000	10.000	10.000	10.000	10.000	10.000	10.000	10.000	110.000	110.000	110.000	110.000	110.000	110.000	110.000	110.000
10.000	10.000	10.000	10.000	10.000	10.000	10.000	10.000	10.000	10.000	10.000	110.000	110.000	110.000	110.000	110.000	110.000	110.000
10.000	10.000	10.000	10.000	10.000	10.000	10.000	10.000	10.000	10.000	10.000	10.000	110.000	110.000	110.000	110.000	110.000	110.000
10.000	10.000	10.000	10.000	10.000	10.000	10.000	10.000	10.000	10.000	10.000	10.000	10.000	110.000	110.000	110.000	110.000	110.000
10.000	10.000	10.000	10.000	10.000	10.000	10.000	10.000	10.000	10.000	10.000	10.000	10.000	10.000	110.000	110.000	110.000	110.000
10.000	10.000	10.000	10.000	10.000	10.000	10.000	10.000	10.000	10.000	10.000	10.000	10.000	10.000	10.000	110.000	110.000	110.000
10.000	10.000	10.000	10.000	10.000	10.000	10.000	10.000	10.000	10.000	10.000	10.000	10.000	10.000	10.000	10.000	110.000	110.000
10.000	10.000	10.000	10.000	10.000	10.000	10.000	10.000	10.000	10.000	10.000	10.000	10.000	10.000	10.000	10.000	10.000	110.000

O^i

Investment liberalized (case IL)

O^j

102.000	102.000	102.000	102.000	102.000	102.000	102.000	100.010	100.010	100.010	100.010	100.010	100.010	100.010	100.000	100.000	100.000	100.000	100.000	100.000	100.000
102.000	102.000	102.000	102.000	102.000	102.000	102.000	100.010	100.010	100.010	100.010	100.010	100.010	100.010	100.010	100.010	100.010	100.010	100.000	100.000	100.200
102.000	102.000	102.000	102.000	102.000	102.000	102.000	100.010	100.010	100.010	100.010	100.010	100.010	100.010	100.010	100.010	100.010	100.010	100.010	100.200	100.200
102.000	102.000	102.000	102.000	102.000	102.000	102.000	100.010	100.010	100.010	100.010	100.010	100.010	100.010	100.010	100.010	100.010	100.010	100.010	100.200	100.200
102.010	102.010	102.010	102.010	102.000	102.010	100.010	0.010	0.010	0.010	0.010	0.010	0.010	0.010	100.011	100.011	100.011	100.011	100.200	100.200	0.200
2.010	2.010	2.010	2.010	2.010	2.010	0.010	0.010	0.010	0.010	0.010	0.010	0.010	0.011	0.011	0.011	0.011	100.011	100.201	0.200	0.200
2.010	2.010	2.010	2.010	2.010	2.000	0.010	0.010	0.010	0.010	0.010	0.010	0.011	0.011	0.011	0.011	0.001	100.001	0.200	0.200	0.200
2.000	2.010	2.010	2.010	2.000	2.000	0.010	0.010	0.010	0.010	0.010	0.011	0.011	0.011	0.011	0.001	0.001	100.001	0.200	0.200	0.200
2.000	2.010	2.010	2.010	2.000	2.000	0.010	0.010	0.010	0.010	0.011	0.011	0.011	0.011	0.001	0.001	0.001	100.001	0.200	0.200	0.200
2.000	2.010	2.010	2.010	2.000	2.000	0.010	0.010	0.010	0.010	0.011	0.011	0.011	0.001	0.001	0.001	0.001	0.201	0.200	0.200	0.200
2.000	2.010	2.010	2.010	2.000	2.000	0.010	0.010	0.010	0.011	0.011	0.011	0.001	0.001	0.001	0.001	0.201	0.201	0.200	0.200	0.200
2.000	2.010	2.010	2.010	2.000	2.000	0.010	0.010	0.011	0.011	0.011	0.001	0.001	0.001	0.001	0.201	0.201	0.201	0.200	0.200	0.200
2.000	2.010	2.010	2.010	2.000	2.000	0.010	0.011	0.011	0.011	0.001	0.001	0.001	0.001	0.201	0.201	0.201	0.201	0.200	0.200	0.200
2.000	12.010	10.010	10.010	10.010	12.010	0.011	0.001	0.001	0.001	0.001	0.001	0.201	0.201	0.201	0.201	0.201	0.201	0.200	0.200	0.200
2.000	12.000	10.010	10.010	10.010	12.000	10.001	10.001	0.001	0.001	0.001	0.201	0.201	0.201	0.201	0.201	0.201	0.201	0.200	0.200	0.200
12.000	12.000	10.010	10.011	10.011	12.000	10.001	10.001	10.001	0.001	0.001	0.201	0.201	0.201	0.201	0.201	0.201	0.201	0.201	10.200	10.200
12.000	12.000	10.001	10.001	10.001	10.001	10.001	10.001	10.001	10.001	10.001	10.001	10.001	10.001	10.001	10.001	10.201	10.201	10.201	10.200	10.200
12.000	12.000	10.001	10.001	10.001	10.000	10.001	10.001	10.001	10.001	10.001	10.001	10.001	10.200	10.200	10.200	10.200	10.200	10.200	10.200	10.200
12.000	12.000	10.001	10.001	10.001	10.000	10.001	10.001	10.001	10.001	10.001	10.001	10.201	10.200	10.200	10.200	10.200	10.200	10.200	10.200	10.200
12.000	12.000	10.001	10.001	10.001	10.000	10.001	10.001	10.001	10.201	10.201	10.200	10.200	10.200	10.200	10.200	10.200	10.200	10.200	10.200	10.200
10.000	10.000	10.000	10.000	10.000	10.000	10.000	10.001	10.001	10.200	10.200	10.200	10.200	10.200	10.200	10.200	10.200	10.200	10.200	10.200	10.200

O^i

$I_i^d = 100$ if type-d_i firms active, 0 otherwise $I_i^v = 2.0$ if type-v_i firms active, 0 otherwise $I_i^h = 0.01$ if type-h_i firms active, 0 otherwise

$I_j^d = 10$ if type-d_j firms active, 0 otherwise $I_j^v = 0.2$ if type-v_j firms active, 0 otherwise $I_j^h = 0.001$ if type-h_j firms active, 0 otherwise

Table 8.3
Types of firms active in equilibrium, low trade costs: Regime (the number in the cell) $= I_i^d + I_j^d + I_i^v + I_j^v + I_i^h + I_j^h$ (I is for "indicator")

Investment prohibited (case TL)

O^j →

110.000	110.000	110.000	110.000	110.000	110.000	110.000	110.000	110.000	100.000	100.000	100.000	100.000	100.000	100.000	100.000	100.000	100.000	100.000	100.000	100.000	100.000	100.000	100.000
110.000	110.000	110.000	110.000	110.000	110.000	110.000	110.000	110.000	110.000	100.000	100.000	100.000	100.000	100.000	100.000	100.000	100.000	100.000	100.000	100.000	100.000	100.000	100.000
110.000	110.000	110.000	110.000	110.000	110.000	110.000	110.000	110.000	110.000	110.000	100.000	100.000	100.000	100.000	100.000	100.000	100.000	100.000	100.000	100.000	100.000	100.000	100.000
110.000	110.000	110.000	110.000	110.000	110.000	110.000	110.000	110.000	110.000	110.000	110.000	100.000	100.000	100.000	100.000	100.000	100.000	100.000	100.000	100.000	100.000	100.000	100.000
110.000	110.000	110.000	110.000	110.000	110.000	110.000	110.000	110.000	110.000	110.000	110.000	110.000	100.000	100.000	100.000	100.000	100.000	100.000	100.000	100.000	100.000	100.000	100.000
110.000	110.000	110.000	110.000	110.000	110.000	110.000	110.000	110.000	110.000	110.000	110.000	110.000	110.000	100.000	100.000	100.000	100.000	100.000	100.000	100.000	100.000	100.000	100.000
110.000	110.000	110.000	110.000	110.000	110.000	110.000	110.000	110.000	110.000	110.000	110.000	110.000	110.000	110.000	100.000	100.000	100.000	100.000	100.000	100.000	100.000	100.000	100.000
110.000	110.000	110.000	110.000	110.000	110.000	110.000	110.000	110.000	110.000	110.000	110.000	110.000	110.000	110.000	110.000	100.000	100.000	100.000	100.000	100.000	100.000	100.000	100.000
110.000	110.000	110.000	110.000	110.000	110.000	110.000	110.000	110.000	110.000	110.000	110.000	110.000	110.000	110.000	110.000	110.000	100.000	100.000	100.000	100.000	100.000	100.000	100.000
10.000	110.000	110.000	110.000	110.000	110.000	110.000	110.000	110.000	110.000	110.000	110.000	110.000	110.000	110.000	110.000	110.000	110.000	100.000	100.000	100.000	100.000	100.000	100.000
10.000	10.000	110.000	110.000	110.000	110.000	110.000	110.000	110.000	110.000	110.000	110.000	110.000	110.000	110.000	110.000	110.000	110.000	110.000	100.000	100.000	100.000	100.000	100.000
10.000	10.000	10.000	110.000	110.000	110.000	110.000	110.000	110.000	110.000	110.000	110.000	110.000	110.000	110.000	110.000	110.000	110.000	110.000	110.000	100.000	100.000	100.000	100.000
10.000	10.000	10.000	10.000	110.000	110.000	110.000	110.000	110.000	110.000	110.000	110.000	110.000	110.000	110.000	110.000	110.000	110.000	110.000	110.000	110.000	100.000	100.000	100.000
10.000	10.000	10.000	10.000	10.000	110.000	110.000	110.000	110.000	110.000	110.000	110.000	110.000	110.000	110.000	110.000	110.000	110.000	110.000	110.000	110.000	110.000	100.000	100.000
10.000	10.000	10.000	10.000	10.000	10.000	110.000	110.000	110.000	110.000	110.000	110.000	110.000	110.000	110.000	110.000	110.000	110.000	110.000	110.000	110.000	110.000	110.000	100.000
10.000	10.000	10.000	10.000	10.000	10.000	10.000	110.000	110.000	110.000	110.000	110.000	110.000	110.000	110.000	110.000	110.000	110.000	110.000	110.000	110.000	110.000	110.000	110.000
10.000	10.000	10.000	10.000	10.000	10.000	10.000	10.000	110.000	110.000	110.000	110.000	110.000	110.000	110.000	110.000	110.000	110.000	110.000	110.000	110.000	110.000	110.000	110.000
10.000	10.000	10.000	10.000	10.000	10.000	10.000	10.000	10.000	110.000	110.000	110.000	110.000	110.000	110.000	110.000	110.000	110.000	110.000	110.000	110.000	110.000	110.000	110.000

O^i ↓

Investment liberalized (case FL).

O^j

102.000	102.000	102.000	102.000	102.000	102.000	102.000	102.000	100.000	100.000	100.000	100.000	100.000	100.000	100.000	100.000	100.000	100.000
102.000	102.000	102.000	102.000	102.000	102.000	102.000	102.000	102.000	102.000	102.000	100.000	100.000	100.000	100.000	100.000	100.000	100.200
102.000	102.000	102.000	102.000	102.000	102.000	102.000	102.000	102.000	102.000	102.000	102.000	100.000	100.000	100.000	100.000	100.000	100.200
102.000	102.000	102.000	102.000	102.000	102.000	102.000	102.000	102.000	102.000	102.000	102.000	102.000	100.000	100.000	100.000	100.000	100.200
102.000	102.000	102.000	102.000	102.000	102.000	102.000	102.000	102.000	102.000	102.000	112.000	112.000	110.000	100.000	100.000	100.000	100.200
2.000	102.000	102.000	102.000	102.000	102.000	102.000	102.000	102.000	112.000	112.000	112.000	110.000	100.000	100.000	100.200	100.200	0.200
2.000	2.000	2.000	2.000	2.000	12.000	12.000	12.000	112.000	110.000	110.000	110.000	100.000	100.200	100.200	100.200	0.200	0.200
2.000	2.000	2.000	2.000	2.000	12.000	12.000	12.000	110.000	110.200	110.200	100.200	100.200	100.200	100.200	0.200	0.200	0.200
2.000	2.000	2.000	2.000	2.000	12.000	12.000	10.000	110.000	110.200	110.200	100.200	100.200	100.200	0.200	0.200	0.200	0.200
2.000	2.000	2.000	2.000	2.000	12.000	10.000	10.000	110.000	110.200	110.200	100.200	100.200	0.200	0.200	0.200	0.200	0.200
2.000	2.000	2.000	2.000	2.000	12.000	10.000	110.000	110.200	110.200	100.200	100.200	0.200	0.200	0.200	0.200	0.200	0.200
2.000	12.000	12.000	12.000	10.000	10.000	10.000	10.000	10.200	10.200	10.200	10.200	0.200	0.200	0.200	0.200	0.200	0.200
2.000	12.000	12.000	12.000	10.000	10.000	10.000	10.200	10.200	10.200	10.200	10.200	0.200	0.200	0.200	0.200	0.200	0.200
2.000	12.000	12.000	12.000	10.000	10.000	10.200	10.200	10.200	10.200	10.200	10.200	10.200	0.200	0.200	0.200	0.200	0.200
12.000	12.000	12.000	12.000	10.000	10.200	10.200	10.200	10.200	10.200	10.200	10.200	10.200	10.200	10.200	10.200	10.200	10.200
12.000	12.000	12.000	12.000	10.000	10.200	10.200	10.200	10.200	10.200	10.200	10.200	10.200	10.200	10.200	10.200	10.200	10.200
12.000	10.000	10.000	10.000	10.000	10.200	10.200	10.200	10.200	10.200	10.200	10.200	10.200	10.200	10.200	10.200	10.200	10.200
12.000	10.000	10.000	10.000	10.000	10.200	10.200	10.200	10.200	10.200	10.200	10.200	10.200	10.200	10.200	10.200	10.200	10.200
10.000	10.000	10.000	10.000	10.000	10.000	10.000	10.000	10.200	10.200	10.200	10.200	10.200	10.200	10.200	10.200	10.200	10.200

O^i

$I_i^d = 100$ if type-d_i firms active, 0 otherwise
$I_j^d = 10$ if type-d_j firms active, 0 otherwise

$I_i^v = 2.0$ if type-v_i firms active, 0 otherwise
$I_j^v = 0.2$ if type-v_j firms active, 0 otherwise

$I_i^h = 0.01$ if type-h_i firms active, 0 otherwise
$I_j^h = 0.001$ if type-h_j firms active, 0 otherwise

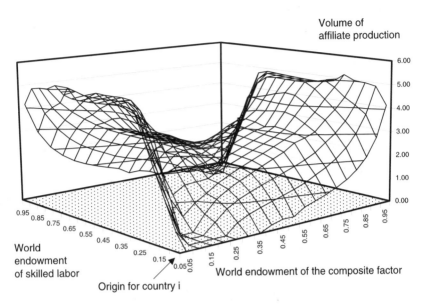

Volume of
affiliate production

Figure 8.1
Volume of affiliate production, investment liberalized, high trade costs (IL)

marginal costs of production in the two countries, each firm's output from its local plant is the same as a foreign firm's output from its branch plant. Since only branch-plant output is classified as affiliate sales, this means that exactly half of all world X output is affiliate sales.

The regions of highest affiliate sales in figure 8.1 occur when one country is small and skilled-labor-abundant. Refer to the second panel of table 8.2. Note that there is a collection of cells where country i has between 30 and 70 percent of the world skilled-labor endowment but only 5 to 15 percent of the unskilled-labor endowment where the equilibrium regime is type-v_i firms only (market regime number 2.0). All firms are headquartered in the small skilled-labor-abundant country i, but all plants are in country j. Thus all world output of X is affiliate output. Although total world output might be slightly smaller here than at the center of the box, this is outweighed by the fact that 100 percent of that output is affiliate output.

Affiliate output in the world economy goes to zero when the two countries have similar endowments but are of very different sizes, or when size differences are less extreme but the smaller country is skilled-labor-scarce. In both the latter cases, the dominant firm type is domestic firms headquartered in the large country.

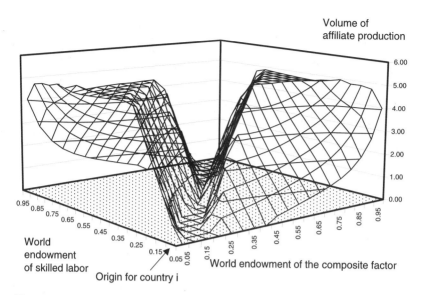

Figure 8.2
Volume of affiliate production, investment liberalized, low trade costs (FL)

Figure 8.2 shows the volume of affiliate production when investment is liberalized and trade costs are low trade/investment regime FL. In this case, there is no affiliate production when relative endowments are similar. With 1 percent trade costs, type-h firms will never exist in equilibrium. A firm will not bear the costs of a second plant when it can almost costlessly ship output from one plant to the other market. Affiliate production is the highest in the same regions as in figure 8.1, when one country is small and skilled-labor-abundant.

Figure 8.3 show the difference between affiliate production in figures 8.1 and 8.2. That is, the vertical axis in figure 8.3 is the change in affiliate production moving from regime IL to FL. Figure 8.3 shows that there are regions in which affiliate production decreases and regions where it increases. The central region, where the fall in trade costs reduces affiliate production, is fairly obvious. When the countries are very similar in size and in relative endowments, falling trade costs lead to type-h firms being replaced by type-d firms. Thus when countries are very similar, one could say that trade and affiliate production are substitutes.

Figure 8.3 also shows, however, that falling trade costs can increase the volume of affiliate production when one country is small and

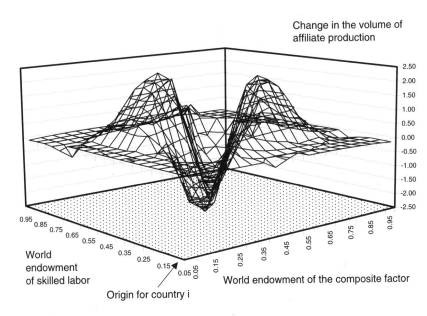

Change in the volume of
affiliate production

Figure 8.3
Change in affiliate production when trade costs are reduced (IL to FL)

skilled-labor-abundant, but the differences between countries are not extreme. Refer to the bottom panels of tables 8.2 and 8.3. Consider a cell such as row-column (0.60, 0.30). With high trade costs (IL), the market regime is .010, meaning that only type-h_i firms are active. The output of these firms in country j is considered affiliate production, but the output in country i is not. The fall in trade costs leads to a market regime shift to 2.0, meaning that only type-v_i firms are active in equilibrium. Now all world production of X takes place in country j with country i served by imports rather than by a local plant. But all firms are headquartered in country i. Thus all world production of X is now affiliate production. In this region, we could say that trade and affiliate production are complements, and indeed the fall in trade costs leads to an increase in both trade and affiliate production.

There are surely other determinants of whether trade and affiliate production are in some sense complements or substitutes, such as the existence of intermediate inputs and multiple final-product lines. But I believe that it is interesting and important to note that complementarity and substitutability also depend on country characteristics in a model with just one final good and no physical intermediate inputs.

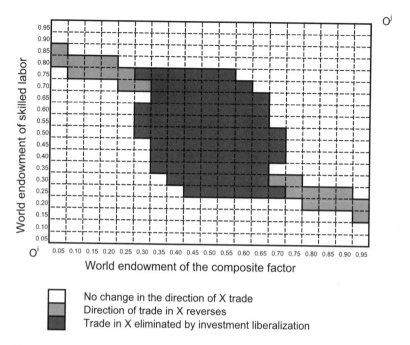

Figure 8.4
Change in the direction of trade, NL to IL

8.5 Effects of Investment Restrictions on the Direction and Volume of Trade

Now I examine the related question of how investment restrictions affect the volume and direction of trade in X. As noted earlier, by "investment restrictions" I simply mean a situation where type-h and type-v firms are banned from entering. In this case, 3-D diagrams are either not very useful or messy, so I simply show qualitative information in figures 8.4–8.7.

Begin with the direction of net trade in X, and liberalization of investment when trade costs are high as shown in figure 8.4. This is a movement from NL to IL, and the change in market regime is shown moving from the top panel of table 8.2 to the bottom panel of that table. First, one sees that trade is eliminated in the central region of figure 8.4. This is due to type-d firms being replaced by type-h firms. Firms serve the foreign market with branch plants rather than by exports, so trade is eliminated.

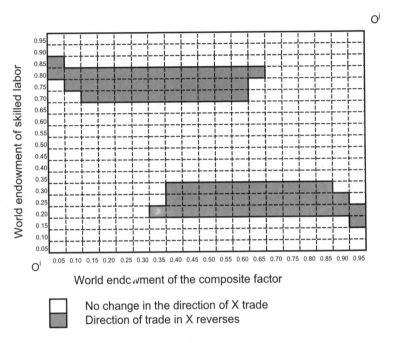

Figure 8.5
Change in the direction of trade, TL to FL

There are small regions in figure 8.4 where the direction of trade is reversed. Consider the shaded points in the northwest region in figure 8.4. Referring to table 8.2, one sees that the region is generally (d_i, d_j) when multinationals are banned (e.g., cell (0.70, 0.10)). Country i is a small net exporter of X in this region as its skilled-labor abundance outweighs its small size. When multinationals are permitted, the regime shifts to v_i. Now all firms are headquartered in region i and all production is by affiliates in country j. Country j exports X to country i, and hence the direction of trade is reversed.

Similar regions appear in figure 8.5, where investment is liberalized in the presence of low trade costs, a movement from trade/investment regime TL to FL. The change in market regime is a movement from the top panel of table 8.3 to the bottom panel. Many of the points in the northwest shaded region of figure 8.5 are a shift from (d_i, d_j) to (d_i, v_i). In the former regime, country i is again a small net exporter of X. Liberalization results in headquarters being shifted to country i, the skilled-labor-abundant country, and plants being shifted to country j, the larger skilled-labor-scarce country. In the shaded regions of figure 8.5, this results in a reversal of the direction of trade in X.

The intuition about these direction-of-trade reversals has to do with the unbundling of trade in goods and services that can occur when multinationals are permitted. When multinationals are banned, exporting X involves the bundling of headquarters services and final production. When one country is small and skilled-labor-abundant, there is some tension as to which country is the net exporter of X. The small skilled-labor-abundant country has an advantage in the service component of the bundle, while the large skilled-labor-scarce country has an advantage in the production component. In the lightly shaded points of figure 8.5, the tension is resolved in favor of the small country that is the net exporter. With unbundling permitted by investment liberalization, the natural pattern of comparative advantage in headquarters services versus production emerges, and the direction of trade reverses. This also helps explain why countries that used to be large exporters of final goods might shift to being large exporters of FDI, such as Japan, as they become more skilled-labor-abundant and/ or investment barriers fall.

Figures 8.6 and 8.7 continue this same analysis by looking at the volume of trade in X as a consequence of investment liberalization. By volume of trade, I mean gross trade, or the sum of the two-way trade if there is any. Liberalization in the presence of high trade costs, NL to IL, is shown in figure 8.6. Liberalization with low trade costs, TL to FL, is shown in figure 8.7. In both diagrams, there is an increase in the volume of trade when one country is skilled-labor-abundant but quite small. The intuition behind these areas is related to that given in the preceding paragraph. When multinationals (and therefore the unbundling of activities) are not permitted, there is not a clear pattern of comparative advantage when one country is small and skilled-labor-abundant. The two determinants of comparative advantage, size and skilled-labor abundance, pull X production in opposite directions. Thus the volume of trade is small. When multinationals and therefore unbundling are permitted, this tension is removed and type-v firms headquartered in the small skilled-labor-abundant country enter, and production shifts to the large skilled-labor-scarce country. The latter country exports to the small country, and the volume of trade increases.

Figure 8.7, showing the movement from TL to FL, also shows regions of increased volume of trade in the top center and bottom center

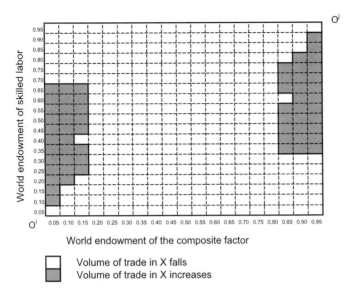

Figure 8.6
Change in the volume of trade, NL to IL

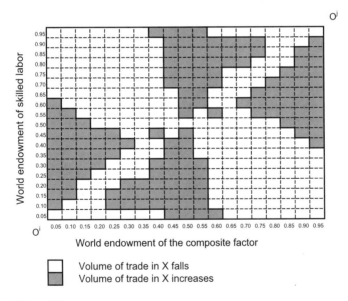

Figure 8.7
Change in the volume of trade, TL to FL

of the box. Referring to table 8.3, one sees that in the absence of multinationals (TL) the regime is (d_i, d_j). Country i exports X in the shaded cells in the top center of the box in figure 8.7. Because country i is also the larger country in these cells, much less than half of all world production of X is exported. The majority of X production occurs in country i and is sold in country i.

World production of X is, in a sense, constrained by the bundling requirements for goods and services. Unbundling permitted by investment liberalization results in a market-regime shift to (d_i, v_i). Production of X falls in country i and is relocated to country j. With low trade costs and the "reciprocal dumping" characteristic of the oligopoly model, X producers export a significant proportion of their output from country j to country i. The loss of a unit of output in country i results in the loss of much less than half a unit of exports. But the increase of a unit of output in the smaller country j results in perhaps more than a half-unit of exports from j to i. Thus increased exports from j to i outweigh the loss of exports from i to j. Gross trade increases at the same time that the volume of net trade might decrease.

Figures 8.6 and 8.7 indicate that trade and affiliate production might be complements in the sense that investment liberalization may increase the volume of trade. This occurs when countries differ in size and/or in relative endowments. Unfortunately however, the points in figure 8.3 where falling trade costs lead to an increase in affiliate production are by and large not the same points as in figures 8.6 or 8.7, where falling investment barriers lead to an increase in gross trade volume. Thus I am left with a somewhat indefinite result. For two arbitrary countries, trade and affiliate production may appear to be complements with respect to falling trade costs but not with respect to falling investment barriers or vice versa. The situation with respect to substitutability is somewhat clearer. One can say that, if countries are very similar, falling trade costs reduce affiliate activity and, if trade costs are moderate to high, falling investment barriers reduce trade (figure 8.6).

8.6   Factor Prices

Investment liberalization has interesting and important effects on factor prices and the internal distribution of income between countries. These effects can be quite different from the standard effects of trade liberalization, because investment liberalization is analogous to

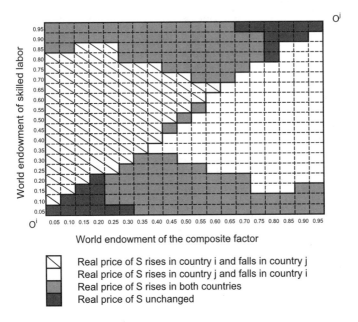

Figure 8.8
Change in the real price of S, NL to IL

changing the active production technology. Some of the consequences are interesting in light of the "trade and wages" debate, which has focused almost exclusively on trade liberalization even though affiliate production has grown faster than trade, as noted in table 1.1.

Figures 8.8–8.11 show the effects of investment liberalization on real and relative factor prices. Figures 8.8 and 8.9 show the effects on the real price of skilled labor, z, which is the "nominal" price (in terms of Y) divided by the unit expenditure function, the cost of purchasing one unit of utility. In the traditional Heckscher-Ohlin model, the real and nominal prices always move in the same direction, but that is not the case with increasing returns and imperfect competition. Changes in scale and markups may mean that nominal prices and the price index can move somewhat more independently.

Figure 8.8 considers investment liberalization in the presence of high trade costs, the movement from *NL* to *IL*. The interesting thing about this figure is the existence of sizable regions in which the real price of S rises in both countries. Consider the light-shaded region at the top of the box in figure 8.8. Refer to table 8.2 and consider, for example, cells near the top of column 0.50. In the top five cells of this column, liberalization results in the regime shift from (d_i) to (d_i, h_i) in the top row, (d_i, d_j) to (d_i, h_i) in rows 2–4 and (d_i, d_j) to (h_i) in row 5.

Consider what is happening in rows 2–4. Liberalization results in the "closure" of type-d_j firms and some type-d_i firms are replaced by type-h_i firms. Because of the lower need for skilled labor in country j, the branch plants actually expand production significantly in country j. There is a net transfer of resources from the Y sector to the X sector, and the real price of skilled labor rises. This larger domestic supply of X is accompanied by a cheaper price, so that the price index falls and unskilled labor may be better off as well. In country i, a transfer of resources from X production to headquarters services occurs since all firms are now headquartered in country i. This results in higher real price for skilled labor. However, the price of X may now rise in country i, so it is likely to result in a fall in the real price of unskilled labor. In summary, what is happening is that resources are shifted toward a more skilled-labor-intensive activity in both countries. This shift is from Y to X production in country j, and from X production to headquarters services in country i. This result is reminiscent of Feenstra and Hanson (1996a,b, 1997), in which investment liberalization results in the shift of activities from the North to South that are unskilled-labor-intensive from the North's point of view, but skilled-labor-intensive from the South's point of view.

Figure 8.9 shows the effect of investment liberalization in the presence of low trade costs, moving from TL to FL. The general pattern is quite similar to that in figure 8.8 except that there are no effects when the countries have identical relative endowments. There is no regime shift when trade costs are low and relative endowments are equal. Consider again the region at the top center of the box in figure 8.9 where the real price of skilled labor rises in both countries. Referring back to table 8.3, investment liberalization generates a regime shift from (d_i) to (d_i, v_i) or more typically from (d_i, d_j) to (d_i, v_i). The effects of the latter shift are quite similar to those described above. In country j, there is a net shift of resources from Y to X production. In country i, there is a shift of resources from X production to headquarters services. In both cases, resources are shifted from a less skilled-labor-intensive activity to a more skilled-labor-intensive activity. In addition, procompetitive effects may mean that the price of X falls in both countries. Thus the real wage of skilled labor can rise in both countries.

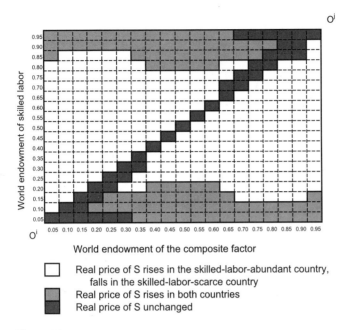

Figure 8.9
Change in the real price of S, TL to FL

Figures 8.10 and 8.11 show the same experiments except that they use the relative price of skilled to unskilled labor. This is what is being measured in the trade-and-wages literature. In general, the z/w ratio moves in the same direction as the real price of S (z over the price index). There are, however, a few points in the northwest and southeast regions of the Edgeworth boxes in which the real price of S rises in both countries but z/w falls in the skilled-labor-scarce country. Obviously, these are then points in which the real prices of both factors must be rising in the skilled-labor-scarce country. On the other hand, if both the real price of S and the price ratio z/w rise, the real price of L may or may not be rising. I provide a more specific example of this later in the chapter.

To summarize then, the knowledge-capital model has something of a "skilled-labor bias" to it, in the sense that investment liberalization may lead to an increase in the real and relative wage of skilled labor in both countries, and there are no pairs of economies (points in the world Edgeworth box) where investment liberalization leads to a fall in the real or relative price of skilled labor in both countries. This is due to a shift toward a more skilled-labor-intensive activity in

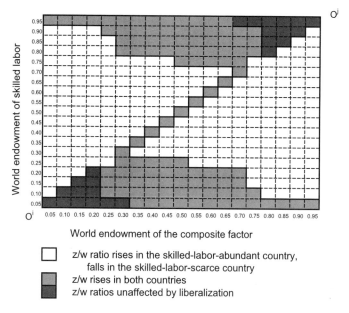

Figure 8.10
Change in z/w ratio, NL to IL

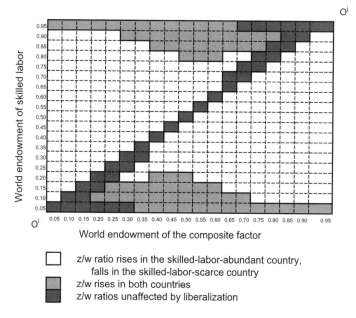

Figure 8.11
Change in z/w ratio, TL to FL

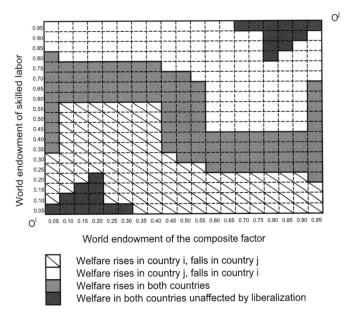

Figure 8.12
Change in welfare, NL to IL

both countries and/or increased efficiency (procompetitive effect) that lowers the price of X.

8.7 Welfare

It might not surprise those readers familiar with the theory of trade under distortions to learn that the welfare effects of investment liberalization are complex and the intuition behind the results difficult. The so-called strategic trade policy literature is a branch of this theory and consists of a seemingly endless series of special cases in which policies have some counterintuitive effect (the intuition being drawn from a distortion-free competitive model). Almost all of that literature is partial equilibrium analysis, and I can report that effects can be even more complicated here due to general-equilibrium effects working through factor markets and factor prices. But at least I will spare you any normative policy analysis as to what is optimal policy, focusing only on the positive economics of the effects of investment liberalization.

Figures 8.12 and 8.13 show the welfare effects of investment liberalization with high trade costs (NL to IL) and low trade costs (TL to FL),

O^j

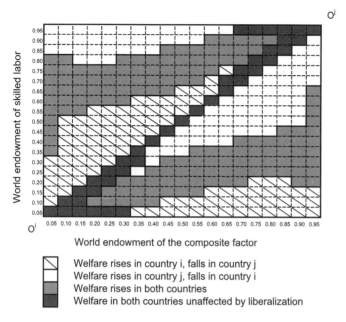

World endowment of the composite factor

☒ Welfare rises in country i, falls in country j
☐ Welfare rises in country j, falls in country i
▨ Welfare rises in both countries
■ Welfare in both countries unaffected by liberalization

Figure 8.13
Change in welfare, TL to FL

respectively. There are clearly significant regions in which one country loses from liberalization. This might seem somewhat surprising, but when one reflects on it, remember that the only strong theorem about gains from trade are for free trade versus autarky. Even in competitive models, one cannot say that both countries are worse off by some small bilateral level of protection relative to free trade, and indeed a large country might be better off. Add the distortions associated with scale economies and imperfect competition, and one is even less certain that bilateral free trade in goods is superior to modest bilateral protection for a large country. Add endogenous firm-location decisions to that, and only an individual ideologically committed to free trade would dare make strong welfare predictions.

Roughly speaking, figures 8.12 and 8.13 suggest that it is the larger country that loses if indeed one country is worse off. Or it could be a slightly smaller country if it is very skilled-labor-abundant. As was the case in figure 7.1 of the previous chapter, the equal-income (equal-size) locus runs from approximately row-column cell (0.95, 0.30) to cell (0.05, 0.70), with slight variations depending on which trade/investment regime one is in. This result that the large country tends to be the loser, if there is a loser, seems to fit nicely with the logic from liberalizing trade in goods, whether in competitive or imperfectly competitive models. But here one is liberalizing restrictions to multinationals, with the consequent unbundling and reorganization of trade in goods and the introduction of trade in services. Furthermore, it seems that different points in the region of losses for one country have somewhat different explanations.

Consider first figure 8.12 and the removal of restrictions on multinationals in the presence of high trade costs. Here there is a large region at the top of the diagram in which country i loses when it is large. Reviewing table 8.2, these points are associated with different market-regime shifts. In the northwest of the region of losses for country i, the shift tends to be from (d_i, d_j) to (d_i, v_i) regimes. In the northeastern region of losses, the shift tends to be from d_i to d_i plus h_i, h_j and/or v_j firms. I have examined many of these points, and in section 8.8 I examine one in detail. Most of these points of losses for country i are associated with a fall in production of X in country i. Investment liberalization results in production becoming more dispersed. The effect of this, given high trade costs, is generally a rise in the price of X in country i and also a rise in the markup on local production. Investment liberalization, in other words, eliminates the "home market effect" for the large country alluded to earlier in the chapter. The consequence of allowing multinationals is that the large country suffers an increased markup for X on domestic production and a higher real price for X.

Figure 8.13 shows the corresponding welfare changes due to investment liberalization when trade costs are low (1%) (TL to FL). In this case, the intuition does not seem to lie in the effects of liberalization on the local price of X via a home-market effect, since the prices are almost the same across countries before and after investment liberalization. After spending much time staring at numbers and equations, I believe that instead the intuition for losses lies with factor-market effects caused by unbundling. A ban on multinationals forces bundling and that can be good for the larger country (or somewhat small, very skilled-labor-abundant country).

Consider the points in the northwest regions of figure 8.13, where country i loses from investment liberalization. A typical regime shift here is from (d_i, d_j) to (d_i, v_i) (table 8.3). I report results for row-column cell (0.85, 0.20), where country i has 85 percent of the world's skilled labor and 20 percent of the unskilled labor in figure 8.13, but the results for other cells in this region are roughly the same. All firms become headquartered in country i following liberalization, but a considerable portion of production is shifted to country j. The price of X relative to Y and the consumer price index (unit expenditure function) falls in country i as well as in country j. Thus, a home-market effect based on the domestic price of X is not responsible for the fall in country i's welfare. While the price of skilled labor rises in country i, the price of unskilled labor falls sufficiently such that real income (factor income divided by the price index) actually falls in country i.

I think that the intuition lies in the unbundling permitted by investment liberalization. Prior to liberalization (TL), the headquarters service and production components of X production must be located together, and it is optimal to locate them mostly in country i in the northwest region of figure 8.13. This makes unskilled labor quite expensive in country i relative to country j. Liberalization permits firms to keep their headquarters in country i but transfer production to country j becoming type-v_i firms. This maintains the demand for skilled labor in the X sector but releases a good deal of unskilled labor, which is absorbed in the Y sector in country i after a sufficient fall in the price of unskilled labor. In row-column cell (0.85, 0.20) of figure 8.3, the price of X falls 10 percent after liberalization, but the price of L falls 20 percent and the price of S rises 10 percent. The changes in the factor prices times factor quantities sums to a negative amount, so country i loses from liberalization.

The other area of loss for country i in figure 8.13 is in the northeast region of the diagram, where country i is large and moderately skilled-labor-scarce. Again, a detailed examination of the results suggests that the explanation lies in the effect of unbundling on factor income. The market-regime shifts in this region are from all or almost all firms being d_i, to regimes such as d_i, v_j. Production is maintained in country i, but headquarters are shifted to country j where skilled labor is cheaper. In this area, the losses to country i skilled labor exceed gains to unskilled labor due to the rearrangement of headquarters versus production activities.

In summary, a prohibition of multinational firms forces firms to bundle headquarters service and production together in one location. This can in fact benefit one country, and this is generally the large country if indeed it benefits either country. This effect can work primarily through a product-market phenomenon, in which the real price of X is lower in the large country as production concentrates there.

This product-market (a.k.a. home market) effect seems important when trade costs are high since that leads to a concentration of production in the large country more than in proportion to size. When trade costs are low, the possible benefits to the large country from a ban on multinationals seems to be more a factor-market effect. When forced to bundle the very skilled-labor-intensive headquarters activity together with the less skilled-labor-intensive production activity, firms are bidding up the price of scarce factors in one or both countries. The unbundling permitted by investment liberalization leads to a fall in the price of the scarce factor and, in certain subregions of the Edgeworth box, this fall is large enough to outweigh real income gains to the other factor.

8.8   A Specific Example

Interesting outcomes occur for many pairs of economies (points in the world Edgeworth box). I have chosen one that occurs when one country is both large and skilled-labor-abundant—for example, the United States and Mexico. In particular, I will use row-column cell (0.80, 0.60) of the Edgeworth box, in which country i has 80 percent of the world's skilled labor and 60 percent of the world's unskilled labor. Tables 8.4 and 8.5 give numerical results for the four trade/investment regimes, while figure 8.14 gives the allocations of country j's factor supplies. That is, figure 8.14 is the Edgeworth box just for country j in this world allocation of the factors with X measured from the southwest corner and Y from the northeast corner.

The top row of table 8.4 indicates the equilibrium market regime corresponding to the four trade/investment regimes. The top half of table 8.4 normalizes all numbers to 1.0 in the NL regime for convenience, while the bottom half presents the raw numbers to permit level comparisons across countries. The lower numbers can be put in perspective by recalling that all of the numbers are calibrated to be 1.0 at the center of the world Edgeworth box in regime IL. Factor prices are real values, the nominal value (in terms of Y) divided by the unit expenditure function.

Figure 8.14 plots the allocations of country j's factors between the X and Y sectors. Production of X in country j is lowest in the no-liberalization (NL) scenario. But interestingly, production increases under trade liberalization (TL). This is not what one would expect from traditional Heckscher-Ohlin logic, in which each country spe-

Table 8.4
Examples of four allocations, country j has 20 percent of world skilled labor, 40 percent of unskilled labor

Trade/investment regime	NL	IL	TL	FL
Market regime (active firm types)	d_i, d_j	d_i, h_i	d_i, d_j	d_i, v_i
Variable, country j *(relative to NL)*				
Welfare	1.000	1.053	1.074	1.083
X production	1.000	2.598	1.436	3.590
z_j	1.000	1.184	1.086	1.105
w_j	1.000	1.027	1.071	1.079
z_j/w_j	1.000	1.152	1.014	1.024
z_j/z_i	1.000	1.110	1.050	0.986
w_j/w_i	1.000	1.061	1.065	1.102
Variable, country i *(relative to NL)*				
Welfare	1.000	0.991	1.009	1.012
X production	1.000	0.766	0.936	0.618
z_i	1.000	1.066	1.017	1.121
w_i	1.000	0.968	1.006	0.979
z_i/w_i	1.000	1.101	1.012	1.145
Variable, country j *(absolute amount)*				
Welfare	0.664	0.699	0.713	0.719
X production	0.637	1.655	0.915	2.287
z_j	1.185	1.403	1.287	1.309
w_j	0.901	0.925	0.965	0.972
z_j/w_j	1.316	1.516	1.334	1.347
z_j/z_i	1.432	1.589	1.504	1.412
w_j/w_i	0.842	0.893	0.897	0.928
Variable, country i *(absolute amount)*				
Welfare	1.293	1.282	1.304	1.309
X production	4.344	3.329	4.065	2.684
z_i	0.828	0.883	0.842	0.928
w_i	1.070	1.036	1.076	1.047
z_i/w_i	0.774	0.852	0.783	0.886

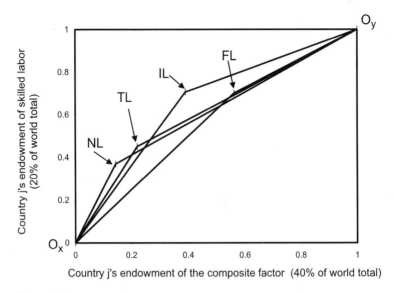

Figure 8.14
Allocations of country j's factors in the four regimes, cell (0.80, 0.60) of the Edgeworth box

cializes in the sector intensively using its abundant factor. I believe that the fall in trade costs eliminates the home-market advantage of the large country, and this outweighs the expected reallocation due to comparative advantage. Production is higher yet under investment liberalization (IL) where type-h_i firms replace type-d_j firms. The branch plants of the type-h_i firms not only displace local production but they also displace the imports from d_i firms that took place under NL. Finally, production of X in country i is highest under full liberalization (FL) in which the regime is (d_i, v_i). The ability to unbundle and locate all headquarters in the large skilled-labor-abundant country leaves ample resources for country j to specialize in actual X production. In figure 8.14, one sees that the overall ratio of S to L used in all X-sector activities is lowest under FL. This is due to most of the resources being devoted to X production which is less skilled-labor-intensive than the headquarters activities which are now concentrated in country i.

Table 8.4 notes that the real prices of both factors of production are higher in country j under any form of liberalization than under NL. This is a comforting characteristic of this type of industrial organization model, in that it escapes the curse of Stolper-Samuelson, in which one factor must lose following liberalization. Another result that differs substantially from Heckscher-Ohlin logic is that the relative price of the scarce factor z_j/w_j, rises in each liberalization scenario above its value under NL. This is the skilled-labor bias built into the model, but note that it also occurs with trade liberalization. Finally, note that country j's welfare is highest under full liberalization.

The ranking of X production in table 8.4 among the scenarios for country i, the large, skilled-labor-abundant country, is the opposite of that for country j, which seems natural. But one still gets these interesting factor-price results that are at odds with Heckscher-Ohlin logic. In both countries, the z/w ratio is higher under any liberalization scenario than under NL, including the trade-liberalization scenario. The only losing factor is unskilled labor in country i in the IL and FL scenarios relative to NL, and these are the scenarios when skilled labor gains the most in country i. This is not very comforting for unskilled workers in the large skilled-labor-abundant country and indeed is consistent with the claim that outward investment to unskilled-labor-abundant countries harms unskilled labor at home, such as claimed by U.S. trade unions in the NAFTA debate.

Table 8.5 looks in detail at the movement from NL to IL and the resulting welfare loss for country i that was mentioned in section 8.7. The left-hand side of the table gives figures at the center of the Edgeworth box for comparison. The IL numbers in this portion of the table are the calibrated values consistent with table 8.1. Investment liberalization at the center of the box reduces the number of firms, increases an efficiency index (total world X production divided by the total number of firms), and reduces the relative price of X and the price index.

The right-hand half of table 8.5 considers the same liberalization experiment in the cell (0.80, 0.60) that is examined in table 8.4. Again, the total number of firms falls and the efficiency index increases in the move from NL to IL. But now the benefits of this liberalization are shared very unevenly. Prior to liberalization, X production is concentrated in country i with a corresponding low price for X in country i. The markup is low in country i for reasons noted earlier. Investment liberalization, by shifting production to country j, lowers the markup, price of X, and price index in country j but increases all of these in country i. The net result is then a small welfare loss for country i and a larger (by 5.3%) welfare increase for country j. Investment liberalization in the presence of high trade costs robs the large skilled-labor-abundant country of its home market advantages and that country is actually worse off.

Table 8.5
Intuition about the efficiency gains from investment liberalization and the distribution of those gains (NL to IL)

	Center of the world Edgeworth box		Cell (0.80, 0.60) as used in table 8.4 (country i has 80% of S, 60% of L)	
	NL	IL	NL	IL
n_j	3.550		1.003	
n_i	3.550		5.876	1.217
h_j		2.500		
h_i		2.500		4.126
Total number of firms	7.100	5.000	6.879	5.343
Efficiency index for X	0.550	0.800	0.560	0.736
mk_{jj}	0.219	0.200	0.295	0.226
mk_{ii}	0.219	0.200	0.164	0.187
p_j	1.281	1.250	1.411	1.252
p_i	1.281	1.250	1.238	1.294
$e_j(p_j, 1)$	1.012	1.000	1.062	1.018
$e_i(p_i, 1)$	1.012	1.000	0.995	1.001
Welfare j	0.988	1.000	0.664	0.699
Welfare i	0.988	1.000	1.293	1.282

Note: Efficiency index for X: World X consumption divided by the total number of firms of all types.

8.9   Summary and Conclusions

This chapter applies the knowledge-capital model to a number of important issues in the positive theory of trade and affiliate production. I consider four combinations of assumptions about trade and investment restrictions: NL (no liberalization), in which trade costs are high and multinational firms are banned; IL (investment liberalization), in which trade costs are high and multinational firms are permitted; TL (trade liberalization), in which trade costs are low and multinational firms are banned; and FL (full liberalization), in which trade costs are low and multinational firms are permitted. I solve each of the cases over the world Edgeworth box as in chapters 5–7.

One issue addressed is the relationship between affiliate production and trade in X as trade and investment restrictions change. A reduction of trade costs tends to reduce affiliate production when countries are similar, but can increase it when one country is small and skilled-labor abundant. Thus whether trade and affiliate production are substitutes or complements in this sense depends upon whether the affiliate production is for local sale or for export. Lower trade costs can encourage vertical firms or force exit of horizontal firms.

I then look at the question the other way around, asking what the effects of investment liberalization on trade are for a given level of trade costs. The results depend somewhat on the level of those trade costs. But for either high or low trade costs, investment liberalization can in fact reverse the direction of trade for some pairs of economies. For both levels of trade costs, investment liberalization can increase the volume of trade in X when countries differ substantially and in particular when one is quite small and skilled-labor-abundant. In the latter case, trade without multinational firms is small because the two determinants of comparative advantage, size, and skilled-labor abundance pull in opposite directions. Investment liberalization leads to an unbundling of production and headquarters services that causes production to be concentrated in the large country. While the results are not easily summarized, I believe it is reasonable to say that trade and affiliate production tend to be substitutes for similar countries but may be complements for dissimilar countries. This result is, in turn, closely tied to the vertical-horizontal distinction and so, alternatively, I could say that trade and horizontal investments are substitutes, but trade and vertical investments are generally complements.

I then look at the effects of investment liberalization on factor prices and suggest that investment liberalization tends to have a pro-skilled-labor bias. This is generally due to unbundling in which one country moves from producing Y to producing X, and the other moves from producing X to specializing in headquarters services. In both countries, resources move toward a more skilled-labor-intensive activity.

I then look at welfare, noting that often both countries gain from investment liberalization. A general result is that the smaller country is virtually assured of gains from investment liberalization. The larger country may, however, lose for some differences in size and in relative endowments. The intuition seems to differ according to whether trade costs are high or low, with a product-market effect responsible when trade costs are high and a factor-market effect responsible when trade costs are low. When trade costs are high, investment liberalization leads the large (or very skilled-labor-abundant) country to lose its home-market advantage in X, which gives it lower X prices and markups in the absence of liberalization. When trade costs are low, the unbundling of activities permitted by investment liberalization allows shifting of an activity intensively using the scarce factor out of the large country with a consequent loss of factor income that outweighs gains to the other factor and a lower price of X. Thus contrary to some conventional arguments, it is generally the host economies that are ensured of gains and the parent countries that could lose from investment liberalization.

9 Traded Intermediate Inputs and Vertical Multinationals

9.1 Introduction

In chapters 7 and 8, I discussed both horizontal multinationals, which build plants in multiple countries to produce the same good or service, and vertical multinationals, which geographically fragment the production process into a headquarters and a final production activity. As I noted earlier, there is probably no such thing as a pure horizontal firm, in that all firms tend to have a one-way trade in the services of knowledge-based assets, typically from the parent to the affiliate. I used the terms *horizontal* and *vertical* with reference to whether or not the firm has two final production plants or one foreign plant and no domestic (headquarters country) plant. The latter are referred to as vertical firms in that headquarters services are exported to the subsidiary and a portion of final output is typically shipped back to the parent country. Horizontal firms maintain final production facilities in both countries, serving local markets by local production.

Chapter 1 presented data that suggests that intrafirm trade is not of major importance relative to local sales (table 1.7), which helped motivate my concentration on horizontal firms in chapters 5 and 6. Nevertheless, vertically integrated firms are important in some industries and surely important to some host countries. Furthermore, vertical operations are often characterized by trade in intermediates within the firm, not just the services of firm-specific assets. A typical example is when a firm ships capital or skilled-labor-intensive parts to an assembly plant in a low-wage country and repatriates most of the output for sale back home. The production structure of the U.S. semiconductor industry is a good example of vertical MNEs. Blueprints and key components such as chips are designed and produced in the parent plants in the United States. Then the chips are shipped to the testing and assembly facilities of subsidiaries in Southeast Asia, where the finished products are assembled using cheap unskilled and semi-skilled labor. Finally, the finished products are shipped back to sales destinations in the United States and elsewhere (Yoffie 1993).

The purpose of this chapter is to extend the previous analysis to consider vertical firms that supply an intermediate input to a final production plant in another country. Final output can be sold in the latter country as well as shipped back to the parent country. In order to focus on some interesting issues at hand, I keep the analysis fairly circumscribed. First, the intermediate input (e.g., microprocessors) can only be produced in skilled-labor-abundant country i. There are only two firm types. Domestic (type-d) firms produce the intermediate and the final good in country i. Vertical firms produce the intermediate in country i and ship it to country j where it is "assembled" into the final output. There are no horizontal firms (with final plants in both countries) in this chapter. Type-d firms export the final good X from i to j and type-v firms ship a portion of it from j to i.

As in the case of the previous two chapters, whether type-d firms or type-v firms dominate in equilibrium depends importantly on factor intensities and factor endowments. I assume that the production of the intermediate is skilled-labor-intensive and that final production is unskilled-labor-intensive relative to the intermediate and relative to the composite rest of the economy (good Y). However, host-country skilled labor is required in the fixed costs of the production plant for managers, technicians, and so forth. These skilled-labor requirements in fixed costs cannot be substituted with unskilled labor, except indirectly by increasing plant scale. This skilled-labor requirement in the host country creates an interesting nonmonotonicity with respect to the number of vertical firms in equilibrium and the relative skilled-labor scarcity of the host country. Results indicate that the number of type-v firms is highest when the host country is moderately, but not extremely, skilled-labor-scarce.

The equilibrium regime also depends on market sizes for reasons that are related to but not quite the same as those in the previous two chapters. Transport costs for the final good, much more so than for the intermediate good, discourage type-v firms. The reason is that as country j shrinks in size, a larger and larger proportion of a type-v firm's output must be shipped back to the parent country i, thereby incurring more transport costs for a given level of output.

Thus the existence of type-v firms depends on both factor abundance and the size of the host country j. The number of type-v firms relative to the size of country j is highest when country j is at an intermediate level of skilled-labor scarcity relative to i, and also at an intermediate level of size. These results fit well with the data presented in tables 1.3 and 1.6, which show that the poorer of the developing countries get little inward investment and that, for a given per capita income (a proxy for factor endowments), the smaller countries get significantly less inward investment.

The chapter ends with some discussion of sensitivity analysis and notes, for example, conditions under which the host-country-size effect can disappear and similarly for the nonmonotonicity of inward investment with respect to relative endowments.

9.2   Technology and Equilibrium Market Structure

In many ways, the model and notation should be familiar. Reducing the reader's transactions costs as he or she moves through the book is an objective. I've noted several principal differences between the current model and the model from previous chapters. There is a traded intermediate that can only be produced in skilled-labor-abundant country i, only type-d and type-v firms are considered. Country subscripts on firm types are not needed since they are all headquartered in country i. The intermediate is only traded intrafirm, so there will be no issues of double marginalization or bilateral monopoly. As has been true to this point, "internalization" is postponed until the final section of the book, so I will not try to justify this assumption that the intermediate is only traded intrafirm. Implicitly, I am assuming that the firm also provides headquarters services with the intermediate, and perhaps the intermediate cannot be used separately from the knowledge embodied in those services.

I find myself running out of letters of the alphabet at this point in the book. I am going to denote the intermediate input as Z. This was the notation used in the original version of this chapter (Zhang and Markusen 1999). Lowercase z will still denote the price of skilled labor, which is again denoted S. I will assume that Z only uses skilled labor in production.

The full specification of the model is as follows:

1. There are two countries, home and foreign (i and j), producing two final goods (Y and X) using two factors, unskilled labor (L) and skilled

labor (S). L and S are required in both sectors and are mobile between sectors but are internationally immobile. Country i is relatively skilled-labor-abundant.

2. Y is produced with L and S under constant return to scale and perfect competition. Y will be used as numeraire, as it has throughout the book.

3. X is produced with increasing returns and imperfect competition in two stages. In the first stage, the intermediate product Z is produced with S alone. In the second stage, X is assembled using unskilled labor, L, and the intermediate product Z. Each unit of X requires one unit of intermediate product Z.

4. We assume that for some exogenous reason, Z can be produced only in country i. Assembly can occur either in country i or in country j.

5. There are two firm types which can produce X. A type-d firm (domestic) produces both Z and X in country i. Some X may or may not be exported to country j.

6. A type-v (vertical multinational) firm produces Z in country i, which is then shipped to an assembly plant in country j. Some X may or may not be exported back to country i.

The term *regime* will denote the set of firm types active in equilibrium. Throughout this chapter, superscripts (d, v) will denote domestic and multinational firms respectively. N^d and N^v indicate the number of active type-d firms and type-v firms. Subscript (i, j) will be used to denote the countries i and j. The cost structure of the X industry is as follows:

c_z Units of skilled labor, S, needed to produce one unit of Z.

c_x Units of unskilled labor, L, needed to produce one unit of X. c_x is assumed to be the same in both countries.

t_x Units of L required to ship one unit of the final good X between markets, assumed to be the same in both directions.

t_z Units of L required to ship one unit of the intermediate good Z from country i to country j (incurred by type-v firms only).

G Units of L required for the fixed costs of an X assembly plant. Incurred in country i for type-d firms, and in country j for type-v firms.

F Units of skilled labor S required for the fixed costs incurred by type-d firms in country i.

F_i Units of skilled labor S required for the fixed costs incurred by type-v firms in country i.

F_j Units of skilled labor S required for the fixed costs incurred by type-v firms in country j.

$$F_i < F < F_i + F_j$$

This last assumption indicates that type-v firms must incur some skilled-labor costs in country j, and that the total skilled-labor cost for a type-v firm are somewhat higher due to the costs of doing business abroad. In the terminology of chapter 7, fragmentation is not costless (perfect). Overall, one assumes that the type-v firm incurs all un-skilled labor costs in country j, except for $t_z Z^v$. A type-d firm incurs all unskilled-labor costs in country i. But type-v firms do have mini-mal skilled-labor requirements in country j (F_j), and this assumption turns out to be crucial to the results.

The output of Y in country i (and similarly j) is a Cobb-Douglas function.

$$Y_i = L_{iy}^\alpha S_{iy}^{1-\alpha} \tag{1}$$

Skilled labor requirements for a single type-d or type-v firm are given by

$$S_i^d = F + c_z Z^d \tag{2}$$

$$S_i^v = F_i + c_z Z^v \qquad S_j^v = F_j \tag{3}$$

Let X_i^d be sales in country i of a type-d firm, while X_i^v be sales in country i of a type-v firm with X_j^d and X_j^v similarly defined. The un-skilled labor used in one X-assembly plant to produce $X^k = X_i^k + X_j^k$, $k = (d, v)$ units of finished good in the two regimes is given by

$$L_j^v = G + c_x X_j^v + (c_x + t_x)X_i^v \qquad L_i^v = t_z Z^v \tag{4}$$

$$L_i^d = G + c_x X_i^d + (c_x + t_x)X_j^d \tag{5}$$

Let w_i and z_i (measured in terms of Y) denote the prices of unskilled and skilled labor in country i, respectively. Then the cost functions for type-d and type-v firms are given by

$$w_i L_i^d + z_i S_i^d = w_i[c_x X_i^d + (c_x + t_x)X_j^d + G] + z_i(c_z Z^d + F) \quad \text{(type-d)} \tag{6}$$

$$w_j L_j^v + z_j S_j^v + w_i L_i^v + z_i S_i^v$$

$$= w_j[c_x X_j^v + (c_x + t_x)X_i^v + G]$$

$$+ z_j F_j + w_i t_z Z^v + z_i(c_z Z^v + F_i) \qquad \text{(type-v)} \qquad (7)$$

where $Z^k = X_i^k + X_j^k$, $k = (d, v)$, because we assume a one-to-one relationship between X and Z.

Let L_i^* and S_i^* be total factor endowments of country i. The adding-up constraints on labor supply—namely, the factor-market-clearing conditions—are then

$$L_i^* = L_{iy} + N^d L_i^d + N^v L_i^v \qquad S_i^* = S_{iy} + N^d S_i^d + N^v S_i^v \qquad (8)$$

$$L_j^* = L_{jy} + N^v L_j^v \qquad S_j^* = S_{jy} + N^v S_j^v \qquad (9)$$

In equilibrium, the X-sector makes zero profits; therefore country incomes, denoted by M_i and M_j, are given by

$$M_i = w_i L_i^* + z_i S_i^* \qquad M_j = w_j L_j^* + z_j S_j^*. \qquad (10)$$

Let X_{ic} and Y_{ic} denote the consumption of X and Y in country i. The utility of the representative consumer in country i is a Cobb-Douglas function, as follows:

$$U_i = X_{ic}^\beta Y_{ic}^{1-\beta} \qquad X_{ic} \equiv N^v X_i^v + N^d X_i^d, \qquad (11)$$

and similarly for country j. Maximizing utility, subject to the income constraint, the first-order conditions give demands for X and Y as follows:

$$X_{ic} = \frac{\beta M_i}{p_i} \qquad Y_{ic} = (1 - \beta)M_i, \qquad (12)$$

where p_i denotes the price of X in country i. p_i is measured in terms of good Y. Corresponding equations apply to country j.

The equilibrium in the X sector is determined by pricing equations and free-entry conditions. Let m be the proportional markups of price over marginal costs, so m_i^v and m_i^d are the markups of type-v and type-d firms in market i, respectively. There are four pricing equations in the model, two for type-d firms (one for each country), and two for type-v firms (one for each market). These are written in complementary-slackness form as follows:

$$p_i(1 - m_i^d) \le w_i c_x + z_i c_z \qquad X_i^d \qquad (13)$$

$$p_i(1 - m_i^v) \le w_j(c_x + t_x) + z_i c_z + w_i t_z \qquad X_i^v \qquad (14)$$

$$p_j(1 - m_j^d) \leq w_i(c_x + t_x) + z_i c_z \qquad X_j^d \tag{15}$$

$$p_j(1 - m_j^v) \leq w_j c_x + z_i c_z + w_i t_z \qquad X_j^v \tag{16}$$

There are two zero-profit conditions corresponding to the numbers of the two types of firms. Given pricing equations, zero profits can be given as the requirement that markup revenues are less than or equal to fixed costs.

$$p_i m_i^d X_i^d + p_j m_j^d X_j^d \leq z_i F + w_i G \qquad N^d \tag{17}$$

$$p_i m_i^v X_i^v + p_j m_j^v X_j^v \leq z_i F_i + w_j G + z_j F_j \qquad N^v \tag{18}$$

In a Cournot model with homogeneous products, the optimal markup formula is given by the firm's market share divided by the Marshallian price elasticity of demand in that market. In our model, the price elasticity is one, since we have a Cobb-Douglas utility function homogeneous of degree one. Unit elasticity reduces the firm's markup to its market share. Using demand equations for country i, results in

$$m_i^d = \frac{X_i^d}{X_{ic}} = \frac{p_i X_i^d}{\beta M_i} \tag{19}$$

$$m_i^v = \frac{X_i^v}{X_{ic}} = \frac{p_i X_i^v}{\beta M_i} \tag{20}$$

and similarly for country j. Substituting the markup equations into the pricing equations gives expressions for demand or output in terms of price.

$$X_i^d \geq \beta M_i \frac{p_i - w_i c_x - z_i c_z}{p_i^2} \qquad X_i^d \tag{21}$$

$$X_i^v \geq \beta M_i \frac{p_i - w_j(c_x + t_x) - z_i c_z - w_i t_z}{p_i^2} \qquad X_i^v \tag{22}$$

$$X_j^d \geq \beta M_j \frac{p_j - w_i(c_x + t_x) - z_i c_z}{p_j^2} \qquad X_j^d \tag{23}$$

$$X_j^v \geq \beta M_j \frac{p_j - w_j c_x - z_i c_z - w_i t_z}{p_j^2} \qquad X_j^v \tag{24}$$

Each of these inequalities holds with equality if the right hand side is positive, otherwise output is zero. If the terms are positive, then the free entry condition (17)–(18) can be rewritten as

$$\beta M_i \left[\frac{p_i - w_i c_x - z_i c_z}{p_i} \right]^2 + \beta M_j \left[\frac{p_j - w_i(c_x + t_x) - z_i c_z}{p_j} \right]^2$$

$$\leq z_i F + w_i G \qquad N^d \tag{25}$$

$$\beta M_i \left[\frac{p_i - w_j(c_x + t_x) - w_i t_z - z_i c_z}{p_i} \right]^2 + \beta M_j \left[\frac{p_j - w_j c_x - w_i t_z - z_i c_z}{p_j} \right]^2$$

$$\leq z_i F_i + w_j G + z_j F_j \qquad N^v \tag{26}$$

This is now a completed general-equilibrium model. The four inequalities (21)–(24) are associated with two output levels (one for each regime), and the two inequalities (25) and (26) are associated with the number of firms in each regime. Moreover, goods prices are given by equation (12), factors prices can be derived from factor-market-clearing condition equations (8) and (9), and income levels from (10).

9.3 Intuition from Partial-Equilibrium Analysis

The inequalities in (25) and (26) contain a large number of simultaneously determined, endogenous variables. In this section, I therefore make some partial-equilibrium assumptions in order to try to develop some intuition about how the model works and the general-equilibrium results to follow. *Assume* that I have an equilibrium in which there are no type-v firms, meaning that country j is specialized in good Y. Then I will inquire as to whether in fact this is an equilibrium.

The dual of the production isoquant in sector Y is zero-profit curve ($\Pi_y = 0$), which can be derived as follows. Let $c_y(w, z)$ be the unit cost function for Y, with $p_y = 1$. The zero-profit locus in factor-price space for Y in country j is given by

$$1 = c_y(w_j, z_j), \qquad 0 = c_{yw} dw_j + c_{yz} dz_j, \qquad -\frac{dz_j}{dw_j} = \frac{c_{yw}}{c_{yz}} = \frac{L_j^*}{S_j^*}. \tag{27}$$

The last equation in (27) is the usual duality result that the ratio of the partial derivatives of the cost function is the ratio of the unit input requirements. If all factors are allocated to Y, this is in turn equal to the factor-endowment ratio of the economy. This isocost curve is shown in the top panel of figure 9.1. Under the assumption that country j is specialized in Y, equilibrium is where the slope of the isocost curve is the endowment ratio as just noted.

Fix the commodity prices and incomes in both countries and factor prices in country i at their values in the "proposed" specialized equi-

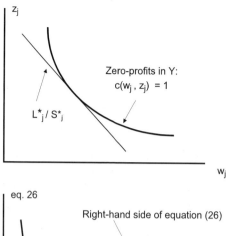

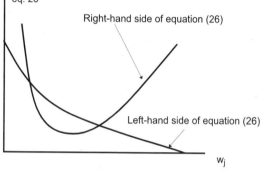

In the lower panel, z_j is implicitly given by $c(w_j, z_j) = 1$

Figure 9.1
Zero-profit loci for Y and X in country j

librium. Consider the set of factor-price combinations traced out by the iso-cost curve in the top panel of figure 9.1, corresponding to different endowment ratios in country j. In the lower panel of figure 9.1, plot separately the values of the two sides of inequality (26), where z_j is implicitly given by (27). The left-hand side of this inequality is monotonically decreasing in w_j, since it doesn't depend on z_j at all. The right-hand side, however, depends on both factor prices. When w_j becomes very small, z_j goes off to infinity (top panel) so the value of the right-hand side does as well. When w_j increases (and therefore z_j falls), the right-hand side falls in value reaching a minimum where $dz_j/dw_j = G/F_j$. Then the right-hand side begins to increase.

The lower panel of figure 9.1 shows a case where there is a "double crossing," indicating that X production in country j is profitable in the central region and unprofitable outside either extreme. Remembering that the factor-price combinations correspond to different endowment ratios (top panel), the result is that X production is profitable over a certain range of endowments. It is unprofitable when skilled labor is too scarce (left region of the lower panel). This is due to the assumption that the firm cannot substitute away from the skilled-labor requirement. Production of X again becomes unprofitable when it is too abundant (right region of the lower panel).

Finally, consider differences in country size, measured by the distribution of total M between M_i and M_j. The proposed equilibrium with country j specialized in Y must have $p_i < p_j$ (transport costs to j), which is a sufficient condition for the left-most bracketed term in (26) to be smaller than the right-most bracketed term. This in turn implies that a shift in income $dM_i = -dM_j > 0$ must reduce the value of the left-hand side of (26). Thus this curve shifts inward in the lower panel of figure 9.1 as country j becomes smaller, narrowing the range of endowments that can support X production. Intuitively, when country i is larger, a higher proportion of final output must be shipped back to country i, incurring added transport costs. In summary then, one can expect that multinational activity will occur when country j is skilled-labor-scarce, but not extremely so, and that this activity will be decreasing as country j becomes small (decreasing proportionally faster than country j's size). Figure 9.1 suggests, at each endowment ratio, that there will be a size below which production in j is eliminated.

9.4   General-Equilibrium Simulations

While some insights are gained section 9.3, the dimensionality of the model and the fact that it contains many inequalities makes the usual analytical techniques of limited value. The full model involves thirty-seven nonlinear inequalities. Thus I will now follow the pattern familiar from the previous four chapters and turn to a numerical simulation of the model. I again use the term regime to denote a set of firm types active (producing positive outputs) in equilibrium. For example, "type-v firms only active" is one regime, while "both type-v and type-d active" is another regime.

Figure 9.2 presents a complete characterization of production regimes with medium transport costs. t_z and t_x are each set at 5 percent of the marginal production cost of Z and X respectively (i.e., t_z and t_x are not equal to each other in units of L). Figure 9.2 and the other figures to follow are not Edgeworth boxes as in chapters 5–8.

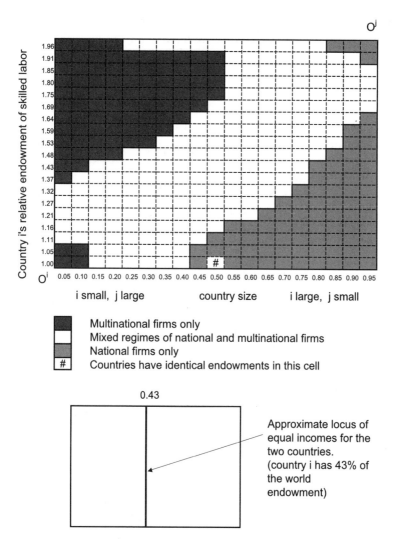

Figure 9.2
Equilibrium regimes $(t_x = t_z = 0.05)$

But they look very much like the boxes in the previous chapters, so I
want to explain carefully what you are looking at. The horizontal axis
of figure 9.2 and those to follow indexes country size, with country i
small and country j large on the left, and country i large and country j
small on the right. But each cell in a given row of figure 9.2 has the
same relative endowments of skilled and unskilled labor in each
country. Thus moving from left to right across a row, I am transferring *both* factors of production from country j to country i. In the bottom row of figure 9.2, countries have identical relative endowments of
skilled and unskilled labor. So in column 0.30 of the bottom row, for
example, country i has 30 percent of the total world endowment of
both factors and country j has 70 percent of both factors.

Moving up a column in figure 9.2, skilled labor is transferred from
country j to country i and unskilled labor in the other direction so as
to approximately preserve the size (measured in GNP) difference at
the bottom of the column. This is why the vertical axis in figure 9.2
and in later diagrams has such apparently odd units. In cell (1.96,
0.30) of the matrix, country i has approximately the same GNP as in
cell (1.00, 0.30), but its ratio of skilled to unskilled labor is 1.96 in the
top row if the ratio is normalized at 1.00 in the bottom row. Conversely, country i has a skilled/unskilled ratio of about 0.05 in the top
row, with the bottom row normalized at 1.00. Thus a very large difference exists in endowment ratios in the top row of the box, with the
S/L ratio in country i being about 38 times higher than in country j. In
the middle row (row 10 or 1.48) of figure 9.2, the S/L ratio for country
i is about 2.8 times higher than in country j.

With respect to empirical relevance, the 2.8 figure in row 10 (1.48) is
well within the range found in the actual labor-force data used in the
three empirical chapters that follow. There the highest ratio is 12.8,
which corresponds to between rows 3 (1.85) and 4 (1.80) of the matrix
in figure 9.2. But the poorest countries in the world are not in that
data set because they have virtually no inward investment, so the top
two rows of figure 9.2 may indeed be empirically relevant. And this is
precisely where the theory suggests that one should find very little
multinational activity so I think that the theory fits well with the data.

The two countries have identical endowments in the middle column
(0.50) of the bottom row of figure 9.2. However, their incomes are not
quite the same in that cell since only country i can produce Z by assumption. Thus the locus of equal incomes is a bit to the left of the
middle column of figure 9.2 (country i has about 43% of the world

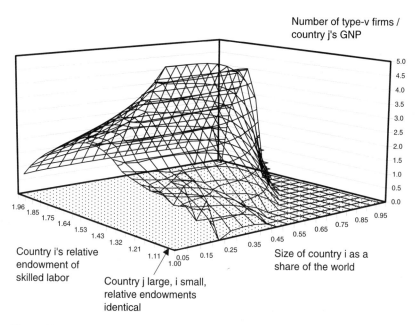

Figure 9.3
Number of type-v firms divided by country j's GNP

endowment when GNPs are equal), and this locus is shown in the small box at the bottom of figure 9.2.

Results in figure 9.2 indicate that all production is by type-v firms if country j is both large and the relative endowment differences are large (northwest region of figure 9.2). In such a case, there is both a strong factor-price motive for locating final X production in country j, and aggregate transport costs are not large since most of the final output stays in country j. All production is by type-d firms if country j is small and the relative endowment difference is small (southeast corner). In this case, there is neither a factor-price motive nor a transport-cost motive for locating final production in country j. Running between these two regions from the southwest to the northeast corner is a mixed regime of type-v and type-d firms.[1]

Figure 9.3 presents a 3-D surface for the number of multinationals in equilibrium divided by the GNP of country j. Since fixed costs are proportional to the number of firms, this is roughly the model equivalent of the data presented in table 1.3 on inward investment divided by GDP. Figure 9.3 shows that this inward "investment" as a

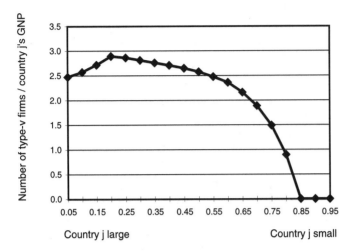

Figure 9.4
Number of type-v firms divided by country j's GNP: row 10 (1.48) of figure 9.3

proportion of GNP is highest when the countries are of similar size and country j is moderately, but not extremely, skilled-labor-scarce. The general-equilibrium simulation is thus nicely consistent with the intuition gained from the partial-equilibrium intuition of figure 9.1. As country j gets extremely skilled-labor-scarce, the fixed costs of a plant in country j become prohibitively expensive. As country j gets quite small, a larger and larger proportion of X must be shipped back to country i, and the range of endowment differences that can support production of X in country j shrinks. These results seem closely consistent with the data presented in tables 1.3 and 1.6.

Figure 9.4 presents the values along row 10 (1.48) of figure 9.3 for clarity, and figure 9.5 does the same thing for column 10 (0.50) of figure 9.3. This shows the relative size effect (figure 9.4) and the relative endowment effect (figure 9.5). Again, what is shown here is consistent with the partial-equilibrium intuition from figure 9.1. I use these diagrams to discuss "robustness" in section 9.5, so further discussion is postponed until then.[2]

Figure 9.6 shows net exports of X by country j over the parameter space. Country j is an exporter of X when the endowment differences are moderate to large. Because country j is necessarily an importer of X in the absence of multinationals (net exports by j must be negative), this diagram can also be used to infer the set of endowment

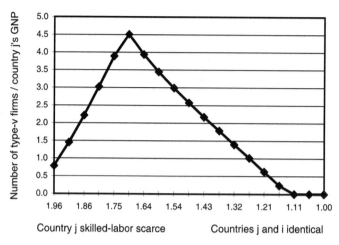

Figure 9.5
Number of type-*v* firms divided by country *j*'s GNP: column 10 (0.50) of figure 9.3

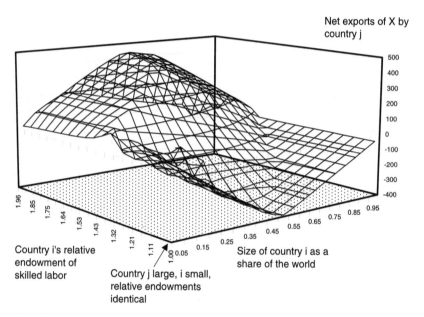

Figure 9.6
Net exports of *X* by country *j*

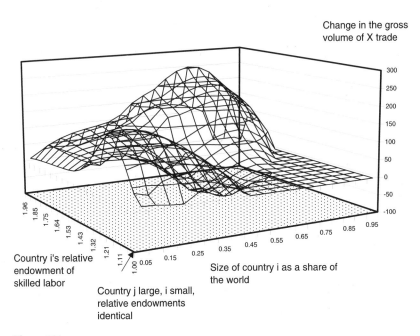

Change in the gross
volume of X trade

Country i's relative
endowment of
skilled labor

Country j large, i small,
relative endowments
identical

Size of country i as a share of
the world

Figure 9.7
Effect of investment liberalization on the volume of gross trade in X

and size differences for which investment liberalization reverses the
direction of trade in X. All points with positive net exports in figure
9.6 are points of direction-of-trade reversal following investment
liberalization.

Figures 9.7 and 9.8 consider the effects of moving from multinationals banned to multinationals allowed on the various measures of
trade volume. This complements the discussion of chapter 8 on trade
and affiliate production as complements or substitutes. Figure 9.7
plots the change in the gross volume of trade in X—that is, the sum of
the two-way trade flows in X (trade in X is only one way in the absence of multinationals of course). There are no negative values in this
diagram so, in a gross sense, trade and affiliate production must be
complements in this model.

Figure 9.8 plots the effect of investment liberalization on the absolute value of the net volume of X trade. Here a rather different result
occurs when factor-endowment differences are not so large and country j is large. The net volume of X trade falls (figure 9.8), while at the
same time the gross volume of X trade generally rises (figure 9.7). In

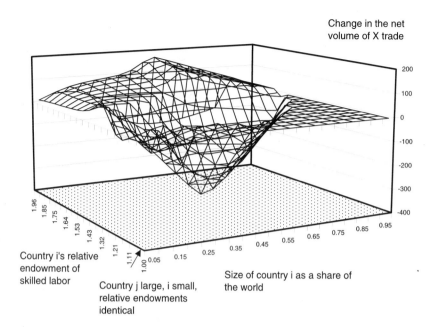

Figure 9.8
Effect of investment liberalization on the volume of net trade in X (Δ in the absolute value of net X trade)

the absence of multinationals, net trade is high and goes from i to j. When multinationals are permitted, a significant share of world X production is transferred from country i to country j. Country i generally remains the net exporter of X in this region (figure 9.6), but net exports from i to j fall significantly. But recalling the "reciprocal dumping" motive, type-v firms producing in country j export to country i and vice versa, so the gross volume of X trade rises even as the net volume falls.

Figure 9.9 presents another way of thinking about whether or not trade and affiliate production are substitutes or complements. This involves considering how investment liberalization and the introduction of affiliate production affect the combined value of X and Z exports from country i. That is, does investment liberalization lead to an increase in the combined value of X and Z exports from country i? Indeed, I have some feeling (largely from seminar discussions) that this is what folks automatically think about when they consider the substitutes/complements question.

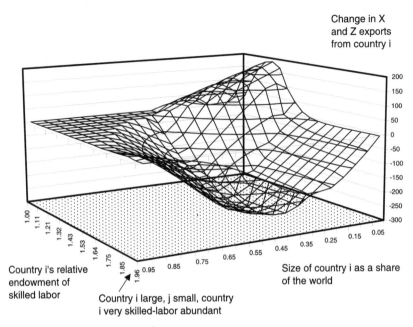

Change in X
and Z exports
from country i

Country i's relative
endowment of
skilled labor

Country i large, j small, country
i very skilled-labor abundant

Size of country i as a share
of the world

N.B., axis rotated 180° from Figures 9.2-9.7

Figure 9.9
Effect of investment liberalization on the exports of X and Z from country i

Note that figure 9.9 has been rotated 180 degrees from the other
diagrams. It is simply unreadable viewed from the same perspective
as the other diagrams: There is confusion about where the positive
and negative points are. Figure 9.9 shows that there is a region where
investment liberalization increases the combined value of X plus Z
exports from country i. This occurs when country i is relatively small
and the endowment differences are not large. In this situation, country
j is a profitable place to produce X for both market size and relative
endowment reasons. But it cannot do so because it cannot obtain Z.
Liberalization leads to a transfer of X production from i to j, but also
of exports of Z from i to j. What happens in the positive region of
figure 9.9 is that Z is very valuable relative to X, and thus the value of
Z exports increases more than the value of X exports falls for country
i. So increased exports of parts and components outweigh the loss in
exports of final output.

When the endowment difference between the countries is much
larger, investment liberalization results in a fall in the total value of X
and Z exports from country i. The dependence on the size of the en-

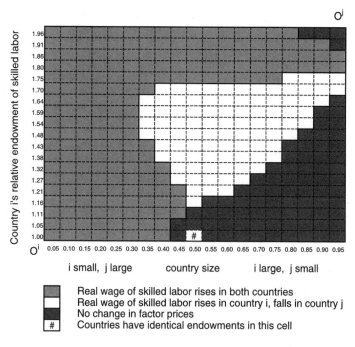

Figure 9.10
Investment liberalization and the return to skilled labor

dowment difference is largely felt through prices. With country i much more skilled-labor-abundant, Z exports are not nearly as valuable relative to X exports. Thus whether or not exports from country i and foreign affiliate sales are complements in the current sense of the term depends on both the relative endowment and size differences. Results suggest that complementarity is more likely when the endowment differences are small but the host country is large. Thus for Swedish, Dutch, or Swiss firms setting up subsidiaries in the United States, the results suggest that a complementary relationship might occur.

The final exercise is to examine the effects of investment liberalization on factor prices, concentrating on the real wage of skilled labor as before. Figure 9.10 shows the effect of moving from multinationals banned to permitted. Over a very large region of the box, the real wage of skilled labor rises in both countries. There are two effects working in this direction, and these are familiar from the previous chapter. First, country i becomes less specialized in X and more specialized in Z, while country j becomes less specialized in Y and more in X. Both countries are then generally moving from a less skilled-labor-intensive activity to a more skilled-labor-intensive activity. Second, production efficiency is generally increasing, so the price index declines. This helps raise the real wages of both factors.

However, a region where the real wage of skilled labor falls in country j (the unshaded points) is also visible. I was puzzled by this, and it took me a lot of time staring at printouts and at the model to understand what was going on. It turns out that the model has a factor-intensity reversal between X and Y, for those of us who are old enough to remember what a factor-intensity reversal is. I didn't intend for this to be the case, but in the end I decided to leave it in and not try to recalibrate the model.

In the numerical model, Y has an elasticity of substitution of 1.0 while X production (plant and marginal costs) has fixed coefficients except insofar as plant scale changes. If the fixed-coefficient isoquant for X intersects the Cobb-Douglas isoquant for Y, there are then two "cones of diversification," one in which X is skilled-labor-intensive and one in which Y is skilled-labor-intensive. When country j is skilled-labor-scarce, it is in the former cone and a movement from Y to X production raises the relative and real wage of skilled labor. But if country j is not very skilled-labor-scarce, the opposite can happen and the relative wage of skilled labor will fall. It turns out that this is what happens in the unshaded region of figure 9.10 where Y is actually skilled-labor-intensive relative to X production. This remains true for points further to the left of the unshaded region, but here the fall in the price index outweighs the fall in the relative wage of skilled labor so the real wage of skilled labor rises along with the unskilled wage.

This is somewhat incidental to the main point, which is similar to that of the previous chapter. Given that Z is skilled-labor-intensive relative to X and given that (in a region in which) X is skilled-labor-intensive relative to Y, the presumption is that investment liberalization will raise the real wage of skilled labor in both countries. As I noted in chapter 8, this is then invariably associated with a rise in the relative wage of skilled labor as well. Thus this model can contribute something to the "trade and wages" debate.

9.5 Robustness

In this section, I briefly consider some alternative parameter values in order to get a clearer idea about which assumptions drive the results concerning country size and relative endowments. I present these alternatives and note how they affect the results shown in figures 9.4 (country size) and 9.5 (relative endowments).

1. All trade costs equal zero.
Figure 9.4:   flattens out
Figure 9.5:   essentially unchanged

Trade costs discourage production in a small country because a larger proportion of output has to be shipped back to country i. The proportion shipped back is irrelevant if there are no trade costs. But trade costs have little to do with the results relating to relative endowments.

2. Trade costs for final output are 10 percent, and for intermediate output 0 percent.
Figure 9.4:   essentially unchanged
Figure 9.5:   essentially unchanged

To clarify further, it is trade costs on final output that matter, not intermediate output. The shipping cost of the latter is simply proportional to final output in country j, irrespective of where the final output is going. But the shipping costs of final output increase as country j gets smaller as just noted.

3. Trade costs for final output are 0 percent, and for intermediate output 10 percent.
Figure 9.4:   flattens out
Figure 9.5:   essentially unchanged

Suppose that a plant has a fixed output of 100,000 units and so needs an input of 100,000 units of Z. Increases in the shipping cost of Z have an effect but this effect does not depend on the country sizes. On the other hand, as country j gets smaller, a larger and larger proportion of X output must be shipped to country j. If shipping costs for X are positive, then shipping costs for a type-v firm rise as country j becomes smaller while shipping costs for a type-d firm fall. It is shipping costs on final output that give rise to the shape of figure 9.4.

4. Lower plant-level fixed costs (holding constant the proportions of skilled and unskilled labor) raise firm-level fixed costs.
Figure 9.4:   essentially no change
Figure 9.5:   curve shifts left

The key to the result in figure 9.5 is the need for country j skilled labor in plant-specific fixed costs. As these costs fall (and holding their composition constant), plants become less skilled-labor-intensive and plants can be supported in a more skilled-labor-scarce country. In the limit as plant-specific fixed costs fall to zero, so do skilled-labor requirements in the plant and the curve in figure 9.5 becomes monotonically decreasing.

5. Make plant-level fixed costs less skilled-labor-intensive.
Figure 9.4:   essentially no change
Figure 9.5:   curve shifts left

Changing the composition of labor requirements for plant-level fixed costs has the same general effect of making plants less skilled-labor-intensive, and hence the qualitative effect is the same as lowering plant-level fixed costs.

6. Lower scale economies (lower both plant and firm-level fixed costs).
Figure 9.4:   flattens out
Figure 9.5:   curve shifts left, flattens out

Scale economies mean that type-v firms have to be a minimum size. But as country j gets smaller, holding a type-v firm's size constant means that it must ship a larger and larger share of output back to country i, so shipping costs rise as per the discussion following point (3) above. This is another way of thinking about figure 9.4. But without scale economies, a type-v firm's profitability depends only on prices, not on output. If scale economies are small, the number of type-v firms in existence falls roughly in proportion to the fall in the size of country j. Hence there is no change in the proportion of output shipped or unit (of output) shipping costs. Hence the size of the economy does not matter to the curve in figure 9.4. This might sound more familiar if I just say that the home-market effect (concentration of the increasing-returns sector in the large country) disappears along with scale economies.

The fact that the curve in figure 9.5 shifts left is an artifact of the assumption that the use of skilled labor is in fixed costs, so as scale economies fall so does the skilled-labor intensity of plant production, with the consequences noted earlier.

7. Fixed and variable costs use factors in the same proportion, and there is smooth substitution between the two labor types.
Figure 9.4:   essentially no change
Figure 9.5:   curve becomes monotonic

It may be reasonably clear from the lower panel of figure 9.1 that the specific nature of the technology chosen is important in producing the nonmonotonicity of figure 9.5: the U-shaped function for the right-hand side of equation (26). The crucial assumption is the fixed skilled-labor requirement that the firm cannot avoid and cannot substitute with unskilled labor. This would disappear with smooth substitution, although a necessary condition for this to be unambiguously true is that the cost function must have the same elasticity of substitution as Y (the old factor-intensity-reversal problem). If fixed and variable costs have the same factor intensities and elasticities of substitution, then the cost function for X has the same shape as that for Y in the upper panel, and the nonmonotonicity in figure 9.5 disappears. However, the position of the iso-cost curve still depends on host-country market size due to scale economies; hence, the general result in figure 9.4 is unchanged.

8. Substitute monopolistic competition for oligopoly.

Although I have not modeled it, I am reasonably certain that the key results would carry through in a standard monopolistic competition model on the basis of results in Markusen and Venables (2000). The results shown in figures 9.4 and 9.5 do not seem to rely on the form of competition or whether or not products are differentiated. To repeat, trade costs and scale economies are the crucial results behind figure 9.4 and the fixed skilled-labor requirement in plant-level fixed costs is the crucial feature behind figure 9.5. I summarize this section on the robustness of the shapes of the curves in figures 9.4 and 9.5 as follows:

· Host country size (country j) matters less if trade costs for final output are low, scale economies are low. Perhaps electronics assembly plants fit this description, in which case plants may be attracted to quite small (but not too skilled-labor scarce) countries.

· The inverted U-shaped relationship with respect to relative endowments (figure 9.5) disappears as the host-country skilled-labor requirements go to zero.

· The inverted U-shaped relationship with respect to relative endowments similarly disappears if fixed and variable costs use skilled and unskilled labor in the same proportions and there is substitution between the two labor types.

9.6   Summary and Conclusions

The purpose of this chapter is to consider an extension to the previous models, allowing for a produced and traded intermediate input. The focus is on vertical activity in which the intermediate is shipped to a foreign plant (e.g., an electronics assembly plant) and the final output shipped back to the parent country. Empirical motivation for the assumptions chosen for the model are found in the data from tables 1.3, 1.6, and 1.7. Among developing countries, the larger and higher-income countries get a significantly larger share of inward investment. Affiliates in developing countries export a larger share back to the parent (table 1.7).

The model helps explain the very low level of direct investment into the small least-developed countries. I believe that there at least two explanations, one involving direct costs and factor requirements of firms and the other indirect requirements. The first involves multi-nationals' needs for local skilled labor, ranging from managers to technicians and engineers to accountants, and so forth. The second involves public or private infrastructure, ranging from utilities to telecommunications to transport services to legal systems. These are not competing explanations, and both could surely be important at the same time.

This chapter tends to focus on the first factor, the direct factor requirements, but of course this could be interpreted as firms generating their own local inputs such as electricity and transport. The model is constrained in that one assumes that a necessary intermediate input can only be produced in the "developed" country, but that final production can take place in either country, using only unskilled labor for marginal costs. But local skilled labor is required in fixed costs. Any final output produced in the developing country is endogenously divided between supply to the local market and shipments back to the multinational's home market.

Results predict that the number of multinational firms active in the developing country relative to that country's GNP bears an inverted U-shaped relationship to the relative endowment differences between the two countries. In particular, investment falls to zero as the developing country becomes extremely scarce in skilled labor. The second result is that this inward investment to GNP ratio is generally, at least eventually, decreasing in the host country's size. Small countries get no investment even relative to their small GNP. The reason is that potential assembly plants would be shipping almost all of their output back to the developed country, thus incurring high aggregate transport costs relative to a situation where a significant proportion of the output remains in the developing country. This may help us to understand, for example, why there is such a large investment boom in China, relative to other much smaller countries with the same per capita income levels.

A final section of the chapter considers variations in parameter values. I note, for example, that the role of country size disappears if the good has low transport costs and there are only small or zero scale economies. This may help explain why some small countries such as Hong Kong and Singapore can compete in electronics assembly. The inverted U-shaped relationship in relative endowments disappears as the local skilled labor requirements go to zero. This may help explain clothing and toy production in very skilled-labor-scarce countries, although those goods are often not produced within multinationals but by contractors, due to other aspects relating to the transfer of knowledge capital (Markusen 1995).

II

Empirical Estimation and Testing

10   Estimating the Knowledge-Capital Model

10.1   Introduction

An attractive feature of the knowledge-capital model as defined in chapters 7 and 8 is that it generates testable predictions about multinational activity. In particular, it suggests relationships between the volume of affiliate production and sales and country characteristics. It predicts how the sales of affiliates of country i firms in country j should be related to the characteristics of both i and j.

The knowledge-capital model allows for both horizontal and vertical multinationals to arise endogenously. Existing evidence points to the horizontal motive as the dominant empirical motive for direct investment. Analyses are found in Brainard (1993b, 1997) and Ekholm (1995; 1998a,b; 2001) and indirect evidence in many papers including Eaton and Tamura (1994), Blonigen (2001), and Blonigen and Davies (2000). Results give good support to the theoretical predictions of the "horizontal" models: Multinational activity should be concentrated among countries that are relatively similar in both size and in relative endowments (or per capita incomes as a proxy for endowments).

The purpose of this chapter and chapters 11 and 12 is to add to this small empirical literature by estimating the knowledge-capital model, attempting to exploit the theory as much as possible in formulating the hypotheses and estimating equations. The focus is on affiliate activity and country characteristics. I use the simulation results in chapters 7 and 8 to predict how multinational activity on a bilateral basis should be related to combined market sizes, differences in size, skilled-labor abundance, and trade and investment costs. This chapter estimates the basic model suggested by the theory. Chapter 11 adds data on affiliate exports versus production for local sale, in an attempt to get at the vertical-horizontal distinction. Chapter 12 considers restricted versions of the general model that correspond roughly to a "pure" horizontal model and a pure vertical model. These restricted versions allow for explicit alternative hypotheses. All results give strong support for the dominance of horizontal motives for multinational activity, although vertical motives may be important for individual host countries.

Readers won't be surprised to learn in advance that the estimation gives good support to the general knowledge-capital model. If that did not turn out to be the case, I doubt that I would have had the heart to produce this book.

10.2 The Theoretical Model

A quick review of the knowledge-capital model and its predictions is necessary. The model assumes the existence of two homogeneous goods (X and Y), two countries (i and j), and two homogeneous factors, unskilled labor (L) and skilled labor (S), which are internationally immobile. Good Y is unskilled-labor-intensive and produced under constant returns to scale in a competitive industry. Good X is skilled-labor-intensive overall, exhibits increasing returns to scale, and is subject to Cournot competition with free entry and exit. Within a firm, headquarters services and plant facilities may be geographically separated and a firm may have plants in one or both countries.

With this structure, there are six firm types, with free entry and exit into and out of firm types. *Regime* denotes a set of firm types active in equilibrium. Firm types are as follows:

Type h_i Horizontal multinationals that maintain plants in both countries with headquarters located in country i.

Type h_j Horizontal multinationals that maintain plants in both countries with headquarters located in country j.

Type d_i National firms that maintain a single plant and headquarters in country i; they may or may not export to country j.

Type d_j National firms that maintain a single plant and headquarters in country j; they may or may not export to country i.

Type v_i Vertical multinationals that maintain a single plant in country j and headquarters in country i; they may or may not export to country i.

Type v_j Vertical multinationals that maintain a single plant in country i and headquarters in country j; they may or may not export to country j.

In the model, national markets for goods are segmented and transport costs are a proportion of marginal costs.

Recall from chapter 7 the defining characteristics of the knowledge-capital model:

• *Fragmentation*: The location of knowledge-based assets may be fragmented from production. Any incremental cost of supplying services of the asset to a single foreign plant versus the cost to a single domestic plant is small.

• *Skilled-labor intensity*: Knowledge-based assets are skilled-labor-intensive relative to final production.

• *Jointness*: The services of knowledge-based assets are (at least partially) joint ("public") inputs into multiple production facilities. The added cost of a second plant is small compared to the cost of the first plant.

The first two properties, fragmentation and skilled-labor intensity motivate vertical (type-v) multinationals that locate their single plant and headquarters in different countries depending on factor prices and market sizes. The third property, jointness, gives rise to horizontal (type-h) multinationals that have plants producing the final good in multiple countries.

10.3   Active Firm Types and Country Characteristics

Different country characteristics favor various firm types producing or maintaining headquarters in country i. Analogous comments apply to firms in country j. Consider first factors that favor national firms headquartered in country i and also producing there. Assumptions of the model developed in chapter 7 suggest that type-d_i firms will be the dominant type active in i (producing in i) if (1) i is both large and skilled-labor-abundant; (2) i and j are similar in size and relative endowments and transport costs are low (type d_j will also sell in i); or (3) foreign investment barriers in j are high (type d_j may also sell in i).

The fact that country i is large supports production there, while skilled-labor abundance favors locating headquarters in i as well.

Thus, an integrated type-d_i firm has a cost advantage over a type-v_i or type-v_j firm. Unless trade costs are very high, a type-d_i firm also has an advantage over a type-h_i firm, which must locate costly capacity in the small j market. Type-d firms should also be dominant when the countries are similar and trade costs are small. If countries are perfectly symmetric, for example, there is no motive for type-v firms. Small trade costs favor type-d firms over two-plant type-h firms.

Type-h_i firms are the dominant type active in country i if the nations are similar in size and relative endowments and transport costs are high (type h_j will also produce in i). Thus, horizontal multinationals firms should be associated with similarities between countries in both size and in relative factor endowments. The underlying intuition is that if countries are dissimilar in either size or relative endowments, one country will be "favored" as a site of production and / or headquarters. For example, if the countries are similar in relative endowments but of different sizes, then national firms located in the large country will be favored because they avoid costly capacity in the smaller market. If the countries are different in relative endowments but of similar size, then there is an incentive to concentrate headquarters in the skilled-labor-abundant country and production in the skilled-labor-scarce country. Thus vertical firms headquartered in the skilled-labor-abundant countries are favored unless trade costs are high.

From this analysis, a prediction about vertical multinationals follows. Type-v_i firms will be dominant in i if country i is small, skilled-labor-abundant, and trade costs are not excessive (in particular, trade costs from the host country back to the parent country).

10.4   Simulation Results

Data exist on the volume of production in host countries by affiliates of firms in parent countries, but not on the number of firms of various types. Accordingly, I need to develop predictions about affiliate production, rather than the numbers of firms of various types. I did this in chapters 7 and 8, so I will refer to the results found there.

A preliminary issue is to define "affiliate production" in the model in a way that relates sensibly to data on affiliate sales. Parents and affiliates in the data are essentially defined in terms of ownership location. Thus, in my model I assume that the country in which a firm's

Volume of
affiliate production

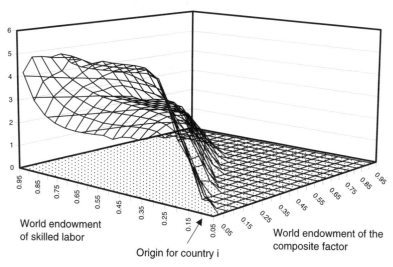

World endowment
of skilled labor

Origin for country i

World endowment of the
composite factor

Figure 10.1
Affiliate production by country-*i*-owned plants in country *j*

headquarters is located is the parent country. Given that assumption, the production of affiliates of country-*i* firms in country *j* is the output of plants in country *j* "owned" by type-h_i and type-v_i firms. Similarly, the volume of production by country-*i* affiliates of country-*j* firms is the production in country *i* of plants owned by type-h_j and type-v_j firms.

Simulation results are demonstrated with a series of world Edgeworth box diagrams in chapters 7 and 8. Here I use the parameterization of chapter 8. Figure 10.1 reproduces the simulation of figure 8.2, but only for production by affiliates of firms headquartered in country *i*, with plants in country *j*. Recall that figure 10.1 is an Edgeworth box, with the total world endowment of skilled labor on one axis and the total world endowment of unskilled labor on the other axis. The origin for country *i* is at the near or "south" (S) corner of the box and the origin for country *j* is at the far or "north" (N) corner. Along the N-S diagonal, the countries have identical relative endowments but differ in size. The locus along which the countries have equal incomes but differ in relative endowments is steeper than the E-W diagonal and is not quite linear. The approximate locus along which the countries have equal incomes is approximately given by the line drawn on the floor of the box in figure 7.1 (although that model is a slightly different calibration from the one used here and in chapter 8). Country i is smaller than country j to the south of this locus and is larger to the north.

Figure 10.1 shows simulation outcomes at high trade costs, with affiliate production being the sum of the outputs of plants in country j of type-h_i and type-v_i firms (figure 8.1 shows the total for affiliate sales by both countries). Moving along the N-S diagonal (relative endowments identical), total affiliate sales have an inverted U shape in figure 10.1, qualitatively very similar to those shown in figure 7.5. The height of this inverted U will depend on the sum of the two countries' incomes.

When the two countries are approximately equal in size, sales by affiliates of country-i-owned firms are increasing in country i's skilled-labor abundance up to a point, and then they begin to fall as the relative endowment differences between the countries become extreme. I discussed this nonmonotonicity at several times in chapters 7–9. It relates to the requirements for skilled labor in fixed costs in the host country, such that when the host becomes very skilled-labor-scarce, the skilled-labor wage rises too high to permit local production and country j is served by exports from country i.

Affiliate production is highest in figure 10.1 when country i is moderately small and highly skilled-labor-abundant. The latter situation is especially reminiscent of Sweden, Switzerland, and the Netherlands, which are small, skilled-labor-abundant countries and important parent countries for multinationals.

In chapter 8 (figure 8.3), I considered the effect of lowering trade costs symmetrically in both directions. Figures 10.2 and 10.3 consider the opposite experiment, raising trade costs but plotting the effects of parent and host-country costs separately. Figure 10.2 considers raising trade costs into host-country j from 0.01 to 0.20 with country i's inward trade costs held at 0.20. Figure 10.2 shows that host-country trade costs encourage affiliate production when the two countries are relatively similar in both size and in relative endowments. There are almost no points in figure 10.2 where host-country trade costs reduce affiliate production. Inward, host-country trade costs encourage type-h_i firms to enter, serving country j by a branch plant rather than by exports. Conversely, in regions where type-v_i firms are important ini-

Change in the volume of
affiliate production

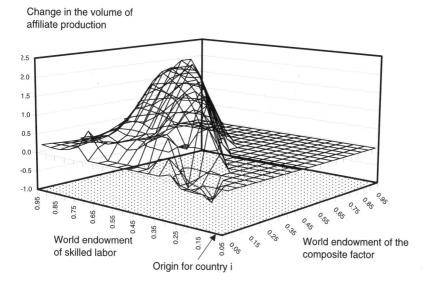

Figure 10.2
Change in affiliate production (by *i*-owned plants in country *j*) when *j*'s trade cost
increases from 0.01 to 0.20

tially, production by those firms is not discouraged by host-country
trade costs since the output shipped back to parent country *i* is not
affected by those costs.

Figure 10.3 shows the effects of increasing parent country *i*'s trade
costs on affiliate production in country *j* by type-h_i or type-v_i firms,
holding trade costs into *j* constant. When home trade costs are low,
type-d_j firms are the dominant firm type in equilibrium, although
type-v_i firms also exist and their production is counted as affiliate
production. However, when the countries are quite similar, these
firms become less profitable with an increase in country *i*'s inward
trade cost, and the regime shifts to a balance of type-h_i and type-h_j
firms, and affiliate sales of country *i* firms in country *j* increase. But
when the countries differ moderately in relative endowments, one sees
that country *i*'s trade costs discourage production by country *i*'s affiliates in country *j* in figure 10.3. The initial dominant firm type in this
region is type-v_i, with all output of these firms counted as affiliate
production. Raising country *i*'s trade costs makes these firms less profitable, and while some type-h_i firms may enter, the net effect on affiliate production in negative.

Change in the volume of
affiliate production

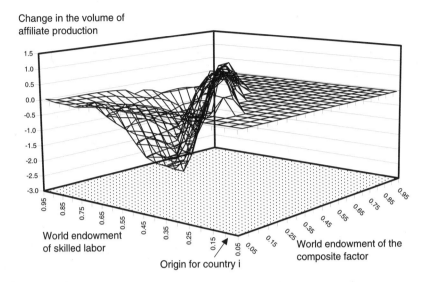

Figure 10.3
Change in affiliate production (by i-owned plants in country j) when i's trade cost
increases from 0.01 to 0.20

Results differ slightly if country j's trade cost is set at 0.01 during
these exercises instead of at 0.20 as in figure 10.3. In particular, the
region of positive change in figure 10.3 disappears. Raising country i's
trade costs leads to type-d_j firms being displaced by type-d_i firms
rather than by type-h_i firms, so there is no affect on country i's affiliate
sales. All changes in figure 10.3 are negative under this alternative assumption and occur when country i is skilled-labor-abundant.

These various results lead us to specify a central equation for estimation purposes.[1] Throughout the empirical analysis, country i will
denote the parent country, and country j the affiliate or host country.
Define the following variables:

$RSALES_{ij}$ real sales by affiliates of country i parents in host-country j

GDP_i real GDP of country i (similarly for j)

SK_i proportion of country i's labor force that is skilled (similarly for j)

$INVCJ$ an index of investment costs/barriers to entering country j

TCJ an index of trade costs/barriers to exporting to country j
(similarly for i)

The central estimating equation is given by

$$RSALES_{ij} = B0 + B1(SUMGDP) + B2(GDPDIFSQ) + B3(SKDIFF)$$
$$+ B4(GDPDIFF * SKDIFF) + B5(INVCJ) + B6(TCJ)$$
$$+ B7(TCJ * SKDIFSQ) + B8(TCI) + u \qquad (1)$$

where

$$SUMGDP = (GDP_i + GDP_j)$$

$$GDPDIFF = (GDP_i - GDP_j)$$

$$GDPDIFSQ = (GDP_i - GDP_j)^2$$

$$SKDIFF = (SK_i - SK_j)$$

$$SKDIFSQ = (SK_i - SK_j)^2$$

The first independent variable is $SUMGDP$, the sum of real GDP in both countries, which I expect to have a positive sign. Indeed, a stronger hypothesis is that the elasticity of affiliate sales with respect to $SUMGDP$ is greater than one. The second variable is $GDPDIFSQ$, the squared difference in real GDP. I expect its coefficient to be negative because our theory says that $RSALES$ has an inverted U-shaped relationship to differences in country size, with a maximum at zero differences. This is demonstrated along the N-S diagonal in figure 10.1, where affiliate sales has an inverted U-shape.

The third variable is $SKDIFF$, which is a measure of skilled-labor abundance in the parent country relative to the host country. I expect its coefficient to be positive because firms tend to be headquartered in the skilled-labor-abundant country. A fourth variable is the interaction between differences in skill endowments and economic size. I anticipate its coefficient (B4) to be negative for reasons shown in figure 10.1. In particular, affiliates sales are highest when the parent country is small and skilled-labor-abundant ($GDPDIFF * SKDIFF < 0$).

The fifth and sixth variables, $INVCJ$ and TCJ, respectively measure costs of investing in, and exporting to, the host country (indices ranging from 1 to 100 as discussed in what follows). I expect the investment-cost coefficient to be negative and the trade-cost coefficient to be positive. The interaction term between trade costs and squared endowment differences is designed to capture the fact that trade costs may encourage horizontal investment but not vertical investment and that horizontal investment is most important when relative endowments are similar. The coefficient should therefore be negative, weakening the direct effect of host-country trade costs. The results in figure 10.2, however, show that the effect of the host-country trade costs (the area of increased affiliate production) is not symmetric around the N-S diagonal and is actually highest when the parent country is moderately skilled-labor-abundant. Thus, this is not a theoretically sharp hypothesis and, indeed, empirical support for this term is weak.

The final regressor is TCI (0 to 100), trade costs in exporting to the parent country. The coefficient should be negative because trade costs diminish the incentive to locate plants abroad for shipment back to the home market, as shown in figure 10.3 (the area of negative change in affiliate production. Recall also that the region of positive change in figure 10.3 disappears as TCJ gets smaller). Figure 10.3 also indicates that TCI should interact with SKDIFF, but the resulting variable is highly colinear with SKDIFF because skilled-labor-scarce countries have high trade-cost indexes.[2] Thus, I exclude this interaction variable in the estimates provided here.

Finally, add geographic distance, DIST, as an independent variable. The sign of this variable is ambiguous in theory, because distance is an element in both export costs and investment and monitoring costs. I specify the regression as linear in levels, with quadratic and interaction terms included.

One can consider the interactive terms in more detail by writing the implied partial derivatives from equation (1). The derivative of RSALES with respect to TCJ has two terms:

$$\frac{\partial RSALES}{\partial TCJ} = B6 + B7(SKDIFSQ).$$

Because B6 should be greater than zero, this derivative is expected to be positive when relative endowments are similar, reflecting the fact that host-country trade costs encourage horizontal direct investment. But it should be smaller when relative endowments differ, in which case horizontal investment is less important. This implies that the expected sign of B7 is negative.

The derivative of RSALES with respect to GDPDIFF has two terms:

$$\frac{\partial RSALES}{\partial GDPDIFF} = B2(2 * GDPDIFF) + B4(SKDIFF).$$

The relationship should be an inverted U as noted above, reaching a maximum when the countries are similar in relative size, which is captured by the first term and an expected negative coefficient $B2$. However, my theory predicts that investment could fall with increases in country i's size if country i is skilled-labor-abundant, which is reflected in the second term and the expected negative sign on B4.

Finally, the derivative of RSALES with respect to SKDIFF has three terms:

$$\frac{\partial RSALES}{\partial SKDIFF} = B3 + B4(GDPDIFF) + B7(2 * TCJ * SKDIFF).$$

The first term is a direct effect that should be positive, capturing both vertical direct investment and headquarters of horizontal firms. The direct effect is weakened as the parent country gets larger, since vertical firms are replaced by national firms, headquartered in the parent nation, that serve the destination country by exports. This effect is also weakened if $SKDIFF$ takes on a large value. The coefficients $B4$ and $B7$ both appear twice in the three derivatives and are predicted to be negative in each case (although the theoretical case for $B7$ is not particularly strong, as noted earlier).

10.5   Data Sources and Estimation Results

Data for the estimation form a panel of cross-country observations over the period 1986–1994. I take real sales volume of nonbank manufacturing affiliates in each country to indicate production activity. The U.S. Department of Commerce provides annual data on sales of foreign affiliates of American parent firms and on sales of U.S. affiliates of foreign parent firms. Thus, the data are bilateral with the United States, and the United States is either country i (parent) or j (host) in every observation. There are thirty-six countries in addition to the United States for which I have at least one year of complete data. Annual sales values abroad are converted into millions of 1990 U.S. dollars using an exchange-rate-adjusted local wholesale price index, with exchange rates and price indexes taken from the *International Financial Statistics* (IFS) of the International Monetary Fund.

Real gross domestic product is measured in billions of 1990 U.S. dollars for each country. For this purpose, annual real GDP figures in local currencies were converted into dollars using the market exchange rate. These data are also from the IFS.

Skilled-labor abundance is defined as the sum of occupational categories 0/1 (professional, technical, and kindred workers) and 2 (administrative workers) in employment in each country, divided by total employment. These figures are compiled from annual surveys reported in the *Yearbook of Labor Statistics* published by the International Labor Organization. In cases where some annual figures were missing, the skilled-labor ratios were taken to equal the period averages for each country. The variable *SKDIFF* is then simply the difference between the relative skill endowment of the parent country and that of the affiliate country (potential range: −1 to 1).

The cost of investing in the affiliate country is a simple average of several indexes of impediments to investment, reported in the *World Competitiveness Report* of the World Economic Forum.[3] The indexes include restrictions on ability to acquire control in a domestic company, limitations on the ability to employ foreign skilled labor, restraints on negotiating joint ventures, strict controls on hiring and firing practices, market dominance by a small number of enterprises, an absence of fair administration of justice, difficulties in acquiring local bank credit, restrictions on access to local and foreign capital markets, and inadequate protection of intellectual property. These indexes are computed on a scale from 0 to 100, with a higher number indicating higher investment costs.

A trade cost index is taken from the same source and is defined as a measure of national protectionism, or efforts to prevent importation of competitive products. It also runs from 0 to 100, with 100 being the highest trade costs. All of these indexes are based on extensive surveys of multinational enterprises. I also incorporate a measure of distance, which is simply the number of kilometers of each country's capital city from Washington, DC. It is unclear whether this variable captures trade costs or investment costs, since both should rise with distance.

Table 10.3 lists the countries for which I have at least one complete yearly set of observations, along with summary statistics. The final data set, after eliminating any row with missing variables, contains 509 observations. An additional 119 observations are complete, except that no foreign affiliate sales are listed in the Commerce Department data. On examination, these countries in all cases are relatively poor and generally small. Thus, I conjecture that the missing observations are in fact zeros. I then perform alternative estimations using a Tobit procedure, adding these cases to the data set for a total of 628 observations.

Results for the central-case regressions are shown in tables 10.1 and 10.2. The regression in the first column of table 10.1 are estimated with a weighted-least-squares (WLS) procedure, employing a WLS correction for heteroskedasticity. The second column is the Tobit equation, adding 119 observations as noted above. The first four variables capture the relationships shown in figure 10.1. All of the coefficients on these variables have the hypothesized signs and are highly significant. The two variables involving *SKDIFF* have much larger magnitudes in the Tobit regression. This seems intuitive: The zero-*RSALES* observations added in the Tobit are overwhelmingly cases where the potential parent nation is skilled-labor-scarce and smaller than the potential affiliate nation (the United States). Excluding them from the WLS estimation in table 10.1 likely biases downward the role of skilled labor.

The next four variables involve the trade and investment cost measures. All signs are consistent with the theory, although *TCJ * SKDIFSQ* is not significant in either regression. *TCI* is not significant in the WLS regression, but it is of marginal significance in the Tobit. Controlling for distance, the decisions of multinational enterprises in setting output levels of affiliates are responsive to perceived costs of investing in the country and the strength of import protection. This outcome is sensible given our measures of investment costs and trade costs, which are indexes of perceived costs and protectionism developed from surveys of multinational managers. The survey questions do not ask about geographical distance, implying that the respondents do not factor it into their answers. Thus, I have conceptually distinctive measures of distance and other border and internal host-country costs.

The results presented above are from a panel data set, and it is of interest to decompose them into cross-section and time-series effects. Before discussing this, I emphasize that the theoretical results apply equally well to time-series and cross-section processes. That is, the theory should correctly characterize both the time-path of the interactions between two countries and the interactions among countries in a single year. For example, as two countries grow in total GDP and become more similar in size over time, direct investment between them should grow in the manner suggested by the theory. Among a

Table 10.1
Results for real sale of affiliates: WLS and Tobit estimation (dependent variable: real sales by affiliates of country i firms in country j)

Variable	WLS estimate (t stat)	Sign as predicted? (marginal significance)	Tobit estimate (χ^2)	Sign as predicted? (marginal significance)
SUMGDP	13.92 (9.80)	Yes (0.0001)	15.04 (105.5)	Yes (0.0001)
GDPDIFSQ	−0.0014 (−8.90)	Yes (0.0001)	−0.0010 (34.67)	Yes (0.0001)
SKDIFF	31044 (4.01)	Yes (0.0001)	61700 (52.98)	Yes (0.0001)
GDPDIFF*SKDIFF	−4.27 (−2.12)	Yes (0.035)	−10.20 (18.81)	Yes (0.0001)
INVCJ	−455.6 (−3.92)	Yes (0.0001)	−378.6 (7.95)	Yes (0.005)
TCJ	190.6 (2.20)	Yes (0.029)	156.2 (2.28)	Yes (0.131)
TCJ*SKDIFSQ	−569.9 (−0.41)	Yes (0.683)	−1264 (0.57)	Yes (0.573)
TCI	−93.3 (−1.14)	Yes (0.256)	−122.0 (2.13)	Yes (0.144)
DIST	−1.34 (−6.63)	? (0.0001)	−1.48 (41.92)	? (0.0001)
INTERCEPT	−5381 (−0.42)	(0.676)	−23282 (2.59)	(0.108)
Observations	509		628	
Adjusted R^2	0.60			
Log Likelihood			−5755	

Notes: WLS is weighted least squares. Figures in parentheses below coefficients are t statistics. Tobit: Figures in parentheses below coefficients are χ^2. Marginal significance levels of the coefficients are indicated in parentheses below sign predictions for both regressions.

Table 10.2
Fixed-effects estimation of basic model: WLS and Tobit (dependent variable: real sales by affiliates of country i firms in country j)

Variable	WLS estimate (t stat)	Sign as predicted? (marginal significance)	Tobit estimate (χ^2)	Sign as predicted? (marginal significance)
SUMGDP	13.72 (13.6)	Yes (0.0001)	16.57 (304.2)	Yes (0.0001)
GDPDIFSQ	−0.0011 (−9.81)	Yes (0.0001)	−0.0009 (64.2)	Yes (0.0001)
SKDIFF	15042 (1.34)	Yes (0.181)	29366 (5.69)	Yes (0.017)
GDPDIFF*SKDIFF	−4.44 (−2.09)	Yes (0.037)	−7.71 (10.4)	Yes (0.0013)
INVCJ	−173.2 (−1.52)	Yes (0.129)	−41.25 (0.10)	Yes (0.752)
TCJ	69.36 (1.02)	Yes (0.310)	144.0 (3.71)	Yes (0.054)
TCJ*SKDIFSQ	−811.6 (−0.57)	Yes (0.572)	−2273 (2.22)	Yes (0.137)
TCI	−75.5 (−1.60)	Yes (0.111)	−112.6 (5.89)	Yes (0.015)
DIST	−0.872 (−4.95)	? (0.0001)	−0.77 (18.3)	? (0.0001)
INTERCEPT	−24552 (−2.57)	(0.011)	−53341 (27.5)	(0.0001)
Observations	509		628	
Adjusted R^2	0.87			
Log Likelihood			−5436	

Notes: Figures in parentheses below coefficients are t statistics for the WLS equation and χ^2 statistics for the Tobit equation. Marginal significance levels of the coefficients are indicated in parentheses below sign predictions.

Table 10.3
Data

Countries (countries for which at least one year is included)		
Argentina	Greece	New Zealand
Australia	Hong Kong	Norway
Austria	India	Panama
Belgium	Indonesia	Philippines
Brazil	Ireland	Portugal
Canada	Israel	Singapore
Chile	Italy	Spain
Colombia	Japan	Sweden
Denmark	Korea	Switzerland
Finland	Malaysia	Turkey
France	Mexico	United Kingdom
Germany	Netherlands	Venezuela

Note: German data are for West Germany before unification and for an estimate of western Germany since unification.

Summary statistics (basic sample; $n = 513$)					
Variable	Mean	Std. Dev.	Minimum	Maximum	
RSALES	15670	24316	0	120070	millions of 1990 US\$
SUMGDP	6125	675	5210	9328	billions of 1990 US\$
GDPDIFF	1146	5219	−6145	6145	billions of 1990 US\$
GDPDIFSQ	2.8e7	0.6e7	0.7e7	3.8e7	
SKDIFF	0.034	0.012	−0.277	0.277	share of the labor force in i (parent) that is skilled minus the skilled share in j (host)
SKDIFSQ	0.016	0.017	5.7e-7	0.077	
INVCJ	34.00	10.59	15.30	79.43	index, 0–100
TCJ	33.62	12.05	6.00	85.08	index, 0–100
TCI	31.74	8.61	6.00	74.34	index, 0–100
DIST	8266	3875	734	16370	km from Washington, DC

Table 10.3
(continued)

Correlation matrix (basic sample; $n = 513$)

	(1)	(2)	(3)	(4)	(5)	(6)	(7)	(8)	(9)	(10)
RSALES	1.00									
SUMGDP	0.53	1.00								
GDPDIFF	0.01	−0.12	1.00							
GDPDIFSQ	−0.52	−0.60	0.07	1.00						
SKDIFF	−0.10	−0.14	0.70	0.11	1.00					
SKDIFSQ	−0.29	−0.07	0.20	0.12	0.33	1.00				
INVCJ	−0.19	−0.18	0.57	−0.02	0.63	0.46	1.00			
TCJ	−0.10	−0.08	0.12	−0.12	0.27	0.33	0.65	1.00		
TCI	−0.02	0.03	−0.05	−0.14	−0.13	0.12	0.01	0.08	1.00	
DIST	−0.36	−0.06	0.07	0.12	0.13	0.37	0.06	0.18	0.03	1

set of countries in a given year, the same bilateral relationships should apply.

One way to isolate the cross-section contribution to the results is to use single-year regressions or to average the years for each variable. But three difficulties emerge. First, there are only sixty-three cross-section observations in the most complete year. Second, *SUMGDP* and *GDPDIFSQ* are highly collinear: They have a correlation coefficient of 0.995 in our cross-section. The time-series variation in U.S. GDP is vital to identifying the separate contributions of these two variables and this information is discarded in the averaging procedure (or in the use of a single year).

Third, there is far less independent information than would appear with 63 observations. The variable *TCI* has the same value for all U.S.-outward investments and *TCJ* and *INVCJ* have the same values for all investments in the United States. Because of these difficulties, standard errors in the cross section regressions are large, although all signs are correct except for *TCJ* * *SKDIFSQ*, which was not significant in the panel regressions of table 10.1. I do not report these results here, but they are available in NBER Working Paper 6773 (see Carr, Markusen, and Maskus 1998).

To distinguish the time-series contributions to the results, I employ country fixed effects. Table 10.2 lists results where the equation contains a dummy variable for each country (regardless if it is the source or recipient country in a given observation) except the United States. The first regression employs WLS, and the second is the related Tobit estimation. I do not report the coefficients of the country dummies, but most are significant.[4]

The results are qualitatively similar to those in table 10.1 for the first group of four variables in the WLS regressions, except that the coefficient on *SKDIFF* is reduced by half. The magnitudes of the coefficients on *INVCJ* and *TCJ* are considerably smaller in table 10.2 as well, and both have lower significance levels. Thus, although the sign pattern is robust to the inclusion of country fixed effects, it is difficult to identify confidently the contribution of trade costs and investment costs to multinational production.

The Tobit results in table 10.2 also show a smaller coefficient for *SKDIFF* with the country dummies added. The variables measuring perceived trade costs are significant in this specification in the hypothesized directions, but the investment-cost variable is not. Overall, it appears that the addition of country fixed effects does not change the results qualitatively, but a smaller role for endowment differences is predicted.[5] It is noteworthy that in the Tobit specification, which incorporates many more developing countries with zero reported affiliate sales, the magnitudes and significance levels of trade costs in both host and parent countries are expanded, as are those of relative endowment differences. This result provides some support for the notion that horizontal and vertical FDI respond differently to host-country and parent-country trade protection.

Overall, I believe the results in tables 10.1 and 10.2 provide strong support to the knowledge-capital model of foreign direct investment. Affiliate sales are strongly sensitive to bilateral aggregate economic activity, squared differences in GDP, differences in skilled labor endowments, and the interaction between size and endowment differences. The evidence suggests more weakly that affiliate activity depends on investment costs and trade costs as hypothesized. I wish to use these results to characterize the various direct and indirect impacts more fully, which is the next task.

10.6 Interpreting the Coefficients

In this section, I interpret the magnitude of the coefficients and interpret the partial derivatives discussed above. For this purpose, I employ the coefficients from the model in table 10.2 (fixed effects included) and apply them to average data values from the year 1991.

First, consider increases in trade costs as measured by the index *TCJ*. It is clear from the estimation that trade costs increase affiliate production when countries have identical relative endowments of skilled labor (*SKDIFF* = 0). This is consistent with horizontal investment. This effect is weakened when the countries differ in relative endowments, but theory suggests it should not be reversed: Vertical investments should be discouraged by *parent-country* trade costs, not so much by *host-country* trade costs. Results from table 10.2 support the following computation:

$$\frac{\partial RSALES}{\partial TCJ} = B6 + B7(SKDIFSQ)$$

$$= 69.4 - 811.6 * SKDIFSQ > 0 \text{ iff } SKDIFF < 0.293 \quad \text{(WLS)}$$

$$= 114 - 2273 * SKDIFSQ > 0 \text{ iff } SKDIFF < 0.252 \quad \text{(Tobit)} \quad (2)$$

In the data, the WLS derivative is always positive for all i-to-j observations, and the Tobit is positive for all but one (United States to Indonesia). I can therefore state the following empirical conclusion:

Result 1: An increase in the host country's trade costs will raise production by affiliates of parent-country firms.

While I do not attempt any measure of trade versus investment, this result suggests that inward trade costs induce a substitution of local production for imports.

Second, consider an equal bilateral increase in trade costs in both i and j. This should encourage horizontal investments but discourage vertical investments. Results from table 10.2 give us the following:

$$\frac{\partial RSALES}{\partial TC} = B6 + B7(SKDIFSQ) + B8 \qquad dTC \equiv dTCI = dTCJ$$

$$= 69.4 - 811.6 * SKDIFSQ - 75.5 < 0 \text{ all } SKDIFF \quad \text{(WLS)}$$

$$= 114 - 2273 * SKDIFSQ - 112.6 > 0 \text{ iff } SKDIFF < 0.118 \quad \text{(Tobit)}$$
$$(3)$$

Using terminology somewhat tautologically, suppose we define trade and investment as "complements" if higher bilateral trade costs discourage investment and "substitutes" if higher trade costs encourage investment. The following result is obtained:

Result 2: A bilateral increase in parent- and host-country trade costs.
1. Weighted least squares: decreases affiliate production, so trade and investment are "complements."
2. Tobit: generally decreases affiliate production when the non-U.S. country is a developing country ("complements") but increases affiliate production when the non-U.S. country is another high-income country ("substitutes").

Part 2, the Tobit result, accords well with the intuition from the theory model. Investment between two developed countries (small *SKDIFF*) is generally horizontal and therefore encouraged by trade costs. Investment between countries of quite different income levels (large *SKDIFF*) is generally vertical, which is discouraged by trade costs.

Third, consider an increase in country i's GDP, holding total world GDP constant (i.e, country j's GDP change is the negative of country i's change). When countries have identical relative endowments ($SKDIFF = 0$), this derivative is positive with $GDPDIFF < 0$, zero at $GDPDIFF = 0$, and negative with $GDPDIFF > 0$. With country i more skilled-labor-abundant than country j, the theory and simulations predicted that this derivative switches sign, from positive to negative, at a lower value of $GDPDIFF$ (see figure 10.1). Results from table 10.2 give us the following results:

$$\frac{\partial RSALES}{\partial GDPDIFF} = B2(2 * GDPDIFF) + B4(SKDIFF)$$

$$= -0.0011 * 2 * (GDPDIFF) - 4.4 * (SKDIFF) \quad \text{(WLS)}$$

$$= -0.0009 * 2 * (GDPDIFF) - 7.7 * (SKDIFF) \quad \text{(Tobit)} \quad (4)$$

An increase in a country's GDP will increase its affiliate sales abroad only if it is small ($GDPDIFF < 0$) and/or skilled-labor-scarce ($SKDIFF < 0$).[6]

One interesting interpretation of these results involves the convergence in income between the United States and its trading partners, holding total two-country income constant ($SUMGDP$ is constant). Using values of $SKDIFF$ from the data, it turns out that the contribution of the last term in equation (4) is small and is always dominated by the first term. Note that $GDPDIFF$ is always positive if the United States is country i and negative if the United States is country j.

Result 3: A convergence in income (GDP) between the United States and country *j* (holding the sum their incomes constant) increases affiliate sales in *both directions.*

This result is connected to results in figure 10.1. Consider the volume of affiliate sales along the N-S diagonal of figure 10.1 and corresponding values for the other direction, *j* to *i* (not shown). Both are inverted U-shaped relationships and while they are not identical, there are regions where convergence toward the center of the box raises affiliate sales in both directions. Moving toward the center, national firms headquartered in the large country (i.e., the United States) are replaced by type-h firms headquartered in both countries. This is seen more clearly in figure 7.5 (although recall that this is a slightly different calibration than this chapter's figures using the calibration of chapter 8). Between 0.30 and 0.70 on the horizontal axis of figure 7.5, movements toward the middle of the box, income convergence, raises affiliate sales in both directions.

Fourth, consider an increase in the skilled-labor abundance of country *i* relative to country *j*. Our results in table 10.2 indicate that this derivative is generally positive for similar countries, but its (absolute) value is reduced by a higher relative endowment difference or a larger GDP difference.

$$\frac{\partial RSALES}{\partial SKDIFF} = B3 + B4(GDPDIFF) + B7(2*TCJ*SKDIFF)$$

$$= 15042 - 4.4*(GDPDIFF) - 811.6*2*(TCJ*SKDIFF) \quad \text{(WLS)}$$

$$= 29366 - 7.7*(GDPDIFF) - 2273*2*(TCJ*SKDIFF) \quad \text{(Tobit)}$$

$$(5)$$

Large values of *SKDIFF* and *GDPDIFF* weaken the effects of an increase in parent-country skilled-labor abundance on outward affiliate sales. To put it the other way around, an increase in *host-country* skilled-labor abundance (*dSKDIFF* < 0) may increase inward investment if that host country is small relative to the parent.

Inserting values for *SKDIFF*, *TCJ*, and *GDPDIFF* for the 1991 data, these results imply the following:

Result 4:
1. When the United States is parent, an increase in country *j*'s skilled-labor abundance increases U.S. affiliate production in country *j* (pro-

duction by U.S. affiliates is attracted to skilled-labor-abundant host countries).

2. When the United States is host, an increase in country j's skilled-labor abundance increases country j's affiliate production in the United States.

Result 1 is consistent with the well-known stylized fact that the poorest countries in the world receive a much smaller share of world direct investment than their share of world income (Zhang and Markusen 1999; see chap. 9).

As a final point, note that the theory suggests a sharper hypothesis on the coefficient of *SUMGDP* than that it is simply positive. Higher total income should lead to some shifting from national firms, which are high marginal-cost suppliers to foreign markets, to horizontal multinationals, which are high fixed-cost suppliers (Markusen and Venables 1998). In regions of parameter space in which regime shifting does not occur, affiliate production should rise in proportion to total world income. Overall, this suggests that affiliate sales should be elastic with respect to world income. I therefore use the results in table 10.2 to calculate the implied elasticity of total affiliate sales (*RSALES*) with respect to total income (SUMGDP) for 1991 in the data. Results are as follows:

Elasticity of production by affiliates of country-i firms in country j with respect to an equal, proportional bilateral income increase.

	Elasticity at $SKDIFF = 0$	Elasticity at $SKDIFF = $ mean
WLS	1.43	1.42
Tobit	4.50	4.50

Result 5: Affiliate production is income elastic: a bilateral increase in parent and host country incomes increases affiliate production by a greater proportion.

This result is consistent with the well-known stylized fact that direct investment, whether measured by stocks or affiliates sales, has risen much faster than world income and trade since the mid-1970s (Markusen and Venables 1998; Markusen 1997; and chap. 1).

10.7 Summary

The knowledge-capital approach to the multinational enterprise as outlined in this chapter is operational and yields clear, testable hypotheses. It this sense, it is more useful that some other theories of FDI, such as the "transactions cost" approach to multinational enterprises.

In this chapter, I test hypotheses regarding the importance of multinational activity between countries as a function of certain characteristics of those countries, particularly size, size differences, relative endowment differences, trade and investment costs, and certain interactions among these variables as predicted by the theory. In my view, the model fits well and gives considerable support to the theory. The panel estimates in tables 10.1 and 10.2 yield correct signs and strong statistical significance for the central variables $SUMGDP$, $GDPDIFSQ$, $SKDIFF$, $GDPDIFF * SKDIFF$, $INVCJ$, and TCJ. Other variables (TCI and $TCJ * SKDIFSQ$) have correct signs but display weak statistical significance. Our efforts to separate the panel results into cross-section and time-series impacts are made problematic by multicolinearity in the cross-section data. Because of the bilateral nature of these data, the time-series variation in the U.S. observations is critical to identification of the contributions of several variables. Estimation with country fixed effects produces results consistent with the panel approach.[7]

According to our findings, outward investment from a source country to affiliates in a host country is increasing in the sum of their economic sizes, their similarity in size, the relative skilled-labor abundance of the parent nation, and the interaction between size and relative endowment differences. Some of these findings are consistent with earlier results, particularly those of Brainard (1997) and Ekholm (1998b). But the precise formulations here are different and closely tied to one particular model. This model allows for simultaneous horizontal and vertical motives for direct investment and emphasizes certain interactions, such as that between size and endowment differences. I should also note that the theoretical model fully endogenizes trade flows in its calculations, allowing direct predictions on affiliate sales without requiring us to worry about questions of trade versus investment. Trade, like factor and commodity prices, is endogenous in generating the predictions of the model.

Subsequent to the estimation, I interpreted the estimates in the language of comparative-statics questions about the world economy. First, the results indicate that increases in host-country trade costs will increase inward affiliate production. Bilateral increases in trade costs produce results that suggest that trade and investment are "complements" but may be "substitutes" (Tobit regression) for similar countries, the latter result consistent with horizontal investment predicted between similar countries. Third, a convergence in country size between the United States and country j will increase affiliate sales in *both* directions. Fourth, an increase in country j's skilled-labor abundance will increase U.S. outward affiliate sales: U.S. investment is attracted to more skilled-labor-abundant countries. Finally, affiliate production is elastic in total two-country GDP as predicted by theory.

In summary, I am enthusiastic about the results and believe that they fit well with theory. I hope that the model will therefore prove useful in future policy analysis.

11

Production for Export versus Local Sale

11.1 Introduction

The knowledge-capital model exposited in chapter 7 and extended in chapter 8 allows for both vertical and horizontal firms to arise in equilibrium as a function of technology and country characteristics. A single theory covers a variety of special cases. Yet it is still of interest to inquire as to whether horizontal firms or vertical firms are more important in actual world multinational activity. It is not, however, a very simple empirical task to sort out how much activity is horizontal and how much is vertical by whatever definition. Vertical activity is closely related to the notion of "outsourcing," but much of this is transacted through contracts with independent local producers, as in the clothing and footwear industries, rather than through subsidiaries. Our affiliate production and sales data does not include this type of activity by definition.

The best one can do with the data set that I assembled with Carr and Maskus and described in chapter 10 is to get at this question indirectly by examining production for local sales versus production for export. One naturally tends to think of production for local sale as suggesting horizontal activity, whereas production for export suggests more vertical activity such as assembly plants. This is clearly an imperfect association. A firm headquartered in a small country may, for example, have a single plant in a large foreign country that supplies both the latter and the parent country. This would be a vertical investment according to the terminology of this book, but a great proportion of the output may be sold in the host country by virtue of the large host-country market size.

The purpose of this chapter is to use the theory model of chapters 7 and 8 in order to generate predictions about production for local sales versus exports. In the theoretical model, production for export is only associated with vertical (type-v) firms, but vertical firms nevertheless have a substantial component of their affiliates' output sold in the local host-country by virtue of the market size as just suggested. Recall that the data in table 1.7 noted that the overwhelming proportion of multinational output is sold in the host-country market. Simulation results are then be used to generate testable predictions as in chapter 10. These predictions are subjected to empirical estimation and tests using the same data set described in chapter 10.

Empirical results fit well with the theoretical hypotheses. Local sales of foreign affiliates are strongly dependent on market size and trade costs into the host country. Skilled-labor abundance between the parent and host country is only weakly related to local affiliate sales in both economic and statistical terms. Export sales are weakly related to market size and to host-country trade costs. They are strongly related to the skilled-labor endowment differences of the parent and host countries, and strongly related to an interaction term between skill differences and country size: Exports by affiliates are particularly important when the parent is both skilled-labor-abundant and small (e.g., Sweden, The Netherlands, Switzerland). Both local sales and export sales are strongly negatively related to a host-country investment barrier (cost) index.

The ratio of exports to local sales is positively related to the relative skilled-labor abundance of the parent, and negatively related to market size, the host-country investment cost index, and the host-country trade-cost index. The findings on trade and investment costs may be due to a substitution phenomenon. If the investment is undertaken to serve the local market, firms bear the trade and investment costs. If the investment is made to serve the market in the parent or third countries, high local trade and investment costs induce the firm to look elsewhere.

11.2   Predictions of the Knowledge-Capital Model

I proceed directly to the results of the simulations that generate the predictions. The model used is exactly the same as the one used in chapters 8 and 10, which differs only slightly in the calibration from the model used in chapter 7.

Figures 11.1–11.3 present results from the simulation of the model for sales by affiliates of country i firms producing in country j. These

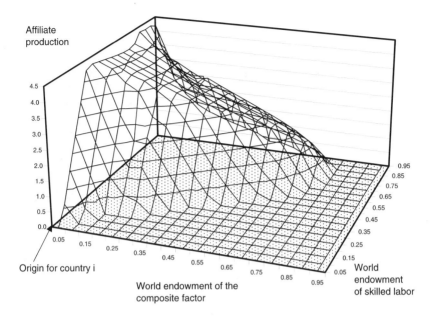

Figure 11.1
Affiliate production for local sale by country-*i*-owned plants in country *j*, high trade costs (20%)

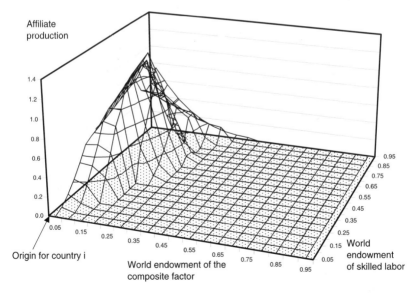

Figure 11.2
Affiliate production for export sale by country-*i*-owned plants in country *j*, high trade costs (20%)

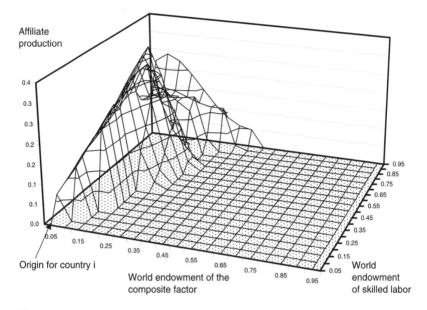

Figure 11.3
Ratio of affiliate production for export to local sale by country-*i*-owned plants in country *j*, high trade costs (20%)

diagrams are oriented somewhat differently from those in chapters 8 and 10, since the information displayed requires a different viewing angle. The origin for country *i* is now at the southwest corner of the Edgeworth box.

Figures 11.1–11.3 present the same simulation as those shown in figures 8.1 and 10.1 but display different data. Trade costs are 20 percent. Figure 11.1 shows only affiliate production for local sale in country *j*. There is an inverted U-shaped relationship along the SW-NE diagonal where countries may differ in size but have identical relative endowments. The highest levels occur when country *i* is both small and skilled-labor-abundant for reasons readers have now come to know and love.

Figure 11.2 shows the export sales of affiliates back to the parent country *i*. This diagram is a "mountain," reaching a maximum when country *i* is small and skilled-labor-abundant, but not extremely small and not too skilled-labor-abundant. The not-too-small requirement is obvious, because little output is exported back to a very small country.

Clear differences exist between figures 11.1 and 11.2. Most notably, only local sales occur if the countries are very similar, and local sales

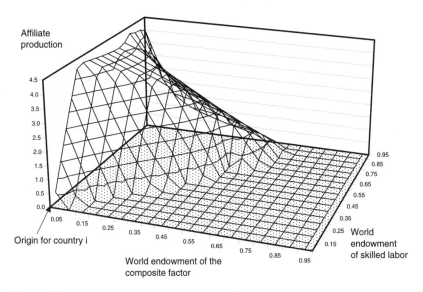

Figure 11.4
Affiliate production for local sale by country-*i*-owned plants in country *j*, low trade costs (10%)

dominate if country *i* is very small and very skilled-labor-abundant. Yet there are some similarities that make it difficult to propose sharply different hypotheses regarding how these two classes of affiliate sales should be related to country characteristics.

Figure 11.3 clarifies this ambiguity a bit by displaying the ratio of affiliate exports back to the parent to local affiliate sales in the host country. The graph suggests that this ratio is most closely related to the skilled-labor abundance of the parent in relation to the host country. Relative size differences play some role, but the ratio clearly is smaller when the parent country *i* is very small. When country *i* is both very small and skilled-labor-abundant, all its X firms are type-v_i but, because of the market-size effect discussed previously, most of the output of those vertical firms is sold in the large (country *j*) market.

For completeness, I should note that the results are somewhat different, at least quantitatively different, when trade costs are low. Figures 11.4–11.6 show the same experiments as the three previous figures but with trade costs 10 percent instead of 20 percent. Figure 11.4 shows production for local sales, and one sees that sales now disappear when the countries are very similar: Type-h firms do not enter even when the countries are identical. Figure 11.5 shows that the surface for

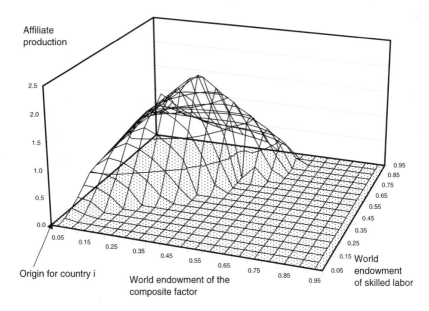

Figure 11.5
Affiliate production for export by country-*i*-owned plants in country *j*, low trade costs
(10%)

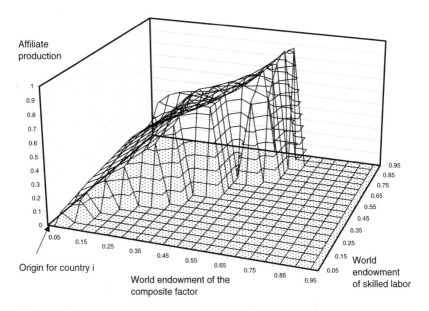

Figure 11.6
Ratio of affiliate production for export to local sale, country-*i*-owned plants in country *j*,
low trade costs (10%)

production for export sale shifts toward the center of the box. Now when country i is just moderately skilled-labor-abundant and slightly smaller or the same size as country j, type-v_i firms are active instead of type-h_i. The former ship part of their output back to country i given the lower trade costs, so production for export sale occurs when the countries are much more similar than when trade costs are high. Figure 11.6 shows the ratio, and here one sees that the ratio peaks when the countries are quite similar in size and indeed when country i is somewhat larger. This is once again the market size effect. Type-h_i firms are never active at the lower trade cost, so all multinationals headquartered in country i are type-v_i. They export a higher proportion of output back to the parent country when the parent country is larger.

These simulation results suggest a number of independent variables that should be used to explain the three dependent variables: local sales by affiliates of country i firms in country j (figures 11.1, 11.4), export sales by the same affiliates (figures 11.2, 11.5), and the ratio of these two variables (figures 11.3, 11.6). Refer to these variables as *RSALESL*, *RSALESE*, and *RATIOEL* (*R* for "real" in the first two). These are obtained from the same Bureau of Economic Analysis data I described in chapter 10. I list the right-hand-side variables, adding a discussion of the hypothesized signs and magnitudes using figures 11.1–11.6 and other more obvious intuition.

Right-hand-side variables have the same definitions as in the previous chapter. *SUMGDP* denotes the sum of two countries' real GDP. This should have a positive coefficient in explaining *RSALESL* and *RSALESE*. However, the effect should be stronger on *RSALESL*. The reason is that growth will, at various points in parameter space, lead to a switch from high marginal-cost single-plant firms to high-fixed-cost multiplant firms, increasing local sales more than in proportion to growth in incomes. Accordingly, I hypothesize that *RATIOEL* should be negatively related to *SUMGDP*.

GDPDIFF is the difference between the two countries' real GDP levels and *GDPDIFSQ* is the squared difference. *GDPDIFSQ* should be negatively related to all three dependent variables, as suggested by all figures. Moving along various loci parallel to the SW-NE diagonal, all three dependent variables are higher near the center than at the extremes, although the maximum point is generally not exactly where the two countries are the same size.

SKDIFF denotes the relative skilled-labor abundance of the *parent* country relative to the host; formally, it is the share of the labor force that is skilled in country i (parent or source) minus the same share in country j (host) ($SKDIFF = SKLI - SKLJ$). $SKDIFF$ should be positively related to both $RSALESL$ and $RSALESE$. However, eye-balling figures 11.2 and 11.3, I notice that it appears to have a stronger impact on $RSALESE$ than on $RSALESL$. Relative endowments and factor-price differences are the primary determinants of export sales, whereas local sales are influenced heavily by country sizes as well. Accordingly, I hypothesize that $SKDIFF$ will have a positive sign in the $RATIOEL$ regression as suggested by figure 11.3. Note that this last theoretical prediction is not robust to the level of trade costs, and the relationship is nonmonotonic especially, when trade costs are small as in figure 11.6. $RATIOEL$ peaks at a very small level of $SKDIFF$, but it remains true that export sales are always higher when country i is skilled-labor-abundant than when it is skilled-labor-scarce (affiliate production is zero).

$INVCJ$ denotes an index of investment barriers (costs) into country j, the host country. Higher numbers indicate higher investment costs. This is hypothesized to be negatively related to both $RSALESL$ and $RSALESE$. However, investments to serve the local market may be less sensitive to these costs than are investments to serve export markets because alternative locations may be selected for the latter; thus I hypothesize that the magnitude of the coefficient in the $RSALESL$ equation should be less than that in the $RSALESE$ equation, and therefore that the sign on $INVJ$ should be negative in the $RATIOEL$ equation as well.

TCJ denotes an index of trade barriers (costs, not including transport costs) into country j. Higher numbers indicate higher barriers or costs. Such barriers should encourage investments to serve the local market, so the hypothesized sign is positive in the $RSALESL$ equation. The effect should be noticeably less in the $RSALESE$ equation and may be negative, insofar as trade costs raise the costs of imported intermediate inputs. The sign of the coefficient in the $RATIOEL$ equation should thus be negative.

TCI is a similar measure of trade barriers back into the parent country. This has little effect on production for local sales in country j, but is expected to have a negative effect on production for export, insofar as much of that may be going back to the home country. This variable should thus have a negative sign in the $RATIOEL$ equation.

$GDPDIFF * SKDIFF$ is an interactive term. Referring to figures 11.1–11.2 the effect of an increase in $SKDIFF$ should be larger when the parent is smaller ($GDPDIFF < 0$), and the effect of an increase in $GDPI$ (parent GDP) should be smaller when the parent country i is skilled-labor-abundant ($SKDIFF > 0$). Both effects imply that the sign of the coefficient on the interactive term should be negative in the $RSALESL$ and $RSALESE$ regressions. Figures 11.3 and 11.6, however, do not suggest a very sharp hypothesis as to whether it should be positive or negative in the $RATIOEL$ equation. Therefore, I am agnostic about the sign in the $RATIOEL$ equation.

$DIST$ denotes a distance measure between pairs of counties. Theory does not offer us much of a prediction about distance. It may lead to a substitution of producing abroad instead of exporting to a distant country. However, distance raises the transactions costs of investments as well as those of exports. It is possible that distance might affect production for export more negatively than production for local sale (which might actually be encouraged), but I am generally agnostic insofar as I do not understand the transactions costs of investing at a long distance.

In addition to examining these hypotheses on two-way data (inward and outward affiliate sales data for the United States), I examine them on U.S.-outward-only data. The advantage of the latter is that it breaks down affiliate export sales into sales back to the parent country and sales to third countries. Sales to the U.S. parent may be closely identified with vertical investments such as foreign assembly plants. One should note, however, that the intuition generated by figures 11.1–11.6 may not always be appropriate, insofar as these diagrams are "compensated" experiments holding the two-country total factor endowment constant. Thus an increase in $SKDIFF$ is an increase in the U.S. skilled-labor abundance and a fall in the host-country skilled-labor abundance in the simulations. For the U.S.-outward data, an increase in $SKDIFF$ is a fall in the host-country skilled-labor abundance holding the U.S. endowment constant. Similar comments apply to $GDPDIFF$, and in the outward regressions I use GDPJ since it is only the latter variable that changes.

A problematic issue with the outward-only data arises from the fact that the United States (the parent) is always far bigger than the host, although not always skilled-labor-abundant relative to the host. This restricts observations to an area in the NE section of the Edgeworth boxes in figures 11.1–11.6, which is a considerable difficulty given the nonlinearity and nonmonotonicity of the theoretical predictions over the parameter space of the Edgeworth box. For example, note that increases in *SKDIFF* could lead to a fall in outward U.S. investment in this region (foreign plants are replaced by U.S. national firms serving the host by exports). Thus one expects some differences in the U.S.-outward-only results versus the two-way results because they are somewhat different experiments and because one is constrained to a subregion of parameter space in the outward-only data.

I don't think it is necessary to say much about the data. It is the same panel as in chapter 10, with added detail only for the dependent variables. The data form a panel of cross-country observations over the period 1986–1994. There are thirty-six countries, in addition to the United States, for which we have at least one year of complete data. As just noted, the "inward" data (U.S. affiliates of foreign parents) only list total exports of the affiliates to all countries. The "outward" data (foreign affiliates of U.S. parents) break down exports of those affiliates into exports back to the United States and exports to third countries. The latter series is particularly valuable, but constrains the analysis to a subarea of the Edgeworth box in which the parent country (the United States) is always very large relative to the host.

11.3 Results

Tables 11.1–11.3 show results for regression equations on the full inward-outward data set. Table 11.1 gives results for dependent variable *RSALESL* (local sales in country j of affiliates of country i firms). Signs are as predicted for direct effects although the two variables involving *SKDIFF* are not statistically significant. Country size, investment costs, and trade costs into the host-country market have strong explanatory power. Trade costs back into the parent country (*TCI*) have little explanatory power, and theory does not hypothesize that they should.

Table 11.2 gives results for dependent variable *RSALESE* (export sales to all countries by affiliates of country i firms in country j). Signs are as hypothesized except for *TCI*, which should be negative, at least for exports going back to the home countries (these cannot be broken out in the data as noted above). The two terms involving *SKDIFF* are both larger in magnitude (economic significance) than in the *RSALESL* regression, and highly statistically significant. The magnitude of the *SUMGDP* coefficient on the other hand is much smaller in the *RSAL-ESE* regression. These results suggest that market size is a more important determinant of production for local sales while differences in

Table 11.1
Results for real sales of affiliates, inward and outward data (dependent variable: local sales of foreign affiliates (*RSALESL*))

Variable	WLS estimate (*t* stat)	Sign as predicted? (marginal significance)
SUMGDP	10.2937 (9.108)	Yes (0.0001)
GDPDIFSQ	−0.0009 (−7.163)	Yes (0.0001)
SKDIFF	10531 (0.877)	Yes (0.3813)
GDPDIFF*SKDIFF	−2.6932 (−1.114)	Yes (0.2658)
INVCJ	−633.397 (−7.119)	Yes (0.0001)
TCJ	366.5574 (6.142)	Yes (0.0001)
TCI	−22.0996 (−0.195)	? (0.8451)
DIST	−1.5326 (−9.293)	? (0.0001)
INTERCEPT	469.216 (0.046)	(0.9631)
Observations	381	
Adjusted R^2	0.722	

Notes: WLS is weighted least squares. Numbers in parentheses below coefficients are *t* statistics. Marginal significance levels of the coefficients are indicated in parentheses below sign predictions.

relative endowments is a more important determinant of production for export.

These comparisons can be misleading, however, due to differences in the size of the dependent variables (local sales are larger than export sales in most observations). Table 11.3 therefore uses the ratio of export sales to local sales. Results confirm that market size is more important for local sales (coefficient on *SUMGDP* is negative) and that skill differences are more important for export sales (coefficient on *SKDIFF* is positive); thus the proportion of export sales increases as host country *j* becomes more unskilled-labor-abundant (skilled-labor-scarce).

Table 11.2
Results for real sales of affiliates, inward and outward data (dependent variable: export sales of foreign affiliates (*RSALESE*))

Variable	WLS estimate (*t* stat)	Sign as predicted? (marginal significance)
SUMGDP	2.9274 (3.971)	Yes (0.0001)
GDPDIFSQ	−0.0003 (−3.504)	Yes (0.0005)
SKDIFF	42961 (5.523)	Yes (0.0001)
GDPDIFF*SKDIFF	−6.952 (−4.434)	Yes (0.0001)
INVCJ	−277.2284 (−4.758)	Yes (0.0001)
TCJ	52.1164 (1.332)	? (0.1836)
TCI	65.6274 (0.892)	No (0.3729)
DIST	−0.6398 (−5.927)	? (0.0001)
INTERCEPT	7501.9364 (1.127)	(0.2604)
Observations	381	
Adjusted R^2	0.473	

The coefficients on the *INVCJ* and *TCJ* variables in the ratio equation of tables 11.3 are negative. This conforms to our intuition about substitutability. Production for local sale, by definition, cannot move to a third country, and thus local sales may be relatively insensitive to these costs. Production for export sale may be more sensitive to investment and trade costs because the firm can choose an alternative location to serve a broader market, as suggested by the negative signs in the ratio equation. *TCI* is positive in this regression, which is consistent with the results in tables 11.1 and 11.2. This outcome is not consistent with my theoretical intuition, but note that the significance level is low. Higher parent-country trade costs should discourage foreign production for export back to the parent but should not affect production for local sale.

Table 11.3
Results for real sales of affiliates, inward and outward data (dependent variable: ratio of export to local sales (*RATIOEL*))

Variable	WLS estimate (*t* stat)	Sign as predicted? (marginal significance)
SUMGDP	−0.000618 (−4.327)	Yes (0.0001)
GDPDIFSQ	−1.92E −08 (−1.209)	Yes (0.2273)
SKDIFF	3.175373 (3.121)	Yes (0.0019)
*GDPDIFF*SKDIFF*	−0.000043 (−0.173)	? (0.863)
INVCJ	−0.043374 (−3.491)	Yes (0.0005)
TCJ	−0.010975 (−1.261)	Yes (0.2082)
TCI	0.014789 (1.094)	No (0.2749)
DIST	0.000055 (2.446)	? (0.0149)
INTERCEPT	6.100586 (4.222)	(0.0001)
Observations	371	
Adjusted R^2	0.319	

Tables 11.4–11.8 present results on the U.S.-outward-only sample, allowing a breakdown of production for export sale into sales back to the United States (*RSALESUS* in table 11.5) and sales to third countries (*RSALESF* in table 11.6). TCI is dropped because it is the same for all observations, and I just use *GDPJ* instead of *SUMGDP*. The most dramatic change in these results relative to tables 11.1–11.3 is the reversal in the signs of *SKDIFF* and *GDPDIFF* * *SKDIFF*. This suggests that U.S.-outward investment is attracted to more skilled-labor-abundant countries both for local production and production for export with strong statistical significance. The latter result is particularly at odds with the two-way results.

Two possible explanations exist, other than just concluding that inward and outward investments follow different models. First, there is

Table 11.4
Results for real sales of affiliates, U.S. outward only (dependent variable: local sales of foreign affiliates (*RSALESL*))

Variable	WLS estimate (*t* stat)	Sign as predicted? (marginal significance)
GDPJ	20.842281 (10.362)	Yes (0.0001)
GDPDIFSQ	−0.00177 (−8.12)	Yes (0.0001)
SKDIFF	−948636 (−11.98)	? (0.0001)
GDPDIFF*SKDIFF	174.58183 (11.905)	? (0.0001)
INVCJ	−517.805597 (−6.546)	Yes (0.0001)
TCJ	314.809228 (5.943)	Yes (0.0001)
DIST	−1.204365 (−7.81)	? (0.0001)
INTERCEPT	73798 (9.863)	(0.0001)
Observations	274	
Adjusted R^2	0.766	

a "compensated" versus "uncompensated" issue. In the U.S.-outward-only data, an increase in *SKDIFF* holds U.S. skilled-labor abundance constant, effectively lowering "world" skilled-labor abundance. This is a somewhat different experiment than that in the two-way data, which includes both such uncompensated observations across different countries, and also a great many "compensated" observation pairs comparing *i*-to-*j* and *j*-to-*i* affiliate production. The response of affiliate production to an increase in host-country skilled-labor abundance (decrease in *SKDIFF*) should be more positive or less negative than if this change is accompanied by a fall in the parent country skilled-labor abundance, and that is what the results tell me.

The second possible explanation relates to the fact that the parent country (the United States) is always much larger than the host in the U.S.-outward data. How this might affect the results is shown most clearly in figure 11.1. When country *i* is quite large relative to country *j*, a (compensated) increase in *SKDIFF* may produce a fall in *RSALESL*:

Table 11.5
Results for real sales of affiliates, U.S. outward only (dependent variable: export sales back to the United States (*RSALESUS*))

Variable	WLS estimate (*t* stat)	Sign as predicted? (marginal significance)
GDPJ	2.195608 (1.445)	Yes (0.1499)
GDPDIFSQ	−0.000218 (−1.332)	Yes (0.1843)
SKDIFF	−177143 (−3.049)	No (0.0026)
GDPDIFF*SKDIFF	33.436762 (3.088)	? (0.0023)
INVCJ	−346.635058 (−5.722)	Yes (0.0001)
TCJ	207.579317 (5.141)	No (0.0001)
DIST	−0.796764 (−6.635)	? (0.0001)
INTERCEPT	20469 (3.616)	(0.0004)
Observations	244	
Adjusted R^2	0.3364	

Heading toward the north edge of the box, one goes over the "hump" and *RSALESL* starts to fall. What is happening in the theoretical model is that host country *j* is becoming sufficiently skilled-labor-scarce such that branch plants there are closed and production is concentrated in national firms headquartered in country *i*. This implies a negative sign on *SKDIFF*, which is the result I get in tables 11.4, 11.5, and 11.6. This finding is in fact consistent with results in chapter 9 and in Zhang and Markusen (1999), which show that the smallest, poorest (skilled-labor-scarce) countries receive a far smaller share of world direct investment than their share of income. These results and associated theory also point out the importance of knowing which part of the box is being examined. Adding more investing countries, as in the two-way sample, allows for a wider range of points over the box.

Table 11.7 shows results for the ratio of affiliate export sales back to the United States to affiliate sales to the local market, and table 11.8 shows results for the ratio of affiliate sales to third markets to affili-

Table 11.6
Results for real sales of affiliates, U.S. outward only (dependent variable: export sales to third countries ($RSALESF$))

Variable	WLS estimate (t stat)	Sign as predicted? (marginal significance)
$GDPJ$	6.894688 (5.69)	Yes (0.0001)
$GDPDIFSQ$	−0.000611 (−4.615)	Yes (0.0001)
$SKDIFF$	−237383 (−4.803)	No (0.0001)
$GDPDIFF*SKDIFF$	44.790718 (4.86)	? (0.0001)
$INVCJ$	−211.320793 (−4.541)	Yes (0.0001)
TCJ	−8.644919 (−0.279)	Yes (0.7805)
$DIST$	−0.270793 (−3.001)	? (0.003)
$INTERCEPT$	29941 (6.715)	(0.0001)
Observations	259	
Adjusted R^2	0.5848	

ate sales to the local market. Results on market size confirm those in table 11.3 (negative sign on $GDPJ$): that a larger market shifts a proportion of sales from exports to local sales. The findings also confirm the two-way results on $INVCJ$ and TCJ. The results on $SKDIFF$ and $GDPDIFF * SKDIFF$ are reversed; however, these point estimates have extremely low statistical significance in table 11.7, while the positive sign on $SKDIFF$ in table 11.3 is highly significant. Both coefficients are statistically significant in table 11.8. Thus the results suggest that U.S.-outward investment is not attracted to low-skilled countries, even investment for production for export back to the United States (table 11.5).

Results on market size and relative endowments must be interpreted carefully since GDP appears in three terms and relative endowments in two terms. Write the first four terms of the regression equation as

$$\beta_1 SUMGDP + \beta_2 GDPDIFSQ + \beta_3 SKDIFF + \beta_4 GDPDIFF * SKDIFF. \quad (1)$$

Table 11.7
Results for real sales of affiliates, U.S. outward only (dependent variable: ratio of exports back to the United States to local sales ($RATIOUSL$))

Variable	WLS estimate (t stat)	Sign as predicted? (marginal significance)
GDPJ	−0.000693 (−3.708)	Yes (0.0003)
GDPDIFSQ	−4.12E−08 (−2.134)	Yes (0.034)
SKDIFF	2.364984 (0.391)	Yes (0.6963)
GDPDIFF*SKDIFF	−0.000186 (−0.165)	? (0.8689)
INVCJ	−0.019319 (−2.831)	Yes (0.0051)
TCJ	−0.004806 (−0.959)	Yes (0.3387)
DIST	0.0000869 (6.225)	? (0.0001)
INTERCEPT	1.947083 (2.925)	(0.0038)
Observations	231	
Adjusted R^2	0.3919	

The derivatives of this equation with respect to host-country variables GDPJ and SKLJ are then as follows (an increase in $GDPJ$ is a negative change in $GDPDIFF$, and an increase in $SKLJ$ is a negative change in $SKDIFF$):

$$\frac{\partial RSALES}{\partial GDPJ} = \beta_1 - 2\beta_2 GDPDIFF - \beta_4 SKDIFF \tag{2}$$

$$\frac{\partial RSALES}{\partial SKLJ} = -\beta_3 - \beta_4 GDPDIFF \tag{3}$$

Table 11.9 computes values of these derivatives at the mean values of SKDIFF and GDPDIFF for the two samples. Table 11.9 gives the absolute change in sales by country i affiliates in j in response to a growth in country j's income and to an increase in country j's skilled-labor abundance (decrease in its unskilled-labor abundance). Effects of increases in country j's investment and trade-cost indices are also listed.

Table 11.8
Results for real sales of affiliates, U.S. outward only (dependent variable: ratio of exports back to third countries to local sales ($RATIOFL$))

Variable	WLS estimate (t stat)	Sign as predicted? (marginal significance)
$GDPJ$	−0.001291 (−3.881)	Yes (0.0001)
$GDPDIFSQ$	−2.36E−08 (−0.683)	Yes (0.4953)
$SKDIFF$	29.904477 (2.63)	Yes (0.0091)
$GDPDIFF*SKDIFF$	−0.005218 (−2.467)	? (0.0144)
$INVCJ$	−0.045391 (−3.517)	Yes (0.0005)
TCJ	−0.003751 (−0.403)	Yes (0.6876)
$DIST$	−0.000026 (−0.841)	? (0.4014)
$INTERCEPT$	3.913419 (3.33)	(0.001)
Observations	236	
Adjusted R^2	0.32	

The top panel gives results for the inward-outward estimation, while the lower panel gives estimates for the U.S.-outward estimation only. Below the level estimates, an elasticity figure is computed. I do not compute elasticities with respect to $INVCJ$ and TCJ, since these are "qualitative" indices.

According to results in the top panel of table 11.9, local sales are elastic with respect to host-country income with an elasticity of $\varepsilon = 1.6$. Export sales are less elastic, at $\varepsilon = 1.1$. Local sales are very insensitive to the skilled-labor ratio in the host country, while export sales have an elasticity with respect to the skilled-labor ratio of $\varepsilon = -.7$. Production for export sales is attracted to less skilled-labor-abundant (more skilled-labor-scarce) countries. Comparing local sales versus export sales, the former respond more to income and export sales respond more to skilled-labor scarcity as suggested by the regression results discussed earlier.

Table 11.9
Effects of host-country size and skilled-labor abundance on foreign affiliate production for local sale and export (derivatives evaluated at the mean of independent variables)

Effect on	$1 billion increase in country j's GDP	One-percentage-point increase in SKLJ*	One-point increase in INVCJ	One-point increase in TCJ
Local sales of country i affiliates in country j (inward and outward data)	$16.7 million $\varepsilon = 1.558$**	−$12.1 million $\varepsilon = -0.017$	−$633.4 million	$366.6 million
Export sales of country i affiliates in j to all countries (inward and outward data)	$4.7 million $\varepsilon = 1.118$	−$189.0 million $\varepsilon = -0.681$	−$277.2 million	$52.1 million
Local sales of U.S. affiliates in country j (U.S. outward data only)	$22.7 million $\varepsilon = 1.044$	$280.5 million $\varepsilon = 0.599$	−$517.8 million	$314.8 million
Export sales of U.S. affiliates in j to the United States (U.S. outward data only)	$1.3 million $\varepsilon = 0.213$ $\Big\}\ \varepsilon_W = 0.681$	$8.3 million $\varepsilon = 0.064$ $\Big\}\ \varepsilon_W = 0.062$	−$346.6 million	$207.6 million
Export sales of U.S. affiliates in j to other countries (U.S. outward data only)	$9.0 million $\varepsilon = 0.989$	$12.0 million $\varepsilon = 0.061$	−211.3 million	−$8.6 million

* A one-percentage-point increase in SKLJ indicates, for example, an increase from 15 percent to 16 percent, not an increase from 15 percent to 15.15 percent.
** ε denotes elasticity.

The pattern for the U.S.-outward-only data (lower panel of table 11.9) is qualitatively similar to the top panel but quantitatively different. Production for local sale has an elasticity with respect to local market size of about 1.0, while the elasticities of exports back to the United States and to third countries are 0.2 and 1.0, respectively. A weighted average of these two elasticities (ε_w) yields a figure of 0.68. Thus the elasticity of exports with respect to host-country size is less than that for local sales by an amount similar to the two-way estimates. The elasticity of local sales with respect to the host-country skilled-labor ratio is about 0.6, while the average of the two export elasticities is 0.06. Production for export back to the United States or to third countries is insensitive to the host-country skilled-labor ratio, at least at the mean of *GDPDIFF*. Again, the pattern is qualitatively similar to that for the two-way estimate in that the export elasticity with respect to local skilled labor is smaller than that for local sales (i.e., less positive or more negative).

Overall, the results in table 11.9, taking into account interactive effects, clearly confirm that production for local sales is more sensitive to local market size than is production for export. Production for local sales has an elasticity with respect to the host-country skilled-labor ratio that is larger (less negative or more positive) than the elasticity for production for export. Production shifts relatively in favor of local sales when the host is more skilled-labor-abundant and relatively in favor of exports when the host is skilled-labor-scarce.

There is an interesting quantitative difference between the two-way and U.S.-outward estimates of the elasticities with respect to the host-country skilled-labor ratio (subject again to the caveats that these are point estimates, evaluated at the mean of *GDPDIFF* in each sample, and the means differ in the two samples). While production for export is attracted by host-country unskilled-labor abundance in the two-way sample, there is virtually no effect in the U.S.-outward sample. One might infer from this that production by U.S. affiliates for export, including that back to the United States, is not primarily attracted to low-skilled countries, contrary to a popular impression of multinationals exporting jobs to low-wage countries. While this may occur in arm's-length outsourcing (e.g., subcontracting), my results suggest that it is not primarily multinationals that are responsible for such a phenomenon if it indeed exists. As I noted earlier, this is consistent with the theoretical assumption that branch-plant production is skilled-labor-intensive relative to the rest of the host economy. Past a certain level of skilled-labor scarcity in the host economy, inward direct investment begins to fall as that country becomes increasingly skilled-labor-scarce (chapter 9; Zhang and Markusen 1999).

11.4   Summary and Conclusions

Part I of this book develops theoretical work that endogenizes multinational firms into general-equilibrium trade models. Part II of the book demonstrates how the models offer predictions about the relationship between affiliate production and parent-country and host-country characteristics. In particular, the knowledge-capital approach to the multinational enterprise identifies motives for both horizontal and vertical multinational activity and predicts how affiliate activity should be related to variables such as country sizes and relative-endowment differences.

This chapter draws implications from the theory as to how production for local sales versus production for export sales relates to country characteristics, then subjects these hypotheses to empirical estimation. Results fit well with the theory in terms of economic and statistical significance. Local (host-country) market size is more important for production for local sales than for production for export sales. Host-country skilled-labor scarcity is important for export production relative to production for local sales. Investment cost barriers in the host country affect production for export more negatively than production for local sales.

Some quantitative difference was found in the two-way (inward and outward) sample versus the U.S.-outward-only sample with respect to host-country skilled-labor abundance or scarcity. In the U.S.-outward-only sample, host-country skilled-labor scarcity (unskilled-labor abundance) had little effect on U.S. affiliate production for export sale, whether back to the United States or to third countries. This suggests that U.S.-outward investment is not primarily drawn to unskilled-labor-abundant countries, contrary to a common fear that "outsourcing" by multinationals is resulting in a loss of U.S. unskilled jobs. (Firms could of course be outsourcing to unaffiliated subcontractors.) In the two-way sample, production for exports is drawn to unskilled-labor-abundant countries. However, the results are qualitatively similar in the two samples insofar as unskilled-labor abundance in the host is *relatively* more important for export sales.

12

Discriminating among Alternative Models of the Multinational

12.1 Introduction

One basic distinction in the theory of the multinational that has been repeatedly emphasized in this book is that between "vertical" and "horizontal" firms. Vertical MNEs are firms that geographically fragment production into stages, typically on the basis of factor intensities, locating skilled-labor-intensive activities in skilled-labor-abundant countries and so forth. Early general-equilibrium treatments of vertical firms include Helpman (1984) and Helpman and Krugman (1985). Horizontal MNEs are multiplant firms that replicate roughly the same activities in many locations. General-equilibrium models of horizontal firms include Markusen (1984), Horstmann and Markusen (1987a, 1992), and Markusen and Venables (1998, 2000).

Throughout the 1980s and much of the 1990s, these two strains of literature remained relatively disjointed, in large part due to technical difficulties. Early papers by Helpman and Helpman-Krugman relied on zero trade costs to produce analytical solutions. But under this assumption, there is no role for horizontal multiplant firms given plant-level scale economies. Papers in the Horstmann-Markusen-Venables tradition typically assumed that there is only one factor used in the MNEs sector, or that different activities (e.g., headquarters and plant) use factors in the same proportion. But under these assumptions, little motivation exists for fragmenting production by stages.

The knowledge-capital model put forward in this book is an attempt to integrate both of these alternative theories, allowing firms the options of having multiple plants or geographically separating a headquarters and single plant. As I have indicated, the hybrid knowledge-capital model seems to get good empirical support. Yet this empirical work does not give us an idea if, in some well-defined sense, the horizontal or vertical formulation is more important or better explains the data. A difficulty with these estimations and indeed a chronic difficulty in empirical work in general is that there is no explicit alternative hypothesis (H1) to the model being estimated. Indeed, authors are generally cautious about referring to "testing" the theory.

This chapter, therefore, attempts an explicit comparison of the knowledge-capital model (henceforth KK) against a restricted horizontal version (henceforth HOR) and a restricted vertical version (henceforth VER). I review the basic theory briefly, and note how each model offers predictions about foreign affiliate production of multinational firms as a function of parent- and host-country characteristics. The HOR and VER models are then nested within an unrestricted KK model and estimated.

Results of this exercise decisively reject the restrictions of the vertical model (VER). Depending upon the specification, the data cannot distinguish between the KK and HOR models. The formal results thus accord well with casual empiricism, which notes that the overwhelming proportion of world direct investment is from high-income developed countries to other similar high-income developed countries.

This does not imply that vertical activity is unimportant for many host countries and in some industries. One reader aptly described what Maskus and I did in Markusen and Maskus (2002) as running a "horserace," trying to see what best explains aggregate world direct investment. Concluding that the vertical model decisively loses the horserace relative to the KK and HOR models does not imply that the vertical activity is nonexistent or unimportant.

12.2   Nesting the HOR and VER Models within an Unrestricted KK Model

Consider the same two-good, two-factor, two-country general-equilibrium model that I have used beginning in chapter 7. For the X sector, the KK model makes three assumptions about technology and costs:

1. There are firm-level as well as plant-level scale economies.

2. Single plant firms may geographically separate plant and headquarters.

3. Headquarters and plants have different factor intensities.

The KK model makes these three assumptions and a more explicit assumption about factor intensities:

KK model

(KK1)   There are firm-level as well as plant-level scale economies.

(KK2)   A single-plant firm may geographically separate headquarters and plant.

(KK3)   Firm-level fixed costs are skilled-labor-intensive relative to plant-level fixed costs and the marginal costs of production.

Specify a horizontal model following chapter 5 and 6 by using the first of these assumptions, but substituting more restrictive assumptions in place of the second and third. By the horizontal (HOR) model, I therefore am referring to the following:

HOR model

(KK1)   There are firm-level as well as plant-level scale economies.

(HOR2) A single-plant firm may *not* geographically separate headquarters and plant.

(HOR3) Firm-level fixed costs, plant-level fixed costs, and the marginal costs of production all use factors in the *same proportion*.

A vertical model is one which there is no motive for horizontal expansion, but which retains the motive for vertical expansion across borders. This is easily done as follows.

VER model

(VER1)   There are *no* firm-level scale economies.

(KK2)   A single-plant firm may geographically separate headquarters and plant.

(KK3)   Firm-level fixed costs are skilled-labor-intensive relative to plant-level fixed costs and the marginal costs of production.

Referring to the definitions in chapter 7, I observe the VER model assumes *fragmentation*, but not *jointness*. The HOR model assumes jointness, but assumes that one plant must be located in the same country as the headquarters. This assumes that fragmentation as defined in chapter 7 does not hold for a single plant. This might be due, perhaps, to the need for feedback and critical revision between the R&D and management personnel in the headquarters and the managers and workers in a nearby plant. One plant needs to be near the headquarters, but then learning from the local plant can be easily transferred abroad.

I should note that the restriction HOR3 above, that all X-sector activities use factors in the same proportions, largely rules out vertical firms arising in equilibrium but not entirely. That is why I have to impose HOR2 as an additional restriction. The intuition is as follows. Suppose that country j is much larger than i, but country i has a slightly lower price for skilled labor, the factor used intensively in the X sector for all fixed and marginal costs. A single-plant firm may want to locate its headquarters in country i for factor-price reasons. But the factor-price and market-size motive conflict for its single plant. If the size difference is sufficiently large relative to the factor-price difference, it may want its single-plant in country j. Thus assumption HOR3 alone is not sufficient to completely rule out type-v firms arising in equilibrium, and a stronger assumption about the prohibitive cost of separating a single plant and headquarters must be made.

What then does theory tell us about the relationship between multinational activity and country characteristics? In the VER model with no firm-level scale economies and no motive for horizontal firms, multinational activity is driven entirely by differences in factor endowments. Type-v firms will be important when countries differ in relative endowments. To make the point directly, multinationals will never exist between identical countries (Helpman 1984).

In the HOR model, one gets more or less the opposite result. MNEs will be most important between similar countries, provided of course that there are positive trade costs. MNEs will be less important as the countries differ in size or in relative endowments (Markusen and Venables 1998, 2000). The intuition here is that when countries differ significantly, one will be a "favored" country as a headquarters for single-plant national firms, either because of a large domestic market (a type-h firm must locate costly capacity in a small market) and/or factor-price differences.

In the KK model, MNEs can exist both when the countries are similar (type-h firms), or different in relative endowments, particularly if the skilled-labor-abundant country is small. In the latter case, the headquarters should be located in the skilled-labor-abundant country and the plant in the large, skilled-labor-scarce country both for a factor-price motive and for a market-size motive (Markusen 1997). These results are summarized as follows:

KK model

1. Both type-h and type-v multinationals can exist.

2. Multinationals are important when countries are similar in size and in relative endowments, and trade costs are moderate to high (type-h multinationals).

3. Multinationals are important when countries differ in relative endowments, particularly if the skilled-labor-abundant country is small.

VER model

1. Only type-v multinationals can exist.

2. Multinationals are important when countries differ in relative endowments.

3. Multinationals do not arise between identical countries.

HOR model

1. Only type-h multinationals can exist.

2. Multinationals are important when countries are similar in size and in relative endowments, and trade costs are moderate to high.

Figures 12.1–12.6 depict simulation results for the three models. The diagrams are once again the world Edgeworth box, with the world endowment of skilled labor on one axis of the base and unskilled labor on the other. The vertical axis measures the real volume of affiliate production.

Figures 12.1–12.3 show total two-way affiliate activity, whereas figures 12.4–12.6 show only the one-way activity of production by affiliates of country-i firms in country j. Figures 12.1 and 12.4 show the unrestricted KK model familiar from the previous two chapters as well as from chapters 7 and 8. Figures 12.2 and 12.5 show the HOR model, assuming that type-v firms cannot enter and that S and L are used in the same proportion in fixed and variable costs. Figures 12.3 and 12.6 give the results for the VER model, raising the fixed costs for type-h firms until they are double the fixed costs for type-d firms (eliminating the jointness property).

Figures 12.1 and 12.4 use the calibration of table 7.1 exactly except that I now assume that foreign branch plants require only three units of local skilled labor instead of four, thus lowering "technology transfer" costs a bit to give vertical firms a bigger role. Figures 12.2 and

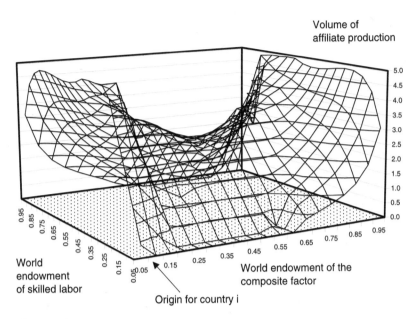

Figure 12.1
Volume of affiliate production, KK model

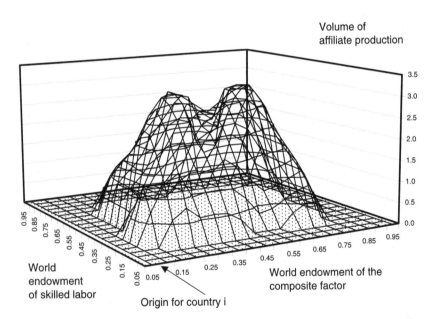

Figure 12.2
Volume of affiliate production, HOR model

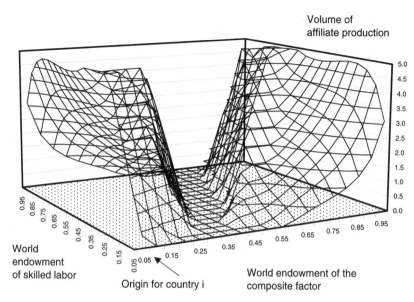

Figure 12.3
Volume of affiliate production, VER model

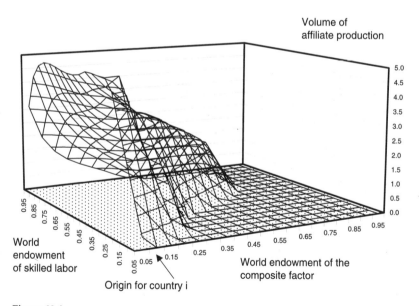

Figure 12.4
Affiliate production by country-*i*-owned plants in country *j*, KK model

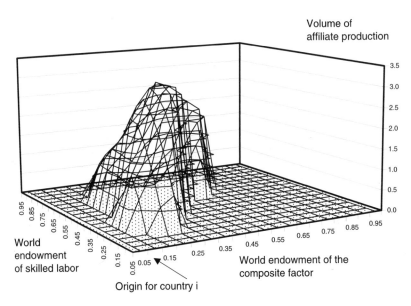

Figure 12.5
Affiliate production by country-*i*-owned plants in country *j*, HOR model

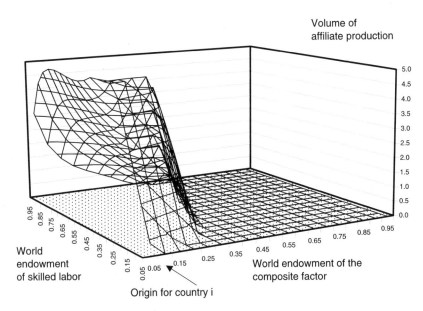

Figure 12.6
Affiliate production by country-*i*-owned plants in country *j*, VER model

12.5 use this same calibration except factor proportions in the sector activities are adjusted to be the same for fixed and variables costs, and then the total factor endowment of each country is adjusted to compensate for this so that all other variables (prices, quantities, numbers of type-h_i and type-h_j firms) take on their same values at the center of the box. Type-v firms are not permitted. Figures 12.3 and 12.6 use the same calibration except that the fixed costs for type-h firms are raised from 20 at the center of the box (where $z = w$) to 26, exactly twice the fixed costs of type-d firms.

The KK and HOR models both show an inverted U-shaped curve along the SW-NE diagonal. Type-h multinationals exist between countries with identical relative endowments, and affiliate production is maximized when the countries are identical. In the VER model, there is essentially no multinational activity along the SW-NE diagonal, and no role for country size or size difference (size ratio) independent of relative endowment differences (i.e., no multinational activity when relative endowments are identical).

Away from the SW-NE diagonal, it is the KK and VER models that are more similar to each other than to the HOR model. In the latter model, type-h firms become disadvantaged when they have to hire costly skilled labor in the skilled-labor-scarce country. Vertical firms on the other hand are encouraged to enter in both the KK and the VER model as relative endowment differences increase. For both the KK and VER models, affiliate activity is highest when one country is small and skilled-labor-abundant. But that is a region where there is very little or no activity in the HOR model.

There are clearly nonlinearities and nonmonotonicities in these results. But some clear ideas emerge. First, in the KK and HOR models there is a role for total income and size differences independent of relative endowment differences (i.e., the SW-NE diagonal). The VER model, on the other hand, gives almost no role for total income and size differences when the countries have identical relative endowments.

The VER model suggests that total income should only have a role when interacting with relative endowment differences. Affiliate activity by country i headquartered firms in country j should be large only when country i is skilled-labor-abundant. Thus there should be a positive sign on an interaction term between skilled-labor abundance and total income. Experiments with the HOR model tend to suggest the opposite, that an increase in total income has a weaker influence on total affiliate production when countries differ in relative endowments, regardless of whether the parent country is the skilled-labor-abundant or skilled-labor-scarce country.

That leaves it somewhat ambiguous as to whether an interaction between skilled-labor abundance and total income should be positive or negative in the KK model. In part, it depends on the level of trade costs. The lower are trade costs, the more that there is going to be a conversion to type-h firms as income grows between similar countries. When trade costs are low to moderate, one predicts that growth in income has a stronger effect between countries with similar endowments for the KK model, which is similar in that respect to the HOR model rather than the VER model. When trade costs are high, growth in total income should lift the whole surface in figure 12.4, so that the effect on affiliate production is roughly the same regardless of whether or not country i is skilled-labor abundant.

An interaction effect between size difference and skilled-labor abundance is predicted by both the VER and KK models, but not by the HOR model. In the former two cases, outward affiliate activity should be high when the country is both small and skilled-labor abundant.

To summarize the simulation results in figures 12.1–12.6, the KK and HOR models predict an important role for total two-country income and the difference in income independent of relative endowment differences, while the VER model predicts no such independent role. The KK and VER models predict a positive interaction between skilled-labor abundance and a small size (or rather a negative interaction between skilled-labor abundance and size) while the HOR model does not. The VER model predicts a positive interaction between skilled-labor abundance and total income, while the HOR model does not. There is some ambiguity with respect to this interaction for the KK model, but at least for low to moderate trade costs it should follow the prediction of the HOR model.

12.3   Estimation and Results

The basic data set is the same as that used in chapter 10. However, I have had to define variables somewhat differently in order to nest the HOR and VER models as restricted versions of the KK model. The estimating equation of chapter 10 remains my first choice for estimating the KK model. But testing the restrictions implied by the HOR and VER models requires me to use a somewhat different (and less preferred) specification.

Table 12.1 gives the estimating equation for the unrestricted KK model and the two restricted models. Variable definitions are given at the bottom of table 12.1. In all regressions, the dependent variable is real affiliate sales of firms headquartered in country i and producing in country j. The $D1$ and $D2$ variables are dummies, taking values depending on whether country i is skilled-labor-abundant relative to country j. $D1$ is negative if country i is skilled-labor-scarce and zero otherwise; D2 is positive if country i is skilled-labor-abundant and zero otherwise.

The first two variables in the estimating equation for KK, $SUMGDP$, and $GDPDIFSQ$ capture the inverted U-shaped relationship along the SW-NE diagonal of the Edgeworth box in figure 12.4. $SUMGDP$ is predicted to be positive and $GDPDIFSQ$ negative for the KK and HOR models, but zero in the VER model. As noted earlier, economic size and size differences have no role in the VER model independent of factor-endowment differences.

The dummy variables $D1$ and $D2$ are designed to capture the results of figures 12.4–12.6 that predictions depend very much on whether the parent country is the skilled-labor-abundant or skilled-labor-scarce country. Variable $D1$ is nonzero if the parent is skilled-labor-*scarce*, and D2 is nonzero if the parent is skilled-labor *abundant* relative to the host.

The complicated variable $D2 * SKDGDPD$ is designed to capture the interaction between being skilled-labor abundant and small that I discussed in connection with the KK and VER models. This variable is predicted to have a negative sign in the KK and VER models (i.e., being small and skilled-labor-abundant increases outward investment) but be zero in the HOR model.

$D2 * SKDSUMG$ is an interaction term between factor abundance and the total size of the "world" economy. This term is positive if the parent is skilled-labor-abundant and zero otherwise. This is the "core variable" in the VER model, figure 12.6. For a given $SUMGDP$, outward investment is increasing in the parent country's skilled-labor abundance, and for a given $SKDIFF$, outward investment is increasing in the total GDP. This variable should have a positive sign in the VER model but a negative sign in the HOR model (figure 12.5). The sign is somewhat ambiguous in the KK model, but my prediction of a negative sign follows the earlier reasoning.

$D1 * SKDSUMG$ is positive if the parent country is skilled-labor-scarce. This term is hypothesized to be negative in all three models.

Table 12.1
Theoretical predictions for three models (i = parent, j = host)

Variable	KK	HOR	VER
SUMGDP	+	+	0
GDPDIFSQ	—	—	0
D2*SKDGDPD	—	0	—
D2*SKDSUMG	—	—	+
D1*SKDSUMG	—	—	—
DISTANCE	?	?	?
INVCJ	—	—	—
TCJ	+	+	+
TCI	—	—	—
SUMGDP	$= GPD_i + GDP_j$		
GDPDIFF	$= (GDP_i - GDP_j)$		
GDPDIFSQ	$= (GDP_i - GDP_j)^2$		
SKDGDPD	$= SKDIFF*GDPDIFF = (SK_i - SK_j)*GDPDIFF$		
SKDSUMG	$= SKDIFF*SUMGDP = (SK_i - SK_j)*SUMGDP$		
D1	$= -1$ if $SKDIFF = SK_i - SK_j < 0$		
	$= 0$ if $SKDIFF = SK_i - SK_j > 0$		
D2	$= 1$ if $SKDIFF = SK_i - SK_j > 0$		
	$= 0$ if $SKDIFF = SK_i - SK_j < 0$		

Notes: D2 is nonzero if the parent country is skilled-labor-abundant, and D1 is nonzero if the host country is skilled-labor-abundant.

Outward investment should be smaller (in fact generally zero) when the parent country is skilled-labor-scarce.

The first control variable (in table 12.1) is distance. Theory does not give a clear prediction as to its sign, since distance increases the costs of both trade (suggesting a substitution toward investment) but also increases the cost of investment. The second variable is the host-country's investment cost index as discussed in chapters 10 and 11; since higher numbers indicate higher costs, this variable is predicted to be negative in all three regressions. TCJ is the host-country's trade cost index and this is expected to be positive, with higher host-country trade costs encouraging inward investment. TCI is the parent-country's trade cost index and this is expected to be negative; it raises the costs of shipping goods back to the parent from a branch plant, although this should not be important in the case of outward horizontal investment.

12.4 Results

Tables 12.2–12.5 present estimation results. In all cases, the dependent variable is production in country j by affiliates of country i parents. Variables listed as zeros in table 12.1 are omitted from the regressions. Tables 12.2 and 12.3 use only distance among the control variables. An initial econometric concern is heteroskedasticity across observations because country sizes are quite different. Thus, I employ in table 12.2 a WLS estimation, where the weights are developed from regressions of first-stage ordinary-least-squares (OLS) residuals on linear functions of *SUMGDP* or square roots of such linear functions. In the WLS regressions, I exclude cases where data on local sales are missing, yielding 509 observations. The first pair of columns in table 12.2 contains results for the WLS version of the unrestricted KK model. This model explains 60 percent of the variation in weighted sales, and all of the coefficients are highly significant, with the expected signs, except that of *D2SKDGDPD*, which is not significant.

As may be seen from the second pair of columns, restricting the coefficient on *D2SKDGDPD* to be zero in the HOR model results in no decline in the adjusted R^2. The remaining coefficients in HOR are close to those in KK. Indeed, the F-test in HOR cannot reject the zero restriction on *D2SKDGDPD*, as shown at the bottom of the table. The negative sign on this F-test stems from the fact that the dependent variables in the two WLS specifications bear different weights, so that the nesting procedure is not, strictly speaking, correct. As indicated in the penultimate row, however, an F-test on the underlying OLS regressions cannot reject HOR relative to KK. In statistical terms, these models are indistinguishable.

The VER model has the right signs on all coefficients, but much lower explanatory power than the KK and HOR models. It is decisively rejected by the F-test for zero restrictions on *SUMGDP* and *GDPDIFSQ*. Indeed, much of the influence of total two-country income is picked up in the intercept, which is large and positive, unlike those in the other regressions. Thus, the VER model, in which economic size and size differences play no independent role in explaining multinational activity, fails to accord with the data.

In the data sample, there are a number of missing observations on local affiliate sales. On inspection these involve potential parent countries that are small and poor and have likely not invested in the United States as discussed in chapter 10. Therefore, a reasonable

Table 12.2
WLS estimation excluding investment and trade costs (509 observations)

Variable	KK WLS estimate (t stat)	KK Sign as predicted? (marginal significance)	HOR WLS estimate (t stat)	HOR Sign as predicted? (marginal significance)	VER WLS estimate (t stat)	VER Sign as predicted? (marginal significance)
SUMGDP	16.241 (11.473)	Yes (0.0001)	16.213 (11.663)	Yes (0.0001)		
GDPDIFSQ	−0.001 (−9.255)	Yes (0.0001)	−0.001 (−9.349)	Yes (0.0001)		
D2SKDGDPD	1.190 (0.365)	No (0.72)			−13.243 (−3.27)	Yes (0.001)
D2SKDSUMG	−8.980 (−2.674)	Yes (0.008)	−7.877 (−4.577)	Yes (0.0001)	5.489 (1.32)	Yes (0.189)
D1SKDSUMG	−13.348 (−5.794)	Yes (0.0001)	−13.228 (−5.779)	Yes (0.0001)	−5.171 (−1.80)	Yes (0.072)
DISTANCE	−1.050 (−5.651)	? (0.0001)	−1.031 (−5.608)	? (0.0001)	−1.668 (−7.09)	? (0.0001)
INTERCEPT	−29670 (−2.810)	(0.005)	−29762 (−2.844)	(0.005)	29947 (13.60)	(0.0001)
Adjusted R^2	0.60		0.60		0.37	
F-Test			−0.65		164.33	
F-Test (OLS)			1.10		448.83	
Critical F 99%			6.65		4.63	

assumption is that these missing values are, in fact, zeroes. In table 12.3 I include these observations with a zero for affiliate production and estimate a Tobit equation on the resulting 722 observations. These results complement the WLS findings. Note that the Tobit coefficients on all variables involving skill differences are considerably larger in magnitude than their WLS counterparts, stemming from the inclusion of more observations from developing nations. Again, in the KK model the coefficient on *D2SKDGDPD* takes the wrong sign and in this case is marginally significant. The likelihood ratio test cannot reject the zero restriction on this variable in the HOR model, again suggesting that KK and HOR are indistinguishable. Finally, note that while the coefficients are correctly signed and significant in VER, implying that skill differences matter importantly for FDI, the model itself is decisively rejected in relation to KK and HOR.

Tables 12.4 and 12.5 repeat the analysis, using all the control variables. The coefficients on *INVCJ* are always significant and have the right sign. Interestingly, those on *TCJ* are positive and significant in the WLS specifications but fall in magnitude and lose significance in the Tobit equations for KK and HOR. On that score, it seems that trade protection loses its attractiveness to FDI in small developing nations in comparison with its effect in developed countries, except in the VER framework. The coefficients on *TCI* always have the right signs as well, although they are generally insignificant.

In terms of the nested testing, results in tables 12.4 and 12.5 are consistent with earlier findings. The HOR model is strongly supported in the WLS regressions in terms of signs and significance of coefficients, and its specification cannot be rejected relative to the KK model at the 99 percent confidence level. It would be rejected at the 95 percent level using the WLS result but would not be so rejected using the OLS F-test. Note, however, that the restriction in HOR is rejected in the Tobit regression in table 12.4. It seems that entering investment costs in the sample that includes more observations from developing countries reduces somewhat the explanatory power of the HOR model relative to KK.

The coefficients have the right signs and strong statistical significance in the VER regressions in tables 12.4 and 12.5, but the zero restrictions of the model are rejected. Note again the reversal in the sign of the intercept term in the VER regression relative to the other two, suggesting that the independent influence of income is being absorbed into the intercept.

Table 12.3
Tobit estimation excluding investment and trade costs (722 observations)

Variable	KK Tobit estimate (χ^2)	KK Sign as predicted? (marginal significance)	HOR Tobit estimate (χ^2)	HOR Sign as predicted? (marginal significance)	VER Tobit estimate (χ^2)	VER Sign as predicted? (marginal significance)
SUMGDP	19.546 (211.201)	Yes (0.0001)	19.108 (208.502)	Yes (0.0001)		
GDPDIFSQ	-0.001 (61.975)	Yes (0.0001)	-0.001 (58.591)	Yes (0.0001)		
D2SKDGDPD	6.762 (3.579)	No (0.059)			-19.661 (19.575)	Yes (0.0001)
D2SKDSUMG	-17.961 (23.995)	Yes (0.0001)	-11.969 (42.446)	Yes (0.0001)	8.006 (3.031)	Yes (0.082)
D1SKDSUMG	-27.824 (165.758)	Yes (0.0001)	-27.486 (163.505)	Yes (0.0001)	-24.826 (82.048)	Yes (0.0001)
DISTANCE	-0.930 (24.410)	? (0.0001)	-0.912 (23.513)	? (0.0001)	-1.003 (16.097)	? (0.0001)
INTERCEPT	-56104 (27.138)	(0.0001)	-55205 (26.337)	(0.005)	26100 (118.556)	(0.0001)
Log Likelihood	-6258		-6260		-6457	
LR Test			4.00		398	
Critical χ^2			7.88		10.6	

12.5 Summary

The econometric results support the KK and HOR models, finding them to be essentially indistinguishable in the data but considerably more descriptive of reality than the VER model in explaining overall world multinational activity. The coefficient estimates in the HOR model have the right signs and are statistically significant, as they are in the KK model with one exception.

These results support what researchers have long believed on the basis of casual empiricism. In particular, direct investment is important between countries that are similar both in size and in relative endowments. It is the "hill" of figure 12.2, rather than the "valley" of figure 12.3, that best describes the world. The VER model clearly should not be taken seriously as a characterization of aggregate multinational activity.

The comparison between the unrestricted KK model and the restricted HOR model is less straightforward. The restriction of the HOR model may be rejected at the 95 percent level when the control variables are included, but overall there is little in the data to distinguish the two models. In this sample, therefore, there do not seem to be strong effects on affiliate sales stemming from the interaction between skilled-labor abundance differences and size differences.

Such impacts are predicted by the KK model and were detected in Carr, Markusen, and Maskus (2001) and in chapter 10. The data are the same in the two, but the estimating equations are different. Carr, Markusen, and Maskus (2001) and chapter 10 use what I consider to be our "ideal" regression equation to estimate the model, without considering an explicit alternative model. In particular, SKDIFF was used as a variable by itself and not interacted with SUMGDP as in this chapter. All the central coefficients had the right sign in chapter 10 and in CMM and were highly significant, indicating an important role for differences in skilled-labor abundance. In this chapter, some compromises to this "ideal" regression equation are made in order to nest the models.

Possibly more relevant, the effect of an increase in *SKDIFF* is complicated because *SKDIFF* appears in two regressors in the KK model. Using the mean values of *GDPDIFF* and *SUMGDP* (which vary with the number of observations), the partial derivatives of the four equations in the KK model with respect to *SKDIFF* are positive for the two Tobit regressions, but negative for the two WLS regressions. For U.S.

Table 12.4
WLS estimation including investment and trade costs (509 observations)

Variable	KK WLS estimate (t stat)	KK Sign as predicted? (marginal significance)	HOR WLS estimate (t stat)	HOR Sign as predicted? (marginal significance)	VER WLS estimate (t stat)	VER Sign as predicted? (marginal significance)
SUMGDP	15.042 (10.352)	Yes (0.0001)	15.001 (10.408)	Yes (0.0001)		
GDPDIFSQ	−0.001 (−9.637)	Yes (0.0001)	−0.001 (−9.594)	Yes (0.0001)		
D2SKDGDPD	5.385 (1.567)	No (0.118)			−7.680 (−1.80)	Yes (0.0729)
D2SKDSUMG	−6.853 (−2.015)	Yes (0.044)	−2.937 (−1.259)	Yes (0.2086)	7.206 (1.72)	Yes (0.0858)
D1SKDSUMG	−12.829 (−5.535)	Yes (0.0001)	−12.534 (−5.441)	Yes (0.0001)	−5.379 (−1.87)	Yes (0.0624)
DISTANCE	−1.309 (−6.548)	? (0.0001)	−1.227 (−6.303)	? (0.0001)	−1.997 (−7.97)	? (0.0001)
INVCJ	−436.630 (−3.500)	Yes (0.0005)	−367.969 (−3.159)	Yes (0.0017)	−552.642 (−3.57)	Yes (0.0004)
TCJ	173.945 (2.215)	Yes (0.0272)	149.962 (1.965)	Yes (0.0499)	285.842 (2.86)	Yes (0.0045)
TCI	−90.693 (−1.121)	Yes (0.2630)	−85.673 (−1.067)	Yes (0.2867)	−43.640 (−0.42)	Yes (0.6716)

INTERCEPT	−7597 (−0.598)	(0.5499)	−10592 (−0.848)	(0.3966)	40736 (7.82)	(0.0001)
Adjusted R^2	0.61		0.61		0.38	
F-Test			6.63		169.19	
F-Test (OLS)			5.16		92.82	
Critical F 99%			6.65		4.63	

Table 12.5
Tobit estimation including investment and trade costs (628 observations)

	KK		HOR		VER	
	Tobit estimate (χ^2)	Sign as predicted? (marginal significance)	Tobit estimate (χ^2)	Sign as predicted? (marginal significance)	Tobit estimate (χ^2)	Sign as predicted? (marginal significance)
SUMGDP	17.402 (132.748)	Yes (0.0001)	17.234 (129.415)	Yes (0.0001)		
GDPDIFSQ	−0.001 (53.688)	Yes (0.0001)	−0.001 (46.135)	Yes (0.0001)		
D2SKDGDPD	11.832 (8.899)	No (0.0029)			−8.688 (3.156)	Yes (0.0756)
D2SKDSUMG	−15.049 (15.441)	Yes (0.0001)	−6.935 (6.689)	Yes (0.0097)	10.112 (4.713)	Yes (0.0299)
D1SKDSUMG	−24.507 (108.127)	Yes (0.0001)	−23.968 (103.462)	Yes (0.0001)	−19.083 (42.170)	Yes (0.0001)
DISTANCE	−1.483 (43.302)	? (0.0001)	−1.361 (37.257)	? (0.0001)	−2.083 (51.244)	? (0.0001)
INVCJ	−386.949 (7.103)	Yes (0.0077)	−227.164 (2.791)	Yes (0.0948)	−607.595 (10.684)	Yes (0.0011)
TCJ	134.054 (2.078)	Yes (0.1494)	76.316 (0.695)	Yes (0.4044)	267.285 (4.778)	Yes (0.0288)
TCI	−136.646 (2.752)	Yes (0.0971)	−125.135 (2.302)	Yes (0.1292)	−88.568 (0.738)	Yes (0.3902)

INTERCEPT	−26270 (3.332)	(0.0679)	−32790 (2.302)	(0.1292)	45884 (64.797)	(0.0001)
Log Likelihood	−5747		−5751		−5909	
LR Test			8.00		324	
Critical χ^2			7.88		10.6	

outward investments (where *GDPDIFF* is large and positive), an increase in *SKDIFF* always increases outward affiliate production. Thus, the results in the KK model are not as clear as they seem from looking at individual coefficients alone, and a positive role for SKDIFF is not rejected here.

I interpret the results as providing strong support for the KK model but not permitting it to be distinguished in aggregate data from the HOR model. A principal message is that the VER model is a poor characterization of the overall pattern of world FDI activity, a finding consistent with the results in Brainard (1993b, 1997). As noted in section 11.1, vertical activities may be important to some host economies in some industries. But in a horserace to pick one model to explain aggregate activity, the VER model loses to the HOR and KK models.

III

Internalization

13

A Reputation Model of Internalization

13.1 Introduction

It has been many pages since I discussed internalization and Dunning's OLI framework in chapter 1. The book to this point has focused, in Dunning's terminology, on ownership (O) and location (L) motives for multinational activity. The theoretical chapters focused on these first two determinants, while the empirical work in chapters 10–12 covered estimating and testing the propositions derived from those models. That is why I placed the empirical chapters before chapters 13–15, which return to theory but focus on internalization.

Recall that internalization refers to motives or reasons why the multinational firm wants to exploit its ownership advantages abroad through an owned subsidiary (and hence FDI) rather than through some arm's-length arrangement such as a licensing agreement. Firm-specific assets are controlled internally within the firm's ownership structure, hence the term *internalization*.

Recall from our literature review in chapter 1 that a consistent empirical theme is that multinationals arise from the existence of knowledge-based assets derived from engineering, management, and/or marketing expertise. These assets often have a jointness or "public-goods" characteristic in that they can be supplied to additional production facilities at very low cost. Blueprints, formulae, managerial procedures, or marketing strategies can be provided to additional plants without reducing the value of them in existing plants. Yet while the existence of these assets gives rise to a motive for foreign expansion, they do not by themselves suggest that arm's-length transfers are inferior to owned subsidiaries or indeed to serving foreign markets by exports.

My view is that the same joint-input property of knowledge capital that creates ownership advantages and multiplant economies of scale also creates the risk of asset dissipation through agent opportunism. In order to preserve the value of the firm's exclusive knowledge, the multinational tends to transfer technology to owned subsidiaries, or in some cases refuses to produce abroad at all.

I am thus suggesting that internalization motives arise from much the same sources as ownership advantages. Yet modeling internalization involves very different economic factors and thus very different analytical tools. Economic factors leading to the risk of asset dissipation include moral hazard, asymmetric information, and incomplete or unenforceable contracts. For this reason, I have chosen to group together the three chapters on internalization at the end of the book. Even though they are conceptually linked to the models presented in chapters 2–9, these chapters use a distinct set of economic tools drawn from game theory, information theory, and the theory of contracts.

Incentives for direct investment in a subsidiary instead of a licensing contract, or for exporting instead of any form of foreign production, can arise from imperfections and opportunism in the production process or from product marketing. The three chapters in this section of the book consider three different motives. All are very specific models and may lack generality, but I believe that is inherent in this type of analysis. Collectively, I hope that they provide some general flavor about the problems of agent opportunism and how they impact firm decision making.

This chapter deals with an imperfection in the product market, assuming that the knowledge-based asset transferred by the multinational to a licensee or subsidiary is a reputation for product quality. The firm must share rents with a licensee in order to induce the licensee to maintain the reputation, and if this becomes sufficiently costly, the multinational chooses a subsidiary. This chapter is a revision of Horstmann and Markusen (1987b) and focuses on the problem of moral hazard.

Chapter 14 turns to the production process and assumes that a foreign manager (whether a licensee or employee) can learn or absorb the knowledge-based asset in the course of producing the multinational's product for one time period, and then can quit or defect from the firm to start a rival business. A contract that preserves the value of the firm's knowledge may have to include rent sharing with the foreign manager, and if this becomes sufficiently costly the multinational dissipates rents through costly exporting rather than share rents in foreign production. Chapter 14 is a revision of Markusen (2001) and earlier work by Ethier and Markusen (1996), which again focuses on moral hazard in an environment where contracts must be self-enforcing.

Chapter 15 returns to product-market considerations with a model of asymmetric information. A local agent has information about local market conditions that would be valuable to the multinational in choosing between serving the market by exports or by local production. The multinational firm does not have this information, and so the local agent may be able to extract an information rent under a licensing contract. If this rent share is sufficiently large, the multinational will choose direct investment initially or may convert to direct investment after an initial licensing period.

In this chapter, however, I focus here on incentives for direct investment that arise from information imperfections in the product market. It is consistent with an observed correlation between advertising expenditures and multinational activity. In the model, the firm-specific asset that must be transferred is the firm's reputation for quality. Because the licensing firm is unable to monitor the licensee costlessly, the licensing agreement must provide incentives for the licensee to maintain the reputation. In effect, the licensing agreement must transfer some of the returns on the reputation to the licensee. FDI avoids the problem, and thus an incentive for FDI is created.

Specifically, the model considers a situation in which a firm (the MNE) possesses a technology capable of producing either a high-quality product or a low-quality one. Other firms can produce only the low-quality one. Consumers cannot ascertain quality prior to purchase and so are assumed to use reputations to make their purchase decisions. The MNE can either license the technology (and along with it the reputation) to a local producer or operate a branch plant of its own. If the licensee and branch plant are equally efficient, then the need to give a licensee the incentive to maintain the reputation results in FDI always dominating licensing. This result is given in section 13.2.

Section 13.3 considers the situation in which the licensee has a cost advantage over the MNE branch plant (as in Buckley and Casson 1981). This advantage arises from economies of scope that the licensee can capture by producing both a high- and a low-quality product. In this situation, the choice of licensing or FDI by the MNE depends on a number of factors. In particular, FDI will be observed in large markets, but licensing will be seen in small (or specialty) markets. Similarly, licensing results if the high- and low-quality goods are close substitutes, FDI results if they are poor substitutes. Finally, high interest rates make FDI more likely when scope economies are small but less likely when these economies are large. Sections 13.4 and 13.5 include a discussion of trade policy issues and a number of extensions to the model of sections 13.2 and 13.3. One extension of particular interest permits the MNE to choose between exporting and foreign operations of some sort. It is shown that, as the market size changes, the MNE may switch from FDI to licensing or from exporting to some form of foreign operations. However, the MNE will never switch from licensing to FDI. Section 13.6 contains a discussion of how the results of these models should be interpreted.

13.2 Licensing versus Foreign Direct Investment: The Symmetric Case

Assume that there are two countries, the home country and the host country. Firms in each country produce a quality-differentiated good q. For simplicity assume that quality can take on two values, q^l and q^h with $q^l < q^h$ indicating that, were goods of quality q^l and q^h to sell for the same price, consumers would strictly prefer q^h.[1] Initially, suppose that a single home country firm has sole access (through a patent, trade secrecy, or the like) to a technology that allows it to produce either q^l or q^h. Host-country firms, on the other hand, have access only to the technology for producing q^l. The home-country firm (MNE) is then faced with the decision of whether or not to enter the host-country market (either with q^h or q^l) and whether to do so by licensing its technology to a host-country firm or by investing directly in the host country. Markets are segmented so that there are no interactions between home- and host-country markets, and scale economies in q^h limit the number of (potential) host-country plants to one.

The host-country market for q^l is assumed to be perfectly competitive. Individual firms produce with identical U-shaped average cost curves. Assume that costs are to take the form of a per-period fixed cost, rk^l and variable costs given by the increasing, convex function $C^l(x) \geq 0$. Here r is the host-country interest rate and x the output of an individual firm producing q^l. Assume that consumers are able to verify that the quality of any product is at least q^l. Free entry implies that the equilibrium price of q^l, then, is given by $\bar{p}^l = [rk^l + C^l(x^{\min})]/$

x^{min}, where x^{min} is the level of x that minimizes average cost. Should the MNE choose to operate a branch plant in the host-country and produce q^l, its costs would be identical to those of any host-country producer of q^l. This is sufficient to guarantee that with perfect information, q^l will not be produced by the MNE.

Should the MNE choose to operate a host-country branch plant and produce q^h, then it would incur a per-period fixed cost of $rk^h > rk^l$ and variable costs given by the increasing convex function $C^h(y) \geq 0$, where y is individual firm output of q^h, in the host country. Assume that these costs are such that, for any $y = x \neq 0$, $C^h(y) > C^l(x)$ and $dC^h/dy > dC^l/dx$. Should the MNE instead choose to license production of q^h to a host-country producer (either an existing q^l producer or a new firm), the licensee would incur exactly the same costs. Thus, in particular, a licensee possesses neither a cost advantage nor a cost disadvantage over a branch plant.

If consumers can perfectly verify quality prior to purchase, then demand for q^h is assumed given by the (stationary) function $Y = D(p^h, \bar{p}^l, q^h, q^l)$, where, since it is assumed that there is only a single host-country producer of q^h, $Y = y$. Consumers are assumed to view q^h and q^l as substitutes, so that increases in q^l (or decreases in $\bar{p}^l$) reduce Y, ceteris paribus.

Assume that decisions occur in each of an infinite number of discrete time periods $t = 0, 1, 2, \ldots$ Each period the licensee/branch plant makes a quality decision (i.e., q^h or q^l) and, if q^h, a price decision p^h in order to maximize the present value of profits. Assume that payments accrue at the end of each period.

Licensing decisions must also be made each period. The admissible licensing contracts in this problem are given by the set of steady-state contracts defined by the pair (F, S). Here F is a one-time, nonrecoverable payment made by the licensee at the time the contract is first entered into, and S is a per-period payment made by the licensee each period the contract continues to be in force. Licensing contracts are negotiated at the end of a given period. If the MNE licenses to a firm that had no contract in the previous period, then the MNE offers a pair (F, S) to the new licensee. Should the licensee accept the contract, it immediately makes a payment F to the MNE. Both parties are bound by the contract through the end of the subsequent period. The contract guarantees the licensee the exclusive right to produce the high-quality product and binds it to a payment of S at the end of the period.[2] At the end of any period during which a licensing contract is in force, the

MNE and licensee decide whether the contract will be renewed for an additional period. If both sides agree to renew the contract, then the licensee again receives exclusive rights to produce the high-quality good in exchange for a payment of S. Should either side decide to terminate the agreement, then the MNE can contract with a new licensee and offer a new (F, S) pair. Recontracting costs are assumed to be zero.[3]

Two points about this contracting problem are worth noting. First, the fact that lump-sum payments are feasible means that conditions are more favorable for licensing. Were lump-sum payments not feasible, licensing fees would introduce distortions that would bias the case toward FDI. Second, while the set of feasible contracts is in some sense quite special, the critical constraint imposed by the above contracting process is on the nature of the commitments firms can make. In particular, it is not possible for either party to commit to payments after the licensing agreement has been terminated. This assumption is crucial to the results on licensing and FDI when quality is unobservable prior to sale.[4] It rules out contracts, for instance, that commit the licensee to payments for all future time even if the MNE's reputation has been dissipated (and so the licensing arrangement terminated). It also rules out the possibility of the MNE committing to refund part of F should it choose to switch licensees. Were such contracts feasible, the licensing/FDI decision for the MNE would be altered.

Given this framework, the decisions of the MNE can be determined easily. Suppose, first, that consumers can perfectly determine quality prior to purchase. Then, should the MNE choose to operate a host-country branch plant each period, its profits would be given by

$$\frac{\pi^*}{r} = \max_{p^h} \frac{p^h D(p^h, \bar{p}^l, q^h, q^l) - C^h[D(p^h, \bar{p}^l, q^h, q^l)] - rk^h}{r}. \tag{1}$$

Should the MNE choose to license its technology in a given period, then, given the MNE's inability to commit to a licensee for more than one period, the contract can extract no more than π^* in payments in any given period. Moreover, in equilibrium, it will extract no less (since a licensee will clearly accept any contract that earns it non-negative profits). Therefore, either the equilibrium contract will specify $F^* = 0$, $S^* = \pi^*$, with each party willing to renew the contract for an additional period or, if $F^* > 0$, a pair (F, S) such that $F^*(1 + r) + S^* = \pi^*$, with the MNE switching licensees each period.[5] In either case, the MNE earns the same profit by licensing each period as by operating a host-country branch plant each period (or any mixture of the two across time). Under the assumptions of the model, therefore, the MNE chooses to license each period.

This result is exactly what should be expected here. Given there exists neither an inefficiency that can be internalized through a non-market transaction nor a special firm asset, the MNE has no incentive to choose a direct investment strategy over a simple licensing arrangement. Therefore, one should expect to observe the MNE licensing the technology to produce q^h.

Suppose, on the other hand, that consumers cannot perfectly determine quality prior to purchase. In situations in which quality warranties are infeasible (due perhaps to difficulties with third-party verification of nonperformance), an equilibrium response to this uncertainty may be for firms to acquire a "reputation" for high quality. This reputation then would become a "special firm asset," the full return on which potentially could not be capturable with a licensing arrangement. If this is so, an incentive arises for the MNE to operate a host-country branch plant.

To explore this, a standard model of reputation equilibrium is adopted. (See, e.g., Klein and Leffler 1981; Allen 1984; Shapiro 1983.) In particular, suppose, while consumers can verify whether a particular firm could produce q^h (and so can verify the quality of the competitive sector good prior to purchase), they cannot verify whether the potential producer of q^h actually produces q^h or q^l without purchasing the good.[6] Instead, in making a purchase decision from the licensee / branch plant, consumers use the fact that price is p^{*h} (defined in equation (1) above) and that q^h has been produced in all previous periods as a signal that quality is q^h this period (it is assumed that consumers ascertain quality correctly after purchase). An observation of quality q^l in any time period leads consumers to assume quality will be q^l in all future periods and so to purchase from the competitive sector. In this sense, the home-country firm, either through its licensee or branch-plant operations, can acquire (or lose) a reputation for high quality in the host country.

Given this setup, it is well known that a reputation equilibrium in which q^h is produced each period exists as long as the present value of producing q^h each period (maintaining a reputation) is at least as large as the value of selling q^l at price p^{*h} for a single period (losing the reputation). In terms of my analysis here, were the home-country firm to operate a host-country branch plant each period, a reputation equilibrium would exist if

$$\pi^*/r \geq (p^{*h}y^* - C^l(y^*) - rk^l)/(1+r) \equiv \pi^c/(1+r), \tag{2}$$

where $y^* = D(p^{*h}, \bar{p}^l, q^h, q^l)$. In what follows, assume that this inequality holds (were it not to hold, the issue of MNE operations in the host country would not arise).

Given that the inequality in equation (2) holds, should the MNE choose to license, it prefers that the licensee maintains its (the MNE's) reputation. If the MNE cannot commit the licensee to producing q^h and the licensee's choice of quality (and so profits) in a given period is private information in that period, then the MNE can accomplish this only by providing the licensee with some incentive to maintain the reputation. It requires that the per-period payment, S, be such that

$$(\pi^* - S)/r \geq (\pi^c - S)/(1+r) \tag{3}$$

or

$$S \leq (1+r)\pi^* - r\pi^c < \pi^*.^7$$

Of particular interest is the fact that the previous equilibria are no longer feasible. If $F^* = 0$ and $S^* = \pi^*$, then no licensee has an incentive to maintain the MNE's reputation. Doing so earns a licensee zero profits, while dissipating the reputation yields

$$(\pi^c - \pi^*)/(1+r) = \{[C^h(y^*) - C^l(y^*)] + r[k^h - k^l]\}/(1+r) > 0. \tag{3'}$$

The same would be true for the other contracts involving $F^* > 0$.

The equilibrium licensing arrangement in this case is the contract given by $F^* = 0$, $S^* = \pi^*(1+r) - r\pi^c$ with each side renewing the contract every period.[8] This equilibrium yields the MNE strictly fewer profits than it earns through FDI. Therefore, in equilibrium, the MNE chooses FDI over licensing.

In contrast to the perfect-information case, the MNE now chooses to transfer the technology internally. This decision arises for two reasons. First, the existence of imperfect quality information results in the creation of the asset "reputation." Second, the inability of the MNE and licensee to write contracts that commit each to certain types of payments even if the contract is terminated results in an inefficiency in the market transfer of the reputation. This inefficiency can be avoided if the transfer is carried out internally. Therefore, the MNE chooses FDI over licensing.[9]

13.3 Licensing versus FDI with Imperfect Information and Asymmetric Costs

Section 13.2 showed that, in the absence of certain forms of commitment (like third-party bonding), the existence of reputations induces the MNE to choose FDI over licensing under all circumstances. This very strong result depends crucially on the assumption that the licensee and host-country branch plant operate with identical costs. This assumption is frequently challenged in the applied literature on MNEs. There it is generally argued that the licensee possesses a cost advantage over the branch plant. If this is the case, licensing may again arise in equilibrium. This possibility is explored later.

To capture the important aspects of the licensee cost advantage while maintaining some degree of simplicity, I modify the production technology in a fairly straightforward way. Specifically, should the MNE operate a host-country branch plant, on the one hand, its costs are assumed to be as before. On the other hand, should it license its technology, it does so to one of the host-country producers of q^l. The licensee can produce q^h along with q^l by upgrading capacity of k^l to a level $\hat{k}$, with $k^h \leq \hat{k} < k^h + k^l \equiv \bar{k}$. This results in the licensee incurring per-period costs for the two goods of $r\hat{k} + C^l(x) + C^h(y)$. Since $\hat{k} < k^h + k^l$, the licensee's production displays economies of scope. In essence, the ability of the licensee to utilize its capacity in both the q^h and q^l markets gives it a cost advantage over the MNE branch plant.[10] If the licensee decides not to produce q^h (i.e., it chooses to dissipate the MNE's reputation by producing q^l), then demand for q^h is assumed to be such that the cost-minimizing solution for the licensee is to make a second capacity investment, k^l, rather than bear the increased marginal costs from using existing capacity. In this case, then, the licensee incurs costs of $2rk^l + C^l(x) + C^l(y)$ (from serving both parts of the host-country market for q^l and all the market for q^h with a good of quality q^l). To maintain the assumption that production of q^l is less costly than production of q^h, assume that $rk^l + C^l(y) < r(\hat{k} - k^l) + C^h(y)$.[11] As before, assume that the MNE cannot monitor the licensee's quality (or capacity) choice prior to sale.

To determine the MNE's equilibrium strategy, again one need only compare the profits from FDI with the equilibrium license fee that the MNE can collect. Then, should the MNE operate a branch plant each period, its profits are given by (1) as previously. Should it license, then, by an argument identical to that in section 13.2, the equilibrium contract has $F^* = 0$ and S^* equal to the maximum per-period payment consistent with the licensee's maintaining the reputation. Licensing dominates FDI as long as $S^* \geq \pi^*$. Since the licensee can continue to produce $x^{\min}$ and receive $\bar{p}^l$ in the market for q^l, its cost of producing q^h is effectively $C^h(y) + r(\hat{k} - k^l)$. If one lets $\pi^L = p^{*h}y^* - C^h(y^*) - r(\hat{k} - k^l)$ and $\pi^{LC} = p^{*h}y^* - C^l(y^*) - rk^l$, then the condition for licensing to be an equilibrium is simply that

$$(\pi^L - \pi^*)/r \geq (\pi^{LC} - \pi^*)/(1 + r). \tag{4}$$

Some simple algebra shows that this condition can be rewritten as

$$\bar{k} - \hat{k} - r(\hat{k} - 2k^l) \geq C^h(y^*) - C^l(y^*). \tag{5}$$

That is, if equation (5) holds, then licensing dominates FDI in equilibrium.

An immediate implication of (5) is that, contrary to the results of section 13.2, licensing now may be an equilibrium strategy. Because the licensee can take advantage of scope economies, it may be possible for the NME to extract at least π^* in license fees and still leave the licensee with enough profits to induce it to maintain the reputation. In such cases licensing becomes an equilibrium strategy for the MNE.

By an analysis of (5), it is possible to obtain a number of predictions regarding the circumstances under which either licensing or FDI will be observed. Consider, for instance, how the size of the market for q^h affects the licensing/FDI decision. Let α parameterize demand for q^h and be such that increases in α lead, in equilibrium, to increases in both p^{*h} and y^*. Further, define the variable z as

$$z \equiv \bar{k} - \hat{k} - r(\hat{k} - 2k^l) - C^h(y^*) + C^l(y^*). \tag{6}$$

Then, it is clear from (6) that increases in α lead to a reduction in z. That is, changes that increase the size of the market for q^h make licensing less desirable. This is because the larger the market, the larger are the cost savings to the licensee from producing q^l rather than q^h (i.e., from dissipating the MNE's reputation). To prevent the licensee from doing this, the MNE must leave it with larger returns from producing q^h. Ultimately the problem can become severe enough that FDI dominates licensing. A prediction of the model, then, is that licensing is more likely to be observed in small markets and FDI in large ones.

In the same vein, a variable that determines demand for q^h is the value of q^l. As I noted earlier, consumers are assumed to view q^h and

q^l as substitutes so that increases in q^l reduce the demand for q^h. The preceding results then imply that the higher the quality of q^l that can be obtained from a given cost, the more attractive licensing becomes for the home-country firm. Further, it is clear from (6) that, should increases in q^l come at the expense of higher costs, this result is merely strengthened. Therefore, where there are good substitutes for the home-country product one should observe licensing, while the lack of substitutes is more likely to result in FDI.

Results can also be obtained concerning the effects of fixed costs on the licensing/FDI decision. From equation (6), should k^l increase relative to $\hat{k}$, z increases and so licensing becomes more attractive. This is simply a result of the fact that an increase in k^l relative to $\hat{k}$ implies larger economies of scope for the licensee. This means that it is more profitable for the licensee to maintain the MNE's reputation, making licensing a more attractive option. Increases in k^h that leave $\hat{k}$ unchanged (or, if not, are such that $dk^h > (1+r)d\hat{k}$) result in a similar outcome. Such a change increases the cost to the MNE of branch-plant operations relative to licensing. This, in turn, reduces the value of S that the MNE must obtain to prefer licensing to FDI, thereby leaving that licensee with a larger return from producing q^h. Again, by essentially increasing the size of the economies of scope, the increase in k^h relative to $\hat{k}$ increases the likelihood that licensing is observed.

Finally, the effect of r on the licensing decision can be considered. From (6), the effect clearly depends on whether $\hat{k} \gtrless 2k^l$. If $\hat{k} > 2k^l$ then increases in r, reduce z and make licensing less attractive. The opposite is true if $\hat{k} < 2k^l$. This ambiguity arises from the fact that increases in r produce counterbalancing effects. One is that increases in r make the dissipation of a reputation more attractive. That is, as the licensee discounts the future more heavily, the one-period gains from the production of q^l become more attractive. The other is that increases in r increase the returns from the scope economies resulting from the production of q^h. If $\hat{k} > 2k^l$, the scope economies are not sufficiently large for the latter to offset the former one. Thus, as r increases, the MNE is less likely to license its technology. The opposite is true if $\hat{k} < 2k^l$ (i.e., large-scope economies).

13.4   Extensions

This section considers a number of extensions to the model in section 13.3. It incorporates that model into a richer framework in which the

MNE must also make an export versus foreign operations decision. As well, it considers both the effects of future uncertainty and the ability of the MNE to monitor the license on the licensing/FDI decision. These extensions generate a number of additional predictions.

Demand Growth and Exporting

To this point, attention has been focused solely on the MNE's decision to license, as opposed to operate, a branch plant. Clearly another alternative is for the MNE simply to export to a host country. One way of adding this additional alternative is to amend the model of section 13.3 to allow for demand growth over time. In particular, suppose that demand at time t is given by the function $Y_t = D(p_t^h, \bar{p}_t^l, q_t^h, q_t^l, t)$. Further, assume that demand function possesses the following properties (in addition to the ones assumed for the stationary case):

1. At $t = 0$, the one-period maximized profits from exporting (π_0^e) exceed the one-period maximized profits from a host-country branch plant (π_0^*).

2. $\pi_t^e - \pi_t^*$ is monotonically decreasing in t. That is, owing to their higher marginal cost, profits from exporting grow more slowly with market size than profits from branch-plant production. Further, there exists a finite time $\bar{t}$ such that, for all $t < \bar{t}$, $\pi_t^e - \pi_t^* > 0$, while, for all $t \geq \bar{t}$, $\pi^e - \pi^* \leq 0$.

3. Demand is bounded for all t.

4. If the home-country firm could choose only to operate a branch plant or export, a reputation equilibrium would exist at every t.

This specification adds the important feature that the home-country firm would prefer to export rather than operate a branch plant for all $t \in [0, \bar{t} - 1]$.

To solve for MNE's optimal strategy, it is useful to define a new variable s_t. This is a per-period licence fee defined such that

$$s_t = \begin{cases} \pi_t^e & t \in [0, \bar{t} - 1] \\ \pi_t^* & t \geq \bar{t}. \end{cases}$$

If, for all $t \geq \hat{t}$, the home-country firm can extract the licence fee s_t from a licensee while still inducing the licensee to maintain a reputation, then licensing will be an equilibrium strategy for all $t \geq \hat{t}$. That is, if at each $t_1 \geq \hat{t}$,

$$\sum_{t=t_1}^{\infty} (\pi_t^L - s_t)[1/(1+r)]^{(t+1-t_1)} \geq (\pi_{t_1}^{LC} - s_{t_1})[1/(1+r)], \tag{7}$$

then licensing will be an equilibrium strategy at each t_1.[12]

Given that π_t^L and π_t^* differ only by a constant, demand condition (2) implies that the left-hand side of (7) is monotonically increasing for all $t < \bar{t}$. Furthermore, it approaches the constant $\bar{k} - \hat{k}$ as t approaches $\bar{t}$. As for the right-hand side of (7), note that for $t < \bar{t}$, it can be written as $(\pi_t^{LC} - \pi_t^*) - (\pi_t^e - \pi_t^*)$. From previous results, the first term of this expression is increasing in t while $-(\pi_t^e - \pi_t^*)$ is increasing in t from (2) above. Therefore, the right-hand side is monotonically increasing in t as well. Furthermore, for $t \geq \bar{t}$, since the left-hand side is a constant, (7) can be expressed as

$$\bar{k} - \hat{k} - r(\hat{k} - 2k^l) \geq C^h(y_t^*) - C^l(y_t^*), \tag{8}$$

with the right-hand side increasing in t.

If it is supposed, then, that at $t = 0$ (7) is violated, the MNE will export rather than license. This is because, even if a licensee were to earn the maximum return possible, it would still dissipate the home-country firm's reputation at $t = 0$. Since the right- and left-hand sides of equation (8) are increasing for all $t < \bar{t}$, two possible outcomes for $t > 0$ exist. One is that the right-hand side increases everywhere more quickly than the left so that at $t = \bar{t}$, (8) is violated. In this case, the results of section 13.3 imply that (8) is violated for all $t > \bar{t}$. Therefore, licensing is not observed. The MNE simply switches from exporting to operating a host-country branch plant.

The other possibility is that the left-hand side increases more quickly so that at $t = \bar{t}$, (8) is satisfied. Further (8) is satisfied for all $t > \bar{t}$ (i.e., while the right-hand side continues to increase, demand never grows large enough for (8) to be violated). In this case, the MNE adopts a policy of switching at some $t \leq \bar{t}$ from exporting to licensing production to a host-country producer.

What might seem to be a third possibility is to observe the home-country firm initially exporting, then switching to licensing and finally FDI. This cannot happen. Were the home-country firm to license for only a finite number of periods, the licensee would always have an incentive to dissipate the reputation before the licence was revoked. The home-country firm, therefore, would never choose this strategy.

Finally, note that the case in which demand for q^h shrinks over time can be dealt with analogously. This might occur, for instance, because q^l is increasing over time (as in section 13.3). In this case, a situation in which the MNE switches from FDI to licensing (as q^l increases) might be observed in equilibrium.

Uncertain Ending Time

In the preceding analysis, it is assumed that the time horizon is infinite and known to be so with certainty. This is easily replaced by an assumption of an uncertain time horizon where the probability that any given period $t = 0, 1, 2 \ldots$ is the last is $\phi(1 - \phi)^t$. Then, if this uncertainty holds both for a host-country branch plant and a licensee, the licensing condition becomes

$$(\pi^L - \pi^*)/(r + \phi) \geq (\pi^{LC} - \pi^*)/(1 + r). \tag{9}$$

Clearly, increases in ϕ make licensing less attractive. The uncertainty about future returns gives the licensee more incentive to produce q^l in the current period and dissipate the MNE's reputation. Therefore, in situations in which the future of the market is very uncertain, either no foreign operations at all or provision of q^h through exports/FDI should be observed.

If, on the other hand, the uncertainty is only as to whether the MNE will be able to continue operating a branch plant (or exporting), then the result is reversed. This uncertainty will have the effect of reducing the minimum licence fee needed to have licensing dominate FDI.

Monitoring the Licensee

In what has preceded, I assumed that the MNE cannot monitor the quality of the licensee's product prior to sale. This assumption can easily be relaxed to allow for monitoring that simply results in increased costs to the licensee should it produce q^l (i.e., try to dissipate the MNE's reputation).[13] Suppose, for instance, that the licensee's variable cost of production for q^l is given by $C^l(y, \sigma)$ where $C^l_\sigma > 0$. Further, suppose that the value of σ is determined by the MNE as part of the licensing agreement at a cost $\chi(\sigma)$ ($\chi' > 0$). Then, as long as the MNE can extract at least $\pi^* + \chi(\sigma)$ in licence fees each period while still inducing the licensee to produce q^h, the MNE will choose to license. That is, licensing is chosen as long as

$$(\pi^L - \pi^* - \chi(\sigma))/r \geq (p^{*h}y^* - C^l(y^*,\sigma) - rk^l - \pi^* - \chi(\sigma))/(1+r). \quad (10)$$

If large increases in $C^l(\ )$ can be achieved at very low cost (i.e., C^l_σ is large) to the home-country firm, then licensing will now be observed in cases where it would not have been observed previously. However, if increases in $C^l(\ )$ are very expensive, then the pattern of licensing and FDI will different little.

13.5 Trade Policy Issues

This section analyzes the welfare implications of several host-country commercial policy actions that seem to be empirically relevant in the context of multinational activity. Rather than examine many possible cases, the discussion is restricted to the case of stationary demand in the host country. This makes it possible to evaluate certain policies through a simple evaluation of their effects on steady-state consumption in the host-country. The assumption that monitoring is prohibitively expensive is also maintained throughout. Finally, the analysis is limited to the case in which the marginal costs functions are the same under licensing and FDI and, for the same level of output, exporting results in a higher total marginal cost (production plus shipping) than either of the other options.

The host-country welfare criterion applied to evaluate the policies will be the sum of the change in consumer surplus (via a change in the availability and price of Y), the change in profits to the host-country licensee (when relevant) and the change in host-country government revenues (if any).

Banning FDI

Banning FDI in the host country may lead to the MNE's choosing either the licensing or the exporting option (or not to serve the host-country at all). Which outcome occurs depends on things such as the host-country market size, discount rate, and so forth. Rather than belabor the point, let me simply assert that each alternative will be chosen for some set of parameter values.

It is clear from the above assumptions and results that the welfare effects of banning FDI depend on which alternative is chosen. Welfare will improve if licensing is chosen, since the host country will capture rents that would otherwise accrue to the MNE (necessary to support the reputation equilibrium) and the price of Y will not change (the equal marginal cost assumption). If exporting is chosen, however, welfare deteriorates as the price of Y increases with no offsetting advantages.

Banning Imports

Suppose that the host country, for whatever reason, wishes to generate domestic production of Y. (One reason is a real or mistaken belief that it will reduce unemployment, something that is outside the scope of this chapter.) Suppose that the host-country market is large enough to support domestic production of Y and that the country levies a sufficiently high tariff to induce the MNE to switch from exporting. Welfare will increase in the host country if the MNE chooses a branch plant and, by transitivity, increase even more if it chooses licensing. Banning imports forces a price reduction and also generates domestic profits if licensing is chosen. This result is, of course, sensitive to the assumption that the marginal cost of domestic production is less than the total marginal cost from the MNE's home plant.

Differential Taxation on FDI

A not-uncommon practice is for countries to penalize foreign firms in subtle or not-so-subtle ways through domestic tax legislation. While the various details of such policies can hardly be captured here, certain principles can be easily illustrated by considering two special cases. First, a pure-profits tax on FDI is welfare improving provided that it does not cause the MNE to switch to exporting. If the MNE absorbs the tax or switches to licensing, p^h stays constant while the host country captures some of the rent. If the MNE switches to exporting, no rent is captured, consumer price rises, and the host country is worse off.

Few countries' corporate taxes are equivalent to a nondistortionary pure-profits tax. An alternative is to model a distortionary tax as a simple output tax on FDI. Comments regarding the MNE's switching to licensing or exporting made with respect to the pure profits tax continue to apply, but more complex outcomes occur when the MNE continues to choose FDI. The problem is that such an output tax generates two conflicting changes for the host country. First, there is a deadweight loss as the distortionary tax increases marginal cost and (generally) reduces output. Second, there is a rent transfer from the MNE to the host-country government. The latter effect could outweigh the former, generating a welfare gain for the host country.

13.6   Summary and Conclusions

This chapter has considered a problem in which, because of imperfect consumer information about quality, a firm acquires a reputation. This is a knowledge-based asset of the firm that is (assumed to be) easily transferred to a new market much like the firm-specific assets discussed throughout this book. But this asset suffers from the problem that it can be easily dissipated through agent opportunism.

Because the firm cannot monitor a licensee to guarantee that the licensee maintain the reputation, the licensing contract must provide incentives for this. This fact may lead the firm to choose a strategy of direct investment rather than licensing. By an ownership arrangement, the firm guarantees that its reputation is maintained.

While the analysis is couched in terms of a reputation model, it may be viewed as applicable to a much broader set of circumstances in which firms (principals) have imperfect control of licensees (agents). A wealth of empirical evidence (see, e.g., Nicholas 1986; Casson 1987; Rugman 1986) suggests the importance of this problem in the firm's decision to operate branch plants and subsidiaries.

Appendix

This appendix contains a formal statement of the results on licensing contained in the section 13.2. The licensing game is as described there. The equilibrium concept is the subgame-perfect Nash equilibrium with each firm's strategy maximizing its stream of profits for every subgame given the strategy of the other firms. It is assumed that a potential licensee earns zero profits in a given period should it not be part of a licensing agreement.

Given these assumptions, a perfect equilibrium strategy for a licensee must involve the licensee accepting/renewing a licensing agreement if that agreement yields non-negative profits. This yields the first result. It is as follows:

LEMMA   For a licensing arrangement (F, S) to be an equilibrium with perfect information, it must be that $F + (S/r) \leq \pi^*/r$.

Proof   Suppose $F + (S/r) > \pi^*/r$, then, should the home-country firm continue the licensing arrangement every period, the licensee would earn negative profits. This, though, implies that the licensee could be better off choosing reject rather than accept. Should the home-country firm terminate the contract after T periods, then since $rF + S > \pi^*$, the licensee would also earn negative profits. Again, it could be made better off by choosing reject. Therefore $F + (S/r) \leq \pi^*/r$.   ∎

In fact, given the equilibrium strategy of a licensee and perfect information, an equilibrium licensing agreement must be such that $F + (S/r) = \pi^*/r$. In addition, the constant (F^*, S^*) must be such that the following is true:

PROPOSITION   With perfect information on quality, the set of equilibrium contracts (F^*, S^*) is unique up to the condition $F(1 + r) + S = \pi^*$.

Proof   It is clear that $F^* = 0$, $S^* = \pi^*$ is an equilibrium and satisfies the above condition. The only issue then is the uniqueness one. Suppose that along the equilibrium path a subgame were reached in which $\hat{F} > 0$, $\hat{S} > \pi^*$. Two possibilities exist for future play of the game. One is that the home-country firm's equilibrium strategy will call for it to continue for T periods and then offer a new (F^*, S^*) pair to another licensee. However, if this is an optimal strategy at time T, it must also be optimal at $T - 1$. If it is optimal at $T - 1$, it must be optimal at $T - 2$, and so on. This, though, implies that continuing for T periods cannot be optimal. Therefore, it must be that continuing is optimal for either all periods or no periods.

Suppose continuing were optimal for all periods. Then, since the home-country firm could earn π^*/r by using the pair $F = 0$, $S = \pi^*$, it must be that $\hat{F} + (\hat{S}/r) = \pi^*/r$. If this is the case, however, then it must be that the home-country firm could offer $(\hat{F}, \hat{S})$ to a new licensee next period and earn larger profits than from continuing. This, though, contradicts the fact that continuing for all periods is optimal.

Therefore, not continuing must be the optimal solution. In this case, for acceptance to be a best reply for the licensee, it must be that $F(1 + r) + S \leq \pi^*$. The optimal strategy for the home-country firm is to set $F(1 + r) + S = \pi^*$.   ∎

Remark Note that were there any recontracting costs, the only equilibrium would be $F^* = 0$, $S^* = \pi^*$. Also, in the case of imperfect information, the set of single-period contracts with $F > 0$ are no longer equilibria. The fact that the licensee would be changed each period would cause any licensee to dissipate the home-country firm's reputation. This leaves only $F^* = 0$, $S^* = (1+r)\pi^* - r\pi^c$ (i.e., the maximum one-period fee consistent with the licensee maintaining reputation).

14

A Learning Model of Internalization, with Applications to Contract and Intellectual-Property-Rights Enforcement

14.1 Introduction

This chapter takes a different tack from the previous one, but they share a common core idea, which is that the multinational firm has an intangible, knowledge-based asset and that the value of this asset can be dissipated by agent opportunism. I again adopt a strategic-behavior approach to the same general problem. The chapter is a revision of Markusen (2001), which in turn builds on Ethier and Markusen (1996) (see also Fosfuri, Motta, and Ronde 2001). An MNE hires a local "agent" (manager) in the host country. The agent learns the technology in the first period of a two-period product cycle and can defect to start a rival firm in the second period. The MNE can similarly dismiss the agent at the beginning of the second period and hire a new agent. The double-sided moral hazard is crucial to some of the interesting results in this chapter.

The multinational introduces a new product in each product cycle, and the old product becomes economically obsolete. There is then the possibility that the MNE and the agent will form a long-term relationship that persists indefinitely over many product cycles. The multinational can choose between simply serving the foreign country by exports or by establishing foreign production. Cases where a subsidiary is chosen can be divided into a case where the MNE captures all rents and one in which it shares rents with the local agent. The former means that both the multinational and the agent are indifferent as to whether to renew the relationship for a second product cycle, so we could think of this case as being something close to a simple product-specific license. Sharing rents with the agent in any product cycle means that there is a positive present value to the agent to maintaining the relationship for future product cycles. This is closer to what we think of as a subsidiary, a long-term relationship involving a credible commitment to continued employment with the firm.

This model is a convenient vehicle for examining the effects of enforcement of contracts and intellectual-property protection (IPP) by the host-country government. Contract enforcement and/or IPP are modeled simply as a cost imposed on the defecting party (or perhaps only on the agent). The institution of contract enforcement may lead to a shift from exporting to a local subsidiary. This is rather obvious, but I want to note its consistency with the recent empirical results of Smith (2001), which therefore lend some support to this type of model.[1]

A mode switch from exporting to a subsidiary improves the welfare of both the MNE and the host country. But if a subsidiary was chosen initially, contract enforcement leads to either no change or to a fall in host-country welfare. In the latter case, there is a rent transfer from the local agent to the MNE. One interesting result is that binding both the MNE and the agent is worse for the agent and better for the MNE than binding the agent alone (as in intellectual property protection). The reason is that a contract-enforceability constraint on the MNE allows it to credibly offer a lower licensing or royalty fee in the second period of a product cycle. But this lower second-period fee then allows it to offer a lower rent share to the agent and still satisfy the latter's incentive-compatibility constraint. The optimal policy for a developing country is to set the level of contract enforcement just high enough to induce entry.

A final section of the chapter considers a few extensions: (1) there are several identical firms, a proxy for the level of competition in inward investment, (2) there are MNEs in different industries that enter at different levels of contract enforcement, and (3) there is a case in which duopoly competition occurs in the second period between the MNE and a (defecting) original agent.

I hope that the chapter captures the essence of the policy debate over IPP and other legal institutions. The model suggests that there is indeed a tension over the benefits of inward investment and the transfer of rents from poor developing countries to first-world MNEs.

14.2   Elements of the Model

Key elements of the model are as follows:

1. The MNE introduces a new product every second time period. Two periods are referred to as a "product cycle." A product is economically obsolete at the end of the second period (end of a cycle).

2. The term r denotes the discount rate between product cycles; to simplify notation I ignore discounting between periods within a product cycle (the longer NBER version of this paper (Markusen 1998b) reproduces key equations with discounting between periods).[2]

3. The MNE can serve a foreign market by exporting, or by creating a subsidiary to produce in the foreign market.

4. Because of the costs of exporting, producing in the foreign country generates the most rents.

5. But any local agent learns the technology in the first period and can quit (defect) to start a rival firm in the second period. Similarly, the MNE can defect, dismissing the agent and hiring a new one in the second period.

6. Initially, no binding contracts can be written to prevent either partner from undertaking such a defection. But the defecting party must pay a penalty P; I assume that this is paid to an outside agent ("government") and not to the other party to the contract. P is taken to be a measure of contract enforcement.

7. Initially, I assume that the MNE either offers a self-enforcing contract or exports. The possibility that second-period duopoly occurs as an equilibrium is allowed later in the chapter.

These assumptions set up a situation where the multinational prefers to produce in the foreign (host) country, but agency costs may force the MNE into rent sharing with the local agent. Thus the multinational may prefer to dissipate rents through exporting rather than to share rents with the agent. Later in the chapter, I consider the case where rents may be dissipated through second-period duopoly competition as just noted.

Notation is as follows:

R Total per period rents from producing in the foreign country.

E Total per period exporting rents ($E < R$).

F Fixed cost of transferring the technology to a foreign partner. These include physical capital costs, training of the local agent, and so forth.

T Training costs of a new agent that the MNE incurs if it dismisses the first one (i.e., if the MNE defects). In general, $F > T$.

G Fixed cost that the agent must incur if he or she quits (defects) to start a rival firm exclusive of legal penalties. This could include costs of physical capital and other real setup costs.

L_i Licensing or royalty fee charged to the subsidiary in period i $(i = 1, 2)$.

V Rents earned by the agent in one product cycle: $V = (R - L_1) + (R - L_2)$.

V/r Present value of rents to the agent of maintaining the relationship (each product cycle is, in value terms, an exact replica of the one before even though the product has changed).

P Defection penalty (proxying contract enforcement) paid to outside agent by the defecting party.

There are two "individual-rationality" constraints (IR): The MNE and the agent must earn non-negative rents. There are two "incentive-compatibility" constraints (IC): the MNE and the agent must not want to defect in the second period. Subscripts a and m refer to the agent and the MNE, respectively. The agent's IR constraint is that the agent must earn his or her opportunity cost over the product cycle from some other outside opportunity (normalized at zero).

$$V = (R - L_1) + (R - L_2) \geq 0 \qquad IR_a \qquad (1)$$

The agent's IC constraint is that second-period earnings $(R - L_2)$, plus the present value of continuing the relationship with the firm (V/r), exceed the returns from defecting to start a rival firm.[3]

$$(R - L_2) + V/r \geq (R - G - P), \ L_2 \leq G + P + V/r \qquad IC_a \qquad (2)$$

The MNE's IR constraint is that the subsidiary yields earnings greater than or equal to exporting.

$$L_1 + L_2 - F \geq 2E \qquad IR_m \qquad (3)$$

The MNE's IC constraint is that the second-period license fee is greater than or equal to the returns from firing the first agent and hiring a second one.

$$L_2 \geq R - T - P \qquad IC_m \qquad (4)$$

Consider first the IC constraints, equations (2) and (4). Combine these to get the inequality

$$R - T - P \leq G + P + V/r. \qquad (5)$$

It is clear that the multinational should minimize V, since that is the same as maximizing $L_1 + L_2$. V is constrained to be greater than or equal to zero by the agent's IR constraint (1). Two interesting cases emerge, the first being that the inequality (5) holds at $V = 0$, implying that the MNE extracts all possible rents. This occurs when $R \leq G + T + 2P$. The optimal contract is then $L_2 = G + P$, satisfying the IC constraint (2), and $L_1 = 2R - G - P$, satisfying the IR constraint (1).

If $R > G + T + 2P$, then the multinational must offer the agent a positive rent share in order to satisfy the two IC constraints summarized by (5). As just noted, the multinational wants to minimize V, so from the second equation in (2), the firm should offer the lowest L_2, which satisfies its own IC constraint (4). Thus

$$L_2 = R - T - P. \tag{6}$$

Minimizing V also implies that equation (5) should hold with equality. Having solved for L_2, (5) is then reduced to one equation in one unknown (L_1). Rearranging (5), and substituting for L_2 from (6) produces

$$R - T - G - 2P = V/r = (2R - L_1 - L_2)/r = (2R - L_1 - R + T + P)/r. \tag{7}$$

This simplifies to

$$L_1 = R + T - r(R - T - G) + (1 + 2r)P. \tag{8}$$

Adding together L_1 and L_2 and subtracting F results in the earnings of the MNE

$$L_1 + L_2 - F = 2R - F - r(R - T - G - 2P). \tag{9}$$

The agent earns

$$V = 2R - L_1 - L_2 = r(R - T - G - 2P). \tag{10}$$

These results can be summarized as follows:

Result 1:
If $R \leq T + G + 2P$, the MNE captures all rents in a product cycle, henceforth referred to as a rent-capture (RC) contract.
If $R > T + G + 2P$, the MNE can credibly offer a long-term commitment, but must share rents with the agent. This is henceforth referred to as a rent-sharing (RS) contract.
The agent's rent share is equal to $V = r(R - T - G - 2P)$.

Note especially that the agent's rent share is *reduced* by tighter contract enforcement (higher P).

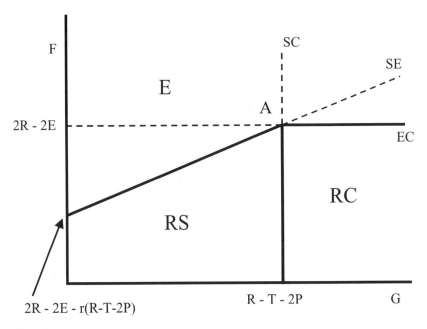

Figure 14.1
Values of F and G supporting alternative modes

Two important parameters of the model are F and G, the multinational's fixed cost of producing locally and the agent's fixed costs of going it alone. Figure 14.1 is a diagram in (F, G) space. The boundary between the area in which a rent-capture contract is possible and the area in which a rent-sharing contract is needed is given by SC in figure 14.1. RC occurs to the right, and RS to the left of SC.

Now consider exporting versus a subsidiary. MNE chooses exporting over the RC contract if $2R - F < 2E$. Indifference between exporting and the RC subsidiary is given by the horizontal line in figure 14.1, $F = 2R - 2E$. I label this line EC.

At point A in figure 14.1, exporting and an RS subsidiary also yield the same profits (by transitivity). Beginning at this point, differentiate the right-hand side of equation (9) holding it equal to zero, in order to derive the locus of indifference between exporting and a subsidiary.

$$dF - r\, dG = 0 \qquad dF/dG = r. \tag{11}$$

The locus of points giving the same profits from a subsidiary as point A in figure 14.1 is given by SE in figure 14.1. These three loci then di-

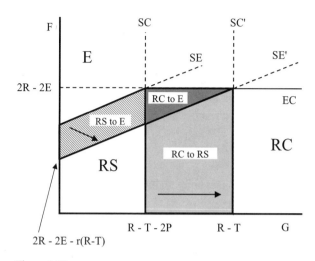

Figure 14.2
Elimination of contract enforcement

vide the space of figure 14.1 into regions of exporting (E), rent-sharing contract (RS), and rent-capture contract (RC).

Figure 14.2 shows show the effect of reducing P to zero. In figure 14.2, the area corresponding to RS expands on its right-hand boundary. At any point inside the rent-sharing region both before and after the elimination of P, equations (9) and (10) tell us that the profits of the MNE decrease and the rents captured by the agent increase. Obviously, points that shift from RC to RS also constitute points of profit loss for the MNE and rent gain for the agent. Thus in the areas labeled "RS" and "RC to RS" in figure 14.2, the agent gains from the elimination of enforcement and the firm loses.

However, in the area of figure 14.2 where RC switches to exporting (labeled "RC to E") the firm's profits decrease while the agent is indifferent (rents were zero in RC). In the area that was a rent-sharing subsidiary and now becomes exporting (labeled "RS to E"), both the MNE and the agent lose from the elimination of P.

Result 2:
Assuming a RC or RS contract initially, the elimination of contract enforcement (P reduced to zero) has the following consequences:
1. The MNE is worse off or indifferent (the latter occurs only when RC remains RC).

2. The agent may be better off (RS remains RS, or RC shifts to RS), indifferent (RC shifts to E), or worse off (RS shifts to E).

An interesting result that deserves emphasis occurs when only the agent has to pay the defection penalty. With reference to equations (2) and (4), P only appears in (2). Adding P is now identical to just increasing G. The new equivalents of (9) and (10) become

$$L_1 + L_2 - F = 2R - F - r(R - T - G - P) \qquad V = r(R - T - G - P).$$
$$(12)$$

The MNE is worse off than if the penalty was binding on both parties, and the agent is better off (unless this induces a shift to exporting). The intuition is as follows. A binding penalty on the MNE means that the MNE can credibly commit to a lower L_2 (higher second-period earnings for the agent). But this in turn relaxes the agent's incentive-compatibility constraint, which in turn allows the MNE to offer lower rent sharing (lower V), as seen in (10) versus (12). By credibly committing not to fire the agent without penalty, the MNE lowers rent sharing. The MNE cannot be better off by elimination of contract enforcement, including elimination of a penalty to itself only. The MNE should wish to bind itself to the rule of law just as much as it wishes to bind the agent.

14.3   Host-Country Welfare

In this section, I develop an underlying model that generates values of R, and E as functions of more primitive parameters, which in turn permits a welfare analysis. I use a well-known model (linear demand and constant marginal cost) of chapters 2, 3, and 4 that has, for better or worse, been popular in the strategic trade policy literature.[4] Let p_x denote the price of X, with the inverse demand function for X given by

$$p_x = \alpha - \beta X.$$
$$(13)$$

Let c denote the marginal cost of production, with the MNE maximizing profits: $p_x X - cX$. Since the results from this simple model are familiar from chapters 2 and 3, I state them here without derivation. If the MNE produces inside the country, the equilibrium values of X, R (profits before fixed costs F), and consumer surplus (CS) are given by

$$X = \left[\frac{\alpha - c}{2\beta}\right] \qquad R = \beta \left[\frac{\alpha - c}{2\beta}\right]^2 \qquad CS = \frac{\beta}{2}\left[\frac{\alpha - c}{2\beta}\right]^2. \tag{14}$$

Host-country welfare is the sum of consumer surplus and the one-period rent share $(V/2)$ of the agent. Denoting welfare as U_c and U_s in the rent-capture and rent-sharing cases, respectively, (14) and (10) give us

$$U_c = \frac{\beta}{2}\left[\frac{\alpha - c}{2\beta}\right]^2 \tag{15}$$

$$U_s = \frac{\beta}{2}\left[\frac{\alpha - c}{2\beta}\right]^2 + r(R - T - G - 2P)/2 \tag{16}$$

Let t be the unit cost of exporting to the host country. Then the equations analogous to (14) for the exporting case are

$$X = \left[\frac{\alpha - c - t}{2\beta}\right] \qquad E = \beta \left[\frac{\alpha - c - t}{2\beta}\right]^2 \qquad CS = \frac{\beta}{2}\left[\frac{\alpha - c - t}{2\beta}\right]^2. \tag{17}$$

Welfare in the exporting regime is just consumer surplus.

$$U_e = \frac{\beta}{2}\left[\frac{\alpha - c - t}{2\beta}\right]^2 \tag{18}$$

The welfare ranking of the three outcomes is clear from these results: $U_s > U_c > U_e$. Investment in the country is preferred by the host to exporting, because the price is lower with the subsidiary, generating a larger consumer surplus. RS is preferred to RC because of the rent capture by the local agent.

14.4 Optimal Policy

The question of what is the optimal P for the host country is conceptually easy, but difficult in practice due to inequality constraints. From (16), (17), and (18), it is clear that the host country wants the MNE to invest in the country. But given investment occurs, the host country wants to maximize local rent capture V, and it does this by minimizing P. The optimal policy is for the host country to minimize P, subject to the MNE investment in the country, and subject to P non-negative (a "commonsense" constraint to not subsidize defection). The requirement that the firm enter is given by (3), requiring that (9) be greater than or equal to $2E$. The optimal policy is thus

Minimize P subject to

$$2R - F - r(R - T - G - 2P) \geq 2E \tag{19}$$

$$P \geq 0 \tag{20}$$

Note that one of these two constraints must hold with equality in the optimal policy. With reference to figure 14.2, the optimal policy is to set P as close to zero as possible without having the firm chose E; that is, the SE and SC boundaries will be shifted to the right (subject to $P \geq 0$) until the parameter point (F, G) lies on the SE boundary. If the constraint $P \geq 0$ binds, then the solution will be $P = 0$ and the parameter point (F, G) below/right of the SE' locus in figure 14.2: (19) is "slack." Finally, if the parameter point (F, G) lies above EC or to the right of SC' in figure 14.2, then the value of P is irrelevant in any case. Note that the host country will always want entry if the parameter point is below EC ($2R - 2E \geq F$). If the parameter point lies "inside" EC and SC', then $P > 0$ should be set such that the parameter point lies on SE.

If this optimal policy is interior ($P > 0$), note that the host country captures all excess profits from the investment over exporting. This is rather obvious from the condition that the solution lies on the policy-shifted SE locus in figure 14.1, implying that the firm is indifferent between investing and exporting. But it can also be verified by solving (19) for P to get

$$2P = (2E - (2 - r)R)/r + F/r - (T + G). \tag{21}$$

Substituting (21) into the expression for the local agent's rent equation $r(R - T - G - 2P)$ gives agent's rents as $(2R - 2E - F)$: the total available surplus.

Result 3: Optimal Policy
1. The host country wishes the MNE to enter if the total returns to doing so exceed the returns from exporting ($2R - 2E \geq F$: (F, G) is below EC in figures 14.1 and 14.2).
2. The host country will set P as low as possible subject to the constraints that the MNE prefers entry to exporting and $P \geq 0$.
3. If the solution is interior ($P > 0$), the local agent captures the entire surplus from investing over exporting.

As a final result, consider the role of host-country market size in determining the optimal level of P. This will also be relevant in section 14.5. Suppose that (19) holds with equality at the optimum (i.e., $P > 0$). There is some ambiguity here. A larger market means more rents from investment relative to exporting, but it also means more rent sharing with the local agent. Note from (14) and (17) that a *growth* in host-country market size, for example, a *fall* in β, means that R and E each grow in proportion to market size, and therefore $R/E > 0$ is constant. From (21), the restriction that an *increase* in market size *lowers* P is equivalent to the restriction that $R/E > 2/(2 - r)$ or $((2 - r)R - 2E > 0)$. This will hold if t is sufficiently large (R/E is large) and/or r is small. A higher t lowers E, increasing the attractiveness of investing without increasing necessary rent sharing. A lower r lowers necessary rent sharing without affecting the total rents from investment versus exporting.

An equivalent way of putting the question is to ask whether or not SE in figure 14.1 shifts up following an increase in market size. While EC and SC unambiguously shift out, this does not necessarily imply that SE shifts up. If SE does shift up with an increase in market size ($R/E > 2/(2 - r)$), this means that smaller countries should have stricter enforcement (higher P).

14.5   Extensions

In this section, I note some results for a few extensions of the model without going into many technical details.

Two Identical Multinationals

Suppose that there were two MNEs, identical with respect to output and costs, that play a Cournot game against one another.[5] In this case, the expressions for R and E given in (14) and (17) are replaced by DR and DE (D for duopoly) given by

$$DR = \beta \left[\frac{\alpha - c}{3\beta} \right]^2 \qquad DE = \beta \left[\frac{\alpha - c - t}{3\beta} \right]^2. \tag{22}$$

Duopoly results in the same proportional reduction in R and E. Given this result, I can draw on the result in (21) and the paragraph that follows it, noting that the introduction of an identical second firm is analogous to a reduction in market size for a single firm. The same condition noted in the paragraph following (21) gives the condition for the introduction of an additional identical firm to result in an *increase* in the optimal value of P, since I am considering an effective *decrease* in the firm's market size. Added competition raises the optimal value of P if $DR/DE > 2/(2 - r)$. Note that this holds if and only if $R/E > 2/(2 - r)$ since $R/E = DR/DE$. In these circumstances, the added competition reduces the incentives to switch from exporting to investment, and the host country must compensate by raising P.

Two Nonidentical Multinationals

There are infinitely many possible cases to consider here. For example, the firms could have identical outputs but different costs, or identical costs but differentiated goods. I have tried a couple of cases such as these two, and the intuition seems to be basically the same. Suppose that P is set such that the "first" firm enters into domestic production while the "second" firm serves the market by exports. So the first firm has perhaps a lower fixed cost of entry or higher demand justifying the fixed cost.

The decision to increase P so as to induce entry of the second firm is a trade-off between the added consumer surplus of having the second product produced domestically plus the rents to the new local agent versus the inframarginal loss of rents to the local agent of the first firm. Clearly, the host-country government will either raise P by exactly the discrete amount necessary to induce entry of the second firm or not at all.

To add a bit of concreteness, consider an extremely simple situation where there are two symmetric but independent products such that each has the inverse demand function given in (13). Suppose X and Y firms differ only in their fixed costs of entry, denoted $F_y > F_x$. Assume that P is set so that the condition (19) holds for the X firm, meaning that X is produced domestically but Y is imported. Then from (19), the change in P necessary to induce the entry of the Y firm is given by

$$\Delta P = (F_y - F_x)/(2r) > 0. \tag{23}$$

This results in lost rents to the X firm's agent of

$$2r\Delta P = (F_y - F_x) > 0. \tag{24}$$

In evaluating total welfare change, it is slightly cleaner to use the two-period product cycle, comparing two-period consumer surplus gains to two-period managerial rent changes. The overall welfare change is then given by twice the added consumer surplus from Y plus the rents to the Y agent minus the loss of rents to the X agent in (24) (there is no consumer surplus change in X). Combine (14) and (17) with the finding in result 3 that the new Y agent captures all the surplus from the mode switch. Increasing P to induce entry of the Y producer is beneficial if

$$\beta \left[\frac{\alpha - c}{2\beta} \right]^2 - \beta \left[\frac{\alpha - c - t}{2\beta} \right]^2 + (2R - 2E - F_y) - (F_y - F_x) > 0. \tag{25}$$

Using the formulae for E and R from (14) and (17), this reduces to

$$3\beta \left[\frac{\alpha - c}{2\beta} \right]^2 - 3\beta \left[\frac{\alpha - c - t}{2\beta} \right]^2 - (2F_y - F_x) > 0. \tag{26}$$

While I have not attempted the analysis, I believe that extensions of this result to a continuum of firms are straightforward: The optimum P is found where the consumer-surplus plus managerial-rent gain of an additional investment equals the inframarginal loss in rents to domestic agents.

Second-Period Duopoly between the MNE and First-Period Agent

In my discussion of the rent-sharing subsidiary contract, I simply *assume* that the MNE would not offer a contract leading to defection in the second period. Here, I consider a situation in which the MNE offers simply a one-period contract, with the MNE and the agent knowing that they will compete as duopolists in the second period. This seems to be an empirically relevant case insofar as a number of studies have documented the fact that agents of locally owned firms in Latin America and in East Asia often originally receive their training in multinational firms. This does not necessarily imply that they become competitors; they may become suppliers to the MNEs, for example (Katz 1987; Hobday 1995; Blomstrom and Kokko 1998). Treatments of duopoly outcomes including the possibility that the MNE and its former agent compete are found in Ethier and Markusen (1996) and in Fosfuri, Motta, and Ronde (2001).

Because (1) this problem has been treated elsewhere (but never in relation to property rights and contract enforcement), (2) the analysis is somewhat lengthy, and (3) the results are somewhat inconclusive,

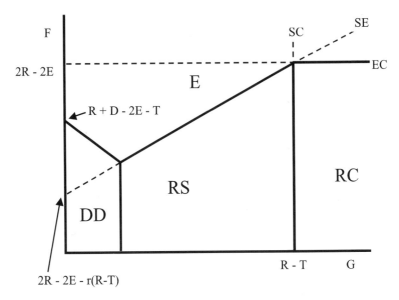

Figure 14.3
Defection occurs in equilibrium

I will simply report the results and refer to a fuller version in my NBER working paper (Markusen 1998b). In it, I show that defection may occur as an equilibrium when both F and G are relatively low. In such a case, the MNE has to pay too much to prevent defection (G is low) but invests anyway since F is low. Figure 14.3 shows a possible outcome at $P = 0$, with the region DD denoting the area where defection occurs and the firm and the first manager play a Cournot duopoly game in the second period (this region need not exist and will not if, e.g., T is sufficiently large).

The welfare difference at the DD-RS boundary in figure 14.3 is ambiguous. Consumer surplus is higher in DD because the price is lower, but the MNE captures all of the (reduced) rents in DD. Thus DD has a higher consumer surplus but lower (i.e., 0) managerial rent.

The effect of raising P is to shift out SE in figure 14.3 as before. The line separating DD and RS is determined by the intersection of SE with the fixed line from $(R + D - 2E - T)$, so the DD region disappears as P increases. Intuitively, a higher P improves the profits for the MNE in RS. A higher P may then induce a regime shift from DD to RS. For reasons just noted, the welfare effects of this are ambiguous.

14.6 Summary and Conclusions

This chapter presents a simple model in order to provide another example of how the transfer of knowledge-based assets to a foreign manager (whether licensee or employee) creates agent opportunism that may inhibit such a transfer. In the model, the local agent learns the necessary technology in order to produce the good in the first period of a two-period product cycle and can quit (defect) to start a rival firm in the second period. The MNE can similarly defect, firing the agent and hiring a new one. I solve for the optimal mode of serving the foreign market as a function of various parameter values. When the multinational does invest in the foreign country, it may be able to extract all rents in a single-product relationship with the manager, which is conceptually close to licensing. Or the multinational may need to share rents with the local manager in a long-term, ongoing relationship that is conceptually close to a subsidiary.

The model is a convenient vehicle for improving our understanding of how contract enforcement, IPP, and so forth influence foreign direct investment into host economies and host-country welfare. The principal result is both MNE profits and host-country welfare are improved by the institution of contract enforcement if it leads to a mode shift from exporting to production within the host economy. Exporting dissipates rents and results in a higher product price in the host country, so domestic production results in a consumer-surplus gain and may result in rent capture by the local agent. Contract enforcement leaves host-country welfare unchanged or reduces welfare, however, if a subsidiary was chosen prior to the policy change. In the latter case, rents are transferred from the local agent to the MNE, precisely the scenario feared by many developing countries.

Other results include the fact that the MNE is better off and the agent worse off if the MNE is bound by a contract than if it is not. A binding contract allows the MNE to credibly commit to a lower second-period licensing fee, which lowers the amount of rent it must share with the agent in order to ensure incentive compatibility for the agent. MNEs thus benefit from a strong commitment to the "rule of law," and benefit as much from their own commitment as they do from bindings on local agents.

The optimal level of enforcement occurs when the level of P is set to just induce entry (subject to a non-negativity constraint on P). Unlike optimal Pigouvian taxes, the optimal P is not given by a marginal condition but requires setting the MNE profits from discrete alternatives equal to one another.

The chapter concludes with a few extensions of the basic argument. These are unfortunately largely ambiguous. For example, it is not clear whether a larger or more competitive environment in the form of several identical foreign MNEs calls for a lower or higher optimal P. A low P may lead to second-period duopoly between the MNE and its original manager, but the welfare effects of this are unclear. More managers are trained under the duopoly outcome and local firms are formed. While these have no welfare implications in this model, they might have in a somewhat richer model with various kinds of spillover effects.

Somewhat clearer results emerge if there are a series of potential investors who would enter a different level of P. Optimality requires that the consumer-surplus plus managerial-rent gain from an additional investment attracted by raising P just equals the inframarginal losses in rents to the agents of existing projects. While that condition is simple in theory, it is not easy to implement or calculate in practice. Ideally, the host-country government could do better with an individual P for each foreign investment project. That is a rather awful thought, but in fact countries or U.S. states do indeed negotiate individual deals on large projects (not necessarily to their benefit). There could be a set legal policy, tax rates, and so forth, with special incentives or discounts offered to certain firms. I do not wish to go on record as advocating this, but it does offer a *theoretical* way out of the dilemma of a single policy balancing marginal gains of a higher P against inframarginal losses. Under a uniform policy, for example, China has to weigh the gains from a new factory against inframarginal rent transfers to Mickey Mouse (Disney).

In summary, I hope that the model captures some of the policy debate over intellectual property rights and other legal institutions. There is clearly some truth in the developed countries' view that developing countries can benefit from more investment that follows stronger legal protection for investors. On the other hand, there is clearly some validity in the developing countries' view that such protection only enriches the MNEs and requires the poor countries to pay more for pharmaceuticals, software, and other products. Results show that which view dominates depends on the initial situation, and whether or not inward investment occurs anyway in the absence of strong investor protection.

15

An Asymmetric-Information Model of Internalization

15.1 Introduction

I have noted several times in the book that a fundamental problem in the theory of the multinational corporation is why these firms exist at all. If there are inherent costs of doing business abroad, then foreign markets should be served either by exports or by local producers in these markets. The traditional explanation for multinational firms rests on the existence of firm-specific, intangible assets that give these firms offsetting cost advantages over foreign-country producers (see Caves 1996). These assets often take the form of knowledge capital within the firm, this capital being either production based and arising from R&D activity and managerial/engineering experience as in chapter 14, or consumer based and the result of product differentiation, brand reputation, and so forth as in chapter 13.

While the existence of knowledge-based capital may explain multinational firms, it does not, by itself, explain why a firm would wish to make a large investment in a foreign branch plant (or even a direct sales branch) versus simply contracting for production and sales with a host-country entrepreneur. Reasons for wishing to directly own foreign facilities is often referred to as "internalization theory," the subject of part III of this book. One reason the firm may choose direct investment over some arm's-length arrangement is that the latter is subject to agency costs that the former avoids. For instance, the public-goods nature of knowledge capital may produce agency problems involving dissipation of that capital by licensees. Horstmann and Markusen (1987b) and chapter 13 argue that, because a licensee will not fully appropriate the returns from maintaining the firm's brand reputation, it will dissipate that reputation in circumstances in which it is in the firm's interest to maintain it. Ethier and Markusen (1996) and chapter 14 support direct investment based on the inability of the multinational to prevent a foreign licensee from "learning by doing" and so defecting to become a local competitor for the firm.[1]

In this chapter, I provide an alternative agency explanation for the multinational firm's choice between direct investment and an arm's-length agreement. Here, the multinational firm may adopt some contractual arrangement with a local agent as a means of exploiting any superior information the agent may possess regarding market characteristics. The cost of such an arrangement to the firm is that the local agent can use this superior information to extract some of the multinational rents. The choice for the multinational then turns on whether the savings that result from learning about the market through the agency arrangement are more than dissipated by the agency costs that the contract produces.

The setting is one in which a firm is seeking to sell its product in a new (foreign) market. Because it is entering a new market, the firm is uncertain about the revenues it can expect to generate. In entering the market, it can either choose to invest immediately in its own sales operation or it can contract for sales via a local agent. The local agent, having experience in the market, has information on market characteristics not available to the multinational. Within this setting, I derive both the optimal multiperiod agency contract and the optimal mode of entry for the multinational. Because one often observes in the data that agency contracts are of limited duration, the model allows for the possibility of short-term contracts that terminate at some predetermined future date. The analysis includes a consideration of the determinants of the decision by the multinational to adopt a short-term (nonrenewable) contract as well as the multinational's choice between the contract and immediate direct investment.

As previous discussion suggests, the multinational's decision regarding initial entry mode depends on the size of the returns to information gathering relative to the rents that the agent can be expected to extract. Things that make investment mistakes more costly, like large setup costs relative to market size/revenues or easy termination of an agency agreement, make a contract more attractive. Things that increase the returns to having superior information, like potentially large but variable sales revenue, increase agency costs and so make immediate investment attractive. Thus, the model predicts that a contractual arrangement is more likely when markets are on average small and investment mistakes are very costly (there is large potential profit variability due to the possibility of very low sales outcomes) and conversion from a contractual arrangement to owned sales operations can be achieved quickly. Further, if conversion from a contract to an owned sales operation occurs, it occurs when past sales are relatively large.

Although there have been no empirical studies (to the best of our knowledge) that explicitly focus on the ideas developed here, considerable evidence points to the empirical relevance of the model. Nicholas (1982, 1983) notes that, among his sample of British multinational firms operating during the pre-1939 period, 88 percent sold their products initially under a contract with a local agent in the foreign country before converting to direct sales or production branches. In instances where conversion to direct investment did occur, the period of agency varied from four to twenty-five years. According to Nicholas, the historical record indicates that the decision to terminate the relationship was a conscious one on the multinational's part (as opposed to being the result of business failure by the agent) based both on a desire by the firm to avoid agency costs and on its having learned, through the agency arrangement, that information on local market characteristics that made the agency contract valuable in the first place.

Zeile (1993) documents a modern tendency for many foreign firms exporting to the United States to use direct sales branches to control the wholesaling and distribution of their products. While he provides no comparable data on the use of agents or licensees, this study at least points to the quantitative importance of the direct sales branch mode of foreign operations. At the same time, survey data on Australian firms' business experiences in East Asia by Thompson (1994) and McIntosh/Baring (1993) provide evidence of the potential problems arising from various contractual arrangements with foreign partners. These problems include the reliability of information, distribution, promotion, and servicing issues. In general, the Australian firms felt disadvantaged by their own ignorance of the Asian markets. The studies recommend the use of local agents only for relatively short-term projects and/or ventures involving commodity products. Direct investment with majority control is found to be important for long-term projects and/or those involving more complex production and servicing.

Finally, Nicholas et al. (1994) provide survey data on direct investment by Japanese multinationals in Australia (a small but high-income market). Of those firms responding, 60 percent indicated that they used an Australian agent for some period of time before making any direct investment, and 69 percent indicated that they exported to Australia using a trading company before making their investment. I should also note a related theoretical literature regarding information gathering in new product markets and the firm's investment decision. McGahan (1993) considers whether a new product monopolist should engage in immediate, large-scale investment that would deter entry by future competitors or explore the market initially with prototypes requiring smaller capacity investments and only invest further if the market proves large. While entry deterrence is not an issue in my model, it has the same information-gathering features as in McGahan's model.

The specifics of my model are detailed in the next section. Section 15.3 provides the optimal agency contract when short-term contracts are not possible, while the optimal contract given the possibility of short-term contracts is derived in section 15.4. The determinants of the multinational's decision regarding direct investment versus contracting is also analyzed in section 15.4. Section 15.5 provides some concluding remarks.

15.2   The Foreign Sales Model

Consider a situation in which a producer (the MNE) of an established product, X, located in Country 1 (the home country) has decided to sell this product in Country 2 (the foreign country), a market in which the MNE has no previous sales experience. Among the options for selling in the foreign country, two are potentially most profitable: contracting with a local sales agent or establishing an owned local sales operation. The foreign market is characterized by a potential pool, N_i, of identical customers with individual demand functions given by the expression $x = f(p)$, where x is the quantity demanded of X by any individual customer if the price of X is p. Because the product is an established one, the characteristics of the demand function are known to both the MNE and any potential local sales agent. Such is not the case for the size of the potential customer pool, N_i. The sales agent is assumed to know the value of N_i, due perhaps to past experience in the local market; the MNE, on the other hand, is initially uninformed as to its actual value. The MNE does know the distribution of values for N_i, however. For simplicity, this distribution is assumed such that N_i may take on one of two possible values: N_1 or $N_2 > N_1$. The probability that $N_i = N_1$ is given by ρ with $0 < \rho < 1$.[2]

While the potential customer pool is of a fixed size (either N_1 or N_2), the number of customers to actually purchase the MNE's product is a variable that depends on sales effort. In particular, one can assume that the number of actual customers is proportional to the size of the potential customer pool, with the variable of proportionality depending on sales effort. Because it is possible that the local sales agent and the MNE's own sales force have differential abilities at generating customers, the variable of proportionality is allowed to depend on whether the product is sold by the local sales agent or via the MNE's owned sales operation. If a local agent is employed and the potential customer pool is N_i, then the number of actual customers, n_i, is given by the expression $n_i = e_a N_i$, where e_a is the local agent's sales effort and is normalized such that $0 \leq e_a \leq 1$. If the MNE uses its own sales force, then the number of actual customers is given by $n_i = \alpha e_m N_i$, where e_m is measured in the same units as e_a, and αe_m gives efficiency units of sales effort by the MNE's sales force. A value of $\alpha > 1$ would indicate that the MNE's sales force is more efficient at producing customers than the local agent, due perhaps to greater experience or familiarity with the product. Alternatively, a value of $\alpha < 1$ would indicate that the MNE's sales force is less efficient, perhaps as a result of less familiarity with local conditions. Sales effort is costly for both the local agent and the MNE's own sales force, with the cost of effort given by the function $C = c(e_j)$, $j = a, m$. The effort cost function is assumed to be increasing and strictly convex with $c'(0) = 0$.

Finally, assume that the cost of establishing a sales operation in the foreign country depends on the choice of sales mode. Should the MNE establish its own sales operation, then it incurs a one-time setup cost of $G \geq 0$. This cost represents a sunk cost and captures such things as legal costs, cost of dealing with bureaucratic red tape, any specific investment costs, and the like. In addition, it incurs a per-period fixed cost of $F \geq 0$, representing various administrative and overhead costs and any costs of compensating its own sales force for foregone alternative opportunities. In contrast, the local sales agent, having already established its operation and already incurring various costs due to other contracts, is assumed able to add the MNE's contract with no additional setup costs ($G = 0$ for the local agent). In essence, setup costs are assumed to result from establishing and operating a sales agency and not from adding an additional product to the sales line. The local agent does incur a lump-sum cost of $R \geq 0$ from adding the MNE's product that represents any added administrative costs for the agent due to adding an additional contract as well as costs of the agent's foregone alternatives (any lost revenues from not entering into an alternative contractual arrangement). Beyond these costs (and the sales effort costs), it is assumed that neither the MNE nor the local agent incurs any other direct costs in producing or marketing the product. It is also assumed that the MNE (or its agent) faces no direct competition (either actual or potential) for its product in the foreign country.[3]

The model implies that, in making a decision on the form of foreign sales operations, the MNE is confronted with a trade-off. The sales agent has the advantage of having better information regarding market size as well as having lower setup costs. These features favor the agency contract. On the other hand, the use of a sales agent must inevitably result in agency costs for the MNE arising from the agent's ability to exploit this better information. In addition, the agent may be less efficient at producing customers than the MNE. These features favor an ownership arrangement. In what follows, I explore the nature of this trade-off, considering it first in a situation in which the MNE can only choose between a once-and-for-all contract with the agent or the permanent establishment of an owned sales operation. I then ask whether (and under what circumstances) the MNE can do better by using a nonrenewable, short-term contract.

15.3 A One-Period Choice Problem

To help define some of the issues involved in the MNE's choice of sales mode, it is useful to consider first a simple one-period problem. One can think of this problem as providing the solution to the optimal multiperiod contracting problem when the MNE is restricted to either contracting once-and-for-all with a local sales agent or permanently establishing an owned foreign sales operation.

To begin, consider the optimal contract should the MNE choose to employ a local sales agent in the foreign country. A contract, in this case, is assumed to specify a price, p, at which X will be sold, a quantity, q, of X that will be sold and a transfer, w, from the MNE to the local sales agent (the sales agent is assumed to remit all sales revenues to the MNE). By the revelation principle,[4] the optimal contract can be found by a consideration of those contracts in which the values of p, q, and w are conditioned only on the agent's report of market size, N_i.

Because the individual demand function is known by both parties and the profit-maximizing price is independent of N_i, the value of p specified in the optimal contract will be independent of N_i. To save on notation, p will, therefore, be suppressed in the description of the optimal contract that follows. The optimal contract, then, is described by a menu $\langle q(N_i), w(N_i) \rangle$ that satisfies both incentive compatibility (IC) and individual rationality (IR).[5] The agent is assumed to choose one (q, w) pair from this menu, choosing the one that maximizes utility. Both the MNE and the local agent are assumed risk neutral, and the menu chosen by the MNE is the one that maximizes its expected profits. It is assumed that the value of R is not so large as to make contracting with the agent always unprofitable for the MNE.

To solve for the optimal contract, note that an agent facing a potential customer pool of size N_i, having contracted to sell a quantity q_i, must engage in sales effort given by the expression $e_a = q_i / f(p) N_i$.[6] If units of X are normalized such that, at the profit-maximizing p, $f(p) = 1$, sales effort simplifies to $e_a = q_i / N_i$. Then, the optimal contract is defined as the solution to the following maximization problem:

$$\max_{q_1, q_2, w_1, w_2} E\pi = \rho(pq_1 - w_1) + (1 - \rho)(pq_2 - w_2) \tag{C1}$$

subject to

$$w_1 - c(q_1/N_1) \geq w_2 - c(q_2/N_1)$$

$$w_2 - c(q_2/N_2) \geq w_1 - c(q_1/N_2)$$

$$w_1 - c(q_1/N_1) \geq R$$

$$w_2 - c(q_2/N_2) \geq R$$

where the first two constraints are the two incentive compatibility conditions and the last two the individual rationality constraints.

The solution to this problem can be illustrated diagrammatically.[7] Consider figure 15.1. The straight lines in the figure represent the MNE's iso-profit curves in (w, q) space, while the curves give the indifference curves for an agent. There are two sets of indifference curves, one when the value of N_i is N_1 and another when $N_i = N_2$. The slope of an indifference curve is given by the expression $(1/N_i)C'(q/N_i)$ so that the indifference curves for $N_i = N_2$ are flatter than those for $N_i = N_1$. Point A gives the MNE's profit-maximizing contract when the customer pool is known to be of size N_1; point B gives the profit-maximizing

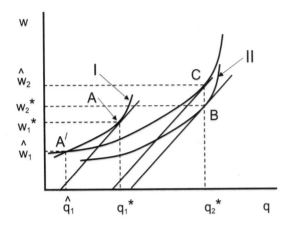

Curve I: $w - c(q/N_1) = R$ Curve II: $w - c(q/N_2) = R$

Figure 15.1
The optimal contract

contract when the pool is known to be N_2.[8] Since a given increase in effort generates a larger increase in sales the larger is N_i, it is profitable for the MNE to have the agent expend more sales effort in the market with the larger customer pool. As a result, $q_2^* > q_1^*$ and $w_2^* > w_1^*$. This same fact regarding the technology of sales production means that, should the agent facing a customer pool of N_2 obtain the contract (q_1^*, w_1^*), utility is larger than R (less sales effort is required to produce q_1^*). Thus, the indifference curve through point B (curve II) passes below point A.

This last feature of the full-information contracts means that the MNE can never implement it if the value of N_i is unknown. If faced with the prospect of (q_2^*, w_2^*), the agent will always select the contract (q_1^*, w_1^*) instead. In general, because the existence of private information means that the contract offer must induce agents to self-select, the MNE will be able to extract all of the surplus from the agent when $N_i = N_1$, but only enough surplus when $N_i = N_2$ to make the agent indifferent between accepting (q_2, w_2) and claiming that the potential customer pool is N_1 (in particular, the surplus must be greater than R). In terms of the problem (C1) above, the profit-maximizing set of contracts will be such that only the first individual-rationality constraint (IR_1) and the second incentive-compatibility constraint (IC_2) are binding. In terms of the diagram, the set of contracts will be such that

(q_1, w_1) lies on indifference curve I (IR_1 binds), and both (q_1, w_1), (q_2, w_2) lie on a single indifference curve for $N_i = N_2$ (IC_2 binds).

The actual profit-maximizing contracts are given by the points C and A'. Note that $q_1 = \hat{q}_1 < q_1^*$ while $q_2 = q_2^*$. This outcome results from the fact that, at point A, a decrease in q and w along indifference curve I has no impact on the MNE's expected profits at the margin when $N_i = N_1$ (this is just an envelope argument). However, because the agent's indifference curves are flatter when $N_i = N_2$, the reduction makes the contract $(\hat{q}_1, \hat{w}_1)$ less attractive to the agent facing a customer pool of N_2 (IC_2 is relaxed). As a result, the MNE can offer a contract (q_2, w_2) with $q_2 = q_2^*$, but w lower than would be needed if $q_1 = q_1^*$, and still have it accepted when $N_i = N_2$. The lower w means that, on net, expected profits rise from the reduction in q_1. Because changes in q_2 relax no constraints, its value remains at q_2^*. For the same reasons as in the full-information contract, $w_2 > w_1$.

How does the MNE rank this contract relative to direct investment via the establishment of an owned sales operation? Suppose that part of the cost of setting up operations for the MNE (i.e., part of the sunk cost, G) is determining the size of the potential customer pool.[9] Suppose, also, that F is not so large as to make selling in the foreign country unprofitable if $N_i = N_1$ (although $F + G$ may well be so) and that $\alpha = 1$. Then, under the equilibrium contract, the quantity sold if $N_i = N_2$ is the same as if the MNE establishes its own sales operation. However, the MNE must compensate the sales agent not only an amount R but some additional amount that is an information rent earned by the local agent. If $N_i = N_1$, while the agent earns no information rent, the quantity sold under the contract is smaller than the amount the MNE would sell with its own sales force $\hat{q}_1 < q_1^*$. Thus, even if $R = 0$, the MNE can expect one of two possible types of agency costs under the equilibrium contract: the information rents earned by the agent should $N_i = N_2$ and the inefficiently low level of sales if $N_i = N_1$. These costs must be traded off against the extra costs of establishing an owned sales operation, $F + G$.

If $\alpha > 1$, so that the MNE's own sales force is more efficient than the local agent, direct investment is additionally desirable relative to the above situation. Conversely, if $\alpha < 1$—the MNE's own sales force is less efficient than the local agent—direct investment is less desirable. Rather than considering here the circumstances under which the MNE prefers a contract to direct investment, I delay this issue until section 15.4 when the MNE has the option of using short-term contracts.

15.4   The Multiperiod Choice Problem

The Contracting Problem

In the contract setting above, should the MNE learn through the agency arrangement that the market is large enough to make an owned sales operation profitable, it is unable to take advantage of this information—the contract is a once-and-for-all contract. This fact makes the contract more costly and makes immediate FDI an attractive alternative. A contract that is of limited duration, on the other hand, allows the MNE to utilize information acquired through the agency relationship by switching to an owned sales operation if this option is found to be more profitable. This feature of a short-term contract makes its initial use an attractive option for the MNE. In what follows, I explore whether and under what circumstances the MNE will choose this short-term contracting option as a means of entering a foreign market.

To proceed, I assume that the MNE is now able to commit to an offer of a nonrenewable contract of finite length in addition to the infinite length contracts available previously. Because of this additional option, a contract is now a triple $\langle q(N_i), w(N_i), T(N_i) \rangle$ where, as before, $q(\cdot)$ gives per-period sales and $w(\cdot)$ the per-period transfer from the MNE to the local agent. The variable $T(\cdot)$ gives the last period for which the contract is in force. In what follows, I will use the abbreviated form (q_i, w_i, T_i) to represent this contract.

As in section 15.3, the MNE's equilibrium contract offer is defined as the one that maximizes its expected profits subject to the appropriate individual rationality and incentive compatibility constraints. This contract is given by the solution to the following maximization problem:

$$\max \rho \left[\sum_{t=0}^{T_1} (pq_1 - w_1)\delta^t + \delta^{T_1+1}\left(\frac{\pi_1}{1-\delta} - G \right) \right] \tag{C2}$$

$$+ (1 - \rho) \left[\sum_{t=0}^{T_2} (pq_2 - w_2)\delta^t + \delta^{T_2+1}\left(\frac{\pi_2}{1-\delta} - G \right) \right]$$

subject to

$$\sum_{t=0}^{T_1} [w_1 - c(q_1/N_1)]\delta^t + \sum_{t=T_1+1}^{\infty} R\delta^t \geq \sum_{t=0}^{T_2} [w_2 - c(q_2/N_1)]\delta^t + \sum_{t=T_2+1}^{\infty} R\delta^t$$

$$\sum_{t=0}^{T_2}[w_2 - c(q_2/N_2)]\delta^t + \sum_{t=T_2+1}^{\infty} R\delta^t \geq \sum_{t=0}^{T_1}[w_1 - c(q_1/N_2)]\delta^t + \sum_{t=T_1+1}^{\infty} R\delta^t$$

$$\sum_{t=0}^{T_1}[w_1 - c(q_1/N_1)]\delta^t + \sum_{t=T_1+1}^{\infty} R\delta^t \geq \frac{R}{1-\delta}$$

$$\sum_{t=0}^{T_2}[w_2 - c(q_2/N_2)]\delta^t + \sum_{t=T_2+1}^{\infty} R\delta^t \geq \frac{R}{1-\delta}$$

In the preceding formulation, π_1 represents the MNE's per-period profit from its owned sales operation should $N_i = N_1$. It is defined by $\pi_1 = \max_q pq - C(q/\alpha N_1) - F$; the variable π_2 is defined analogously. The variable $\delta \in (0, 1)$ is a common discount factor. Also built in to the above problem is the assumption that the local sales agent can take advantage of the best alternative opportunity once the MNE terminates the sales contract. The alternative assumption that the local sales agent loses this opportunity upon contracting with the MNE could easily be incorporated into the above problem.

By arguments identical to those employed in section 15.3, one can show that IR$_1$ and IC$_2$ bind (the second and third constraints above) and that IR$_2$ (the last constraint) does not bind. In contrast to the previous problem, IC$_1$ (the first constraint) may or may not bind; however, a necessary condition for IC$_1$ to bind is that $T_1 > T_2$.[10] In what follows, I assume that IC$_1$ does not bind. However, I note at various points in the discussion to follow how our results would be affected were IC$_1$ binding. Given these observations and letting λ_1 be the Lagrange multiplier for IR$_1$ and λ_2 the multiplier for IC$_2$, the conditions defining the pairs (q_1, w_1), (q_2, w_2) for the equilibrium multiperiod contract are

$$\frac{\partial L}{\partial q_1} = \left[pp + \lambda_2 c'(q_1/N_2)\frac{1}{N_2} - \lambda_1 c'(q_1/N_1)\frac{1}{N_1} \right]\frac{1 - \delta^{T_1+1}}{1-\delta} = 0 \tag{1}$$

$$\frac{\partial L}{\partial w_1} = [-p - \lambda_2 + \lambda_1]\frac{1 - \delta^{T_1+1}}{1-\delta} = 0 \tag{2}$$

$$\frac{\partial L}{\partial q_2} = \left[(1-p)p - \lambda_2 c'(q_2/N_2)\frac{1}{N_2} \right]\frac{1 - \delta^{T_2+1}}{1-\delta} = 0 \tag{3}$$

$$\frac{\partial L}{\partial w_2} = [-(1-p) + \lambda_2]\frac{1 - \delta^{T_2+1}}{1-\delta} = 0 \tag{4}$$

The reader can check that these conditions are identical (up to a multiplicative constant) to those that would define the optimal values of q_1 and q_2 in the once-and-for-all contracting problem of section 15.3. Thus, as before, $q_2 = q_2^*$ while $q_1 = \hat{q}_1 < q_1^*$. The values of w_1 and w_2 are those that make IR_1 and IC_2 hold as equalities.[11]

More interesting are the results regarding the optimal values of T_1 and T_2. The impacts on the Lagrangean of a one-period increase in T_1 or T_2 are given by (5) and (6), respectively, as

$$\{\rho(pq_1 - w_1 - \pi_1 + (1-\delta)G) - \lambda_2[w_1 - c(q_1/N_2) - R]$$
$$+ \lambda_1[w_1 - c(q_1/N_1) - R]\}\delta^{T_1+1} \tag{5}$$

$$\{(1-\rho)(pq_2 - w_2 - \pi_2 + (1-\delta)G) + \lambda_2[w_2 - c(q_2/N_2) - R]\}\delta^{T_2+1} \tag{6}$$

The first thing to note about the above expressions is that their signs are independent of T_i. This follows from the fact that the values of q_1, q_2, λ_1, and λ_2 determined in equations (1)–(4) are all independent of T_i.[12] As a result, the optimal values of T_i must be either 0 or ∞, with $T_1 = 0$ if the sign of (5) is negative and $T_1 = \infty$ if (5) is positive. The sign of (6) determines the value of T_2 in a similar fashion.

Substitution for λ_1, λ_2, $\hat{q}_1$, and q_2^* from conditions (1)–(4) allows the bracketed expressions in (5) and (6) to be written as

$$\rho[(p\hat{q}_1 - c(\hat{q}_1/N_1) - R) - (\pi_1 - (1-\delta)G)]$$
$$- (1-\rho)[c(\hat{q}_1/N_1) - c(\hat{q}_1/N_2)] \tag{7}$$

and

$$(1-\rho)[(pq_2^* - c(q_2^*/N_2) - R) - (\pi_2 - (1-\delta)G)]. \tag{8}$$

Inspection of (8) reveals that $T_2 = 0$ if the total one-period returns from utilizing a local agent when $N_i = N_2$ (the first term in parentheses) are smaller than the one-period returns from the MNE employing its own sales force (the second term). $T_2 = \infty$ if the opposite is true. The MNE will find an owned sales operation more profitable the smaller are F and G relative to R and the larger is α.

As for T_1, it also is zero if the MNE finds an owned sales operation more profitable when $N_i = N_1$ than utilizing a local agent (the first bracketed term). However, unlike the situation with T_2, the opposite ranking of returns does not guarantee that $T_1 = \infty$. This is because an increase in T_1 results in an increase in the information rents that must be paid to the agent to induce self-selection when $N_i = N_2$. This increment in expected information rents is given by the second term in (7). These rents represent per-period payments to the agent over and above opportunity cost (R) when $N_i = N_2$ and are required to induce the agent to select the appropriate contract. The rents arise because, when $N_i = N_2$, the agent can always generate a given amount of sales with less effort than when $N_i = N_1$. As a consequence, the agent can always select the contract designed for the situation $N_i = N_1$ and meet the sales requirement with sufficiently little effort to earn a return above R. The information rents exactly compensate the agent for this return when the N_2 contract is chosen. Information rents will be small either when N_1 is close to N_2 (the effort cost savings for the agent from choosing the N_1 contract when, in fact, $N_i = N_2$ are small) or when N_1 is very small (effort costs for $\hat{q}_1$ are small regardless of the value of N_i).[13] Thus, in addition to having F and G large relative to R and/or α small, N_1 being either small or close to N_2 will result in $T_1 = \infty$. These results are summarized in the following proposition:

PROPOSITION 1: If F and G are small relative to R and α large, then $T_1 = T_2 = 0$. If F and G are large relative to R and α small and, in addition, either (a) N_1 close to N_2 or (b) N_1 small, then $T_1 = T_2 = \infty$.

Two other possibilities are (c) $T_1 = 0$, $T_2 = \infty$ and (d) $T_1 = \infty$, $T_2 = 0$. The former case arises when F and G are sufficiently large relative to R and/or α sufficiently small that the returns from utilizing the local agent are larger than from the MNE employing its own sales force when $N_i = N_2$. However, when $N_i = N_1$, information rents are sufficiently large as to offset any profit advantage the local agent might provide.

The latter case is perhaps the most interesting of the four possibilities and one often found in the data. For this situation to arise, it must be that, when $N_i = N_1$, the returns from utilizing a local agent are sufficiently large relative to those from an owned sales operation that the differential swamps any costs the MNE expects to incur from paying information rents. At the same time, it must be that, when $N_i = N_2$, the returns from an owned sales operation are larger than those from utilizing a local agent. The fact that the costs of operating an owned sales operation are lumpy suggests that this outcome is feasible if N_2 is sufficiently large and N_1 sufficiently small. The following proposition confirms this intuition by providing conditions on N_1 and N_2 sufficient to guarantee the outcome $T_1 = \infty$, $T_2 = 0$.[14]

PROPOSITION 2: Suppose that (a) $R = 0$, (b) $\alpha > 1$, and (c) F, G such that $\quad 0 < F + (1 - \delta)G < \{pq_2^*(\alpha) - c[q_2^*(\alpha)/\alpha N_2]\} - \{pq_2^* - c(q_2^*/N_2)\}$.

Then there exists a value $\underline{N}_1 > 0$, such that, for all $0 < N_1 < \underline{N}_1$, the optimal contract has $T_1 = \infty$, $T_2 = 0$.

Proof: Conditions (a) and (c) guarantee that (8) is negative and so $T_2 = 0$. Condition (b) guarantees that there are values of F and G such that (c) can be satisfied. Condition (a) also guarantees that the program (C2) defines the optimal contract for all values of N_1, N_2. From (1), this program has the feature that $\hat{q}_1 > 0$ for all $N_1 > 0$ and $\hat{q}_1 \to 0$ as $N_1 \to 0$. This fact implies that (7) approaches the value $F + (1 - \delta)G > 0$ as $N_1 \to 0$. Thus, for N_1 sufficiently small, (7) is positive and therefore $T_1 = \infty$.

Two features of this contract make it of particular interest. First, the MNE uses a short-term contract to gather information about market size. The contract allows the MNE to convert to an owned sales operation when this sales mode is more profitable and to keep the agency contract when this arrangement is the more profitable one. Second, conversion to FDI occurs when the value of shipments is large while retention of the agency contract occurs when the value of shipments is small. This predicted behavior conforms well to observed outcomes on FDI.

The Choice between Contracting and FDI

Of course, rather than entering the market initially via a contractual arrangement, the MNE may choose immediate direct investment. Should the MNEs choose this latter option, then I assume as previously that it learns the value of N_i in the process of establishing its operations. I also assume that, having established operations, it pays the MNE to operate for at least one period regardless of the value of N_i.[15] After this one period of operation, the MNE may choose to remain in the foreign country for additional periods or withdraw and sell via a contracted sales agent. In the case of MNE withdrawal from the foreign country, the agency contract will be the full information one since the MNE has learned the value of N_i.

As for the MNE's choice of initial sales mode, when the optimal contract has either $T_1 = T_2 = 0$ or $T_1 = T_2 = \infty$ (the situations described in proposition 1), the MNE's decision is implied by the values of T_i. In the former case, the MNE prefers FDI over any contract with a local sales agent while, in the latter, it prefers a contract involving a permanent arrangement with a local sales agent over FDI. Thus, when the MNE's costs are low relative to those of the agent and its sales force is more efficient, direct investment will occur initially. If the MNE's costs are high and its sales force less efficient, a permanent agency arrangement will result.

What about the remaining situations—namely, those for which (a) $T_1 = 0$, $T_2 = \infty$, and (b) $T_1 = \infty$, $T_2 = 0$? While both types of contracts are legitimate given the MNE's assumed ability to commit, I focus on those situations in which the latter contract is the optimal one. This is done both because I think this case is more relevant empirically and because the former contract suffers from time-inconsistency problems that make it unattractive. In particular, this contract has the feature that it would be in both agents' interest to renegotiate the contract to a long-term contract when $N_i = N_1$. Of course, for those interested in this case, an analysis similar to that which follows could be carried out for this contract.

Turning to the situation in which the optimal contract is $T_1 = \infty$, $T_2 = 0$,[16] the MNE's expected profits under this contract are

$$V^a = \rho \frac{p\hat{q}_1 - \hat{w}_1}{1 - \delta} + (1 - \rho)\left[(pq_2^* - \hat{w}_2) + \frac{\delta\pi_2}{1 - \delta} - \delta G\right]. \qquad (9)$$

If the MNE chooses FDI initially, then it earns profits of π_2 each period if $N_i = N_2$. If $N_i = N_1$, then the MNE earns profits, π_1, in period 1 and profits given by $\max[\pi_1, pq_1^* - w_1^*]$ in each subsequent period. This latter expression takes into account the possibility that the MNE may find it more profitable to shut down its operations in the foreign country and sell via a local sales agent. The expression $pq_1^* - w_1^*$ gives the MNE's per-period profits should it choose this option.[17] The MNE's expected profits from choosing FDI initially are therefore given by the expression

$$V^I = \rho\left(\pi_1 + \delta \max\left[\frac{\pi_1}{1 - \delta}, \frac{(pq_1^* - w_1^*)}{1 - \delta}\right]\right) + (1 - \rho)\left(\frac{\pi_2}{1 - \delta}\right) - G. \qquad (10)$$

If $V^I > V^a$, then the MNE chooses FDI initially, while it chooses a contract with the local agent initially if $V^I < V^a$.

As in the case of the single-period problem, the MNE's decision to contract initially with a local agent or invest in an owned sales operation turns on the balance between the savings arising from lower setup costs ($G = 0$) and the losses due to lower efficiency at generating customers and agency costs created by the imperfect information. The exact nature of the trade-off between these different elements can be quantified by noting that the difference $V^I - V^a$ can be expressed as[18]

$$V^I - V^a = [\rho\pi_1 + (1 - \rho)\pi_2]$$

$$- [\rho(pq_1^* - w_1^*) + (1 - \rho)(pq_2^* - w_2^*) - [G(1 - \delta + \rho\delta)]$$

$$+ \frac{\delta\rho}{1 - \delta} \max[0, \pi_1 - (pq_1^* - w_1^*)] + (1 - \rho)(\hat{w}_2 - w_2^*)$$

$$+ \frac{\rho}{1 - \delta} [(pq_1^* - w_1^*) - (p\hat{q}_1 - \hat{w}_1)]. \tag{11}$$

The first two lines of (11) plus the first term in the third line give the difference between the MNE's expected profits, should it choose FDI, and its expected profits, were it able to contract with a local sales agent and implement the full-information outcomes. These terms capture the relevant gains and losses from the use of the different selling technologies implied by the local agent as opposed to an owned sales operation. The last two terms in (11) are the agency costs resulting from the fact that the contract with the local agent cannot implement the full-information outcomes. The first of these terms is the information rent that the agent extracts if $N_i = N_2$, while the second is the profit loss resulting from the fact that q_1 is distorted away from the full-information level.[19]

If one substitutes out for w_1^*, $\hat{w}_1$, w_2^* and $\hat{w}_2$ using IR$_1$, IC$_2$, and the IR constraints for the full-information contracting problem, (11) can be rewritten as

$$V^I - V^a = [E\pi^I - E\pi^a] - [G(1 - \delta + \rho\delta)]$$

$$+ \frac{\delta\rho}{1 - \delta} \max[0, \pi_1 - [pq_1^* - c(q_1^*/N_1) - R]]$$

$$+ \frac{1 - \rho}{1 - \delta} [c(\hat{q}_1/N_1) - c(\hat{q}_1/N_2)]$$

$$+ \frac{\rho}{1 - \delta} ([pq_1^* - c(q_1^*/N_1)] - [p\hat{q}_1 - c(\hat{q}_1/N_1)]) \tag{12}$$

where the value of $E\pi^I$ is given by the expression $E\pi^I = \rho\pi_1 + (1 - \rho)\pi_2$ and that of $E\pi^a$ by $E\pi^a = \rho[pq_1^* - c(q_1^*/N_1)] + (1 - \rho)[pq_2^* - c(q_2^*/N_2)] - R$. Because (12) contains the maximized value of profits under the two selling modes and also incorporates the relevant constraints from the contracting problem (IC_2 and IR_1), envelope properties can be exploited to determine how the MNE's choice of sales mode is affected by the various parameters of the problem. In particular, any desired comparative-statics result can be obtained by simply taking the partial derivative of (12) with respect to the relevant variable. With this fact in hand, I turn to a consideration of the determinants of the MNE's sales mode choice for this case.

Entry via FDI versus Local Agent
First, note that both initial entry via FDI and via an agency contract in which $T_1 = \infty$, $T_2 = 0$ are possible outcomes. To see this, consider the case in which $R = 0$, $F, G > 0$, $\alpha > 1$, and N_1 small. Recall from Proposition 2 that, as $N_1 \rightarrow 0$, so do $\hat{q}_1$ and q_1^*. As a result, the last two terms in (12) are small when N_1 is small. In this case, then, the choice between immediate FDI and an agency contract turns essentially on the relative per-period returns of the two modes. That $T_1 = \infty$ implies that an agency contract yields higher per-period returns when $N_i = N_1$ while $T_2 = 0$ means that FDI is more profitable when $N_i = N_2$. Therefore, when the market is likely small (ρ large), the agency contract will be adopted. In this case, if the market proves small, the agency relationship persists. However, if the market proves large, the agent is replaced by an owned sales operation. If it is likely the market is large (ρ small), immediate FDI is the preferred mode. In this case, it is possible that the MNE discovers that the market is, in fact, small after entry. If so, the MNE may choose subsequently to exit the market and continue serving it via a local agent. That is, failed FDI may occur.

Market Size and the Entry Decision
Consider the MNE's entry decision in two distinct markets: a large market and a small market. The potential customer pool in the large market is β times that in the small market, $\beta > 1$ (implying that N_1/N_2 is the same in both markets). How might this difference in market size affect the MNE's mode of entry? To answer this question, note first that, if $\alpha > 1$ (as was assumed in proposition 2), $E\pi^I - E\pi^a > 0$ and increasing in both N_1 and N_2. The same is true of the third term in (12). Large markets allow the MNE to exploit its superior selling ability more than small markets do. This fact makes immediate FDI more likely in the larger market.

What about the effect of market size on agency costs? These costs are given by the last two terms in (12). Differentiation of these terms with respect to N_1 and N_2, holding the ratio N_1/N_2 constant, shows that the impact on agency costs of an increase in market size is given by the expression

$$-\frac{1-\rho}{1-\delta}\left[c'\left(\frac{\hat{q}_1}{N_1}\right)\frac{\hat{q}_1}{N_2N_1} - c'\left(\frac{\hat{q}_1}{N_2}\right)\frac{\hat{q}_1}{N_2^2}\right]$$

$$+\frac{\rho}{1-\delta}\left[c'\left(\frac{q_1^*}{N_2}\right)\frac{q_1^*}{N_1N_2} - c'\left(\frac{\hat{q}_1}{N_1}\right)\frac{\hat{q}_1}{N_1N_2}\right]. \tag{13}$$

The first term in (13) represents the change in information rents to the agent when $N_i = N_2$ and is negative (i.e., information rents are lower in the larger market). The second term represents the change in foregone profits due to the distortion in q_1 and is positive. Adding and subtracting $\rho p \hat{q}_1/N_2(1-\delta)$ and noting that $c'(q_1^*/N_1)/N_1 = p$, (13) can be expressed as

$$\frac{\hat{q}_1}{N_2(1-\delta)}\left\{\left[\rho(p-c')\left(\frac{\hat{q}_1}{N_1}\right)\frac{1}{N_1}\right] - (1-\rho)\left[c'\left(\frac{\hat{q}_1}{N_1}\right)\frac{1}{N_1} - c'\left(\frac{\hat{q}_1}{N_2}\right)\frac{1}{N_2}\right]\right\}$$

$$+\frac{\rho p}{N_2(1-\delta)}(q_1^* - \hat{q}_1).$$

From (1)–(4), the first term is zero while the second is positive; that is, the net change in agency costs is positive. Thus, the higher agency costs in the larger country also make FDI more attractive. As a result, both because of the greater profitability of FDI in the large country and the greater costs of an agency contract, the MNE is more likely to enter the larger market with FDI and the smaller market with an agency contract.

Profit Variability and FDI

In addition to considering how differences in the size of the potential customer pool (average revenues) across markets affects the MNE's entry decision, one might consider how variability in the size of the potential customer pool (variance in revenues) within a market affects the MNE's decision. Imagine, for instance, an increase in N_2 and a corresponding decrease in N_1 such that $E\pi^I$ remains constant.[20] Such a change leaves expected profits constant should the MNE choose FDI, but increases the variance in profits. In general, nothing unambiguous can be said about how such a change affects the MNE's decision. However, if the effort cost function is assumed to be quadratic, then interesting implications can be obtained. I proceed under this assumption.

Under quadratic costs, the ratio $q_1^*(\alpha)/q_2^*(\alpha) = N_1^2/N_2^2$ for all α. This implies that, if $E\pi^I$ remains constant under the proposed changes in N_1 and N_2, so does $E\pi^a$. Therefore, the first term in (12) remains unchanged while the third term is weakly decreasing. Thus, the increase in profit variability weakly decreases the direct profitability of FDI. In essence, the return to maintaining an owned sales operation when $N_i = N_1$ becomes smaller as N_1 falls and so, in present value terms, FDI looks less attractive.

How are agency costs affected? The last two terms of (12) capture these costs. Differentiation of these two terms and use of the definitions of q_1^* and $\hat{q}_1$ reveal that the impact on agency costs is given by the sign of the expression $\rho N_1^4 - (1 - \rho)(N_2^2 - N_1^2)$. If N_1 is small, as is assumed for the contract $T_1 = \infty$, $T_2 = 0$ to be optimal, then increasing profit variability decreases agency costs. The reason is that, as I noted earlier, information rents become small as N_1 becomes small; in addition, the distortion in q_1 becomes small, and so losses attributed to this distortion are small.

The implication then is that, when effort costs are quadratic, the MNE will choose to enter initially with an agency arrangement in markets that are risky in the sense given here. When the market proves profitable, the MNE converts to an owned sales operation; otherwise, the agency relationship persists. In markets that are less risky, entry via immediate FDI is the more likely outcome.

Costs and FDI

As F and G increase or α decreases, FDI becomes less profitable relative to an agency arrangement. Indeed, as I demonstrated earlier, FDI may be sufficiently costly relative to the agency contract that the MNE simply chooses to enter initially with a contract that is maintained regardless of the size of N_i.

Contract Length and FDI

Previously, one assumed that the length of time over which profits accrue and the length of time required for the MNE to break the contract and establish its own sales operation are the same. There is no obvious reason that this should be the case (i.e., periods have no natural length). This equivalence can be broken by assuming that profits accrue at $t = 1, 2, \ldots$ while the contract period is Δt, $\Delta \geq 1$. For instance, one might assume that if the MNE wishes to implement a short-term contract followed by conversion to an owned sales operation, the shortest feasible such contract lasts until $t = 2$. What effect will increasing the length of the initial contract period have? From section 15.3, one observes that if the MNE cannot convert until $t = 2$, then the value to it of the contract is diminished. As a result, V^a falls and the value of (12) increases. In essence, increasing the length of the initial contract makes it a less valuable tool for gathering information about the market. As a result, the MNE is less likely to choose the contract over FDI.

15.5 Summary and Conclusions

This chapter considers the decision of a multinational firm either to enter a new market via immediate direct investment or through some contractual arrangement with a local firm. If the contractual arrangement is chosen, the contract can be a short-term or long-term one. The gain from contracting with a local agent is that the multinational can avoid possibly costly investment mistakes arising from its unfamiliarity with market characteristics. The cost of contracting is that the firm must transfer some of its rents to the agent due to the superior information the agent possesses (the agency costs of contracting). The multinational may prefer a short-term contract because such a contract allows it to exploit the information it gathers via the agency arrangement. The cost is that the contract results in additional agency costs due to the agent's recognition of ultimate termination.

I find that, if the MNE uses a contract initially, it will use a (potentially) short-term contract when its fixed costs are high relative to the agent's, its sales force is more efficient, and there is risk of large losses due to the market being small. In these circumstances, the contractual arrangement will be a permanent one if the market proves small (low sales), while it will be a temporary one if the market proves large (high sales). As for the MNE's choice of initial entry mode, it is more likely to enter via immediate direct investment (rather than the potentially short-term contract) the larger the expected market size, the less the variability in potential profits, and the longer the time required to convert to owned operations should the market prove large.

Technical Appendices

Preface to Technical Appendices

Many branches of both pure and applied mathematics are in great need of computing instruments to break the present stalemate created by the failure of the purely analytical approach to nonlinear problems.

—John Von Neumann, 1945

I discussed the use of numerical models briefly in the preface, but some bit of repetition might not hurt. I became frustrated with traditional analytical methods for comparative statics quite a number of years ago because of two difficulties. First, the problems I wanted to solve had many dimensions (equations and unknowns), generally at least forty, and it is hard to get answers to comparative-statics exercises this large. Second, I was very interested in "regime-shifting" problems, in which production took place in different locations by different types of firms. This meant that the underlying problem of interest was a set of inequalities with associated non-negative variables. These are called complementarity problems in mathematical programming language. But our traditional textbook comparative-statics methods are not much help in large-dimension, nonlinear complementarity problems.

Several traditional ways out of these difficulties exist if one sticks to analytical methods. The first is to avoid the inequalities and regime shifting. The second is to allow for regime shifting, but drastically limit the number of regimes and the dimensionality of the problem. This last alternative is what I did in chapters 2–4 and later in chapters 13–15. But this second alternative generally requires the modeler to sacrifice general-equilibrium models, for example. The first alternative assumes away the whole objective of the exercise.

The third alternative is to turn to simulations, using numerical models to do "theory with numbers." Much of this book chooses this third way. This alternative also has limiting features, such as the use of specific functional forms. But the use of specific functional forms pervades the trade-IO and strategic trade policy literatures in any case. In addition, it can be hard for readers to know exactly what is going on and exactly how the problem is formulated and solved. I try to deal with these problems by showing more or less exactly what equations and inequalities are solved for what variables. In addition, I try to provide partial-equilibrium "thought experiments" to help understand the general-equilibrium simulation results.

But that is not enough, and many interested scholars want to get under the hood and see exactly what is making the motor run. The purpose of these appendices is to give an introduction to solving nonlinear complementarity problems using GAMS (general algebraic modeling system) software. I cannot show every feature, subtlety, and nuance of this software. I try to show instead the basics of what the code looks like and how it can be used. My goals are (1) to let readers know how the models in the book are formulated and solved, and (2) give enough of an introduction to let readers know whether or not this is something they would like to pursue further.

I can tell readers that this software dramatically changed, extended, and deepened my research agenda. I have been able to solve problems and arrive at insights that I would not have been able to achieve otherwise. Often a general-equilibrium model has produced results that I don't quite understand and, after taking incredible care that there were no errors, I would go back and work on the basic theory until I understood the outcome. And, quite frankly, it's a lot of fun to produce those pictures in chapters 5–12.

Readers will want to visit the GAMS Web site (⟨www.gams.com.⟩) for more details, tutorials, sample models, and other information.

Appendix 1: Stop Avoiding Inequalities and Complementarity Problems: A Simple Partial-Equilibrium Model Illustrating the GAMS MCP Solver

This appendix introduces GAMS using the MCP (mixed complementarity problem) solver, which solves sets of equations and/or inequalities with associated variables. Variables corresponding to inequalities are generally non-negative ones with a minimum value of 0, but other minimum values could be set.

The problem I have chosen is rather simple, four inequalities in four unknowns, and it also has the advantage of being relevant to many of the theoretic models in the body of the book. It is a simple partial-equilibrium model. There is one good X, produced by firms who have a constant marginal cost (mc) and a fixed cost (F). p_x is the price of X. Consumers spend a constant share α of fixed income I on good X. There is free entry and exit of firms until profits are zero, so the number of firms is a continuous variable. X is output per firm, and N the number of firms. mk denotes the equilibrium markup, which in a Cournot model with unitary elasticity of demand is just given by a firm's market share, or $1/N$.

In this problem, there are four inequalities for the four endogenous variables: p_x, X, N, and mk. I follow the tradition from applied general-equilibrium modeling in how variables are associated with inequalities. The quantity variable X is associated with the marginal-revenue equal marginal cost pricing inequality. The number of firms N is associated with the zero-profit condition that markup revenues are less than or equal to fixed cost. The markup is given by the Cournot formula (with unitary elasticity), and finally the price of X is associated with the market-clearing condition that demand is less than or equal to supply.

Inequality	Complementary variable	Name of inequality
$p_x(1 - mk) \leq mc$	X	(pricing inequality)
$p_x mk X \leq F$	N	(free entry inequality)
$1/N \leq mk$	mk	(markup formula)
$\alpha I/p_x \leq NX$	p_x	(market-clearing inequality)

This complementarity problem can be thought of as composed of PARAMETERS, VARIABLES, and EQUATIONS that are key words in GAMS. The equations are actually inequalities, but "equation" is the key word. The equations must be given equation names (which must differ from the names of variables).

I call the four equations (inequalities) *MRMC, ZEROP, MKUP,* and *DS* (for demand = supply).

```
PARAMETERS:

    MC        - MARGINAL COST
    F         - FIXED COST
    ALPHA     - SHARE OF INCOME SPENT ON X
    I         - INCOME

VARIABLES:

    PX        - PRICE OF X
    MK        - MARKUP
    X         - OUTPUT PER FIRM
    N         - NUMBER OF FIRMS

EQUATIONS:

    MRMC      -    MARGINAL REVENUE LESS THAN / EQUAL TO
                   MARGINAL COST
                       COMPLEMENTARY VARIABLE: X
    ZEROP     -    ZERO PROFITS: FIXED COSTS GREATER THAN/
                   EQUAL TO MARKUP REV
                       COMPLEMENTARY VARIABLE: N
    MKUP      -    COURNOT MARKUP FORMULA
                       COMPLEMENTARY VARIABLE: MK
    DS        -    DEMAND EQUAL SUPPLY OF X
                       COMPLEMENTARY VARIABLE: PX
```

GAMS then requires us to specify a MODEL and give it a name. The specification of a model is the key word "model," followed by the model name, followed by a slash (/). Then there is a list of equations, each equation followed by a period and then the name of the complementary variable. Then comes a closing slash and a semicolon. For the above model, I name it EQUIL. The model statement is then

```
MODEL EQUIL /MRMC.X, ZEROP.N, MKUP.MK, DS.PX /;
```

Finally, I have to tell GAMS what we want to do, since GAMS also does optimization, linear programming, and so forth. In our case, the command line I want is:

```
SOLVE EQUIL USING MCP;
```

A few final points, with respect to the actual program that follows.

1. The program begins with two text lines preceded by a *. GAMS ignores any line beginning with a *.

2. I declare the parameter names, then assign them values (note where semicolons do and do not go).

3. Next I declare positive variables and then equation names. Then I write out the equation names in the syntax shown, [equation name].., the equation itself ending with a semicolon.

4. Note that GAMS was written to use greater-than-or-equal-to syntax (=G=), so the above inequalities are written "backwards." Note also that I have avoided having variables in denominators, since if a variable (even temporarily during the execution of the algorithm) has a value of zero, this causes a divided-by-zero problem and *may* crash the solver.

5. Then the model name and specification, then starting values.

6. Before the solve statement, I am going to help the solver by giving starting values for the variables. The syntax is, for example X.L, where the "L" stands for "level." Default values are 0, and in nonlinear problems it is very helpful and indeed sometimes necessary to help the solver with some initial guesses. I constructed this problem knowing the answer, so I give those values as .L values.

7. Finally, the solve statement.

Now I am ready to go. After the first solve statement, I specify a new value for income, tripling the size of the economy. Then I have a second solve statement.

```
* EXAMPLE1.GMS
* this illustrates the use of the GAMS MCP solver
```

```
PARAMETERS
 MC
 F
 ALPHA
 I;

MC    = 1;
F     = 1;
ALPHA = 0.5;
I     = 8;

POSITIVE VARIABLES
 PX
 MK
 N
 X;

EQUATIONS
 MRMC
 ZEROP
 MKUP
 DS;

MRMC..    MC =G= PX*(1 - MK);

ZEROP..   F =G= PX*MK*X;

MKUP..    MK*N =G=1;

DS..      N*X*PX =G= ALPHA*I;


MODEL EQUIL /MRMC.X, ZEROP.N, MKUP.MK, DS.PX /;

**** give the solver starting values of the variables****

PX.L = 2;
N.L = 2;
X.L = 1;
MK.L = 0.5;

SOLVE EQUIL USING MCP;

**** now a counterfactual in which we triple income****

I = 24;

SOLVE EQUIL USING MCP;
```

I save this file under the name EX1.GMS. The solver will return a file called EX1.LST (the extension meaning listing file). The equilibrium values of the variables will be

```
PX = 2.0
MK = 0.5
N  = 2.0
X  = 1.0
```

The total X production is thus $N^*X = 2$.

In the counterfactual experiment, the value of income is tripled to 24. The listing file tells me that the equilibrium values of the variables will be

```
PX = 1.406
MK = 0.298
N  = 3.464
X  = 2.464
```

Total X production is now 8.535; the price of X has fallen as has the markup on X. This is a simple illustration of the pro-competitive effect of a larger economy when there is free entry and exit. Total output of X more than quadruples when the size of the economy triples.

This example doesn't really show the solver's strength in solving complementarity problems. So I jazz it up a little, in a way that is relevant to much of the book. Suppose that there are two choices of technologies. There is a high-marginal-cost, low-fixed-cost technology, denoted technology 1, which is identical to the technology in the previous example. Then there is a low-marginal-cost, high-fixed-cost technology denoted technology 2. Firms can choose their technology, and equilibrium requires that all active firms earn nonpositive profits.

The way to model this is as I did it throughout the book. Think of there being two firm "types," with free entry and exit into and out of firm types. There are thus type-1 and type-2 firms. For each firm type, there will have to be three inequalities, $MRMC$, $ZEROP$, and MK. There is only one price since the good is homogeneous. Thus the model now has seven inequalities in seven unknowns. The inequalities and complementary variables are as follows:

```
MRMC1        X1
ZEROP1       N1
MKUP1        MK1
```

```
MRMC2      X2
ZEROP2     N2
MKUP2      MK2
DS         PX
```

The markup equations are now more complicated, but they still equal
an individual firm's market share. Here is the program.

```
*EXAMPLE 1A:
* same example as in EXAMPLE 1 except
* here there are two technologies for X,
* technology 2: low marginal cost, high fixed cost
* technology 1: high marginal cost, low fixed cost

PARAMETERS
 MC1
 F1
 MC2
 F2
 ALPHA
 I;

MC1     = 1;
F1      = 1;
MC2     = 0.5;
F2      = 3;
ALPHA   = 0.5;
I       = 8;

POSITIVE VARIABLES
 PX
 MK1
 N1
 X1
 MK2
 N2
 X2;

EQUATIONS
 MRMC1
 ZEROP1
 MKUP1
 MRMC2
 ZEROP2
 MKUP2
 DS;
```

```
MRMC1..      MC1 =G= PX*(1 - MK1);

ZEROP1 .     F1 =G= PX*MK1*X1;

MKUP1..      MK1*(X1*N1 + X2*N2) =G= X1;

MRMC2..      MC2 =G= PX*(1 - MK2);

ZEROP2..     F2 =G= PX*MK2*X2;

MKUP2..      MK2*(X1*N1 + X2*N2) =G= X2;

DS..         (N1*X1 + N2*X2)*PX =G= ALPHA*I;


MODEL EQUIL /MRMC1.X1, ZEROP1.N1, MKUP1.MK1,
               MRMC2.X2, ZEROP2.N2, MKUP2.MK2, DS.PX /;

**** give the solver starting values ****

PX.L = 2;
N1.L = 2;
X1.L = 1;
MK1.L = 0.5;



SOLVE EQUIL USING MCP;



**** now a counterfactual in which we triple income ****



I = 24;

**** new starting values ****

N2.L = 2;
X2.L = 6;
MK2.L = .5;



SOLVE EQUIL USING MCP;
```

I save this file under the name EX1A.GMS. The solver returns a file called EX1A.LST. The equilibrium values of the variables are

```
PX   = 2.0

MK1  = 0.5
N1   = 2.0
X1   = 1.0

MK2  = 0.75
N2   = 0.0
X2   = 1.5
```

The total X production is thus $N1^*X1 = 2$ as in the previous example. Only type-1 firms are active (i.e., only technology 1 is used).

The solver returns positive values for $MK2$ and $X2$, but they really don't mean anything because no type-2 firms are active. Refer back to equation $MRMC2$; the equilibrium price is greater than MC2, so the solver will find a positive value of $MK2$ and a positive value of $X2$, but they have no significance.

In the counterfactual experiment, the value of income is tripled to 24. The listing file tells me that the equilibrium values of the variables will be

```
PX   = 1.0

MK1  = 0.0
N1   = 0.0
X1   = 0.0

MK2  = 0.5
N2   = 2.0
X2   = 6.0
```

Total X production is now 12, and the price of X has fallen. A "regime switch" in the larger economy results. Technology 2 is now the only technology used, or alternatively only type-2 firms are active. Comparing this result to the same counterfactual in the previous example where only technology 1 was available (total production of X: 8.535), one sees that the alternative technology is socially as well as privately the efficient choice in the larger economy.

Note in this case the solver does return zero values for $MK1$, $N1$, and $X1$. The equation $MRMC1$ is satisfied only at $MK1 = 0$, which in turn is only consistent with $X1 = 0$, which are in turn only consistent with $N1 = 0$.

Appendix 2: Who's Afraid of Applied GE Modeling? A General-Equilibrium Version of Appendix 1 Using the MCP Solver

This appendix adds a new layer of complications, reformulating the problem of appendix 1 as a general-equilibrium model. The model is still a closed economy. However, it has two goods (X and Y), and two factors (L and K). Y has constant returns and perfect competition. The X sector is the same as in appendix 1. There is free entry and exit of firms, who have a constant marginal cost (for given factor prices) and a fixed cost. Markets are determined by the Cournot rule that the markup equals a firm's market share divided by the Marshallian price elasticity of demand, the latter equal to one due to the assumption that preferences are Cobb-Douglas.

The first thing one does in an applied GE model is to organize the dimensionality of the model. I do this by formatting the model as a "social accounting matrix." The columns of the matrix are production activities or sectors and agents in the economy. The rows of the matrix are markets. Here is the matrix I use in this appendix and in appendix 3.

	X	Y	N	W	CONS	ENTRE	ROW SUM
PX	100			−100			0
PY		100		−100			0
PL	−25	−70	− 5		100		0
PK	−50	−30	−20		100		0
MKREV	−25					25	0
PW				200	−200		0
PF			25			−25	0
COLUMN SUM	0	0	0	0	0	0	

Consider first the columns of this matrix. Sector X is the "marginal acitivity" for producing X. Sector Y produces goods Y. Sector N

produces fixed costs for good X, and the activity level of this sector corresponds to the number of firms in the industry. W is the activity that takes commodities and produces utility. This is a useful way to think about utility and welfare in a general-equilibrium model.

CONS is the representative consumer who owns factors and buys goods. ENTRE is a single representative agent for the group of "owners" who receive markup revenues and demand fixed costs.

Positive entries in a column denote receipts by a sector, and negative entries denote payments. A condition of general equilibrium is that each column sum must equal zero. A zero column sum indicates *product exhaustion* or *zero profits* (net of markup payments, etc.). All receipts of a sector or agent must go to some payment. The X sector in the matrix receives receipts of 100 from sales and pays 25 for labor (PL), 50 for capital (PK), and 25 to markup revenues ($MKREV$).

Positive entries for an agent are typically endowments, tax or transfer receipts, or markups. The negative entry for CONS is the "purchase" of utility financed by the positive entries, which are the value of the consumer's endowment of labor and capital. The positive entry for the entrepreneurs is markup receipts, and the negative entry is the purchase of fixed costs.

Now consider the rows of the matrix. These are markets, and I have used "P" before the commodity name since the complementary variable is typically a price (commodities and activities must have different names). A positive entry can be thought of as a supply and a negative entry a demand. Thus sectors X and Y produce supplies of PX and PY, and consumers demand these goods. The "welfare sector" (W) demands commodities and supplies the utility good (PW).

Labor (PL) and capital (PK) are supplied by households, and demand by the X and Y sectors. Markup revenue is supplied by the ENTRE and demand by the X sector. This seems odd, so another way to think of a positive entry is an income, and a negative entry is an expenditure. ENTRE spends money buying fixed costs (PF), the output of activity N, to obtain income, the markup revenues. CONS purchases utility (PW) from income received from factor sales.

A condition for general equilibrium is market clearing or, loosely, supply equal to demand in each market. A zero row sum in the accounting matrix indicates that *market clearing* is satisfied. All receipts in a market are payments somewhere else.

If a data set is consistent with general equilibrium in the economy, then it is micro-consistent. A micro-consistent data set can in turn be reproduced as a general equilibrium for the economy. Let me summarize this as follows:

1. A data set is *micro-consistent* if it satisfies *product exhaustion* and *market clearing*.

2. In the accounting convention adopted earlier, a zero column sum satisfies product exhaustion for an activity or agent.

3. In the accounting convention adopted earlier, a zero row sum satisfies market clearing for a commodity.

The next task in constructing a general-equilibrium model is to make the model consistent with the data. This is known as *calibration*. If the model is properly constructed and calibrated, then the data can be reproduced as an equilibrium to the model. This is known as the *calibration check*. There is no need to construct a general-equilibrium model with calibrated, micro-consistent data. Just give it inputs and let it rip. But starting with micro-consistent data and a calibrated solution is a good idea and extremely good discipline for the researcher, and I strongly recommend it for novices. Getting the model to pass the replication check helps the researcher uncover many errors in model construction and coding.

Calibrating a model with increasing returns and imperfect competition is much trickier than calibrating a standard Arrow-Debreu competitive model. I reproduce some of the key inequalities from the previous section.

$p_x(1 - mk) \leq mc$	X	(pricing inequality)
$p_x mkX \leq F$	N	(free entry inequality)
$1/N \leq mk$	mk	(markup formula)

I am going to begin my calibration of the above data assuming that as many things as possible equal 1. The activity levels for X, Y, and W equal 1. The prices of PW, PY, PL, and PK are equal to 1. The data for the X sector allow us to solve directly for the markup, and thus for the number of firms that is consistent with the initial data. The value of output is 100, and the value of inputs of L and K is 75, which produces

$$100(1 - mk) = 75 \Rightarrow mk = 1/4 \Rightarrow N = 4.$$

The value of the markup implies $N = 4$. So in the initial calibration, N is set at 4. I also interpret the value of X output equal to 100 as being

75 units of X with a price of $4/3$. Actually, I code X output in the file as X^*75, so $X = 1$ in the initial calibration. The value of X is referred to as the "activity level" of the industry, where running the industry at unit activity means 75 units of output and requires 25 units of labor and 50 units of capital. These values then imply an output of $75/4$ per firm. Total fixed costs are 25 or $25/4$ per firm. Note then that the free-entry equation is satisfied (where X is the number of units of output, not the activity level): $p_x mk X = F$.

$$(4/3)(1/4)(75/4) = (25/4)$$

If this model is correctly calibrated, then the first run of the model should produce the following results:

Activity levels	Prices	Auxiliary variables
$X = 1$	$PX = 1.333$	$MK = 0.25$
$Y = 1$	$PY = 1$	
$N = 4$	$PF = 1$	
$W = 1$	$PW = 1$	
	$PL = 1$	
	$PK = 1$	

A few other details not mentioned are that the endowments of labor and capital are 100 units each, consistent with the unitary price calibration, and that the production functions for the X, Y, N, and W activities are assumed to be Cobb-Douglas.

The price level is not determined in this model as is usual, so I choose Y as numeraire. The syntax for this is $PY.FX = 1$, where FX stands for fix(ed).

A block of text is ignored by GAMS if each line starts with a $*$ as noted in the appendix 1, or if the block is written

```
$ontext

    text ignored by GAMS

$offtext
```

Equations (actually inequalities) of the model are named as follows. The complementary variables associated with each equation are generally quantities for cost equations and prices for market-clearing (supply = demand) equations. Please note that in the program that follows PX, PY, and so forth are prices.

Equation	Definition	Comple-mentary variable
COSTX	(marginal) cost for X = marginal revenue	X
COSTY	unit cost of Y = price of Y	Y
COSTN	unit cost of fixed costs = price of fixed costs N	
COSTW	unit cost of utility = price of utility	W
MARKETX	supply equal demand for X	PX
MARKETY	supply equal demand for Y	PY
MARKETN	supply equal demand for fixed costs	PF
MARKETW	supply equal demand for utility	PW
MARKETL	supply equal demand for labor	PL
MARKETK	supply equal demand for capital	PK
CONSINC	consumer expenditure = endowment income	$CONS$
ENTREINC	entrepreneur expenditure = markup revenue	$ENTRE$
MKUP	markup formula	MK

The model thus solves 13 inequalities in 13 unknowns.

```
*EXAMPLE 2:
* this is a simple closed economy GE model with one sector having
* increasing returns, Cournot competition, and free entry
* it uses the mcp solver


$ONTEXT

            X       Y       N       W       CONS    ENTRE
PX        100                     -100
PY                100             -100
PL        -25     -70     - 5              100
PK        -50     -30     -20              100
MKREV     -25                                       25
PW                               200     -200
PF                        25                       -25
```

```
$OFFTEXT

PARAMETERS
 ENDOWL
 ENDOWK;

ENDOWL = 100;
ENDOWK = 100;

POSITIVE VARIABLES
 X
 Y
 N
 W
 PX
 PY
 PL
 PK
 PW
 PF
 CONS
 ENTRE
 MK;

EQUATIONS
 COSTX
 COSTY
 COSTN
 COSTW
 MARKETX
 MARKETY
 MARKETN
 MARKETW
 MARKETL
 MARKETK
 CONSINC
 ENTREINC
 MKUP;


COSTX..    (PL**(1/3))*(PK**(2/3)) =G= PX*(1 - MK);

COSTY..    (PL**.70)*(PK**.30) =G= PY;

COSTN..    (PL**.20)*(PK**.80) =G= PF;

COSTW..    ((3/4)**.5)*(PX**.5)*(PY**.5) =G= PW;

MARKETX..  PX*X*75 =G= 0.5*CONS;
```

```
MARKETY..   PY*Y*100 =G= 0.5*CONS;

MARKETN..   PF*N*6.25 =G= ENTRE;

MARKETW..   PW*W*200 =G= CONS;

MARKETL..   ENDOWL*PL =G= (1/3)*PX*(1-MK)*X*75 + 0.70*PY*Y*100 +
                          0.20*PF*N*6.25;

MARKETK..   ENDOWK*PK =G= (2/3)*PX*(1-MK)*X*75 + 0.30*PY*Y*100 +
                          0.80*PF*N*6.25;

CONSINC..   CONS =G= PL*ENDOWL + PK*ENDOWK;

ENTREINC..  ENTRE =G= PX*X*75*MK;

MKUP..      MK*N =G= 1;

MODEL EX2  /COSTX.X, COSTY.Y, COSTN.N, COSTW.W, MARKETY.PY,
            MARKETX.PX, MARKETN.PF, MARKETW.PW, MARKETL.PL,
            MARKETK.PK, CONSINC.CONS, ENTREINC.ENTRE, MKUP.MK/;


**** give the solver starting values ****

X.L = 1;
Y.L = 1;
N.L = 4;
W.L = 1;
PX.L = 4/3;
PY.L = 1;
PF.L = 1;
PL.L = 1;
PK.L = 1;
PW.L = 1;
MK.L = 0.25;


PY.FX = 1;

SOLVE EX2 USING MCP;


**** counterfactual: double the size of economy ****

ENDOWL = 200;
ENDOWK = 200;

SOLVE EX2 USING MCP;
```

The listing file returns the following solution values. The only constrained variable is *PY*, which was chosen as numeraire as noted.

	LOWER	LEVEL	UPPER	MARGINAL
---- VAR X	.	1.000	+INF	.
---- VAR Y	.	1.000	+INF	.
---- VAR N	.	4.000	+INF	.
---- VAR W	.	1.000	+INF	.
---- VAR PX	.	1.333	+INF	.
---- VAR PY	1.000	1.000	1.000	1.421E-14
---- VAR PL	.	1.000	+INF	.
---- VAR PK	.	1.000	+INF	.
---- VAR PW	.	1.000	+INF	.
---- VAR PF	.	1.000	+INF	.
---- VAR CONS	.	200.000	+INF	.
---- VAR ENTRE	.	25.000	+INF	.
---- VAR MK	.	0.250	+INF	.

The counterfactual experiment is to double the factor endowment of the economy. Here are the solution values.

	LOWER	LEVEL	UPPER	MARGINAL
---- VAR X	.	2.204	+INF	.
---- VAR Y	.	1.992	+INF	.
---- VAR N	.	5.674	+INF	.
---- VAR W	.	2.095	+INF	.
---- VAR PX	.	1.205	+INF	.
---- VAR PY	1.000	1.000	1.000	5.684E-14
---- VAR PL	.	1.006	+INF	.
---- VAR PK	.	0.986	+INF	.
---- VAR PW	.	0.951	+INF	.
---- VAR PF	.	0.990	+INF	.
---- VAR CONS	.	398.449	+INF	.
---- VAR ENTRE	.	35.114	+INF	.
---- VAR MK	.	0.176	+INF	.

Welfare more than doubles, which is the pro-competitive effect of the larger economy. Note the fall in the markup, from 25 percent to 17.6 percent. The number of firms increase, but only by about 40 percent, not double. Dividing the activity level for *X* by the number of firms, one sees that output per firm has increased substantially, by about 55 percent, thus increasing technical efficiency through lower average cost per firm.

As I said earlier, it is not necessary to start with micro-consistent data and a calibrated model. But it is good training and discipline to do so. In chapters 5, 6, and 7, I present the initial calibration at the center of the world Edgeworth box for the central-case models of those chapters. Appendices 5 and 6 present the actual models for chapters 5 and 6.

Appendix 3: Doing It the Easy Way: General-Equilibrium Problem of Appendix 2 Using the MPS/GE Subsystem of GAMS

In addition to having written the MCP solver in GAMS, my colleague Tom Rutherford has written a high-level language called MPS/GE, which stands for mathematical programming system for general equilibrium. MPS/GE uses the MCP solver. This higher-level language permits extremely efficient shortcuts for modelers, allowing them to concentrate on economics rather than coding.

There are several great features of MPS/GE. First, the program has routines for calibrating and writing all constant-returns CES and CET functions, up to three levels of nesting. All the modeler has to do is specify the nesting structure, the elasticity of substitutions in each nest, and a representative point on the function consisting of output quantities, input quantities, and prices. This one such point and price vector uniquely determines the function, and MPS/GE then generates the cost function (or expenditure function). In the simple simulation models presented in this book this does not save time or prevent errors, but it is a wonderful feature for larger models.

Second, and closely related, the form of the data required to specify a CES/CET function is exactly the data modelers have, so there is a swift and easy move from an accounting matrix as described in appendix 2 to the calibration of the model.

Third, a lot of market-clearing and income-balance equations are written automatically by MPS/GE so the modeler doesn't have to worry about doing so. Fourth and closely related, a lot of errors that can occur when a modeler writes out his or her equations cannot occur in MPS/GE. If there is a tax or markup, for example, the revenues must be assigned to some agent and will be allocated automatically to that agent by the income-balance properties of the coding. I once refereed a paper in which the author claimed to have some weird numerical result. It turned out that the modeler had a tax, but forgot to put the tax revenue in the representative agent's income balance equation. That cannot happen in MPS/GE. In short, MPS/GE automatically checks for and ensures many of the product-exhaustion and income-balance requirements discussed in appendix 2.

In this appendix, I give a short and unfortunately superficial introduction to the MPS/GE subroutine of GAMS. I use exactly the same problem as in the previous appendix, so that readers can see the connection. First, a few key words.

Sector (activity) Production activities that convert commodity inputs into commodity outputs. The variable associated with a sector is the activity level.

Commodity (markets) A good or factor. The variable associated with a commodity is its price, not its quantity.

Consumers Individuals who supply factors and receive tax revenues, markups, and pay subsidies. In imperfectly competitive models, firm owners can be designated as consumers. A government that receives tax revenue and buys public goods is also designated as a consumer. The variable associated with a consumer is income from all sources.

Auxiliary Additional variables, such as markup formulae or taxes with endogenous values that are functions of other variables such as prices and quantities. Please note the spelling of auxiliary; mistakes will cause MPS/GE to crash.

Constraint An equation that is typically used to set the value of an auxiliary variable. In these appendix programs, constraint equations will be used to set the values of markups, which are auxiliary variables.

Here is what an MPS/GE program, embedded in a GAMS file, looks like, where the model name is EX3.

```
GAMS statements such as declaring sets, parameters,
  parameter values, etc.
**** now control is passed to the MPS/GE subsystem ****
$ONTEXT  [this tells the GAMS compiler to ignore what follows,
          but the MPS/GE compiler will recognize the model
          statement that follows and will begin to pay
          attention]
$MODEL: EX3
Declaration of sectors, commodities, consumers, auxiliary
  variables
```

```
Production Blocks
Demand Blocks
Constraint equations
$OFFTEXT  [control is passed back to GAMS]
**** now we are back in GAMS ****
$SYSINCLUDE MPSGESET EX3
GAMS statements such at setting starting values of variables,
other parameter values, etc.
$INCLUDE EX3.GEN
SOLVE EX3 USING MCP;
GAMS statements processing output
```

What follows is the MPS/GE version of the MCP in appendix 2. It is not only a lot cleaner, but note how easy it is to take the numbers from the accounting matrix and slot them into the actual program.

I show first the actual program and results, then guide readers through the specification of production and demand blocks, and constraint equations for those interested.

```
* EXAMPLE 3:
* same as example 2, except this uses mps/ge

$ONTEXT
```

	X	Y	N	W	CONS	ENTRE
PX	100			-100		
PY		100		-100		
PL	-25	-70	- 5		100	
PK	-50	-30	-20		100	
MKREV	-25					25
PW				200	-200	
PF			25			-25

```
$OFFTEXT


PARAMETERS
 ENDOWL
 ENDOWK;

ENDOWL = 100;
ENDOWK = 100;


**** now the MPS/GE file starts.
**** MPS/GE will recognize $MODEL:EX3
```

```
$ONTEXT

$MODEL:EX3

$SECTORS:
 X
 Y
 N
 W

$COMMODITIES:
 PX
 PY
 PL
 PK
 PW
 PF

$CONSUMERS:
 CONS
 ENTRE

$AUXILIARY:
 MK

$PROD:X  s:1
        O:PX     Q: 75     A:ENTRE   N:MK
        I:PL     Q: 25
        I:PK     Q: 50

$PROD:Y  s:1
        O:PY     Q:100
        I:PL     Q: 70
        I:PK     Q: 30

$PROD:N  s:1
        O:PF     Q: 6.25
        I:PL     Q: 1.25
        I:PK     Q: 5.00

$PROD:W s:1
        O:PW     Q:200
        I:PX     Q: 75    P:(4/3)
        I:PY     Q:100

$DEMAND:CONS
        D:PW     Q:200
        E:PL     Q:(ENDOWL)
        E:PK     Q:(ENDOWK)
```

```
$DEMAND:ENTRE
        D:PF     Q: 25

$CONSTRAINT:MK
        MK * N   =G= 1;


$OFFTEXT


**** now control is returned from MPS/GE to GAMS


$SYSINCLUDE mpsgeset EX3

**** starting values ****

N.L = 4;
PX.L = 4/3;
MK.L=0.25;

PY.FX = 1;

$INCLUDE EX3.GEN
SOLVE EX3 USING MCP;

***** counterfactual double the size of economy ****

ENDOWL = 200;
ENDOWK = 200;

$INCLUDE EX3.GEN
SOLVE EX3 USING MCP;
```

Here is the output from the first run of the model. It successfully reproduces the data in the accounting matrix and therefore passes the consistency or replication check. Note that it is identical to the solution to the MCP in appendix 2.

	LOWER	LEVEL	UPPER	MARGINAL
---- VAR X	.	1.000	+INF	.
---- VAR Y	.	1.000	+INF	.
---- VAR N	.	4.000	+INF	.
---- VAR W	.	1.000	+INF	.
---- VAR PX	.	1.333	+INF	.
---- VAR PY	1.000	1.000	1.000	EPS
---- VAR PL	.	1.000	+INF	.
---- VAR PK	.	1.000	+INF	.

---- VAR PW	.	1.000	+INF	.
---- VAR PF	.	1.000	+INF	.
---- VAR CONS	.	200.000	+INF	.
---- VAR ENTRE	.	25.000	+INF	.
---- VAR MK	.	0.250	+INF	.

Here are the results from the counterfactual experiment, in which the country's endowment is doubled. Again, it matches the output of appendix 2.

	LOWER	LEVEL	UPPER	MARGINAL
---- VAR X	.	2.204	+INF	.
---- VAR Y	.	1.992	+INF	.
---- VAR N	.	5.674	+INF	.
---- VAR W	.	2.095	+INF	.
---- VAR PX	.	1.205	+INF	.
---- VAR PY	1.000	1.000	1.000	EPS
---- VAR PL	.	1.006	+INF	.
---- VAR PK	.	0.986	+INF	.
---- VAR PW	.	0.951	+INF	.
---- VAR PF	.	0.990	+INF	.
---- VAR CONS	.	398.449	+INF	.
---- VAR ENTRE	.	35.114	+INF	.
---- VAR MK	.	0.176	+INF	.

Now I offer some more details for those interested. I can't do everything in this appendix, but I can help readers understand what they are looking at.

Production Blocks

The terminology here is a bit confusing, since MPS/GE takes the information in a production block and generates a cost function, not a production function. But the variable associated with a production block (cost function) is an activity level. Let's take an example from the previous program.

```
$PROD:Y   s:1
        O:PY     Q:100    P:1
        I:PL     Q: 70    P:1
        I:PK     Q: 30    P:1
```

First Line

Name of activity (Y), values of substitution and transformation elasticities $(s:1)$. Default elasticity of substitution is 0 (not 1!).

First Column

Names of commodity outputs (O:) and inputs (I:).

Second Column

Reference commodity quantities (Q:), used for calibration. Default $= 1$ if none specified.

Third Column

Reference commodity prices (P), used for calibration. Default $= 1$ if none specified.

MPS/GE then takes this information to construct a cost function and, as a feature of CES functions, it is globally defined by a single reference point. Think of putting an isoquant labeled 100 units of output, with elasticity of substitution 1, though input points $L = 70$, $K = 30$, with slope $PL/PK = 1$. That is what MPS/GE does. In this simple case, it constructs the cost function:

```
100*(PL**.70)*(PK**.30) =G= 100*PY;
```

Why the reference output quantity appears on both sides will become clear shortly. The saving from using MPS/GE might not seem like a big deal, but with many inputs, different prices for all inputs, and an elasticity of substitution of 3.5, it is a huge saving indeed.

Now consider the production block for W.

```
$PROD:W s:1
        O:PW     Q:200
        I:PX     Q: 75    P:(4/3)
        I:PY     Q:100
```

The price field must be there for PX because the reference (benchmark) price is not equal to 1. This information causes MPS/GE to generate the cost function:

```
200*((3/4)**.5)*(PX**.5)*(PY**.5) =G= 200*PW;
```

The term $((3/4)\text{**}.5)$ is a scaling term on the cost function such that the cost function is consistent with the data in the production block. Let A be this scaling parameter. The data in the production block tell us that $p_w = 1$, $p_x = 4/3$, and $p_y = 1$. The share of X and Y in the Cobb-Douglas function are each 0.5, which results in

$$A p_x^\alpha p_y^{1-\alpha} \le p_w \qquad A(4/3)^{.5}(1)^{.5} \le 1 \Rightarrow A = (3/4)^{.5}.$$

MPS/GE automatically calculates this scaling parameter from the data.

Finally, consider the production block for X.

```
$PROD:X   s:1
        O:PX      Q: 75      A:ENTRE   N:MK
        I:PL      Q: 25
        I:PK      Q: 50
```

The information "A:ENTRE N:MK" is read as "assign to agent *ENTRE* the revenues from an endogenous 'tax rate' (N:) whose value is given by the auxiliary variable *MK*." This causes MPS/GE to generate the cost function

```
75*(PL**(1/3))*(PK**(2/3)) =G= 75*PX*(1 - MK)
```

and to automatically assign the markup revenue to consumer *ENTRE*.

Now back to the reason that the reference output quantities appear in the cost functions. This is because MPS/GE uses Shepherd's lemma to generate factor demands that are automatically put into the market clearing equations for factors. For the Y-sector cost function, Shepherd's lemma tells us that the demand for labor in the Y sector is the derivative of the unit cost function with respect to PL, which is

```
70*(PL**(-.30))*(PK**.30) = 70 at benchmark PL = PK = 1.
```

Total demand for labor in X is then given by the unit demand above times the activity level X. MPS/GE generates factor demands for us, and take factor supplies from the demand blocks. Factor prices are the complementary variables for factor-market clearing equations.

Now consider the *DEMAND* block for agent *CONS*.

```
$DEMAND:CONS
        D:PW      Q:200
        E:PL      Q:(ENDOWL)
        E:PK      Q:(ENDOWK)
```

This is rather straightforward. The consumer receives income from endowments (the E: field) of labor (*ENDOWL*) and capital (*ENDOWK*) and uses that income to demand (the D: field) the utility good *PW*. As in the case of factor-market-clearing equations, MPS/GE will create an equation for the supply and demand of the utility good whose complementary variable will be the price of a unit of utility (PW).

The demand block for agent *ENTRE* is given by

```
$DEMAND:ENTRE
     D:PF    Q: 25
```

The agent *ENTRE* demands fixed costs (*PF*) and receives income from the markup (literally, endogenous tax rate), *MK*. Again, the income-balance equation is automatically generated by MPS/GE. Finally, there is the constraint equation that sets the value of the auxiliary variable *MK*.

```
$CONSTRAINT:MK
     MK * N   =G= 1;
```

Constraint equations are written in the GAMS syntax, always using the greater-than-or-equal-to (=G=) syntax and a semicolon at the end. I have written it this way rather than $MK = 1/N$ to avoid divide-by-zero problems for the solver.

This is a rather superficial introduction to MPS/GE, but it should (1) give readers some feel for what is actually going on, and (b) tell readers whether or not they would like to learn more. I have found it a wonderful tool for doing general-equilibrium simulations. Amazing things can be done with the auxiliary variables and constraint equations, and the built-in features generating income balances and market-clearing equations are a tremendous help and prevent many errors.

Others doing larger, high-dimension problems have found it a life-saver. Try writing out a fairly simple CES cost function if you are skeptical: three inputs in two nests, all inputs have different reference prices. You are given reference input quantities and prices only, plus elasticities of substitution for the two nests. I can do it in 30 seconds with an MPS/GE production block. Writing it out algebraically takes me maybe 30 mintues if I am really lucky. The next appendix introduces sets and conditionals, which are other great tools.

Appendix 4: Fun with Sets and Conditionals: GAMS Program Generating the Nash Equilibria in Figures 3.6 and 3.7

GAMS has a number of features that make high-dimension problems or looping-over parameter values quite easy. The set notation in GAMS is clear and simple in my opinion. I have also made extensive use of conditional statements that set values of parameters or variables depending on whether or not some condition is true or false.

This appendix illustrates the use of sets and conditionals, using the policy experiment in figures 3.6 and 3.7 as an example. Set notation can also be used in MPS/GE, but I won't go into its complications, subtleties, and options here. However, it is immensely useful in large-dimension problems. While I cannot provide a general tutorial, as in the case of the other appendixes I want to illustrate the use of GAMS and inspire readers to pursue it further.

The program that generates the numbers for figures 3.6 and 3.7 begins with the following statement:

```
SETS
R /0*2/
C /0*2/
S /1*10/;

ALIAS (R,RR);
ALIAS (C,CC);
```

I use three sets, R (for row), C (for column), and S (for scenario, namely different trade costs). There are many ways to order and specify the elements of a set, using numbers and/or letters, and I use just one simple way here. /0*2/ means that the set has three elements (0, 1, 2). (0, 1, 2) are the three strategies each firm can adopt: zero plants, one plant, or two plants. The rows and columns comprise a 3×3 payoff matrix as in (29) of chapter 3. Set S has 10 elements, $(1, \ldots, 10)$, which are different levels of tc_j in this example. "Alias" allows a set to have a second name, which is useful.

The parameters of this model are

$PI(R, C, S)$	Profits of firm i when i chooses strategy R, firm j chooses strategy C, and the trade cost is S
$PJ(R, C, S)$	Profits of firm j
$WI(R, C, S)$	Welfare of country i
$WJ(R, C, S)$	Welfare of country j
$ROWMAX(R, C, S)$	Largest element of row R, for trade cost S
$COLMAX(R, C, S)$	Largest element of column C, for cost S
$NE(R, C, S)$	Nash equilibrium: an element of matrix $R \times C$ will be assigned a value of 1 if it is a Nash equilibrium, 0 otherwise
$PINE(S)$	Nash equilibrium profits of firm i for trade costs S
$PJNE(S)$	Nash equilibrium profits of firm j
$WINE(S)$	Nash equilibrium welfare of country i
$WJNE(S)$	Nash equilibrium welfare of country j
$ALPHA$	Demand intercept (see chapter 3)
G	Plant-fixed cost
F	Firm-fixed cost
T	Cost of exporting to country i
TJ	Cost of exporting to country j
$TCJ(S)$	Vector of different values of TJ

Now the program loops over set S. Each iteration of the loop increases the trade cost TJ by 0.25, beginning with $TJ = 1$. $ORD(S)$ is the ordinal value of the current element of S and allows the element to be written as a number (i.e., element 1 of the set S becomes the number 1).

```
LOOP(S,
TJ =   0.75 + 0.25*ORD(S);
TCJ(S) = TJ;
```

$TCJ(S)$ just stores the values of TJ as a vector for display later in the listing file. Then the program sets the values of profits for each element of the 3×3 payoff matrix, for each level of the trade cost TJ.

These values are found in chapter 3, equations (23)–(28). The loop is closed with the syntax ");".

Next comes three lines of code that find all the pure-strategy Nash equilibria for each value of S. These use the conditional operator "$". Consider a couple of simple examples:

```
X = 1$Y;      X = 1$(Y GE 4);
```

The first is read "set the value of X equal to 1 if Y is nonzero, otherwise set $X = 0$." The second is read "set the value of X equal to 1 if Y is greater than or equal to 4, otherwise set $X = 0$." Note that when the conditional is on the right-hand side, it will override all previous assignments of values to X, in this case setting it at either 1 or 0. My program reads:

```
ROWMAX(R,C,S) = 1$(PI(R,C,S) EQ SMAX(RR, PI(RR,C,S)));
COLMAX(R,C,S) = 1$(PJ(R,C,S) EQ SMAX(CC, PJ(R,CC,S)));
NE(R,C,S) = ROWMAX(R,C,S)*COLMAX(R,C,S);
```

The first line says "set $ROWMAX(R, C, S) = 1$ if $PI(R, C, S)$ is the largest element (over the rows) of column C for trade cost S, otherwise set it to zero." SMAX stands for "set max." "Alias" is used here to distinguish what we are searching over from what we are assigning. $ROWMAX$ is finding firm i's best response to strategy C played by firm j. $COLMAX$ similarly finds firm j's best response to a strategy R played by firm i. A best response gets a value of 1, and all other values in the row get 0s.

$NE(R, C, S)$ multiplies together the corresponding elements of the matrices $ROWMAX$ and $COLMAX$. For a given value of S, $NE(R, C, S)$ will be a matrix of zeros and ones, with a one indicating a Nash equilibrium. There will 10 of these matrices 3×3 payoff matrices, one for each element of S (each level of tc_j).

Now consider the Nash equilibrium levels of profits and welfare. Here a conditional is on the left-hand side of the equation. This means something different.

```
X$Y = 1;
```

means "set X equal to 1 if Y is nonzero, otherwise leave the current value of X unchanged." When the conditional is on the left-hand side, it does not override the current value of X (i.e., set it to 0) *when the condition is false*; the statement is just ignored *when the condition is false*.

```
LOOP(R,
LOOP(C,

PINE(S)$NE(R,C,S) = PI(R,C,S);
PJNE(S)$NE(R,C,S) = PJ(R,C,S);
WINE(S)$NE(R,C,S) = WI(R,C,S);
WJNE(S)$NE(R,C,S) = WJ(R,C,S);

);
);
```

This statement loops over the payoff matrix for a given S, and give
$PINE(S)$ the value of firm i's profits when it hits the Nash equilibrium
and so forth for the other variables. This is a bit sloppy; it only works
if the Nash equilibrium for a given value of S is unique, but that holds
in this problem ($NE(R, C, S)$ is printed out so I can check). If there
is more than one Nash equilibrium, the parameters are assigned the
values from the last Nash equilibrium encountered over the payoff
matrix.

It is important that the conditional appear on the left, otherwise
GAMS will override the correct assignment with a zero assignment
when it moves on to the next element after the Nash equilibrium.

The following statement causes the output to be displayed in the
listing file:

```
DISPLAY TCJ, NE, PINE, PJNE, WINE, WJNE;
```

The set designators are not used in the display statement.

A great feature of GAMS is that the output in a listing file can be
dumped into several types of graphics packages. I use Excel (but I
wrote the book in WordPerfect, I might add). The statements to dump
to Excel sheets are as follows:

```
$LIBINCLUDE SSDUMP PINE PROFI.XLS
$LIBINCLUDE SSDUMP PJNE PROFJ.XLS
$LIBINCLUDE SSDUMP WINE WELI.XLS
$LIBINCLUDE SSDUMP WJNE WELJ.XLS
```

This gives four separate spreadsheets, but they can be quickly combined to generate figures 3.6 and 3.7.

Here is the actual program.

```
* EXAMPLE 4
* this is the code for Figures 3.6 and 3.7
* it shows some of the set features of GAMS
```

```
* finding Nash equilibria over a 3×3 payoff matrix, for different
* values of trade costs

* REGIME CHANGES AS COUNTRY J RAISES ITS TRADE COSTS.

SETS
R /0*2/
C /0*2/
S /1*10/;

ALIAS (R,RR);
ALIAS (C,CC);

PARAMETERS
PI(R,C,S)
PJ(R,C,S)
WI(R,C,S)
WJ(R,C,S)
ROWMAX(R,C,S)
COLMAX(R,C,S)
NE(R,C,S)
PINE(S)
PJNE(S)
WINE(S)
WJNE(S)
ALPHA
G
F
T
TJ
TCJ(S);

ALPHA = 12;
T = 1;
F = 10;
G = 12;


**** here is the loop over values of trade costs ****


LOOP(S,

TJ =    0.75 + 0.25*ORD(S);
TCJ(S) = TJ;
PI('2','2',S) = 2*(ALPHA/3)**2 - 2*G - F;
PI('1','2',S) = (ALPHA/3)**2 + ((ALPHA - 2*TJ)/3)**2 - G - F;
PI('0','2',S) = 0;
```

```
PI('2','1',S) = (ALPHA/3)**2 +((ALPHA + T)/3)**2 - 2*G - F;
PI('1','1',S) = ((ALPHA + T)/3)**2 + ((ALPHA - 2*TJ)/3)**2
                   - G - F;
PI('0','1',S) = 0;
PI('2','0',S) = 2*(ALPHA/2)**2 - 2*G - F;
PI('1','0',S) = (ALPHA/2)**2 + ((ALPHA - TJ)/2)**2 - G - F;
PI('0','0',S) = 0;

WI('2','2',S) = (1/2)*(2*ALPHA/3)**2 + PI('2','2',S);
WI('1','2',S) = (1/2)*(2*ALPHA/3)**2 + PI('1','2',S);
WI('0','2',S) = (1/2)*(ALPHA/2)**2;
WI('2','1',S) = (1/2)*((ALPHA + T + ALPHA - 2*T)/3)**2
                   + PI('2','1',S);
WI('1','1',S) = (1/2)*((ALPHA + T + ALPHA - 2*T)/3)**2
                   + PI('1','1',S);
WI('0','1',S) = (1/2)*((ALPHA - T)/2)**2;
WI('2','0',S) = (1/2)*(ALPHA/2)**2 + PI('2','0',S);
WI('1','0',S) = (1/2)*(ALPHA/2)**2 + PI('1','0',S);
WI('0','0',S) = 0;


*


PJ('2','2',S) = 2*(ALPHA/3)**2 - 2*G - F;
PJ('2','1',S) = (ALPHA/3)**2 + ((ALPHA - 2*T)/3)**2 - G - F;
PJ('2','0',S) = 0;
PJ('1','2',S) = (ALPHA/3)**2 +((ALPHA + TJ)/3)**2 - 2*G - F;
PJ('1','1',S) = ((ALPHA + TJ)/3)**2 + ((ALPHA - 2*T)/3)**2
                   - G - F;
PJ('1','0',S) = 0;
PJ('0','2',S) = 2*(ALPHA/2)**2 - 2*G - F;
PJ('0','1',S) = (ALPHA/2)**2 + ((ALPHA - T)/2)**2 - G - F;
PJ('0','0',S) = 0;

WJ('2','2',S) = (1/2)*(2*ALPHA/3)**2 + PJ('2','2',S);
WJ('2','1',S) = (1/2)*(2*ALPHA/3)**2 + PJ('2','1',S);
WJ('2','0',S) = (1/2)*(ALPHA/2)**2;
WJ('1','2',S) = (1/2)*((ALPHA + TJ + ALPHA - 2*TJ)/3)**2
                   + PJ('1','2',S);
WJ('1','1',S) = (1/2)*((ALPHA + TJ + ALPHA - 2*TJ)/3)**2
                   + PJ('1','1',S);
WJ('1','0',S) = (1/2)*((ALPHA - TJ)/2)**2;
WJ('0','2',S) = (1/2)*(ALPHA/2)**2 + PJ('0','2',S);
WJ('0','1',S) = (1/2)*(ALPHA/2)**2 + PJ('0','1',S);
WJ('0','0',S) = 0;

   );
```

```
** now we find the Nash equilibrium for each value of
** trade costs **


ROWMAX(R,C,S) = 1$(PI(R,C,S) EQ SMAX(RR, PI(RR,C,S)));
COLMAX(R,C,S) = 1$(PJ(R,C,S) EQ SMAX(CC, PJ(R,CC,S)));

NE(R,C,S) = ROWMAX(R,C,S)*COLMAX(R,C,S);


** set profits and welfare at the Nash equilibrium value for
** each trade cost **


LOOP(R,
LOOP(C,

PINE(S)$NE(R,C,S) = PI(R,C,S);
PJNE(S)$NE(R,C,S) = PJ(R,C,S);
WINE(S)$NE(R,C,S) = WI(R,C,S);
WJNE(S)$NE(R,C,S) = WJ(R,C,S);

);
);


DISPLAY TCJ, NE, PINE, PJNE, WINE, WJNE;


**** dump the output to be plotted to EXCEL spreadsheets ****

$LIBINCLUDE SSDUMP PINE PROFI.XLS
$LIBINCLUDE SSDUMP PJNE PROFJ.XLS
$LIBINCLUDE SSDUMP WINE WELI.XLS
$LIBINCLUDE SSDUMP WJNE WELJ.XLS
```

The listing file gives the following solution values. To save space in high-dimension problems, zero rows or columns of a matrix or zero values of scalars are not listed by GAMS.

```
----     120 PARAMETER TCJ

1  1.000,    2  1.250,    3  1.500,    4  1.750,    5  2.000,
6  2.250,    7  2.500,    8  2.750,    9  3.000,   10 3.250
```

```
----    120 PARAMETER NE

                1           2           3           4           5

1.1         1.000       1.000       1.000       1.000       1.000

  +           6           7           8           9          10

1.1         1.000       1.000       1.000
2.1                                             1.000       1.000



----    120 PARAMETER PINE

1    7.889,   2    6.806,   3    5.778,   4    4.806,   5    3.889,
6    3.028,   7    2.222,   8    1.472,   9    0.778,  10    0.778



----    120 PARAMETER PJNE

1    7.889,   2    8.618,   3    9.361,   4   10.118,   5   10.889,
6   11.674,   7   12.472,   8   13.285,   9    5.111,  10    5.111



----    120 PARAMETER WINE

1   37.278,   2   36.194,   3   35.167,   4   34.194,   5   33.278,
6   32.417,   7   31.611,   8   30.861,   9   30.167,  10   30.167



----    120 PARAMETER WJNE

1   37.278,   2   37.372,   3   37.486,   4   37.622,   5   37.778,
6   37.955,   7   38.153,   8   38.372,   9   37.111,  10   37.111
```

Note that there is no instance of multiple equilibria over the 10 elements of set S. The (unique) Nash equilibria change from (1,1) to (2,1) when one hits $S = 9$ ($tc_j = 3$). The Nash equilibrium profit and welfare levels are dumped to Excel and do not have to be retyped.

Appendix 5: How to Stop Worrying and Love the Computer: Program Generating Figures 5.1 and 5.2 Using the MPS/GE Subsystem of GAMS

This appendix gives the code for the central-case model in chapter 5. This is the "four-firm-type" model established in Markusen and Venables (1998). The calibration of this model is somewhat different from the original, so don't puzzle over it if the results do not quite match those in the original research. They do match the results in chapter 5 exactly. Review appendix 3 for information on the basic syntax and structure of MPS/GE.

National (type-d) and horizontal multinationals (type-h) are permitted, but vertical firms (type-v) are not. Thus there are four possible firm types: d_i, d_j, h_i, and h_j. A second simplifying assumption is that the X sector uses only one factor, skilled labor. The other factor, referred to as the "composite factor" or "unskilled labor" is used only in the Y sector. This helps "convexify" the model, in that the X sector must draw skilled labor from the Y sector at an increasing cost in terms of Y.

The initial calibration of the model is to the center of the world Edgeworth box, where the solution is symmetric and all firms are type-h. The top of the file gives the accounting matrix in table 5.1, except that here I add together a couple of columns exploiting symmetry at the point of initial calibration. Because a type-h_i and type-h_j firm have the same technologies and output in both countries, I need only specify one multinational agent, *ENTM*, but two technologies for producing fixed costs. The equilibrium activity levels for these technologies corresponds to the number of type-h_i and type-h_j firms active in equilibrium.

Here are definitions of sectors (activities), commodities (prices), and consumers (agents), and auxiliary variables (markups).

Sector	Activity level gives
YI	Output of Y in country i
YJ	Output of Y in country j
WI	Welfare of country i (output of utility)
WJ	Welfare of country j (output of utility)
XMI	Output of X by multinational firms in country i
XMJ	Output of X by multinational firms in country j
XDI	Output of X by national firms headquartered in i
XDII	Supply of a type-d_i firm to market i
XDIJ	Supply of a type-d_i firm to market j
XDJ	Output of X by national firms headquartered in j
XDJI	Supply of a type-d_j firm to market i
XDJJ	Supply of a type-d_j firm to market j
NMI	Output of fixed costs for type-h_i firms
NMJ	Output of fixed costs for type-h_j firms
NI	Output of fixed costs for type-d_i firms
NJ	Output of fixed costs for type-d_j firms

Commodity	Variable gives
CY	Price of good Y
UTILI	Price of a unit of utility in country i
UTILJ	Price of a unit of utility in country j
SI	Price of skilled labor in country i
SJ	Price of skilled labor in country j
LI	Price of unskilled labor in country i
LJ	Price of unskilled labor in country j
CXI	Consumer price of X in country i
CXJ	Consumer price of X in country j
CXDI	Marginal cost of X in country i
CXDJ	Marginal cost of X in country j
FCM	Price of fixed costs for multinational firms
FCI	Price of fixed costs for national firms in country i
FCJ	Price of fixed costs for national firms in country j

Consumer	Variables gives
CONSI	Income of representative consumer in country i
CONSJ	Income of representative consumer in country j
ENTM	Income (markup revenue) of multinational "owner"
ENTI	Income (markup revenue) of owners of type-d_i firms
ENTJ	Income (markup revenue) of owners of type-d_j firms

Auxiliary	Variable gives
NMIT	Number of type-h_i firms (explained below)
NMJT	Number of type-h_j firms (explained below)
NIT	Number of type-d_i firms (explained below)
NJT	Number of type-d_j firms (explained below)
MARKMI	Markup of type-h_i and h_j firms in country i
MARKMJ	Markup of type-h_i and h_j firms in country j
MARKDII	Markup of a type-d_i firm in market i
MARKDIJ	Markup of a type-d_i firm in market j
MARKDJI	Markup of a type-d_j firm in market i
MARKDJJ	Markup of a type-d_j firm in market j

I explain the variables NMIT, NMJT, NIT, and NJT at the end of this appendix. They are basically there to avoid a potential zero/zero division problem in the constraint equations, which is disliked by the solver. They take on the values of NMI, NMJ, NI, and NJ except when one of the latter is 0, in which case the auxiliary variables are bounded slightly above zero to avoid a 0/0 expression.

Near the top of the GAMS files, one sees

```
SET C /1*19/;
SET R /1*19/;

ALIAS (R,RR);
SCALAR UP /0/;
```

The sets C and R stand for column and row, and I use these to generate the Edgeworth box, moving in 5 percent steps, from 0.05 to 0.95, which is where the number 19 comes from (19 steps). I do not go into detail about the alias statement and the scalar "UP" (set initially at $UP = 0$) but mention their use below.

After the MPS/GE block of the problem, set starting values of the variables with the .L (for level) syntax. These help the solver find the first solution. Then come to the loop statement that repeatedly solves the model $19 \times 19 = 361$ times to generate the Edgeworth box. I explain this complicated loop statement at the end of the appendix; basically, it causes the program to "snake" through the Edgeworth box rather than jumping from the bottom of one column to the top of the next column. I could replace it with just

```
LOOP(C,
LOOP(R,

);
);
```

but the solver has trouble with the big jumps that result.

Inside the loop are four factor endowment parameters (ENDOW) being set for each point in the Edgeworth box:

```
ROW = ORD(R);
COL = ORD(C);

ENDOWJS = (ROW)*.1;
ENDOWJL = (2 - .1*COL);
ENDOWIS = (2 - .1*ROW);
ENDOWIL = (COL)*.1;
```

where "ORD" stands for the ordinal value of the set and converts the set index into an actual number. The ENDOW parameters are seen in the consumer demand blocks

```
$DEMAND:CONSI
 D:UTILI
 E:SI      Q:(150.*ENDOWIS)
 E:LI      Q:(50.*ENDOWIL)

$DEMAND:CONSJ
 D:UTILJ
 E:SJ      Q:(150.*ENDOWJS)
 E:LJ      Q:(50.*ENDOWJL)
```

Note that when $R = C = 1$, the first value of the loop for example, the endowments of the two countries are

$SI = 150^*1.90 = 285$ (95% of the world endowment of S)

$LI = 50^*0.1 = 5$ (5% of the world endowment of L)

$SJ = 150^*0.1 = 15$ (5% of the world endowment of S)

$LI = 50^*1.90 = 95$ (95% of the world endowment of L)

This is therefore the top left-hand (northwest) corner of the Edgeworth box.

Ignore the ".L" statements that follow, which are to avoid a certain divide-by-zero problem that can arise when an agent has zero income. (I discussed them briefly at the end of the program.)

Following the SOLVE statement, I manipulate the output before going on to the next element of the box. I see the statements

```
MNIE(R,C)$(NMI.L GE 0.3) = 10.;
MNJE(R,C)$(NMJ.L GE 0.3) = 1.0;
NEI(R,C)$(NI.L GE 0.3) = .1;
NEJ(R,C)$(NJ.L GE 0.3) = .01;

REGIME(R,C) = MNIE(R,C) + MNJE(R,C) + NEI(R,C) + NEJ(R,C);
```

These statements generate an "indicator function" that indicate what types of firms are active in equilibrium. (Ignore the $ conditionals, which are also discussed at the end of this appendix.) There are various ways to do this, but I just assign a 10 if type-h_i firms are active, and so forth. The parameter matrix $REGIME(R, C)$ is then the sum of these assignments. A $REGIME$ value of 10.1, for example, tells us that type-h_i and type-d_i firms are active in equilibrium at that point in the world Edgeworth box. The values of $REGIME$ in the central case in chapter 5 are shown in table 5.2.

Finally, I calculate the volume of affiliate sales (VAS), shown in figure 5.2.

```
MI(R,C) = NMI.L$(NMI.L GE 0.3);
MJ(R,C) = NMJ.L$(NMJ.L GE 0.3);
DI(R,C) = NI.L$(NI.L GE 0.3);
DJ(R,C) = NJ.L$(NJ.L GE 0.3);

SHAREJM(R,C)$(MI(R,C) + MJ(R,C)) = MJ(R,C)/(MI(R,C) + MJ(R,C));
SHAREIM(R,C)$(MI(R,C) + MJ(R,C)) = MI(R,C)/(MI(R,C) + MJ(R,C));

VAS(R,C) =(CXI.L*XMI.L*SHAREJM(R,C) +
           CXJ.L*XMJ.L*SHAREIM(R,C))/CY.L;
```

$SHAREJM$ is the share of multinational firms (if any) headquartered in country j. Of the total output of multinationals in country i, only the portion produced by type-h_j firms counts as affiliate sales, as discussed in chapter 5. Thus, out of the value of output of type-h firms in country i, only

```
CXI.L*XMI.L*SHAREJM(R,C)
```

counts as affiliate output (CXI is price, XMI is the quantity (activity level), and CY is the price of good Y, used here as numeraire). At the center of the box in figures 5.1 and 5.2, the share parameters are both one-half, so exactly half of all world output of X is affiliate output.

Near the end of the program is the statement

```
MODELSTAT(R,C) = BOX.MODELSTAT - 1;
```

Model name (BOX in the this case), followed by a period and the keyword MODELSTAT, produces a statistic that indicates if the model solved properly. It takes a value of 5 if the model does not solve and a value of 1 if it does solve (don't ask me why). Subtracting 1 and storing all values in a matrix results in a matrix where the only nonzero values indicate a failure to solve that element. GAMS will only display nonzero values of matrices and parameters, which is very beneficial in this case. If a solution is found every time, it will just report "ALL ZERO" instead of 361 zeros.

Here is the actual program that generates table 5.2, figure 5.1, and figure 5.2 using the initial calibration of table 5.1. Note that the numbers in the accounting matrix are values. In many cases the initial price is chosen as one, so they are also physical quantities. The exceptions are X_i and X_j. Note that the 100 units in the initial data are interpreted as 80 physical units at a price of 1.25 (marginal cost is 1, and the markup is 0.2: $1.25(1 - 0.2) = 1$). This is where the "80s" come from in the MPS/GE program. Note that the price 1.25 is used in calibrating the utility functions, activities WI and WJ.

```
* EXAMPLE 5
* this produces Figure 5.1 of Chapter 5
* it uses mpsge

* four firm types, no type-v firms
* Oligopoly model of Markusen and Venables, JIE 1998
* calibrated to the center of the Edgeworth box
```

$ONTEXT

	YI	YJ	XMI	XMJ	NMI	NMJ	WI	WJ	CONSI	CONSJ	ENTM
CYI	100						-100				
CYJ		100						-100			
CXI			100				-100				
CXJ				100				-100			
FCM					20	20					-40
LI	-50								50		
SI	-50		-80		-15	-5			150		
LJ		-50								50	
SJ		-50		-80	-5	-15				150	
UTILI							200		-200		
UTILJ								200		-200	
MKI			-10	-10							20
MKJ			-10	-10							20

$OFFTEXT

SET C /1*19/;
SET R /1*19/;

ALIAS (R,RR);
SCALAR UP /0/;

PARAMETERS
  FMI
  FMJ
  ENDOWIS
  ENDOWJS
  ENDOWIL
  ENDOWJL
  FDI
  FDJ
  TCOST
  ROW
  COL
  SCALE(R)
  TMC(R,C)
  MNIE(R,C)
  MNJE(R,C)
  NEI(R,C)
  NEJ(R,C)
  MI(R,C)
  MJ(R,C)

```
DI(R,C)
DJ(R,C)
VAS(R,C)
REGIME(R,C)
SHAREIM(R,C)
SHAREJM(R,C)
WELFAREI(R,C)
WELFAREJ(R,C)
MODELSTAT(R,C);

FMI = 8;
FMJ = 8;
FDI = 5.5;
FDJ = 5.5;
TCOST = .15;


**** now control passes to the MPS/GE compiler ****

$ONTEXT
$MODEL:BOX

$SECTORS:
 YI     YJ
 WI     WJ
 XMI    XMJ
 XDI
 XDII
 XDIJ
 XDJ
 XDJI
 XDJJ
 NMI    NMJ
 NI     NJ

$COMMODITIES:
 CY
 UTILI  UTILJ
 SI     SJ
 LI     LJ
 CXI    CXJ
 CXDI
 CXDJ
 FCM
 FCI    FCJ
```

```
$CONSUMERS:
 CONSI    CONSJ
 ENTM
 ENTI    ENTJ

$AUXILIARY:
 NMIT
 NMJT
 NIT
 NJT
 MARKMI
 MARKMJ
 MARKDII
 MARKDIJ
 MARKDJI
 MARKDJJ

$PROD:YI    s:5.0
 O:CY     Q:100.0
 I:SI     Q:50.0
 I:LI     Q:50.0

$PROD:YJ    s:5.0
 O:CY     Q:100.0
 I:SJ     Q:50.0
 I:LJ     Q:50.0

$PROD:XMI
 O:CXI    Q:80.      A:ENTM    N:MARKMI
 I:SI     Q:80.

$PROD:XMJ
 O:CXJ    Q:80.      A:ENTM    N:MARKMJ
 I:SJ     Q:80.

$PROD:XDI
 O:CXDI   Q:80.
 I:SI     Q:80.

$PROD:XDII
 O:CXI    Q:80.      A:ENTI    N:MARKDII
 I:CXDI   Q:80.

$PROD:XDIJ s:0.0
 O:CXJ    Q:80.      A:ENTI    N:MARKDIJ
 I:CXDI   Q:80.
 I:SI     Q:(80.*TCOST)
```

```
$PROD:XDJ
 O:CXDJ   Q:80.
 I:SJ     Q:80.

$PROD:XDJI
 O:CXI    Q:80.     A:ENTJ    N:MARKDJI
 I:CXDJ   Q:80.
 I:SJ     Q:(80.*TCOST)

$PROD:XDJJ s:0.0
 O:CXJ    Q:80.     A:ENTJ    N:MARKDJJ
 I:CXDJ   Q:80.

$PROD:NMI  s:0.0
 O:FCM
 I:SI     Q:(FMI*3/4)
 I:SJ     Q:(FMI/4)

$PROD:NMJ  s:0.0
 O:FCM
 I:SJ     Q:(FMJ*3/4)
 I:SI     Q:(FMJ/4)

$PROD:NI
 O:FCI
 I:SI     Q:FDI

$PROD:NJ
 O:FCJ
 I:SJ     Q:FDJ

$PROD:WI   s:1.0
 O:UTILI  Q:200.
 I:CXI    Q:80.    P:1.25
 I:CY     Q:100.

$PROD:WJ   s:1.0
 O:UTILJ  Q:200.
 I:CXJ    Q:80.    P:1.25
 I:CY     Q:100.

$DEMAND:CONSI
 D:UTILI
 E:SI     Q:(150.*ENDOWIS)
 E:LI     Q:(50.*ENDOWIL)

$DEMAND:CONSJ
 D:UTILJ
 E:SJ     Q:(150.*ENDOWJS)
 E:LJ     Q:(50.*ENDOWJL)
```

```
$DEMAND:ENTM
 D:FCM

$DEMAND:ENTI
 D:FCI

$DEMAND:ENTJ
 D:FCJ

$CONSTRAINT:NMIT
 NMIT =G= NMI;

$CONSTRAINT:NMJT
 NMJT =G= NMJ;

$CONSTRAINT:NIT
 NIT =G= NI;

$CONSTRAINT:NJT
 NJT =G= NJ;

$CONSTRAINT:MARKMI
 MARKMI*(NMIT+NMJT)*(XMI + XDII + XDJI) =G= XMI;

$CONSTRAINT:MARKMJ
 MARKMJ*(NMIT+NMJT)*(XMJ + XDIJ + XDJJ) =G= XMJ;

$CONSTRAINT:MARKDII
 MARKDII*(NIT)*(XMI + XDII + XDJI) =G= XDII;

$CONSTRAINT:MARKDIJ
 MARKDIJ*(NIT)*(XMJ + XDIJ + XDJJ) =G= XDIJ;

$CONSTRAINT:MARKDJI
 MARKDJI*(NJT)*(XMI + XDII + XDJI) =G= XDJI;

$CONSTRAINT:MARKDJJ
 MARKDJJ*(NJT)*(XMJ + XDIJ + XDJJ) =G= XDJJ;

**** now control goes back to GAMS ****

$OFFTEXT
$SYSINCLUDE MPSGESET BOX

**** set starting values (these are guesses) ****

NMI.L = 0;
NMJ.L = 0;
NMIT.L = 0;
NMJT.L = 0;
```

```
NI.L = 2.0;
NJ.L = 2.0;
NIT.L = 2.0;
NJT.L = 2.0;

CXI.L = 1.25;
CXJ.L = 1.25;

MARKMI.L = .2;
MARKMJ.L = .2;

MARKDII.L = .2;
MARKDIJ.L = .2;
MARKDJI.L = .2;
MARKDJJ.L = .2;

XMI.L = .0;
XMJ.L = 0.;

XDI.L = 1.0;
XDII.L = 1.0;
XDIJ.L = 1.0;
XDJ.L = 1.0;
XDJI.L = 1.0;
XDJJ.L = 1.0;

CY.FX = 1.0;

NMIT.LO = 0.001;
NMJT.LO = 0.001;
NIT.LO = 0.001;
NJT.LO = 0.001;

**** now do some stuff, to reduce the size of the listing file

BOX.ITERLIM = 5000;
OPTION MCP=MILES;
OPTION SOLPRINT=OFF;
OPTION LIMROW=0;
OPTION LIMCOL=0;
$OFFSYMLIST OFFSYMXREF OFFUELLIST OFFUELXREF


**** now come the loops that repeatedly solve the model over the
**** world Edgeworth box ****

LOOP(C,

    LOOP(RR,
```

```
*     If we are going down a column, then R=RR.

*     If we are going up a column, then R = NR - RR + 1

   LOOP(R$(  (1-UP)$(ORD(R) EQ ORD(RR)            ) +
             UP$(ORD(R) EQ CARD(R)-ORD(RR)+1)  ),


ROW = ORD(R);
COL = ORD(C);

ENDOWJS = (ROW)*.1;
ENDOWJL = (2 - .1*COL);
ENDOWIS = (2 - .1*ROW);
ENDOWIL = (COL)*.1;

UTILI.L = MAX(UTILI.L, 1.E-4);
UTILJ.L = MAX(UTILJ.L, 1.E-4);
FCM.L = MAX(FCM.L, 1.E-4);
FCI.L = MAX(FCI.L, 1.E-4);
FCJ.L = MAX(FCJ.L, 1.E-4);

$INCLUDE BOX.GEN
SOLVE BOX USING MCP;

MODELSTAT(R,C) = BOX.MODELSTAT - 1.;

MNIE(R,C)$(NMI.L GE 0.3) = 10.;
MNJE(R,C)$(NMJ.L GE 0.3) = 1.0;
NEI(R,C)$(NI.L GE 0.3) = .1;
NEJ(R,C)$(NJ.L GE 0.3) = .01;

REGIME(R,C) = MNIE(R,C) + MNJE(R,C) + NEI(R,C) + NEJ(R,C);

MI(R,C) = NMI.L$(NMI.L GE 0.3);
MJ(R,C) = NMJ.L$(NMJ.L GE 0.3);
DI(R,C) = NI.L$(NI.L GE 0.3);
DJ(R,C) = NJ.L$(NJ.L GE 0.3);

SHAREJM(R,C)$(MI(R,C) + MJ(R,C)) = MJ(R,C)/(MI(R,C) + MJ(R,C));
SHAREIM(R,C)$(MI(R,C) + MJ(R,C)) = MI(R,C)/(MI(R,C) + MJ(R,C));
VAS(R,C) = (CXI.L*XMI.L*SHAREJM(R,C) + CXJ.L*XMJ.L*SHAREIM(R,C))
           /CY.L;


WELFAREI(R,C) = WI.L;
WELFAREJ(R,C) = WJ.L;
```

```
   );
   );

*     We have finished a column, so the next column
*     changes direction:

   IF (UP, UP = 0; ELSE  UP = 1; );

);

DISPLAY WELFAREI, WELFAREJ;
DISPLAY MI, MJ, DI, DJ;
DISPLAY VAS;

DISPLAY REGIME;
DISPLAY MODELSTAT;

$LIBINCLUDE SSDUMP REGIME FIG1REG.XLS
$LIBINCLUDE SSDUMP VAS FIG2VAS.XLS
```

The variables *NMIT*, *NMJT*, *NIT*, and *NJT* need a few words of explanation, which can be skipped over by those readers not interested in the finer points. The difficulty with the markup equations is that the sales of a given firm type in a market are total output of that group of firms divided by the number of those firms. That is, the *X* variables above are total output of a firm type, not the output of an individual firm. If that firm type is not active, then this is a ratio of zero/zero. The computer doesn't like this much, and the solver can crash when asked to evaluate 0/0. So I have a second set of variables for the number of firms, those ending in "T," which are set in constraint equations to be greater than or equal to the actual number of firms but have minimum values constrained at 0.001 to avoid the division-by-zero problem. So in the MPS/GE block one sees, for example,

```
$CONSTRAINT:NIT
  NIT =G= NI;
```

where NI is the activity level for production of fixed costs for type-d_i firms. The auxiliary variable *NIT* appears in the markup equation, such as

```
$CONSTRAINT:MARKDII
  MARKDII*(NIT)*(XMI + XDII + XDJI) =G= XDII;
```

and NIT is constrained with a minimum value by a later statement,

```
NIT.LO = 0.001;
```

where "LO" stands for "lower bound on the variable named." Thus when firm type-d_i is not active in equibrium, $NI = 0$, $XDII/NIT = 0/0.001$ instead of $0/0$.

Now a few comments on the loop statements. These are given by

```
LOOP(C,

  LOOP(RR,

  LOOP(R$(  (1-UP)$(ORD(R) EQ ORD(RR)              ) +
            UP$(ORD(R) EQ CARD(R)-ORD(RR)+1)  ),

  );
  );

  IF (UP, UP = 0; ELSE  UP = 1; );

);
```

I do not go into this in detail. Basically, if I just specified

```
LOOP(C,
LOOP(R,

);
):
```

the program would go down the first column and jump back to the top of the second column and go down that column. The problem with that is that the solver begins looking for the solution at the top of the second column using the solution values at the bottom of the first column as starting values. But these starting values are way off from the new solution values. What the complicated loop statement above does is snake its way through the Edgeworth box. When it reaches the bottom of the first column, it just moves over to the bottom element of the second column and then works its way up. This avoids the big "jumps" that sometime cause the solver to fail.

Endowments are the first thing specified within the loop statement, and then, one sees the statements

```
UTILI.L = MAX(UTILI.L, 1.E-4);
UTILJ.L = MAX(UTILJ.L, 1.E-4);
FCM.L = MAX(FCM.L, 1.E-4);
FCI.L = MAX(FCI.L, 1.E-4);
FCJ.L = MAX(FCJ.L, 1.E-4);
```

These avoid another possible division-by-zero problem. When there is a good, such as fixed costs, which is only demanded by a single agent and that agent has zero income (e.g., an inactive firm type), the price of that good will be zero. (Note that the left-hand-side variables are all prices here.) But this price can appear in a denominator of some equation in the solution algorithm, so an initial assignment of a minimum starting value for each of these goods avoids a divide-by-zero problem.

One unexpected consequence of the use of the auxiliary variables such as *NIT* is that the solver can leave little pieces of firms around. With reference to the determination of the equilibrium regimes (*REGIME*), conditionals such as $(NI.L GE 0.3) set the reported number of firms of a given type equal to zero, unless there is a least 0.3 firms in equilibrium, in which case the reported number equals the actual number. This is a somewhat sloppy way of ignoring a firm type when there is only a small fraction of one firm in equilibrium.

Appendix 6: Chef's Special for Dixit-Stiglitz Lovers: Program Generating Figures 6.1 and 6.2 Using MCP

The monopolistic-competition model in chapter 6 uses the same dimensionality and same calibration data as the model in chapter 5. Exactly the same data is calibrated to a different model. Thus one can free-ride on what was learned in the previous chapter to a great extent.

In this case, I used the MCP solver writing out all of the inequalities explicitly. Monopolistic competition is a bit awkward for MPS/GE, since the changing number of varieties leads to some problems with the standard way a utility function is specified in MPS/GE. There are ways around this, but in the end I just decided to do this as an MCP.

Here are the definitions of the variables. The notation is hopefully very close to that in chapter 6.

Variable	Definition
EI	Price index for differentiated goods in country i
EJ	Price index for differentiated goods in country j
MI	Income of country i
MJ	Income of country j
$XDII$	Output of a variety by firm type d_i sold in market i
$XDIJ$	Output of a variety by firm type d_i sold in market j
$XDJJ$	Output of a variety by firm type d_j sold in market j
$XDJI$	Output of a variety by firm type d_j sold in market i
$XHII$	Output of a variety by firm type h_i sold in market i
$XHJI$	Output of a variety by firm type h_j sold in market i
$XHJJ$	Output of a variety by firm type h_j sold in market j
$XHIJ$	Output of a variety by firm type h_i sold in market j

YI	Output of Y in country i
YJ	Output of Y in country j
NDI	Number of type d_i firms
NDJ	Number of type d_j firms
NHI	Number of type h_i firms
NHJ	Number of type h_j firms
PI	Consumer price of an X variety in country i
PJ	Consumer price of an X variety in country j
PY	Consumer price of Y
ZI	Price of skilled labor in country i
WI	Price of unskilled labor in country i
ZJ	Price of skilled labor in country j
WJ	Price of unskilled labor in country j

One feature of the standard large-group monopolistic-competition model that makes it simpler than the oligopoly model is the fixed markup, so it is not necessary to solve for these variables here. In addition, output per firm takes on a very simple formula. There is a price to this of course, which is that there are no firm-scale effects and therefore no market-size effects as I noted in chapter 6. Simplicity has a price. Here are the equations of the model.

Equation	Definition	Complementary variable
INDEXI	Price index for differentiated goods in i	EI
INDEXJ	Price index for differentiated goods in j	EJ
EXPI	Income of country i	MI
EXPJ	Income of country j	MJ
DXDII	Demand for a type-d_i firm's good in country i	XDII
DXDJI	Demand for a type-d_j firm's good in country i	XDJI
DXDJJ	Demand for a type-d_j firm's good in country j	XDJJ
DXDIJ	Demand for a type-d_i firm's good in country j	XDIJ
DXHII	Demand for a type-h_i firm's good in country i	XHII
DXHJI	Demand for a type-h_j firm's good in country i	XHJI
DXHJJ	Demand for a type-h_j firm's good in country j	XHJJ

$DXHIJ$	Demand for a type-h_i firm's good in country j	$XHIJ$
DY	World demand for good Y	PY
NNI	Zero profits for type-d_i firms	NDI
NNJ	Zero profits for type-d_j firms	NDJ
$NNMI$	Zero profits for type-h_i firms	NHI
$NNMJ$	Zero profits for type-h_j firms	NHJ
$PRICEI$	$MR = MC$ for X varieties produced in country i	PI
$PRICEJ$	$MR = MC$ for X varieties produced in country j	PJ
$PRICYI$	Price = marginal cost for Y produced in i	YI
$PRICYJ$	Price = marginal cost for Y produced in j	YJ
$SKLABI$	Supply = demand for skilled labor in i	ZI
$UNLABI$	Supply = demand for unskilled labor in i	WI
$SKLABJ$	Supply = demand for skilled labor in j	ZJ
$UNLABJ$;	Supply = demand for unskilled labor in j	WJ

Below is the GAMS file for the model that generates the data for figures 6.1 and 6.2. Many of these equations are quite simple for this reason: markups are fixed and outputs per firm take on very simple expressions. What the MCP formulation will not do, however, is all of the automatic generation of the market-clearing and income-balance equations that are automatically generated (error free) by MPS/GE. If the modeler makes an error in one of these while writing out the equations, no one will ever know, including the author. This is one reason in favor of MPS/GE but also a reason why the modeler should start with a calibrated problem so as to make sure that it can pass the replication check. This leads to the discovery of most errors.

The factor-market-clearing equations $SKLABI$, $UNLABI$, $SKLABJ$, and $UNLABJ$ use Shepard's lemma for factor demands on the right-hand side. A really ambitious reader can check that the demand for skilled labor in Y in country i, for example, is equal to derivative of marginal cost for Y with respect to ZI in equation $PRICYI$ times the level of Y production in $i(YI)$.

Here is the program.

```
* EX6.GMS
* This file produces Figures 6.1 and 6.2 of Chapter 6
* four firm-type model adapted from the
* monopolistic-competition model of Markusen and Venables,
* JIE 2000.
```

```
$ontext
        YI    YJ   XMI  XMJ  NMI  NMJ    WI    WJ CONI CONJ ENI   ENJ

CYI    100                        -100
CYJ          100                        -100
CXI               100             -100
CXJ                    100             -100
FCI                          20                            -20
FCJ                               20                            -20
SI    -50    -80        -15   -5             150
SJ          -50        -80   -5  -15             150
LI    -50                                     50
LJ          -50                                     50
UTILI                                  200  -200
UTILJ                                       200  -200
MKI         -10  -10                                    10    10
MKJ         -10  -10                                    10    10

$offtext


SET R /1*19/;

*     The following are used to manipulate the order in which
*     we loop through the cases in order to assure that we take
*     small steps:

ALIAS (R,RR,C,CC);
SCALAR UP /0/;

PARAMETERS
EP
EY
TC
FCD
FCH
ENDOWIS
ENDOWIL
ENDOWJS
ENDOWJL
ROW
COL
MODELSTAT(R,C)
MNIE(R,C)
MNJE(R,C)
NEI(R,C)
NEJ(R,C)
MNI(R,C)
```

```
MNJ(R,C)
DI(R,C)
DJ(R,C)
REGIME(R,C)
VAS(R,C)
VASC(R,C)
WELFAREI(R,C)
WELFAREJ(R,C);


EP = 5;
EY = 3;
TC = 1.35;
FCD = 13.75;
FCH = 20;
ENDOWIS = 150;
ENDOWIL = 50;
ENDOWJS = 150;
ENDOWJL = 50;

POSITIVE VARIABLES
EI
EJ
MI
MJ
XDII
XDIJ
XDJJ
XDJI
XHII
XHJI
XHJJ
XHIJ
YI
YJ
NDI
NDJ
NHI
NHJ
PI
PJ
PY
ZI
WI
ZJ
WJ;
```

```
EQUATIONS
INDEXI
INDEXJ
EXPI
EXPJ
DXDII
DXDJI
DXDJJ
DXDIJ
DXHII
DXHJI
DXHJJ
DXHIJ
DY
NNI
NNJ
NNMI
NNMJ
PRICEI
PRICEJ
PRICYI
PRICYJ
SKLABI
UNLABI
SKLABJ
UNLABJ;
```

```
INDEXI..    EI =E= (NDI*PI**(1-EP) + NDJ*(PJ*TC)**(1-EP)
                   + (NHI+NHJ)*PI**(1-EP))**(1/(1-EP));

INDEXJ..    EJ =E= (NDI*(PI*TC)**(1-EP) + NDJ*PJ**(1-EP)
                   + (NHI+NHJ)*PJ**(1-EP))**(1/(1-EP));

EXPI..      MI =E= ZI*ENDOWIS + WI*ENDOWIL;

EXPJ..      MJ =E= ZJ*ENDOWJS + WJ*ENDOWJL;

DXDII..     XDII =E= PI**(-EP)*(EI**(EP-1))*MI/2;

DXDJI..     XDJI/TC =E= (PJ*TC)**(-EP)*(EI**(EP-1))*MI/2;

DXDJJ..     XDJJ =E= PJ**(-EP)*(EJ**(EP-1))*MJ/2;

DXDIJ..     XDIJ/TC =E= (PI*TC)**(-EP)*(EJ**(EP-1))*MJ/2;

DXHII..     XHII =E= PI**(-EP)*(EI**(EP-1))*MI/2;

DXHJI..     XHJI =E= PI**(-EP)*(EI**(EP-1))*MI/2;

DXHJJ..     XHJJ =E= PJ**(-EP)*(EJ**(EP-1))*MJ/2;
```

```
DXHIJ..    XHIJ =E= PJ**(-EP)*(EJ**(EP-1))*MJ/2;

DY..       YI + YJ =E= MI/(2*PY) + MJ/(2*PY);

NNI..      FCD*(EP-1) =G= XDII + XDIJ;

NNJ..      FCD*(EP-1) =G= XDJJ + XDJI;

NNMI..     FCH*(.75*ZI + .25*ZJ)*EP =G= PI*XHII + PJ*XHIJ;

NNMJ..     FCH*(.25*ZI + .75*ZJ)*EP =G= PJ*XHJJ + PI*XHJI;

PRICEI..   PI*(1-1/EP) =E= ZI;

PRICEJ..   PJ*(1-1/EP) =E= ZJ;

PRICYI..   (ZI**(1-EY) + WI**(1-EY))**(1/(1-EY))*(2**(1/(EY-1)))
           =G= PY;

PRICYJ..   (ZJ**(1-EY) + WJ**(1-EY))**(1/(1-EY))*(2**(1/(EY-1)))
           =G= PY;

SKLABI..   ENDOWIS =E= YI*ZI**(-EY)
              *(ZI**(1-EY) + WI**(1-EY))**(EY/(1-EY))
              *(2**(1/(EY-1)))
              + NDI*(XDII + XDIJ + FCD)
              + NHI*(XHII + 15) + NHJ*(XHJI + 5);

UNLABI..   ENDOWIL =E= YI*WI**(-EY)
              *(ZI**(1-EY)
              + WI**(1-EY))**(EY/(1-EY))*(2**(1/(EY-1))));


SKLABJ..   ENDOWJS =E= YJ*ZJ**(-EY)
              *(ZJ**(1-EY) + WJ**(1-EY))**(EY/(1-EY))
              *(2**(1/(EY-1)))
              + NDJ*(XDJJ + XDJI + FCD)
              + NHJ*(XHJJ + 15) + NHI*(XHIJ + 5);

UNLABJ..   ENDOWJL =E= YJ*WJ**(-EY)
              *(ZJ**(1-EY)
              + WJ**(1-EY))**(EY/(1-EY))*(2**(1/(EY-1))));


MODEL BOX /INDEXI.EI, INDEXJ.EJ, EXPI.MI, EXPJ.MJ,
              DXDII.XDII, DXDJI.XDJI, DXDJJ.XDJJ, DXDIJ.XDIJ,
              DXHII.XHII, DXHJJ.XHJJ, DXHIJ.XHIJ, DXHJI.XHJI,
              DY.PY, NNI.NDI, NNJ.NDJ, NNMI.NHI, NNMJ.NHJ,
              PRICEI.PI, PRICEJ.PJ, PRICYI.YI, PRICYJ.YJ,
              SKLABI.ZI, SKLABJ.ZJ, UNLABI.WI, UNLABJ.WJ/;
```

```
OPTION MCP=MILES;
OPTION SOLPRINT=OFF;
OPTION LIMROW=0;
OPTION LIMCOL=0;
$OFFSYMLIST OFFSYMXREF OFFUELLIST OFFUELXREF

EI.L = 1;
EJ.L = 1;
MI.L = 150;
MJ.L = 150;
XDII.L = 40;
XDIJ.L = 40;
XDJJ.L = 0;
XDJI.L = 0;
XHII.L = 0;
XHJJ.L = 0;
XHJI.L = 0;
XHIJ.L = 0;
YI.L = 10;
YJ.L = 100;
NDI.L = 2;
NDJ.L = 0;
NHI.L = 0;
NHJ.L = 0;
PI.L = 1.25;
PJ.L = 1.25;
PY.L = 1;
ZI.L = 1;
WI.L = 1;
ZJ.L = 1;
WJ.L = 1;


PY.FX = 1;

TC = 1.35;

LOOP(C,

  LOOP(RR,

*    If we are going down a column, then R=RR.

*    If we are going up a column, then R = NR - RR + 1

    LOOP(R$(  (1-UP)$(ORD(R) EQ ORD(RR)          ) +
           UP$(ORD(R) EQ CARD(R)-ORD(RR)+1) ),
```

```
ROW = ORD(R);
COL = ORD(C);

ENDOWIS  = 300 - 15*ORD(R);
ENDOWIL  = 5*ORD(C);
ENDOWJS  = 15*ORD(R);
ENDOWJL  = 100 - 5*ORD(C);


SOLVE BOX USING MCP;

MODELSTAT(R,C) = BOX.MODELSTAT - 1.;

MNIE(R,C)$(NHI.L GE 0.3) = 10.;
MNJE(R,C)$(NHJ.L GE 0.3) = 1.0;
NEI(R,C)$(NDI.L GE 0.3) = .1;
NEJ(R,C)$(NDJ.L GE 0.3) = .01;

MNI(R,C) = NHI.L$(NHI.L GE 0.3);
MNJ(R,C) = NHI.L$(NHJ.L GE 0.3);
DI(R,C) = NDI.L$(NDI.L GE 0.3);
DJ(R,C) = NDJ.L$(NDJ.L GE 0.3);

REGIME(R,C) = MNIE(R,C) + MNJE(R,C) + NEI(R,C) + NEJ(R,C);

VAS(R,C)$(MNJ(R,C) + MNI(R,C)) = PJ.L*XHIJ.L*NHI.L
    + PI.L*XHJI.L*NHJ.L;
VASC(R,C)$(MNJ(R,C) + MNI(R,C)) = XHIJ.L*NHI.L + XHJI.L*NHJ.L;

WELFAREI(R,C) =((1/2)**.125)*(1.25**0.5)*(1/EI.L)**0.5*(MI.L/2);
WELFAREJ(R,C) =((1/2)**.125)*(1.25**0.5)*(1/EJ.L)**0.5*(MJ.L/2);

  );
  );

*  . We have finished a column, so the next column
*    changes direction:

  IF (UP, UP = 0; ELSE UP = 1; );

);

DISPLAY WELFAREI, WELFAREJ;
DISPLAY MNI, MNJ, DI, DJ;
DISPLAY VAS, VASC;


DISPLAY REGIME;
DISPLAY MODELSTAT;
```

```
$LIBINCLUDE SSDUMP REGIME MCREG.XLS
$LIBINCLUDE SSDUMP VAS FIG1VAS.XLS
```

I don't have much to add to the program, since the looping and the use of output is the same as in appendix 5. Note here that I don't solve for utility in the main model (which I could), but find *WELFAREI* and *WELFAREJ* after the main problem has been solved.

The model concludes with the dumping of the parameters REGIME and VAS to Excel sheets as in the case of appendix 5, which are then used to generate figures 6.1 and 6.2.

I hope that you have gotten something out of this little tour through GAMS and numerical modeling. If nothing else, it is a lot of fun producing nifty 3-D diagrams. The lines between production and consumption, and work and play, can get blurry; but having fun leads to better output, in my opinion.

Notes

Chapter 1   Statistics, Stylized Facts, and Basic Concepts

This chapter draws from James R. Markusen, "The Boundaries of Multinational Firms and the Theory of International Trade," *Journal of Economic Perspectives* 9 (1995): 169–189; and James R. Markusen, "Multinational Firms, Location and Trade," *The World Economy* 21 (1998): 733–756.

1. Documentation of country characteristics 1–3 can be found in a number of sources. All are demonstrated in various articles found in Froot (1993). See also Hummels and Stern (1994), the UNCTAD World Investment Report (1993), and Markusen and Venables (1998). Julius (1990) reports that the share of all direct investment outflows generated by G-5 countries absorbed by other G-5 countries has been rising and amounted to 70 percent by 1988. Hummels and Stern report that in 1985 the developed countries were the source of 97 percent of direct investment flows and the recipient of 75 percent. See also tables 1.1–1.4 presented in section 1.3.

2. Brainard (1997) shows that intra-industry affiliate sales indices are somewhat lower than intra-industry trade indices, but they are still significant (the intra-industry affiliate sales index measures the degree of international cross-investment in a particular industry: production and sales abroad by US MNEs and production and sales in the United States by foreign MNEs). Grubel-Lloyd indices of cross or intra-industry investment are present in table 1.7.

3. Brainard (1997) reports that foreign affiliates owned by U.S. multinationals export 13 percent of their overseas production to the United States, while the U.S. affiliates of foreign multinationals export 2 percent of their US production to their parents. Affiliate-parent trade figures are presented in table 1.7 and discussed more in section 1.3.

4. UNCTAD (1993) reports that intrafirm trade is about one-third of world exports. Brainard (1993b) reports that, for the United States, the share of both imports and exports accounted for by intrafirm transfers is roughly equal to one quarter. Total trade mediated by affiliates is 32 percent of imports and 37 percent of exports. See Blomstrom, Lipsey, and Kulchycky (1988) and Denekamp and Ferrantino (1992) concerning the complementarity of exports and overseas production. Markusen and Maskus (2001) and Blonigen (2001) discuss some aspects of this issue.

5. Brainard (1997) rejects factor-proportions explanations of FDI except for that portion of FDI production explicitly for export back to the home country. Carr, Markusen, and Maskus (2001) and Markusen and Maskus (1999, 2001) find strong support for the

positive role of skilled labor in explaining outward FDI. Studies by Morck and Yeung (1991) and Wheeler and Mody (1992) reject explanations of multinationality based on risk and portfolio diversification, and on tax variables. Although it is essentially a macro-oriented volume, I found little support in Froot (1993) for macro-oriented explanations of FDI such as international risk diversification. A great deal of evidence on taxation and multinationals is found in Hines (1997) and Feldstein, Hines, and Hubbard (1995).

6. Outward affiliate sales relative to exports and inward affiliate sales relative to imports for 64 industries in the United States are given in Brainard (1997).

7. These stylized facts appear in many studies, and I have never seen any of them contradicted in any study. Much discussion, data, and many references are found in Caves (1996). Buckley and Casson (1985) remains an important study on this question. For more recent evidence, see Morck and Yeung (1991, 1992), Brainard (1993b, 1997), Grubaugh (1987), and Beaudreau (1986). For events in which firms do transfer technology abroad, articles by Davidson and McFetridge (1984), Mansfield and Romeo (1980), Teece (1986), and Wilson (1977) show technology is more likely to be transferred internally within the firm by R&D-intensive firms producing new and technically complex products. Blomstrom and Zejan (1991) get similar results with respect to joint ventures: Firms are less likely to seek a foreign partner when intangible assets are important.

8. Morck and Yeung (1991).

9. Brainard (1997) and Beaudreau (1986).

10. Morck and Yeung (1991) and Beaudreau (1986).

11. Regression coefficients on tariffs and transport costs or distance have often been insignificant and/or had the wrong sign in equations with some measure of multi-nationality as the dependent variable (e.g., Beaudreau 1986 using extensive firm-specific data). Brainard (1997) has mixed results for equations explaining the level of affiliate sales abroad. Part of the explanation seems to be that many firms have substantial imported content in their foreign production and export modest amounts (on average as noted above) back to their parent. In these respects tariffs and transport costs discourage affiliate production just like they discourage exports. However, using share equations, the *share* of affiliate sales in the total of affiliate sales and exports is increasing and significant in both freight charges and tariffs. Carr, Markusen, and Maskus (2001) and Markusen and Maskus (2001, 2002) find host-country protection levels positive and significant determinants of inward affiliate activity using a broader index of protection, and they find distance a significant negative determinant.

Chapter 2   A Partial-Equilibrium, Single-Firm Model of Plant Location

1. X_{ii} and X_{ji} will never both be positive. If the firm finds it profitable to serve country i from a plant in country j (e.g., the marginal cost plus transport cost from j is less than the marginal cost in i) then the firm should shut its plant in i and save the fixed cost G.

2. This efficiency parameter γ plays no important role in this chapter. It is inserted to patch a potential technical problem that is often ignored in these models. Researchers generally assume an interior solution to the model with both X and Y produced. But with the demand for X income inelastic, the demand for labor in the X sector at the "proposed" interior solution may exceed the economy's labor supply, so that the correct

solution is a corner solution with only X produced. A large enough choice of γ eliminates this possibility. I will not refer to this problem again.

3. At this point I might mention that the aggregate budget constraint (4) can be written in an alternative way. Let $\gamma = 1$ for simplicity and suppose that it is a type-d firm, exporting X to country j and importing good Y. c, G, and F are all in units of good Y and therefore also in units of L. Substitute in for profits in (4):

$$L_i + (p_i X_{ii} + p_j X_{ij} - c_i X_{ii} - (c_i + t)X_{ij})) - G - F = p_i X_{ii} + (Y_{ii} + Y_{ji}).$$

Simplify:

$$L_i - c_i X_{ii} - (c_i + t)X_{ij} - G - F - Y_{ii} = [Y_{ji} - p_j X_{ij}] = 0.$$

The left-hand side is labor supply minus labor demand in the X and Y sectors. The right-hand side is balance of trade: Y imports minus X exports. If the aggregate budget constraint income equals expenditure is satisfied and trade balances, the labor market clears. Trade balance is always imposed in static models.

4. For anyone interested in replicating these results, the base-case parameter values in figure 2.1 are as follows: $\alpha = 10$, $\beta = 1$, $c_i = 2$, $c_j = 2$, $t = 2$, $G = 22$, $F = 16$, $L_i + L_j = 10$ ($L_i = L_j = 5$ in the middle of the horizontal axis in figure 2.1).

5. Equal marginal costs in the two markets is a sufficient condition for this result.

Chapter 3   International Duopoly with Endogenous Market Structures

This chapter draws from Ignatius J. Horstmann and James R. Markusen, "Endogenous Market Structures in International Trade (natura facit saltum)," *Journal of International Economics* 32 (1992): 109–129; it appeared in J. Peter Neary, ed., *International Library of Critical Writings in Economics: International Trade* (London: Edward Elgar, 1995), 381–401.

Chapter 4   Incumbency, Preemption, and Persistence

This chapter relates to Ignatius J. Horstmann and James R. Markusen, "Strategic Investments and the Development of Multinationals," *International Economic Review* 28 (1987): 109–121; it appeared in Mark Casson, ed., *Multinational Corporations* (London: Edward Elgar, 1990), 126–140, and in Melvin Greenhut and George Norman, eds., *The Economics of Location, Vol. 3: Spatialmicroeconomics* (London: Edward Elgar, 1995), 499–511.

Chapter 5   A General-Equilibrium Oligopoly Model of Horizontal Multinationals

This chapter draws from James R. Markusen and Anthony J. Venables, "Multinational Firms and the New Trade Theory," *Journal of International Economics* 46 (1998): 183–203.

1. The assumption of no transport costs in Y is frequently made in both the oligopoly and monopolistic-competition literatures, and I make that assumption here to facilitate comparisons with those models. Although it has been pointed out that this assumption is important in some models (e.g., those with agglomeration economies), I do not think that it is important for the principal results of this chapter.

2. The fact that MNEs do not ship between markets is imposed as an *assumption* in the computer simulation model. But it is also a *result*, given that MNEs view factor prices as fixed. If an MNE supplies market i from both a local plant and by exports from j, optimality requires that the delivered marginal cost from i and j are equal. But if this is true (given constant marginal cost), then the MNE should shut the plant in i, saving the fixed cost G, and become a type-d_j firm.

3. I use the segmented markets assumption simply because most of the oligopoly literature has done so, and I want to make a clear comparison with that literature. In general, arbitrage constraints are not binding, but I am unsure if this is always the case. If NE (national enterprise, type-d) firms in i export to j, they will have market share in j no larger than in i due to the transport costs. (10)–(13) then imply that their markups are at least as large in i as in j, which in turn implies that the type-n_i firms absorb some of the transport costs in their pricing and arbitrage constraints do not bind.

4. Note that this effect would not occur in a Dixit-Stiglitz or Helpman-Krugman type of monopolistic-competition model. Higher world income has no effect on firm scale in the large-group monopolistic-competition model and would not induce a shift to multinational production. I will return to this point in chapter 6.

Chapter 6   A General-Equilibrium Monopolistic-Competition Model of Horizontal Multinationals

This chapter draws from James R. Markusen and Anthony J. Venables, "The Theory of Endowment, Intra-Industry and Multinational Trade," *Journal of International Economics* 52 (2000): 209–234.

Chapter 7   The Knowledge-Capital Model

This chapter relates to James R. Markusen, "Trade versus Investment Liberalization," NBER Working Paper No. 6231, October 1997.

1. I am tempted to call this property "separability," but I don't want to confuse things with very different concepts in economics that use the term separability.

2. Evidence supporting the assumption that multinational branch plants are more skilled-labor-intensive than the overall economy (at least for developing economies) is inferred from Feenstra and Hanson (1996a,b, 1997), and Aitken, Harrison, and Lipsey (1996). Slaughter (2000) gives data on the labor-force composition of U.S. multinationals' home operations versus their affiliates abroad, but no comparable data is available for the overall economy.

Chapter 8   Extensions to the Knowledge-Capital Model: Trade versus Affiliate Production, Factor-Price Effects, and Welfare Effects of Trade and Investment Liberalization

This chapter relates to James R. Markusen, "Trade versus Investment Liberalization," NBER Working Paper No. 6231, October 1997; James R. Markusen and Anthony J. Venables, "The Role of Multinational Firms in the Wage-Gap Debate," *Review of International Economics* 5 (1997): 435–451; and James R. Markusen and Anthony J. Venables, "Multinational Firms, Skilled Labor and Real Wages," in *Dynamic Issues in Applied Commercial Policy Analysis*, ed. Richard Baldwin (Cambridge: Cambridge University Press, 1999), 138–172.

Chapter 9   Traded Intermediate Inputs and Vertical Multinationals

This chapter draws on Kevin Honglin Zhang and James R. Markusen, "Vertical Multinationals and Host-Country Characteristics," *Journal of Development Economics* 59 (1999): 233–252.

1. "Reversals" are visible in the extreme southwest and northeast corners of figure 9.2. The reversals in the northeast corner moving down columns 0.85–0.95 are precisely what I discussed in connection with figure 9.1. In the northeast corner, country j is so scarce in skilled labor and so small that it is not profitable to produce any X in j. In the southwest corner, country i is so small that the skilled-labor requirements for producing all the Z for both countries drives the price of S_i sufficiently high that all final production is located in country j (reducing the demand for skilled labor in i from F to F_i per firm).

2. The initial rise in figure 9.4 is due to the fact that, with country i extremely small, its skilled-labor endowment is a constraint on producing Z, thus leading to a smaller world output of X than when the countries are somewhat more equal in size.

Chapter 10   Estimating the Knowledge-Capital Model

This chapter is a revised version of David Carr, James R. Markusen, and Keith E. Maskus, "Estimating the Knowledge-Capital Model of the Multinational Enterprise," *American Economic Review* 91 (2001): 693–708.

1. I wish to emphasize again, especially from this point forward, that this chapter is largely a replication of Carr, Markusen, and Maskus (2001). It was awkward choosing between using "we" and "I" in the text as it was in other chapters with different coauthors. In some cases where I am adding new comments or references to other chapters "I" is correct, but in many other cases it should be "we" (meaning Carr, Markusen, and Maskus). In the end, I chose "I," but I emphasize my debt to my coauthors, especially with respect to the empirical work that I could never have done alone and for which they deserve most of the credit.

2. The partial correlation coefficient between them is −0.96.

3. Some of these data were kindly provided by staff of the United States International Trade Commission.

4. Results are available on request. I also tried country-pair dummies, but with the United States as a partner in each case this procedure could not distinguish well individual country effects. I should note that the variable DIST is a perfect linear combination of the country dummies, so one dummy is dropped in the fixed-effects regressions.

5. Most of the countries in the sample are less skilled-labor-abundant than the United States. It may be that the country dummies are capturing some of this effect that should

be correctly attributed to endowment differences, as it is in the panel and in the cross-section.

6. There are 66 country pairs $(i, j$ observations) with positive affiliate sales from i to j in 1991. Of these, 59 have complete data for this exercise; 36 of the 59 are affiliate sales of U.S. firms in some country j; and 23 are country i affiliate sales in the United States.

7. For comparison purposes, I ran a simple gravity equation estimation on the panel data set, with log-real affiliate sales regressed on log-real GDP in host and parent countries and log distance. The gravity equation displayed a considerably lower adjusted R^2 (0.46) than the panel equation based on the theoretical model (0.60).

Chapter 11   Production for Export versus Local Sale

This chapter is a revised version of James R. Markusen and Keith E. Maskus, "Multinational Firms: Reconciling Theory and Evidence," in *Topics in Empirical International Economics: A Festschrift in Honor of Robert E. Lipsey*, ed. Magnus Blomstrom and Linda Goldberg (Chicago: University of Chicago Press, 2001), 71–95.

Chapter 12   Discriminating among Alternative Models of the Multinational

This chapter is a revised and expanded version of James R. Markusen and Keith E. Maskus, "Discriminating among Alternative Theories of the Multinational Enterprise." Forthcoming in *Review of International Economics* (2002).

Chapter 13   A Reputation Model of Internalization

This chapter is a revised version of Ignatius J. Horstmann and James Markusen, "Licensing Versus Direct Investment: A Model of Internalization by the Multinational Enterprise," *Canadian Journal of Economics* 20 (1987): 464–481.

1. The analysis that follows would hold equally well were q a continuous variable and part of a firm's optimization problem. The assumption that q can take on only two values simply removes the additional complication that would otherwise result.

2. Clearly, as long as this is possible, it will generally be in the MNE's interest to commit to an exclusive licensing arrangement.

3. This and the assumed stationarity of demand and costs imply that little (if anything) is lost by restricting the contract to a constant, per-period payment, S, for as long as the contract is in effect.

4. To be precise, if the quality choice and profits of a licensee are private information in a given period (as will be assumed), then a general licensing contract can only condition on past information. Given the reputation equilibrium that is employed when consumers cannot ascertain quality, such a contract will dominate the contracts assumed here only if payments can be committed to after the contract has been terminated (either by the licensee dissipating the MNE's reputation or the MNE switching licensees). The commitment contracts given as examples in the text have this property and dominate a simple (F, S) pair. A similar contract that would also have this property would be one

that required the licensee to pay to the MNE all profits obtained from dissipating the reputation. Since the dissipation of its reputation could only be ascertained by the MNE in the subsequent period, the MNE would need some way of recovering these gains after the fact. The contracting problem considered here assumes that this is not possible.

5. $F > 0$, and $F(1 + r) + S > \pi^*$ could not be an equilibrium, since, were a licensee to accept this contract, it would pay the MNE to switch licensees after one period. Given F is not refundable, the licensee would make negative profits. Anticipating this, the licensee would not accept such a contract. The complete details of the licensing equilibrium are provided in the appendix.

6. This can be thought of as capturing a situation in which the MNE is identified by some brand name that it can keep from being employed by anyone other than its branch plant/licensee. Alternatively, one can think of this assumption as being the appropriate approximation to a model in which q is a continuous variable and consumers can perfectly ascertain quality only so long as $q \le q^l$. Then, consumers could perfectly ascertain the quality of the competitive sector. However, the licensee/branch plant could claim to have quality q^h and produce quality $q^l + \varepsilon$ and go undetected. For a model in which other q^l producers could claim to have the q^h technology, see Grossman and Shapiro (1988).

7. It is assumed here that $S/r \ge \pi^c/(1 + r)$, so that the MNE can extract enough in license fees to make its reputation valuable to it.

8. Were the MNE to switch licensees, no licensee would have an incentive to maintain the reputation. Therefore, the MNE and licensee must have incentives to renew the contract each period. This occurs only if $F = 0$. See the appendix for details.

9. As argued above, the inefficiency of licensing would be removed if some scheme like third-party bonding were possible. Such a scheme would require the licensee to make a nonrecoverable payment $F > 0$ to a third party, who would transfer the entire amount to the MNE only if the contract were renewed *every* period. The same result would occur if the licensee could commit to paying penalties should it dissipate the MNE's reputation. If such commitments are not possible, then the essentials of the analysis presented here would continue to hold in more general settings.

10. An implicit assumption here is that the multinational branch plant chooses not to produce both q^h and q^l. Production of both q^h and q^l could be achieved through either acquisition of a host-country producer of q^l or new entry into the host-country market for q^l. It is assumed here that FDI or licensing dominates either of these options. This could be the case if, for instance, significant acquisition costs existed, and entry into the host-country market for q^l required a larger sunk cost. The latter would imply that, were the home-country firm simply to enter the host-country market for q^l, the existing producers would not exit. This would drive price below average cost (inclusive of the sunk entry cost). Were the sunk entry cost large enough, this could make entry into the q^l market undesirable.

11. It is assumed here that, should the licensee sell q^l in both markets, it must produce x and y in separate production runs to avoid detection by the MNE. This assumption could be dropped with no cost other than the proliferation of additional notation. The same is true were the licensee assumed to produce all output with existing capacity.

12. It is assumed here that the licensing agreement now simply specifies an initial payment F at the beginning of the agreement and a single-period payment s_t determined each period that the agreement is renewed.

13. This sort of monitoring would be such that the licensee could circumvent the process only by expending some amount of resources. If, for instance, cost savings from the production of q^l arise from the use of inferior (and lower-priced) inputs, monitoring might take the form of the MNE requiring the licensee to buy inputs from him. Then, to obtain the cost savings from the production of q^l, the licensee must resell these inputs and acquire the lower-priced ones. The resale costs are captured here.

Chapter 14 A Learning Model of Internalization, with Applications to Contract and Intellectual-Property-Rights Enforcement

This chaper relates to Wilfred Ethier and James R. Markusen, "Multinational Firms, Technology Diffusion and Trade," *Journal of International Economics* 41 (1996): 1–28; it is a revised version of James R. Markusen, "Contracts, Intellectual Property Rights, and Multinational Investment in Developing Countries," *Journal of International Economics* 53 (2001): 189–204.

1. Theory papers that are more focused on intellectual property protection per se include Chin and Grossman (1988), Glass and Saggi (1995), Diwan and Rodrik (1991), Helpman (1993), Grossman and Helpman (1991), Lai (1998), Segerstrom (1991), Taylor (1994), and Yang and Maskus (2001). The papers closest to this chapter, focusing more on internalization, are Ethier and Markusen (1996) and Fosfuri, Motta, and Ronde (2001).

2. The term r has an alternative interpretation. Assume that there is no discounting, but that there is uncertainty over whether or not the firm will successfully develop the next generation of product. Let the probability of successfully developing a new product in the next cycle be $1/(1 + r)$ if there is a product in the current cycle, zero otherwise (i.e., once the firm fails to develop a new product, it is out of the game). The probability of having a product in the third cycle is $1/(1 + r)^2$, and so forth. The algebra in the chapter is valid under either interpretation of r.

3. I am modeling this as a contracting problem, not explicitly as a game. Nevertheless, we do need to define "defecting" and its payoff in order to derive the incentive-compatibility constraints. Basically, I have in mind that both the agent and the MNE must plan and undertake the costs for a defection during the first period, with their "rival's" move only revealed at the beginning of the second period. Thus if one party defects and the other does not, the latter is out of the game and the defecting party collects all rents.

4. Recall that we developed this model in chapters 2 and 3. The partial-equilibrium model has a general-equilibrium analogue, with a second good Z, one factor of production labor (L), and a quadratic utility function $U = \alpha X - (\beta/2)X^2 + Z$. The one-period budget constraint for the "representative consumer" is $L + V/2 = p_x X + Z$, where L is labor income and the production of Z requires one unit of labor. $V/2$ is single-period managerial rent.

5. I am simply going to assume a symmetric outcome in which both firms export or both enter. It is beyond the scope of this chapter to expand the "game" to an earlier stage with simultaneous entry decisions. See chapters 3 and 4 for relevant algebra.

Chapter 15   An Asymmetric-Information Model of Internalization

This chapter is a revised version of Ignatius J. Horstmann and James R. Markusen, "Exploring New Markets: Direct Investment, Contractual Relations and the Multinational Enterprise," *International Economic Review* 37 (1996): 1–19.

1. Good collections of articles that examine investment and internalization are found in Casson (1987) and Buckley (1990). Casson (1990) presents a comprehensive study of FDI. An interesting survey on multinationals is presented in *The Economist*, March 27–April 2, 1993. In a section of this survey article titled "Creatures of Imperfection," the authors note that the principal paradox is why we have seen such a tremendous expansion of direct investment in a world where trade barriers have fallen dramatically. "The solution to this puzzle is that multinationals are not exploiters of purity but rather creatures of market imperfections, or failures."

2. The assumption that the asymmetric information involves the size of the potential customer pool is not crucial to what follows. The analysis would apply equally well to a situation in which the potential customer pool is of a known size but some parameter of the demand function is known only to the agent.

3. This assumption means that the MNE's decision regarding sales mode turns purely on the magnitude of the agency costs implied by different contract forms relative to the costs of establishing an owned sales operation. The use of particular agency contracts by the MNE as a means of deterring entry (à la Aghion and Bolton 1987) is not an issue here.

4. The revelation principle states that any allocation that would arise as a Nash equilibrium outcome of a game with communication can be recovered via a game in which (a) allocations depend only on agents' reports of type (their private information) and (b) the allocation rule satisfies incentive compatibility (agents report types truthfully) and individual rationality (agents are willing to participate). For more details, see Myerson (1991, 255n).

5. The assumption that the parties are able to contract on the actual quantity sold may seem somewhat unrealistic. However, a contract specifying an initial payment by the MNE to the sales agent when the contract is signed as well as a quantity of the good that the agent must purchase from the MNE each period and a purchase price would exactly mimic the contract defined below.

6. In what follows, I will use the notation (q_i, w_i) as a shorthand to describe the contract $\langle q(N_i), w(N_i) \rangle$, the pair offered should the agent report a customer pool of size N_i.

7. For a formal treatment of this problem, see Horstmann and Markusen (1996).

8. It is assumed that the effort cost function is sufficiently convex that the profit-maximizing contract is an interior point. In this case, the contract occurs where the MNE's iso-profit line is tangent to the indifference curve giving R units of utility.

9. This assumption simply makes comparisons easier in that it implies that the MNE's sales force is making effort choices with the same information as the local agent.

10. The condition for IC_1 not to bind is that

$$\sum_{t=0}^{T_2} [c(q_2/N_1) - c(q_2/N_2)]\delta^t > \sum_{t=0}^{T_1} [c(q_1/N_1) - c(q_1/N_2)]\delta^t.$$

This condition is derived by subtracting the left-hand side of IC_1 from the right-hand side of IC_2 and vice versa (recall that IC_2 holds as an equality). If $q_2 > q_1$, as will be the case in the optimal contract, then convexity of $C(\cdot)$ implies that a sufficient condition for the above to be satisfied is that $T_2 \geq T_1$. Clearly, it may also be satisfied if $T_2 < T_1$.

11. Had IC_1 been binding, the only difference in the results would be that q_2 would be larger than q_2^*. Otherwise, the results would be unaffected.

12. In particular, $q_2 = q_2^*$, $q_1 = \hat{q}_1$ (as depicted in figure 15.1), $\lambda_1 = 1$ and $\lambda_2 = 1 - \rho$.

13. Indeed, $\lim_{N_1 \to N_2}[c(\hat{q}_1/N_1) - c(\hat{q}_1/N_2)] = \lim_{N_1 \to 0}[c(\hat{q}_1/N_1) - c(\hat{q}_1/N_2)] = 0$. The reason in the former case is obvious. In the latter case, substitution for λ_1 and λ_2 in (1) reveals that $\hat{q}_1$ must be such that

$$\rho\left[p - c'(\hat{q}_1/N_1)\frac{1}{N_1}\right] - (1 - \rho)\left[c'(\hat{q}_1/N_1)\frac{1}{N_1} - c'(\hat{q}_1/N_2)\frac{1}{N_2}\right] = 0.$$

Because $c'(0) = 0$, $\hat{q}_1$ is strictly positive for all N_1 positive and $\hat{q}_1 \to 0$ as $N_1 \to 0$. Of course, for this contract to continue to be optimal when N_1 is small, R must be small also. In particular, if R were zero, this contract would be optimal even as N_1 approached zero.

14. In the following proposition, the variable $q_2^*(\alpha)$ refers to the profit-maximizing output of the MNE's owned sales operation when $N_i = N_2$.

15. This is an assumption that, by the time the MNE has learned the value of N_i, F is sunk for the one period.

16. This is the situation described in proposition 2.

17. Recall that the situation under consideration is one in which an owned sales operation is more profitable for the MNE than the agency contract if $N_i = N_2$, while the opposite is true if $N_i = N_1$. Because the cost G is sunk once the MNE has invested, however, it may nonetheless find it more profitable to maintain its owned sales operation even if $N_i = N_1$.

18. In calculating the expression below, the value $(\rho/(1 - \delta))(pq_1^* - w_1^*)$ has been added and subtracted to the difference $V^I - V^a$ from (9) and (10). The addition appears in the last term in (11) while the subtraction occurs in the second and fourth terms. The value $(1 - \rho)w_2^*$ has also been added and subtracted.

19. Where IC_1 is binding, there would be an additional agency cost resulting from the fact that q_2 would be distorted away from q_2^*. In addition, it may be that $T_2 > 0$, implying a further cost under the contract.

20. This change would be given by the expression

$$\frac{dN_1}{dN_2} = -\frac{(1 - \rho)c'[q_2^*(\alpha)/\alpha N_2]\frac{q_2^*}{\alpha N_2^2}}{pc'[q_1^*(\alpha)/\alpha N_1]\frac{q_1^*}{\alpha N_1^2}}.$$

Preface to Technical Appendices

Special thanks again to my colleague and friend Tom Rutherford, who made this all happen.

References

Note: Some references are included for general information even though they may not be discussed in the text. I follow this practice throughout the book.

Aghion, P., and P. Bolton. 1987. "Contracts as Barriers to Entry." *American Economic Review* 77: 388–401.

Aitken, Brian, Ann Harrison, and Robert E. Lipsey. 1996. "Wages and Foreign Ownership: A Comparative Study of Mexico, Venezuela, and the United States." *Journal of International Economics* 40: 345–371.

Allen, F. 1984. "Reputation and Product Quality." *Rand Journal of Economics* 15: 311–27.

Beaudreau, Bernard C. 1986. *Managers, Learning and the Multinational Firm: Theory and Evidence.* Ph.D. diss., University of Western Ontario.

Beckman, Martin J., and Jacques-Francois Thisse. 1986. "The Location of Production Activities." In *Handbook of Regional and Urban Economics*, ed. P. Nijkamp, 21–95. Amsterdam: Elsevier Science Publishers.

Blomstrom, Magnus. 1991. "Host Country Benefits of Foreign Investment." NBER Working Paper No. 3615.

Blomstrom, Magnus, and Ari Kokko. 1998. "Foreign Investment as a Vehicle for International Technology Transfer." In *Creation and Transfer of Knowledge*, ed. G. B. Navaretti, P. Dasgupta, K.-G. Maeler, and D. Siniscalco, 279–311. Berlin: Springer-Verlag.

Blomstrom, Magnus, and Mario Zejan. 1991. "Why Do Multinational Firms Seek Out Joint Ventures." *Journal of International Development* 3, no. 1: 53–63.

Blomstrom, Magnus, Robert Lipsey, and Ksenia Kulchycky. 1988. "U.S. and Swedish Direct Investment and Exports." In *Trade Policy Issues and Empirical Analysis*, ed. Robert E. Baldwin, 259–297. Chicago: University of Chicago Press.

Blonigen, Bruce A. 2001. "In Search of Substitution between Foreign Production and Exports." *Journal of International Economics* 53: 81–104.

Blonigen, Bruce A., and Ronald B. Davies. 2000. "The Effect of Bilateral Tax Treaties on US FDI Activity." Working paper, University of Oregon.

Brainard, S. Lael. 1993a. "A Simple Theory of Multinational Corporations and Trade with a Trade-Off between Proximity and Concentration." NBER Working Paper No. 4269.

Brainard, S. Lael. 1993b. "An Empirical Assessment of the Factor Proportions Explanation of Multinationals Sales." NBER Working Paper No. 4580.

Brainard, S. Lael. 1997. "An Empirical Assessment of the Proximity-Concentration Trade-Off between Multinational Sales and Trade." *American Economic Review* 87: 520–544.

Brander, James R., and Paul Krugman. 1983. "A 'Reciprocal Dumping' Model of International Trade." *Journal of International Economics* 15: 313–323.

Brander, James A., and Barbara J. Spencer. 1985. "Export Subsidies and International Market Share Rivalry." *Journal of International Economics* 18: 83–100.

Braunerhjelm, Pontus, and Karolina Ekholm, eds. 1998. *The Geography of Multinational Firms*. Boston: Kluwer Academic Publishers.

Buckley, Peter J., ed. 1990. *International Investment*. Aldershot: Edward Elgar.

Buckley, Peter J., and Mark Casson. 1981. "The Optimal Timing of a Foreign Direct Investment." *Economic Journal* 91: 75–87.

Buckley, Peter J., and Mark Casson. 1985. *The Economic Theory of the Multinational Enterprise*. London: Macmillan.

Carr, David, James R. Markusen, and Keith E. Maskus. 1998. "Estimating the Knowledge-Capital Model of the Multinational Enterprise." NBER Working Paper 6773.

Carr, David, James R. Markusen, and Keith E. Maskus. 2001. "Estimating the Knowledge-Capital Model of the Multinational Enterprise." *American Economic Review* 91: 693–708.

Casson, Mark. 1984. "The Theory of Vertical Integration: A Survey and Synthesis." *Journal of Economic Studies* 11: 3–43.

Casson, Mark. 1986. *Multinationals and World Trade: Vertical Integration and the Division of Labor in World Industries*. London: Allen and Unwin.

Casson, Mark. 1987. *The Firm and the Market: Studies in Multinational Enterprise and the Scope of the Firm*. Oxford: Blackwell, and Cambridge, MA: The MIT Press.

Casson, Mark, ed. 1990. *Multinational Corporations*. Aldershot: Edward Elgar.

Caves, R. 1982. *Multinational Enterprise and Economic Analysis*. London: Cambridge University Press.

Caves, Richard E. 1996. *Multinational Enterprise and Economic Analysis*, 2d ed. London: Cambridge University Press.

Caves, Richard E., and William F. Murphy II. 1976. "Franchising: Firms, Markets, and Intangible Assets." *Southern Economic Journal* 42: 572–586.

Chin, Judith C., and Gene M. Grossman. 1988. "Intellectual Property Rights and North-South Trade." In *The Political Economy of International Trade: Essays in Honor of R. E. Baldwin*, ed. R. W. Jones and A. O. Kueger, 90–107. Oxford: Blackwell.

Contractor, F. J. 1985. *Licensing in International Strategy: A Guide for Negotiations and Planning*. Westport, CT: Quorum Books.

Davidson, William H., and Donald G. McFetridge. 1984. "International Technology Transactions and the Theory of the Firm." *Journal of Industrial Economics* 32: 253–264.

Denekamp, Johannes, and Michael J. Ferrantino. 1992. "Substitution and Complementarity of U.S. Exports and Foreign Based Affiliate Sales in a Demand Based Gravity System." USITC working paper.

Diwan, Ishak, and Dani Rodrik. 1991. "Patents, Appropriate Technology, and North-South Trade." *Journal of International Economics* 30: 27–48.

Dixit, Avinash K. 1984. "International Trade Policy for Oligopolistic Industries." *Economic Journal* (Suppl.) 94: 1–16.

Dixit, Avinash K., and A. S. Kyle. 1985. "The Use of Protection and Subsidies for Entry Promotion and deterrence." *American Economic Review* 75: 139–152.

Dixit, A. K., and J. E. Stiglitz. 1977. "Monopolistic Competition and Optimum Product Diversity. *American Economic Review* 67: 297–308.

Dunning, John. 1958. *American Investment in British Manufacturing Industry*. London: Allen and Unwin.

Dunning, John H. 1977. "The Determinant of International Production." *Oxford Economic Papers* 25: 289–330.

Dunning, John H. 1981. *International Production and the Multinational Enterprise*. London: Allen and Unwin.

Dunning, John H. 1988. *Explaining International Production*. London: Unwin Hyman.

Eastman, Harry, and Stefan Stykolt. 1967. *The Tariff and Competition in Canada*. Toronto: Macmillan.

Eaton, B. Curtis, and Richard Lipsey. 1979. "The Theory of Market Preemption: The Persistence of Excess Capacity and Monopoly in Growing Spatial Markets." *Economica* 46: 149–158.

Eaton, Jonathan, and Gene Grossman. 1986. "Optimal Trade and Industrial Policy under Oligopoly." *Quarterly Journal of Economics* 101: 383–406.

Eaton, Jonathan, and Akiko Tamura. 1994. "Bilateralism and Regionalism in Japanese and U.S. Trade and Foreign Direct Investment Relationships." *Journal of Japanese and International Economics* 8: 478–510.

Ekhlom, Karolina. 1995. *Multinational Production and Trade in Technological Knowledge*. Lund Economic Studies No. 58, Lund University.

Ekholm, Karolina. 1998a. "Headquarter Services and Revealed Factor Abundance." *Review of International Economics* 6: 545–553.

Ekholm, Karolina. 1998b. "Proximity Advantages, Scale Economies, and the Location of Production." In *The Geography of Multinationals*, ed. Pontus Braunerhjelm and Karolina Ekholm, 59–76. Boston and Dordrecht: Kluwer Academic Publishers.

Ekholm, Karolina. 2001. "Factor Endowments and Intra-Industry Affiliate Production." In *The Frontiers of Intra-Industry Trade*, ed. Peter Lloyd, Herbert Grubel, and Hyun-Hoon Lee. London: Macmillan.

Ekholm, Karolina, and Rikard Forslid. 2001. "Trade and Location with Horizontal and Vertical Multi-Region Firms." *Scandinavian Journal of Economics* 103: 101–118.

Ethier, Wilfred. 1982. "National and International Returns to Scale in the Modern Theory of International Trade." *American Economic Review* 72: 389–405.

Ethier, Wilfred. 1986. "The Multinational Firm." *Quarterly Journal of Economics* 101: 805–833.

Ethier, Wilfred, and James R. Markusen. 1996. "Multinational Firms, Technology Diffusion and Trade." *Journal of International Economics* 41: 1–28.

Feenstra, Robert C., and Gordon H. Hanson. 1996a. "Foreign Investment, Outsourcing, and Relative Wages." In *The Political Economy of Trade Policy: Papers in Honor of Jagdish Bhagwati*, ed. R. C. Feenstra, G. M. Grossman, and D. A. Irwin, 89–127. Cambridge, MA: The MIT Press.

Feenstra, Robert C., and Gordon H. Hanson. 1996b. "Globalization, Outsourcing, and Wage Inequality." *American Economic Review* 86, 240–245.

Feenstra, Robert C., and Gordon H. Hanson. 1997. "Foreign Direct Investment and Relative Wages: Evidence from Mexico's Maquiladoras." *Journal of International Economics* 42: 371–393.

Feldstein, Martin, James R. Hines Jr., and Glenn R. Hubbard, eds. 1995. *The Effects of Taxation on Multinational Enterprises.* Cambridge, MA: The MIT Press.

Fosfuri, Andrea, Massimo Motta, and Thomas Ronde. 2001. "Foreign Direct Investments and Spillovers through Workers' Mobility." *Journal of International Economics* 53: 205–222.

Froot, Kenneth A., ed. 1993. *Foreign Direct Investment.* Chicago: University of Chicago Press.

Fujita, Masahisa, Paul Krugman, and Anthony J. Venables. 1999. *The Spatial Economy: Cities, Regions, and International Trade.* Cambridge, MA: The MIT Press.

Glass, Amy J., and Kamal Saggi. 1995. "Intellectual Property Rights, Foreign Direct Investment, and Innovation." Working paper, Ohio State University.

Graham, Edward M., and Paul R. Krugman. 1993. "The Surge in Foreign Direct Investment in the 1980s." In *Foreign Direct Investment*, ed. Kenneth A. Froot, 13–33. Chicago: University of Chicago Press.

Grossman, Gene M., and Elhanan Helpman. 1991. "Quality Ladders and Product Cycles." *Quarterly Journal of Economics* 106: 557–586.

Grossman, Gene, and Carl Shapiro. 1988. "Counterfeit Product Trade." *American Economic Review* 78: 59–75.

Grubaugh, S. 1987. "Determinants of Direct Foreign Investment." *Review of Economics and Statistics* 69: 149–151.

Helpman, Elhanan. 1981. "International Trade in the Presence of Product Differentiation, Economies of Scale and Monopolistic Competition; A Chamberlinian-Heckscher-Ohlin Approach." *Journal of International Economics* 11: 305–340.

Helpman, Elhanan. 1984. "A Simple Theory of Trade with Multinational Corporations." *Journal of Political Economy* 92: 451–471.

Helpman, Elhanan. 1985. "Multinational Corporations and Trade Structure." *Review of Economic Studies* 52: 443–458.

Helpman, Elhanan. 1993. "Innovation, Imitation, and Intellectual Property Rights." *Econometrica* 61: 1247–1280.

Helpman, Elhanan, and Paul Krugman. 1985. *Market Structure and Foreign Trade*. Cambridge, MA: The MIT Press.

Hines, James R. Jr. 1997. *Tax Policy and the Activities of Multinational Corporations*. Cambridge, MA: The MIT Press.

Hobday, Michael. 1995. *Innovation in East Asia: The Challenge to Japan*. London: Aldershot.

Horstmann, Ignatius J., and James R. Markusen. 1986. "Up the Average Cost Curve: Inefficient Entry and the New Protectionism." *Journal of International Economics* 20: 225–248.

Horstmann, Ignatius J., and James R. Markusen. 1987a. "Strategic Investments and the Development of Multinationals." *International Economic Review* 28: 109–121.

Horstmann, Ignatius J., and James R. Markusen. 1987b. "Licensing Versus Direct Investment: A Model of Internalization by the Multinational Enterprise." *Canadian Journal of Economics* 20: 464–481.

Horstmann, Ignatius J., and James R. Markusen. 1992. "Endogenous Market Structures in International Trade (natura facit saltum)." *Journal of International Economics* 32: 109–129.

Horstmann, Ignatius J., and James R. Markusen. 1996. "Exploring New Markets: Direct Investment, Contractual Relations and the Multinational Enterprise." *International Economic Review* 37: 1–19.

Hummels, David L., and Robert M. Stern. 1994. "Evolving Patterns of North American Merchandise Trade and Foreign Direct Investment, 1960–1990." *The World Economy* 17: 5–29.

Hymer, Stephen. 1976. *The International Operations of National Firms: A Study of Direct Foreign Investment*. Cambridge, MA: The MIT Press.

Julius, DeAnne. 1990. *Global Companies and Public Policy*. London: Royal Institute of International Affairs.

Katz, J. M. 1987. *Technology Generation in Latin American Manufacturing Industries*. New York: St. Martin's Press.

Klein, B., and K. Leffler. 1981. "The Role of Market Forces in Assuring Contractual Performance." *Journal of Political Economy* 89: 615–641.

Kravis, Irving B., and Robert E. Lipsey. 1982. "The Location of Overseas Production and Production for Export by U.S. Multinational Firms." *Journal of International Economics* 12: 210–223.

Krugman, Paul. 1979. "Increasing Returns, Monopolistic Competition, and International Trade." *Journal of International Economics* 9: 395–410.

Krugman, Paul. 1984. "Import Protection as Export Promotion: International Competition in the Presence of Oligopoly and Economies of Scale." In *Monopolistic Competition and International Trade*, ed. Henryk Kierzkowski, 180–193. London: Oxford University Press.

Lai, Edwin L.-D. 1998. "International Intellectual Property Rights Protection and the Rate of Product Innovation." *Journal of Development Economics* 55: 133–153.

Levinsohn, James A. 1989. "Strategic Trade Policy When Firms Can Invest Abroad: When Are Tariffs and Quotas Equivalent?" *Journal of International Economics* 27: 129–146.

Lipsey, Robert E., and Merle Yahr Weiss. 1981. "Foreign Production and Exports in Manufacturing Industries." *Review of Economics and Statistics* 63: 210–23.

Lipsey, Robert E., Magnus Blomstrom, and Eric Ramstetter. 1995. "Internationalized Production in World Output." NBER Working Paper No. 5385.

Mansfield, Edwin, and Anthony Romeo. 1980. "Technology Transfer to Overseas Subsidiaries by U.S. Firms." *Quarterly Journal of Economics* 94: 737–750.

Markusen, James R. 1981. "Trade and the Gains from Trade with Imperfect Competition." *Journal of International Economics* 11: 531–551.

Markusen, James R. 1983. "Factor Movements and Commodity Trade as Complements." *Journal of International Economics* 13: 341–356.

Markusen, James R. 1984. "Multinationals, Multi-Plant Economies, and the Gains from Trade." *Journal of International Economics* 16: 205–226.

Markusen, James R. 1995. "The Boundaries of Multinational Firms and the Theory of International Trade." *Journal of Economic Perspectives* 9: 169–189.

Markusen, James R. 1997. "Trade versus Investment Liberalization." NBER Working Paper No. 6231, October.

Markusen, James R. 1998a. "Multinational Firms, Location and Trade." *The World Economy* 21: 733–756.

Markusen, James R. 1998b. "Contracts, Intellectual Property Rights, and Multinational Investment in Developing Countries." NBER Working Paper No. 6448.

Markusen, James R. 2001. "Contracts, Intellectual Property Rights, and Multinational Investment in Developing Countries." *Journal of International Economics* 53: 189–204.

Markusen, James R., and Keith E. Maskus. 2001. "Multinational Firms: Reconciling Theory and Evidence." In *Topics in Empirical International Economics: A Festschrift in Honor of Robert E. Lipsey*, ed. Magnus Blomstrom and Linda Goldberg, 71–95. Chicago: University of Chicago Press.

Markusen, James R., and Keith E. Maskus. 2002. "Discriminating among Alternative Theories of the Multinational Enterprise." Forthcoming in *Review of International Economics*.

Markusen, James R., and Anthony J. Venables. 1988. "Trade Policy with Increasing Returns and Imperfect Competition: Contradictory Results from Competing Assumptions." *Journal of International Economics* 24: 299–316.

Markusen, James R., and Anthony J. Venables. 1997. "The Role of Multinational Firms in the Wage-Gap Debate." *Review of International Economics* 5: 435–451.

Markusen, James R., and Anthony J. Venables. 1998. "Multinational Firms and the New Trade Theory." *Journal of International Economics* 46: 183–203.

Markusen, James R., and Anthony J. Venables. 1999. "Multinational Firms, Skilled Labor and Real Wages." In *Dynamic Issues in Applied Commercial Policy Analysis*, ed. Richard Baldwin, 138–172. Cambridge: Cambridge University Press.

Markusen, James R., and Anthony J. Venables. 2000. "The Theory of Endowment, Intra-Industry and Multinational Trade." *Journal of International Economics* 52: 209–235.

Mathewson, G. Frank, and Ralph A. Winter. 1985. "The Economics of Franchise Contracts." *Journal of Law and Economics* 28: 503–526.

McGahan, A. M. 1993. "The Effect of Incomplete Information about Demand on Preemption." *International Journal of Industrial Organization* 11: 327–46.

McIntosh/Baring. 1993. *The Kangaroo Hops North: An Analysis of Australian Business Opportunities in Asia*. Melbourne: McIntosh & Company.

Morck, Randall, and Bernard Yeung. 1991. "Why Investors Value Multinationality." *Journal of Business* 64: 165–187.

Morck, Randall, and Bernard Yeung. 1992. "Internalization: An Event Study Test." *Journal of International Economics* 33: 41–56.

Motta, Massimo. 1992. "Multinational Firms and the Tariff-Jumping Argument." *European Economic Review* 36: 1557–1571.

Myerson, R. B. 1991. *Game Theory: Analysis of Conflict*. Cambridge, MA: Harvard University Press.

Nicholas, Stephen. 1982. "British Multinational Investment Before 1939." *Journal of European Economic History* 11: 605–630.

Nicholas, Stephen. 1983. "Agency Contracts, Institutional Modes, and the Transition to Foreign Direct Investment by British Manufacturing Multinationals Before 1939." *Journal of Economic History* 43: 675–686. Reprinted in *Multinational Corporations*, ed. Mark Casson, 473–484. Aldershot: Edward Elgar, 1990.

Nicholas, Stephen. 1986. "Theory of the Multinational Enterprise as a Transactional Mode: Pre-1939 British Overseas Investment." Working paper, University of New South Wales.

Nicholas, S., W. Purcell, D. Merritt, and A. Whitwell. 1994. "Foreign Direct Investment in Australia in the 1990's." Mimeo., University of Melbourne.

Rao, R., and D. Rutenberg. 1979. "Preempting an Alert Rival: Strategic Timing of a First Plant by Analysis of Sophisticated Rivalry." *Bell Journal of Economics* 10: 412–428.

Rugman, Alan. 1986. "New Theories of the Multinational Enterprise: An Assessment of Internationalization Theory." *Bulletin of Economic Research* 38: 101–118.

Rutherford, Thomas F. 1995. "Extensions of {GAMS} for Complementarity Problems Arising in Applied Economics." *Journal of Economic Dynamics and Control* 19: 1299–1324.

Rutherford, Thomas F. 1999. "Applied General Equilibrium Modeling with MPSGE as a GAMS Subsystem: An Overview of the Modeling Framework and Syntax." *Computational Economics* 14: 1–46.

Segerstrom, S. Paul. 1991. "Innovation, Imitation, and Economic Growth." *Journal of Political Economy* 99: 807–827.

Shapiro, Carl. 1983. "Premiums for High Quality Products as Returns to Reputation." *Quarterly Journal of Economics* 98: 659–679.

Slaughter, Matthew J. 2000. "Production Transfer within Multinational Enterprises and American Wages." *Journal of International Economics* 50: 449–472.

Smith, Alasdair. 1987. "Strategic Investment, Multinational Corporations, and Trade Policy." *European Economic Review* 31: 89–96.

Smith, Pamela. 2001. "Patent Rights and Bilateral Exchange: A Cross-Country Analysis of U.S. Exports, FDI, and Licensing." *Journal of International Economics* 55: 411–440.

Swenson, Debra. 1998. "The Tradeoff between Trade and Foreign Investment." Working paper, University of California, Davis.

Taylor, M. Scott. 1994. "Trips, Trade, and Technology Transfer." *International Economic Review* 35: 361–381.

Teece, David. 1977. "Technology Transfer By Multinational Firms: The Resource Cost of Transferring Technological Know-How." *Economic Journal* 87: 242–261.

Teece, David. 1986. *The Multinational Corporation and the Resource Cost of International Technology Transfer.* Cambridge, MA: Ballinger.

Thompson, Allan G. 1994. "Relationship Problems in Australian Business Ventures in Southeast Asia." Mimeo., University of Melbourne.

Tyson, Laura. 1992. *Who's Bashing Whom? Trade and Conflict in High-Technology Industries.* Washington, DC: Institute for International Economics.

UNCTAD. 1992–2000. *World Investment Report,* years 1993–2000. New York: United Nations.

Venables, Anthony J. 1985. "Trade and Trade Policy with Imperfect Competition: The Case of Identical Products and Free Entry." *Journal of International Economics* 19: 1–19.

Wang, Jian-Ye, and Magnus Blomstrom. 1992. "Foreign Investment and Technology Transfer: A Simple Mode." *European Economic Review* 36: 137–155.

Wheeler, David, and Ashoka Mody. 1992. "International Investment Location Decisions." *Journal of International Economics* 33: 57–76.

Williamson, Oliver E. 1981. "The Modern Corporation: Origins, Evolution, Attitudes." *Journal of Economic Literature* 19: 1537–1568.

Wilson, Robert W. 1977. "The Effect of Technological Environment and Product Rivalry on R&D Effort and Licensing of Inventions." *Review of Economics and Statistics* 59: 171–178.

Yang, Guifang, and Keith E. Maskus. 2001. "Intellectual Property Rights, Licensing, and Innovation in an Endogenous Product-Cycle Model." *Journal of International Economics* 53: 169–188.

Yoffie, David B. 1993. "Foreign Direct Investment in Semiconductors." In *Foreign Direct Investment,* ed. K. A. Froot, 197–222. Chicago: University of Chicago Press.

Zeile, William J. 1993. "Merchandise Trade of U.S. Affiliates of Foreign Companies." *Survey of Current Business* 73: 52–65.

Zhang, Kevin H. 1995. "Determinants of Foreign Direct Investment in China: 1979–1995." Working paper, University of Colorado.

Zhang, Kevin Honglin, and James R. Markusen. 1999. "Vertical Multinational and Host-Country Characteristics." *Journal of Development Economics* 59: 233–252.

Index